THE

BUNAU-VARILLA BROTHERS

AND

THE

PANAMA CANAL

GABRIEL J. LOIZILLON

THE BUNAU-VARILLA BROTHERS AND THE PANAMA CANAL

1st Edition August 2008

2nd Edition (enlarged and revised) January 2013

Copyright © 2013 by GABRIEL J. LOIZILLON

I S B N # 978 – 1 – 300 – 55 840 – 8

To my family

When Michelet, a French writer, was asked what method he used to create his historical works, he replied : " I always start first by gathering the facts and then I list them rigorously in a chronological order. Thus, having extracted the essential lines, I try to narrate the history, as if it was a novel. "

This is how, in all modesty, I have attempted to narrate the fight for the best route for an interoceanic canal: Panama or Nicaragua; fight which, at times, turned into a real thriller.

BUSTE DE PHILIPPE BUNAU-VARILLA par MALVINA HOFFMANN

TABLE OF CONTENTS

* The figures found in parenthesis, like (5) for example, refer to the books
or documents listed in the reference list shown in Appendix 4, page 303.

FOREWORD

Philippe Bunau-Varilla, a graduate of the prestigious French *École Polytechnique*, class of 1878, was a major partaker in the victory of Panama against Nicaragua, to win the Interoceanic Canal of Central America.

Involved in the French venture as a young engineer in 1886, and disappointed when the French failed in 1889, he continued his fight with determination by supporting the project with eagerness for the next fourteen years.

In 1903, appointed Plenipotentiary Minister by the Panamanian revolutionists, he signed the treaty, which recognized the new Republic and allowed the assets of the French Canal to be purchased by the Government of the United States. The U. S. Army completed the work in 1914.

This treaty is remembered as the ***Hay/Bunau-Varilla Treaty***, associating the name of our hero with John Milton Hay, the American Secretary of State, serving under the 26th President, Theodore Roosevelt.

This treaty remained in force until 1977, when it was replaced by the *Torrijos/Carter Treaty*, valid until December 31, 1999, when the "Canal Zone" was finally returned to Panama.

Philippe Bunau-Varilla did not only lobby in favor of Panama against her rival Nicaragua, but he also helped finance with his own money the secession/independence of the Province of Panama, then part of Colombia.

At first, Philippe Bunau-Varilla was recognized as a *libertador* in Panama.

When Manuel Amador died - he had been the leader of the 1903 insurgents -, José Domingo de Obaldia, the Panamanian President, wrote to Bunau-Varilla on May 13, 1909: "Our people will keep eternally engraved in their memories your fruitful services and will put in a pre-eminent place the names of Amador and your own. The national gratitude gives them the title of benefactors of Panama."

This was five years before the United States completed the canal in August 1914.

However, Philippe Bunau-Varilla's fame would erode slowly with time. Soon after the canal's completion, the terms of the 1903 treaty appeared unfair and unbearable to Panamanian nationalists. For them it was highly unjust that Panama's sovereignty on the "Canal Zone" had been transferred to the United States in a perpetuity clause, in exchange of an insignificant annual payment.

Gradually with time, Bunau-Varilla's accomplishments were discredited by the nationalists' ingratitude, until in January 1927, he officially became "a foreigner prejudicial to our country . . . exposed to the aversion of the Panamanian people," according to a resolution of the Chamber of Deputies of Panama.

He was thus deprived of his moral heritage. He became a scapegoat for the unacceptable, leonine, infamous treaty he had imposed upon Panamanians. Every time a negotiating session of the treaty came up with the United States, which happened at regular intervals all along the 20th Century, his name was cursed by Panamanians.

Panamanian history books describe Philippe Bunau-Varilla as a "vile speculator, acting solely for his own interests", under the false belief that he was a shareholder of the French New Company. He was, but for less than 1%!

Philippe Bunau-Varilla died in May 1940, in his Parisian home, quite forgotten by French historians.

With his brother Maurice, they had set up a construction company to work on the French canal and in only four years (1886 to 1889), amassed an enormous profit. They later purchased a successful French newspaper, *Le Matin,* which Maurice managed with an iron fist; it became one of the largest Parisian newspapers from 1900 to 1944.

Sadly and unfortunately, Maurice collaborated with the Germans during the Second World War; he was judged and condemned in 1944, deprived of his civil rights; his huge fortune was confiscated.

The Bunau-Varilla family had been downgraded from fame to infamy.

On December 31, 1999, the United States returned the ownership of the Canal to Panama. Logically, the passions between Panamanians and Americans subsided.

One hundred years after the opening of the Panama Canal, time has now come to tell the true story of Philippe Bunau-Varilla.

This book demonstrates with indisputable evidence that without Philippe Bunau-Varilla, the excavations done by the French in Panama would have been left useless and abandoned; the Interoceanic Canal would have been built in Nicaragua.

Most Panamanians ignore that they owe to Philippe Bunau-Varilla their independence from Colombia.

They do not fully appreciate that Bunau-Varilla:
- spent five years of his life supporting Panama's cause and opposing the Nicaraguan project - 1899 to 1904;
- spent a million francs - in gold - of his wealth, travelling and lobbying to ensure that the Interoceanic Canal be built in Panama, and not in Nicaragua, which had been designated as the "American Canal";
- spent $ 100,000 of his own money to support the revolutionaries of Panama.
- developed a rare ingenuity to sign with Hay the treaty that ratified the independence of the new nation.

For all that, Panamanians owe him their current independence and booming economy. Thanks to Philippe Bunau-Varilla, they own a canal, which produces today enough revenues to lift them into the flock of developed countries.

Using references from historians, as well as from Philippe Bunau-Varilla's memoirs, this book endeavors to tell how this Frenchman acted so successfully in favor of Panama.

However, until now, the part played by Philippe Bunau-Varilla had not been fully recognized, partly because many questions had remained unanswered. The author deemed essential to seek the answers to these questions.

Our investigations have allowed the unraveling of all the secrets left hidden by Philippe Bunau-Varilla in his memoirs. Documents from the French Archives (2) prove without any doubt that his motivations were not covetous, nor inspired by greed, but that he was totally unselfish and devoted mostly to the success of the Panama Canal.

This book demonstrates in full detail that Philippe Bunau-Varilla did not intend to speculate, when he negotiated in Washington the sale of the French Company.

He did not need money; with his brother Maurice, they had earned enough to satisfy their family needs for several generations: 8 million francs in gold - about $ 50 million in today's value.

Most historians who have written about the history of the Panama Canal ignore how the Bunau-Varilla brothers built their fortune. This book reveals the origin of the brothers' wealth. The secret had remained well kept in the dusty boxes of the French Archives in Paris and in Roubaix, a small provincial town in the North of France. The author is most grateful to its custodians.

Philippe Bunau-Varilla's actions had been vital to decide where to build an Interoceanic Canal in Central America: in Panama and not in Nicaragua. Without being excessive, it can be said that without Philippe Bunau-Varilla, the Panama Canal would be in Nicaragua!

Panamanians owe their independent Republic to Philippe Bunau-Varilla and should show him some appreciation.
It is not too late for such recognition.

1

PANAMA BEFORE THE CANAL

When, in 1453, the Turks seized Constantinople, today called Istanbul, they also acquired control of the terrestrial commercial routes from Western Europe to Asia. To escape this constraint, it became vital for Europeans to discover a shorter western route to the Indies.

This was why Christopher Columbus, half a century later, in search of the "secret of the strait", had run into the coasts of the Caribbean Sea islands and of Central America. On his fourth and last travel, in 1502, he stopped in Panama while sailing along her Atlantic coast. There, he lost a caravel, the *Vizcaina*, whose wreck had been recently discovered.

In 1513, Vasco Nunez de Balboa, a Spanish explorer, was the first European to cross the Panama Isthmus on foot, in the Darien jungle, east of today's canal. It was quite an extraordinary achievement for the time and after struggling through the thick jungle and across the high mountains, he reached the shores of an ocean that he named Pacific.

To the west of Darien, in the narrowest part of the Isthmus, the Spaniards established in 1517 a footpath, called *El Camino Real* - Spanish for "The Royal Path" -, through which most of the Inca gold would be sent to Spain. It started from the Old Panama City on the Pacific Ocean to Nombre de Dios - later to Portobelo, "the Great Emporium of South America"-, on the Atlantic Ocean.

Although it had been "finally completed and paved, wide enough for two wagons to pass" (10), this *Camino* would not allow cumbersome loads to be transported. In Spain, entrepreneurs were dreaming that their caravels could cross the Isthmus through a sea-level canal.

When Philip the Second, King of Spain, "forbade any modification of what God had created, the junction of oceans remained in the realm of dreams." (7)

Almost three centuries later, the idea of an Interoceanic Canal in Central America was revived. Among the explorers who mulled this idea, was the famous German scientist Alexander Von Humboldt. He mentioned the nine possible routes that he had explored during his peregrinations in Central America from 1799 to 1804.

In his ranking of those feasible routes, Humboldt put Nicaragua first, Panama coming only in fourth place, behind Darien and Tehuantepec - Mexico.

In 1823, following Simon Bolivar's campaign against Spain, all Central American Republics attained their independence. "Thus all the possible routes passed beyond control of the mother country and ended for all time the chance of Spain to participate in the great undertaking." (10) A few years later, Bolivar "attempted the project himself. . . He commissioned a British engineer, John Lloyd." (10) But no action was taken owing to the death of Bolivar in 1830.

Following her emancipation from Spain, in 1821, the province of Panama, after much wavering, finally and voluntarily joined Colombia*. However, the remains of an independent spirit among its inhabitants lingered in the Isthmus. This would come to light at regular intervals during the second half of the century, provoking many riots, and it did mark the Panamanians with an image of constantly agitated characters. For that reason, they were carefully watched by the Colombian Government - set in Bogota.

More explorers followed and, in 1835, we note the first French interest for the Panama Isthmus, then a province of Colombia. Charles de Thierry, a businessman born from French parents who had emigrated to London during the French Revolution, entered into a partnership with rich Jewish merchants, led by Augustin Solomon. In 1838, they obtained a land concession from Colombia "for all roads, railways or canals". However, French investors were seduced by other developments and, lacking funds, the partnership abandoned its project.

* This final choice had followed four periods where independence alternated with a union to the southern neighbor: 1830, 1831, 1832 and 1840. For reasons of simplicity, we shall use the name of Colombia for the country, which has her capital in Bogota and was successively named:
- Before 1831: the Republic of Great Colombia,
- From 1831 to 1863: the Republic of New Granada,
- From 1863 to 1886: the United States of Colombia ; after 1886: the Republic of Colombia.

At almost the same time, Charles Biddle, an ex-U. S. Army Colonel, visited Panama on a mission for President Andrew Jackson and, discouraged by the thick jungle, concluded that digging a canal there was impossible. Nevertheless, being a practical man, he obtained a private concession from Colombia for a railway project across the Isthmus, which displeased Jackson.

In Bogota, the Colombian Government delayed its decision to choose a contractor to dig the canal. We understand why: the Colombian historian Eduardo Lemaitre explained that, in 1840, "there were three concessions simultaneously active: Thierry, Solomon and Biddle." (15) What a confusion!

In the future, we shall encounter many more examples of such procrastination, as political chaos was endemic in Bogota.

When Biddle suddenly died, the Colombians decided to make a clean sweep and cancelled all current concessions.

DuVal explained that, from 1840 to 1860, a great number of explorers came to Central America. (10) We shall limit our story to the most noteworthy of them. A French mining engineer, Felix-Napoleon Garella, commissioned by Guizot, the French Prime Minister, visited Panama from 1838 to 1843. In a detailed study*, he recommended the starting point for a potential Interoceanic Canal to be in the Bay of Limon, close to where is today the City of Colon, on the Atlantic Coast. It was an excellent choice, as today the existing canal starts in the Bay of Limon. The British engineer Hill reached the same conclusion in his 1845 book - "A succinct view of forming a ship canal in Panama".

North Americans were intrigued by these projects. As the United States were climbing up into the leading nation pack, they looked unfavorably upon any foreign intervention on the American continent. The Monroe doctrine was only a few years old - 1823. This doctrine stated fundamentally that "Old World powers should abstain from settlement or occupation" (8) into America, in exchange for which Americans would not interfere into European affairs. Americans wanted to bar the Europeans from intervening in what they called the "western hemisphere" - a term describing the half-section of our planet containing the American continent. However, they did not yet have the means of such politics, lacking a strong navy.

France and Great Britain were still the most powerful nations on earth and remained so until the end of World War I, in 1918.

On their side, despite their trailing behind the major powers, the United States sent several explorers in the Central American Isthmus, such as Oersted in 1848 and Childs in 1850. However, no specific project came out of their exploratory missions.

---

* Garella's book "Project of a junction canal from the Pacific Ocean to the Atlantic Ocean through the Panama Isthmus", 260 pages long, studied a route through Mexico (Tehuantepec) and another through Nicaragua, but Garella favored the Panama route, at a cost of $ 50 million, to be built by 7,000 workers, during 10 years. Its original feature was a tunnel (sic) across the hills.

Now that Spain was out of the race for the Interoceanic Canal, America's main adversary remained Great Britain. For centuries, the British had traded with the Mosquito* Indians, on the Atlantic Coast of Belize and Nicaragua. This "Mosquito Coast" had its capital in Greytown - also called San Juan del Norte, at the mouth of the Rio San Juan -, which explorers had earmarked as a possible entry point for an Interoceanic Canal. For Americans, it was essential that Greytown be purged from all British influence.

This was 30 years before the opening of the Suez Canal and Great Britain was looking for a passage to send her commercial fleet to Asia. (10)

"While Britain appeared indifferent to a Panama Canal, it was much more assertive in Nicaragua, where in 1844 it had established a protectorate over the Mosquito Coast, at the Atlantic end of the projected canal." (20) After this indigenous kingdom, along the Atlantic Coast, had proclaimed itself independent, Great Britain declared it a protectorate, part of the British Empire. The Mosquito Indians became good friends of Great Britain.

"With the British in possession of the eastern slope of Nicaragua, the United States were in an embarrassing situation. . . fortunately, they had in Bogota, a man of initiative, Benjamin Bidlack. He was engaged in adjusting a controversy regarding differential duties imposed by Colombia in favor of her own shipping. . . Although without any instructions from his government, he negotiated with the Foreign Minister, Manuel Mallarino, a treaty. " (10) Colombia and the United States were both opposed to Great Britain, the intruder in their sphere of influence, and they pledged by this treaty their firm intent to collaborate in maintaining peace and free trade in the Central American Isthmus. On December 12, 1846, was signed the *Mallarino-Bidlack* agreement, "act of simple generosity from the new Colombian Government to Uncle Sam." (15) It was in fact a military alliance, designed to guarantee movements of goods and passengers in the Central American area. As a consequence of this treaty, "a constant military force, in the form of U. S. war ships, will cruise along the Panamanian coasts." (20)

"After a lengthy hesitation, the Senate sanctioned that treaty on June 3, 1848," (20) a year and a half after its signature by Ambassadors. We shall see all along many examples of this procrastination, typical of the Senate.

To follow historians' tradition, we shall refer to it as the **1846** treaty.

As this treaty is essential for the rest of our story, we ought to cover here its main features, which surprisingly come under Article 35 - out of 36 – the first 34 articles addressing the "perfect, firm and sincere friendship between the United States and Colombia", as well as free trade rules, smuggling practices, representatives of both countries - ministers, consuls, and so on.

* DuVal (10) preferred "Mosquito, but other authors use "Miskito".

Wyse quoted the entire text in his 1885 book. (3)

Article 35 was titled "Special Formal Conventions":

- "Colombia guarantees to the United States Government that the right of way or transit across the Isthmus of Panama, upon any modes of communication that now exist, or that may be, hereafter, constructed, shall be open and free to the Government and U. S. citizens;
- In order to secure to themselves the tranquil and constant enjoyment of these advantages, the U. S. guarantee positively and efficaciously to Colombia the perfect neutrality of the before mentioned Isthmus;
- In consequence, the United States also guarantee, in the same manner, the rights of sovereignty and property which Colombia has and possesses over the said territory." (10)

Much later, in 1903, we shall see how this pact would have dramatic consequences for Colombia. It was a good example - valid even today - showing that a country should not permit foreign battleships to protect its territory for too long, without running into major trouble.

Commenting on the 1846 treaty, McCullough concluded that: "An American military presence would continue, in the form of gunboats standing off the coasts of Colon and Panama City." (16)

Having found in Colombia an ally for maintaining free passage through the Isthmus of Panama, Americans' next goal was to free the Nicaragua route from British influence. This would not be so easy, because both American and British agents were very active on the Mosquito Coast and inside Nicaragua.

War had even been avoided on several occasions. "Both countries had become involved by work of their agents, rather than by the desires of the governments of the two nations." However, reason prevailed. "Washington and London recognized the importance of the matter and that neither desired war." (10) They reached a compromise, which "neutralized" British ambitions in the region.

In **1850**, the United States signed with Great Britain a treaty called *Clayton-Bulwer,* by which both nations recognized Colombia and pledged to build jointly a future Interoceanic Canal in "any part of Central America", according to the terms of the treaty. Such treaty being as important for this story as the one signed with Colombia, let us summarize here some of its terms:

- "The Governments of the U. S. and Great Britain hereby declare, that neither one nor the other will ever obtain or maintain for itself any exclusive control over the ship canal, which may be constructed between the Atlantic and the Pacific Oceans, by the way of the River San Juan de Nicaragua;

- The contracting parties further engage that, when the said Canal shall have been completed, they will protect it from interruption, seizure or unjust confiscation, and that they will guarantee its neutrality, so that the said Canal may forever be open and free." (10)

Americans were thus tied to the British in Nicaragua; they were also committed to maintain order in Panama. They would have many difficulties to truthfully respect the terms of those two treaties. We shall see how they used their commitments to their advantage. The disputes over some of their terms would bring endless diplomatic battles with Great Britain or with Colombia.

During these treaties' negotiation, exploration of the region did not stop. American engineers Orville Childs and Aniceto Menocal - of Cuban origin - surveyed the Nicaragua route. In their March 1852 report, they recommended to start from Greytown - San Juan del Norte -, on the Atlantic Ocean, from there to climb with 12 locks the Rio San Juan, then go across Lake Nicaragua - located 100 feet above sea level - , and from there descend with 13 locks to Brito, on the Pacific Ocean. The project would cost $ 31.5 million and would take 6 years to be completed. "Two eminent British engineers concurred, with minor changes, with Childs' report. It was the first accurate survey of the Nicaraguan route and formed the basis of all subsequent explorations." (10)

Having dealt with Colombia and Great Britain, Americans had almost forgotten about other influences in Central America.
In 1847, the French company of Martin and Klein (10) obtained from Colombia a concession for a railway line across the Isthmus.
Together with Great Britain and other European nations, the French already had over twenty years' experience in building railways. It had become the preferred passenger transportation system all over the old continent. Of course, Americans had also mastered this new technology.
For the second time - after Thierry in 1838 - , probably because they preferred investing in other projects, the French did not follow up on the deal and let their concession expire. Colombians transferred it to a group of American businessmen led by William Henry Aspinwall and John Lloyd Stevens.
On April 15, 1850, was signed in Bogota the *Stephens/Paredes* convention, which gave the *Panama RailRoad Company* - PRR -, that Aspinwall and his associates had registered in New York, the exclusive right to build a railway across the Isthmus of Panama.

This railway project across the Isthmus very opportunely. In 1848 gold has been discovered in California and many adventurers - mostly North-Americans - were moving from the East towards the West. These fortune hunters were commonly called the *Forty Niners* - from 1849. Following this *Gold Rush*, the population of San Francisco would grow from only 460 inhabitants in 1848 (17) to 15,000 by the end of 1849.

The Californian population reached a million just ten years later. There were quite a lot of greedy travelers looking for gold. To go west, these adventurers had a few choices. "To reach California, the traveler had three choices of routes: the Panama route, called "of the two seas", or cross the immensity of the North American continent, or last, the Cape Horn route," told us Bénard de Russailh, a French trader who used this last route in 1851. He explained: "Panama was the shortest route and also the most expensive, but it was also the most dangerous, as only a few voyagers, whether rich or poor, escaped from the redoubtable fever or cholera." (17)

As for crossing the immense plains to go west on a horse-pulled wagon, praying not to encounter some hostile Indians, it was not obviously the preferred way: "This trail is staked out with tombs." (17)

A more expensive way was to buy a ticket on a clipper - a three-masts sailing ship -, where hundreds of poor passengers were packed in filthy cabins at the bottom of the hull. This was not exempt from danger either, as during the eight-week trip around the southern tip of America, many ship-wrecks happened when passing the Cape Horn. (17)

Being a *Forty-Niner* required unusual courage.

Awaiting for the Panama railway to be built, an easy route was being sought through the Central American Isthmus. It still needed to be developed, but where? The choice was between Nicaragua and Panama.

To understand the geography of the area, let us have a look on these two countries. A map of the Central American Isthmus is shown in Appendix 7.

Nicaragua is 2,500 kilometers* (1,500 miles) south of New Orleans, while Panama is a further 500 kilometers (300 miles) south. In Nicaragua, the Isthmus is 230 kilometers (140 miles) wide, this distance being divided almost equally between the land and Lake Nicaragua, whose smaller adjunct in the North is called Lake Managua. From both oceans, the access to Nicaragua is easy, through partly navigable rivers running among hills, not exceeding an altitude of 50 meters (160 feet). These rivers act as overflows to the oceans for Lake Nicaragua, itself at an altitude of 32 meters (100 feet). In Nicaragua, the passage looked encouraging, but it stood in a country of jungle forests with some scattered pastures and was scarcely populated. Only some small fishermen huts were found on its oceans' shores. The country's main cities, Leon and Managua, located north of Lake Nicaragua, were way out of a potential canal route. And last, everything needed to be created there, while in Panama the footpath *Camino Real* has been used almost continually since Columbus' trip.

So, how was the best route selected?

* 1 meter = 0.305 feet. 1 kilometer = 0.62 mile.

New York capitalist Cornelius Vanderbilt had built a huge fortune by exploiting his monopoly of the *Big Apple* ferries. He hoped to expand his domain by running maritime passenger lines on both oceans, which called for the opening of the Nicaragua "land and lake" route.

As Vanderbilt was not known to take his decisions lightly, this was a sign that he considered it to be the best route.

In 1849, Vanderbilt signed a contract with the Government of Nicaragua, granting him the exclusive right to cross the country, and also the right to build a canal within the next twelve years. It was a great opportunity for Vanderbilt to expand his fleet.

A passenger transit was put into place. Using carved trees as canoes, mule-pulled carts or on donkey backs, the *Accessory Transit Company* of Vanderbilt transported up to 2,000 passengers a month, each paying $ 300 to go one-way from New York to San Francisco, - later reduced to $ 150. The trip lasted a whole month, half the time it took to go around Cape Horn. Vanderbilt successfully offered a full door-to-door service, what we would call today a "package".

At first, this route operated well, but did not really flourish, as there were numerous problems. Passengers crossing the Nicaraguan Isthmus complained about the perilous sailing across Lake Nicaragua, often subject to violent storms, because of its enormous size: 150 kilometers (94 miles) long and 60 kilometers (38 miles) wide. As for its land portion, the roughly built paths, across a heavy tropical jungle, were not much safer.

Further South, in the Isthmus of Panama, the *Camino Real* - Spanish for Royal Path - had been well maintained for two centuries, allowing the transit of the Inca gold from Peru and Equator to Spain. After the old Panama capital was ravaged by fire in 1671, the city was reconstructed a few kilometers to the west and the path relocated too.

At about the same time, a better landing was found on the Atlantic coast: San Lorenzo, protected by a fort, at the mouth of Rio Chagres. This new path was called the *Camino de Cruces* - Spanish for: The Path of the Crosses.

In the middle of the 18th Century, this route was however abandoned, as pirates, who operated in the Caribbean area, made it an unsafe trade route. Gold was sent from South America to Spain through the fortified port of Cartagena in Colombia or - rarely - around the southern tip of America, through the inevitable Cape Horn.

The *Camino de Cruces* slowly sank into the tropical jungle.

In Panama, the width of the Isthmus is about one third of what it is in Nicaragua: 70 kilometers (45 miles) instead of 230 kilometers (140 miles). On the Atlantic side, a canoe traffic had been developed along the Rio Chagres, a barely navigable stream, constituting an alternate route to the *Camino de Cruces*, for about half of the Isthmus route.

Coming back to the adventurers who wished to travel from the East Coast to California, they could now choose freely between Nicaragua and Panama. A more or less equally split flow of passengers resulted. In 1853, 20,000 passengers crossed the Isthmus through Nicaragua and 27,000 through Panama. (16)

These two routes would be rendered obsolete by the railway planned in Panama. We have seen that Aspinwall had obtained from Colombia an exclusive concession for a railway, which, through an amicable gesture towards the United States, was also allowing for a future canal to be built. This Colombian "gift" would play an important part in the events to come.

The *Panama RailRoad Company* (PRR) was funded with 100% American money. Lemaitre believed that "this company was a mask" (15) for the *Pacific Mail Steamship Company*, the rival company of Vanderbilt's *Accessory Transit Company*. Competition was tough.

In the 1850s, Central America was quite disorganized. Most of the small nations - from Guatemala in the North to Panama in the South - had acquired their independence from Spain in 1821. As John Major put it: "The isthmian republics - Mexico, Central America and New Granada - were poor, backward, and unstable, incapable of engineering and defending a transit themselves, and dependent on foreign money, expertise, and protection to do it for them." (20) Additionally, the Central American governments were not strong enough to pacify their frontiers, which were not yet well defined at this time.

In 1854, the Government of Nicaragua, short of money, wanted to take control of the profitable business run by the *Accessory Transit Company*. The natives were witnessing the great number of rich Americans en route to California and decided to have a piece of the pie. To protect Vanderbilt's interests, according to the *Mallarino-Bidlack* agreement, U. S. battleships had to intervene. They bombed the City of San Juan del Norte - Greytown - on the Atlantic Ocean and this temporarily restored order in the country.

This incident shows the enormous pressure American magnates were exerting on their Government. We shall see more of it along this story, proof that money was already reigning in the United States.

At that time, the major world powers - Great Britain, Spain, France and, to a smaller extent, the United States - were ruling the entire planet, thanks to their powerful battleships. The strategic importance of a modern war fleet was paramount.

It was also the time of colonization. Let us just remember a few of the colonies: Natal 1843, Algeria 1843, Punjab 1845, Texas 1846, Senegal 1854, Cochinchin 1862, etc.

Here we find the reason behind our story of the Interoceanic Canal. These colonies were obviously a major source of trade and it was logical to optimize that trade by using quicker vessels - and/or shorter maritime routes.

Fortunately, technology was developing at a fast pace. Soon appeared on the seas monster ships 300 to 500 feet long (100 to 150 meters), built in steel and propelled by steam engines, fired with coal.

Among the routes mulled by the engineers to cut maritime distances, the Suez Canal would obviously shorten the eastern route from Europe to Asia and, as far as the western route was concerned, there was no obvious solution and a site in Central America would still have to be selected.

In January 1855, after five years of hard work and with expenses reaching $ 8 million, the PRR - *Panama RailRoad* - was inaugurated. It ran between Aspinwall - on the Atlantic coast, on the Island of Manzanillo, for better protection, near the actual city of Colon - and reached the City of Panama on the Pacific coast, after a 48-mile trip - an additional mile long junction led to the port of La Boca, now Balboa. A one-way ticket was $ 25. The PRR was a 100% American company, managed from its New York offices.

The PRR came at the right time for shortening by a whole week the *Forty Niners'* trip from the East Coast to California. It was quite a luxury, compared to the old means of transportation: passengers only had to jump from ship to train and to another ship.

The completion of the PRR announced the end of the Nicaragua route.

In the fight for an Interoceanic Canal route, Panama had won the first round against Nicaragua.

Panama had won because there the Isthmus is narrower – 45 miles (70 kilometers) against 140 miles (230 kilometers) in Nicaragua - and therefore better suited for a railway. What tilted the decision in favor of Panama was the tract's length, which was the major factor determining the cost of a railway line. However the hills of Panama were higher - 110 meters against 50 in Nicaragua -, but it did not matter, as trains could climb hills easily.

The contest between Panama and Nicaragua would continue for the entire second half of the 19th century. Strangely, neither country really took a decisive advantage in that race - until Panama won - and this will certainly spice up our story.

The second round of this contest will take place with the decision to select a route for an Interoceanic Canal. We have already mentioned that in 1852 American engineers had recommended a canal in Nicaragua. However, through incredible and sudden changes of fortune, Panama would win, as we shall explain later on.

The attentive reader had certainly noticed that it took five years to build the 78 kilometer-long (49 miles) railway in Panama. Even at the time, it was an incredibly long time. The ground of the region was found very unstable, subject to landslides, and that caused many problems to the engineers. The rivers were extremely irregular, coming up or down in matter of hours, a consequence of the torrential rains. In particular, the floods of the largest river along the PRR, the *Rio Chagres*, often carried away the railroad wooden bridges, which needed constant repair. Furthermore, the unfortunate workers were decimated by fevers. Panama was too small a country to supply the large working force required by the PRR's construction. Laborers had to be brought from all over the world, even from as far away as China.

Historians quote various numbers for the casualties during the PRR's construction, from 1,000 to 5,000. Totten's official figure - 840 - seems too low.

When 25 years later, the French started digging the canal, they would again be facing the same problems – landslides and fevers.

That same year 1855, events became somewhat hectic in Nicaragua. William Walker, an American adventurer, proclaimed himself President of the country. He wanted to annex the territory in favor of the United States, as it had happened for Texas and California; he dreamed of expanding the Southern American border down to Panama; he also wanted to enslave the natives to dig a transoceanic canal.

Walker seized the *Accessory Transit Company*, a large source of revenues. This time, there was a conflict of interest between Vanderbilt and the *Panama RailRoad Company* of Aspinwall, two powerful and rival financial groups of New York City. The American Government hesitated to send a battleship and Walker ruled undisturbed for a while.

Since the opening of the PRR, in Panama, the superior passenger car's comfort dealt a fatal blow to the Nicaragua route and Vanderbilt hesitated between withdrawing completely and involving the American Government in defending his interests.

In 1857, Vanderbilt finally convinced his Government to send troops in Nicaragua in 1857, Walker was captured, but did not lose his momentum. Sent back to the States, Walker came back with new recruits, but was finally caught and executed in September 1860.

Bringing peace to Nicaragua was not enough to revive the *Accessory Transit Company*. It had not only suffered from the competition opened by the *Panama RailRoad Company* but also from the PRR's contracted services: two other maritime services, the *Pacific Mail Steamship* and the *U. S. Mail Companies*. Unfortunately, Vanderbilt could not do anything to prevent this. His company, the *Accessory Transit Company*, could not compete and had to withdraw. It was the end of the land route across Nicaragua.

Devastated by this loss, from then on Vanderbilt would invest exclusively in continental U. S. railways. He built the first New York to Chicago line.

When he died in 1877, his company, the *NY Central System* was carrying passengers over more than 4,000 miles.

With the Monroe doctrine in mind, Americans were still contemplating an Interoceanic Canal of their own, but they did not favor Panama, judged to be too restless. They recalled that on April 15, 1856, a ridiculous fight concerning the robbery of a watermelon from the market in the City of Panama went sour and that Panamanians had murdered 15 *gringos* - citizens of North America. (16) As recommended by American engineers, Nicaragua was favored, but, there, no serious project would emerge for the next ten years, the Civil War having deferred all American investments abroad.

Once the war over, on March 19, 1866, the Senate voted a resolution requesting the Marine Secretary to gather all existing information on the possible canal routes across the Central American Isthmus. Rear-Admiral Charles H. Davis, who knew the area well, prepared the report. He had been first in command on the *Saint Mary*, in 1857, when he accepted Walker's surrender in Greytown.

Davis's report was honest. He frankly stated that there were not enough data available to choose the best canal route and recommended to send more expeditions to the area. (10)

A year later, in 1867, Andrew B. Dickinson for the United States and Tomas Ayon for Nicaragua signed a treaty, by which the neutrality of the future canal would be guaranteed. This clearly showed that the United States favored Nicaragua. However, they showed no haste in organizing new expeditions. (10)

In 1869, President Grant, already familiar with Nicaragua, which he had crossed on his way to his California's garrison, named Daniel Ammen as the expedition leader. This was the *First Isthmian Canal Commission*.

Ammen did not leave immediately. He believed that the Nicaragua project would encourage the world commerce and that, as such, it should interest scientists from all nations.

In order to convince the entire world of the viability of his project in Nicaragua, Ammen attended in 1871 the First International Geographic Congress. "It gathered in Antwerp, Belgium. Ferdinand de Lesseps was the French delegate. The delegates were to examine various possible routes across the Central American Isthmus and favored the project submitted by Gorgoza, a French engineer, who worked together with the explorer Lacharme. This project consisted in a canal with locks through the Isthmus of Panama. However, Congress did not reach any firm agreement and the project remained purely virtual." (2)

Evidently, Ammen did not have enough information to be fully convincing about Nicaragua.

These Geographic Congresses would meet every four years in a European city; the next one was to be held in Paris in 1875.

In preparation for the next Congress, Ammen led a large American expedition to Nicaragua in 1872/1873. With him were Commanders Edward P. Lull and Alexander F. Crosman, and the engineer Aniceto G. Menocal, - whom we shall meet again, as the most fervent supporter of Nicaragua.

They explored the entire country and met with President Jose Santos Zelaya, who asked a Nicaraguan expert, Maximiliano Sonnenstern, to join the American team for a survey. Together, they did an excellent job. Ammen and Menocal came home with a detailed route, which would be considered for years as the best reference for a canal project in Nicaragua. (10)

Here were the main features of Ammen and Menocal's proposed route, which differed slightly from the 1852 project:

Starting from the Atlantic coast, in the city of San Juan Del Norte - as the capital of the British protectorate, it was also called Greytown -, the proposed canal went westwards near the village of Boca San Carlos, where it met the Rio San Carlos. The canal route then followed this "almost navigable" river until it reached Lake Nicaragua. On the other shore of the lake, it crossed the Rivas Isthmus, through the valley of the Rio del Medio, instead of the Rio Las Lajas, as proposed by Childs.

For this detailed route, Ammen and Menocal produced an estimated cost of $ 65.7 million, with a contingency of 25% included.

Ammen, Lull and Menocal also visited Panama and came up with an estimated cost of $ 94.5 million, along a route closely following the PRR.

Panama's cost came out 40% more expensive than Nicaragua's.

Strangely, this difference would remain unchanged for all the estimated costs that would be calculated in the following years.

In 1875, Ammen and Menocal attended the International Geographic Congress in Paris, where they made a presentation of their findings. Having failed to be convincing in Antwerp, Menocal was saddened that here again, no agreement was reached.

Although, at the time, the scientists exchanged their information freely, the existing data was not found detailed enough to determine with accuracy the budget of the future canal. The engineers could not agree with Ammen and Menocal figures. They lacked detailed topographic surveys, hydrographic measures, and many other important details. They expressed many reservations on the estimates of Ammen and Menocal – who did not divulge the entirety of their calculations.

Upset by their failure to convince the congressmen that Nicaragua had superior advantages, the *First Isthmian Canal Commission*, chaired by Daniel Ammen, assisted by Andrew A. Humphreys and C. P. Patterson, studied once again the Nicaragua route and unanimously recommended it as being the less expensive in a meeting with President Ulysses Grant, on February 7, 1876. Again, the Americans showed their persistence and their resolve to build their own canal.

The *Isthmian Commission* issued its formal report on October 21, 1876 - see *American Inter-Oceanic Ship Canal Question*, by Rear–Admiral Daniel Ammen (L. R. Hamersly, Philadelphia, 1880).

One would have thought that the thorough knowledge of Panama's terrain, where the PRR had been in operation for more than twenty years, would have influenced the opinion of the members of the Commission. Not at all.

Although it was difficult to explore Nicaragua, with its inaccessible paths in the jungle, now abandoned for twenty years - Vanderbilt had left in 1856 -, its small harbors on the coasts, the dangerous navigation on its large lake, the *Isthmian Commission* nevertheless recommended the Nicaragua route.

The conclusions of the Ammen Commission proved without a shadow of any doubt that the Nicaragua route was the best.

The Commission produced the first estimate for the canal and all estimates in the future would confirm this preference for Nicaragua, always found simpler and costing less than Panama.

At this point, we are logically led to ask ourselves: so, why is the canal in Panama?

Despite what history tells us, all engineers were certain that the simplest and cheapest route across the Central American Isthmus was and has remained today: Nicaragua.

What follows will show how Americans remained committed to the recommendation of the Ammen Commission for decades and finally selected Panama as a last resort, in 1903, thanks to the intervention of Philippe Bunau-Varilla, the champion of Panama.

The Panama Canal had been opened in 1914, but since, Nicaragua had never completely disappeared from the Interoceanic Canal race.

In 1929, the U. S. *International Canal Board* led by Colonel Daniel I. Sultan headed a Corps of Engineers' delegation, 300 strong, and after two years of studies, came up with a detailed project for a canal through Nicaragua, for a cost of $ 722 million. However, this alternative route stayed on the drawing boards.

More recently, in 2006, when Panama was preparing an expansion of its canal, Nicaragua came up again with a very serious proposal for a new canal, but failed to find the money for such a huge undertaking - the figure of $ 18 to 25 billion was quoted. At the time we write these lines, this Nicaragua Canal is still under consideration.

Would there be some day a second canal in Nicaragua?

Let us go back to 1876 and briefly summarize the situation of the contenders in the Interoceanic Canal race:
- Panama had won the first round, when a railroad was built there in 1855,
- Nicaragua had won the second round, when the U. S. *Isthmian Commission* recommended it to Congress in 1876.

The Washington Government just had to act on it.

2
THE BUNAU FAMILY

After the above historical reminders, we are now ready to meet the hero of this book.

First, we have to recognize that his name, Bunau-Varilla, with its Spanish touch, makes it perfect to become involved in the Panama Canal project - Panama's official language being Spanish. The origin of his name has been tickling the imagination of many authors because, in his writings, Philippe Bunau-Varilla has remained totally silent about his ancestors; there is not a single word in all his books.

Anguizola believed that the Bunau-Varilla family went back to ancient and noble origins, on one side: German - Bunau - and on the other: Basque - Varilla -, both genealogies having been traced up to the 18th Century. (18)

Another author, De Diesbach, suggested that the brothers could be the out-of-wedlock sons of Ferdinand de Lesseps, who happened to be a widower between 1853 and 1868, the exact period when the brothers were born. (22)

Both theories could make sense, but there is no evidence for either.

The reader may appreciate that these romantic stories belong rather to a novel than to this serious book.

Our sources of information are three fold:

- The Paris City Hall Archives, (2) recently transcribed into a digital form and made accessible through the Internet, where the birth certificates of Philippe and Maurice can be found. Some other certificates - marriage, death - related to the Bunau-Varilla family are also available. Without the Internet, this search would have been a long and tedious task.

- The engravings on the Bunau-Varilla's funeral monument in Passy cemetery. Maurice, the eldest brother, had bought the burial vault in 1888 to bury his grandmother. Passy was a small town west of Paris; later, the area was developed and became part of the City of Paris; it is called the 16th ward - *arrondissement*.

- François-Ignace Mouthon's book: "From Bluff to Blackmail. The Great Campaigns of *Le Matin*", edited by Pauwels, Paris, 1910, confirmed the above information. Mouthon knew intimately the Bunau-Varilla family, having worked from July 1900 to January 1908, as a journalist of *Le Matin*, the newspaper owned by Maurice Bunau-Varilla, Philippe's brother; Mouthon had evidently investigated the origin of the Bunau-Varilla family.

- Various sources quoted in Pinsolle's book. (30)

In Paris' City Hall archives, we can read the birth certificates of:
- "Philippe Jean <u>Bunau</u>, born on July 26, 1859, in the 1st ward of Paris, file # 421553" (2); that same file was surcharged by a handwritten mention: Philippe Jean Bunau Varilla, where "Varilla" had been added.

- His elder brother, "Maurice Jules <u>Varillat</u>, born on September 18, 1856, 9 Rue Casimir Périer, in the 10th ward of Paris, file # 423795" (2); the certificate has been surcharged with the handwritten mention: "Bunau Varilla".

The Passy funeral monument of the Bunau-Varilla family, which still exists today, shows:
"Caroline Pamela Bunau, born Coche, on May 21, 1804 and died March 12, 1888." She was the grandmother of Maurice and Philippe. She married Jean Baptiste Bunau on May 7, 1823 - their marriage certificate can be found in the digitalized Paris City Hall Archives. (2)

"Ms. Widow Bunau-Varilla, born Bunau, on May 31, 1826 and died July 1st, 1895." Ms Bunau-Varilla's death certificate indicates that she died on July 3 (and not 1st) and that her official name was Caroline Pamela Bunau. (2)

She was the brothers' mother and had kept her mother's name Bunau, because she never officially married Varillat.

According to Mouthon and to the Paris City Hall Archives, when Maurice was born in 1856, he was recognized by his father William Jean-Jules Varillat. However, evidently, he never married the mother, Caroline Pamela, who remained Bunau. This could indicate the modest origin of the Bunau family, as more affluent people would have been married in City Hall.

The brothers' mother, Ms. Widow Bunau-Varilla kept a haberdasher shop - also called men's outfitter. "She was a dark brunette, with some silver threads in her hair. She had a gleam in her eyes." The Bunau family lived Rue Saint-Augustin, near the Paris *Bourse* - the Stock Market. (30)

In 1859, when Philippe was born, his father William Jean-Jules Varillat had either died or disappeared. Philippe therefore had to take his mother's name, Bunau.

By putting all this information together, we found that from 1859 to 1882, the brothers bore two different family names:

- Maurice Jules Varillat,
- Philippe Jean Bunau.

According to Mouthon's book, Maurice's father, "William Jean-Jules Varillat, was a merchant originating from Auvergne, a region in the center of France." Pinsolle (30) indicated that Varillat was preparing chemical products and selling his production. He had filed many patent claims from 1850 to 1860.

There are few records of the origin of the Bunau family. It probably came from the East of France, Alsace or Lorraine.

The name of Bunau is found in these regions in the early 19th Century and around 1830 in the Paris *Almanach* - the *Who's Who* of the time -, which listed the names of about 25,000 celebrities. We have found in the City records that there was a Mr. Alfred Jean Baptiste Bunau - born in Paris on Oct. 14, 1804 and died 1836 -, who had married Caroline Pamela Coche on May 7,1823. He was the grandfather of Philippe and Maurice; he died young at only 32.

A serious setback or reverse of fortune in the family could have left Caroline Pamela Coche/Bunau poverty stricken, with her young daughter - she was 10 when her father died.

The brothers Philippe and Maurice spent a quiet childhood in Paris, sustained by the love of their mother and grandmother. They attended High School in the Condorcet and Saint-Louis *lycees*.

Mouthon indicated page 145 of his book that "on March 22, 1882, a presidential decree authorized Maurice Varillat to change his name to Maurice Bunau Varilla - without the *t*. This decree was validated on June 4, 1884. He thus gave his patronymic from Auvergne a consonance more in line with his future mission: Grandee of Spain, Inca of Peru . . . nobody knows."

Why did the brothers apply for changing their names?

One possible explanation is that the name Bunau sounded too German. The 1870 defeat was fresh in the French people's memory and must certainly have attracted some derogatory remarks to the brothers. In the years following 1870, a revengeful spirit was in the air in France, two of its eastern provinces - Alsace and a major part of Lorraine - had been taken by Germany.

Another motivation could have been a desire to move up the social scale.

The addition of Varilla surely made Bunau sound more exotic.

Alike his brother, Philippe changed his name from Bunau to Bunau Varilla.

Their mother remained Bunau, as shown on her death certificate.

The origin of the Bunau-Varilla family has been for most authors a mystery. It is now solved.

Using the Paris Archives, Mouthon's book and the engravings of the Passy cemetery, we can summarize our findings by the equation:

Bunau + Varillat = Bunau Varilla.

With or without a hyphen?

In the first years after the concatenation, the two patronymics stood next to each other without a hyphen. With time, both Maurice and Philippe have added the hyphen, as shown in their signatures of the early years of the 20th century.

From the above demonstration, we can now write the real name of this book's hero:

Philippe Jean Bunau-Varilla.

We will refer to him as **B-V,** and to avoid any confusion, we shall refer to his brother simply as **Maurice**.

Philippe was an extremely gifted child, with an exceptional mental ability. He was a good student, always first of his class, easily passing all his high school exams, until being successfully admitted to the prestigious École Polytechnique* in 1878. Napoleon called this school: "The hen with the golden eggs". Its motto was: "For the country, its science and its glory". (11)

At only eighteen, Philippe's admission to this prestigious school was a truly amazing performance. "Although this institution is a military school, it is exclusively devoted to the study of pure science, such as mathematics, physics, geometry, astronomy and so on. Its aim is to provide the military and the civil services of the nation scientifically educated officers."(18)

There we find more information about the man who will occupy all our attention in the following pages. His record has been kept in the École Polytechnique files and states that Philippe was a protestant and that his "full name" was Philippe Jean Bunau, changed later on the same file to "usual name": Bunau Varilla.

Mirella Ricciardi, a granddaughter of Philippe Jean Bunau-Varilla (B-V), mentioned his "abject poverty" in a recent book. (24) It is certainly an understatement.

---

*According to some authors, B-V had been admitted to Polytechnique with a scholarship. This does not make much sense, as tuition was and is still free for French students.

The Bunau family lived on the meager revenues of the two ladies, who were not really poor. B-V mentioned in his memoirs that when he was ten, "a young student of the *École Polytechnique*, was visiting my mother." (7) This could add credibility to his mother's men outfitting occupation. Or it could be a sign of some wealth, as all the alumni of this prestigious school had a high social status.

Later, when B-V was twenty-five and working as an engineer on the Panama Canal, he did not behave at all like a pauper when he was faced with the sumptuous spending of the French Company. Quite the opposite: he tried to minimize the lavish expenses. In his memoirs, he mentioned the cottage built for the French Company's General Manager and luxuriously decorated at a cost of more than one million francs, as just: "a wooden cottage, a country house for the Company's General Manager, was baptized *Folie Dingler;* the word applied in the eighteen Century to *secret pavilions* in the outskirts of Paris."(7) And B-V was not particularly enthralled by a luxurious passenger car of the PRR, specially equipped for the same General Manager: "the car ordered for the inspections of the works was called the *Wagon Palais*. It was a wicked translation of the word *Palace Car*," (7) used in America to designate simple sleeping cars. As he did not show any surprise in discovering these extravagances, B-V must have certainly been accustomed to a certain level of luxury within his previous living environment in Paris.

In summary, let us just recall that the Bunau-Varilla brothers came from a lower middle class family, neither poor nor wealthy, just comfortably well off. They were raised, in the absence of a father, by their mother and grandmother, living frugally of their revenues, widow pensions or other.

In 1880, after two years of studies, B-V graduated from Polytechnique.

Some questions arise about his knowledge of foreign languages. He certainly spoke good enough English to present a series of conferences in the United States in 1900. And later, he supervised the translation of his books in English; they were printed by Constable in England in 1913 and by Doubleday in the U. S. in 1920. (9) He had studied English in school and had become quite fluent by practicing it on the Panama Canal works, where, in his position as General Manager of the works, he would often meet American representatives - marine and railway -, and perhaps some Jamaican supervisors: at that time, Jamaica was a British Commonwealth protectorate.

We also have the testimony of one of his friends, who wrote that: "Philippe lamented to have to express his ideas in a foreign tongue, but in fact, his English was *quite good*" - from a letter by Sir Edwyn Dawes dated December 24, 1900. Later, during World War I, B-V met an English officer who "congratulated him of his knowledge of the English language." (9)

As for Spanish, he did not speak it well. His correspondence with Marroquin, the President of Colombia, was mainly in French, the diplomatic language of the time - although a few cables were sent in Spanish. (11)

We have to pause briefly here to explain how skeptical one ought to be when reading B-V's memoirs. As we are going to quote these books abundantly (references 5, 7, 9 and 11), the reader should be warned beforehand about their veracity.

B-V's memoirs are often difficult to believe, as his writing is quite sophisticated, bombastic and grandiloquent. Even some of his friends pointed it out: "The Frenchman (B-V) had a penchant for literary license and dramatic hyperbole in his writings," (Edward P. Mitchell, editor of the New York Sun).

Let us, for example, read the first few lines of B-V's memoirs published in 1913: "The object of this book is not to wreak vengeance on certain men . . . They are entitled to the contempt of oblivion. The upshot of the lesson of this book should be to show to the nation and to her leaders that the primary virtue of democracy is resistance to calumny. The reader of this book will understand how many disasters we would have been spared if this virtue had inspired some of our leading men."(7)

It should be noted that "resistance to calumny" is rarely mentioned as a virtue.

B-V was extremely verbose, he loved writing about his achievements. The 1913 edition is an enormous book, 800 pages in French and 700 in English.

Was B-V honest? Among the huge amount of details quoted in the book, we have never been able to find a single lie or even a contradiction. However, there are many - indeed many - omissions, most of the time the result of a voluntary decision.

B-V often remained silent about some events and certainly about his motivations. In his memoirs we read a lot of "I decided, I left, I felt, I was compelled to, etc.", without any reason being given for such action. We will encounter many such examples along this story.

In the absence of a straightforward explanation by B-V, we have always tried to determine a logical reason for his actions, selecting the most probable one, among those quoted by the historians, which we have selected as the best historical sources of information and are listed in Appendix 4.

For B-V, words had to be chosen very carefully. As an example, let us examine how he justified himself to have arrived in New York on September 22, 1903, at the exact moment when Panamanian revolutionaries were looking for help - which he provided for them.

In his statement of March 29, 1912, B-V wrote: "When I arrived, I had not the slightest precise hint as to a revolution being started, though press dispatches made probable that the state of discontent on the Isthmus would burst out at the first instance." (6)

Now, let us examine what was written in *Le Matin*, newspaper of his brother Maurice, on Wednesday September 2, 1903, just below an article written by B-V: "Panama in Revolution. Travelers report that the Isthmus is in full revolution. . . . Indians have rebelled. . . . Guns are being distributed in the mountains." (2)

B-V was certainly cautious about newspaper's information, but his goal in 1912 was to hide the fact, that, in 1903, he had supported the Panamanian revolutionaries, as his solution to the rupture between the United States and Colombia in their negotiation for the Interoceanic Canal.

Not only his character was special, but B-V had unusual physical features that need to be mentioned.

According to McCullough, B-V was "a small man. He stood only 5' 4" (1.63 meters) and probably weighed no more than 130 pounds (60 kilograms). However, he had a square, high brow, a good chin, extremely pale blue eyes - so intense they were piercing -, a luxuriant dark-red mustache, and his posture was always perfect. He was, as well, proud, ambitious, phenomenally energetic, blatantly self-confident, and, for all that, quite likable, in an eager and direct way." (16)

Some authors differed on B-V's physical aspect. For Morris, he was seen as an eccentric character: "It was hard for Americans not to laugh at B-V's bristling, so Gallic was he in his gamecock fierceness, all frown and spiked mustaches. Had he stood a foot taller, he might have looked as formidable as he in fact was."(25)

McCullough described our hero: "B-V's table manners were impeccable. He was the cultivated, upper-class European *par excellence* and he knew exactly how to gain attention wherever he went. "He just did not just come into a room, he made an *entrance*," recalled Alice Roosevelt Longworth admiringly." (16) Nevertheless, B-V was recognized as having "the bruising willpower and aristocratic intelligence of the best French *éducation d'élite*."(25)

Morally, he was impeccable. He wrote in his memoirs: "A nation alike a man, cannot live without honor." And also: "The honor of our fatherland is a thousand times more precious than all the goods I could acquire." And lastly: "The graduates of Polytechnique ought to permanently serve their country." (7 and 9) These were not just words, as we shall discover later when we narrate his heroic conduct during the "Great War" - World War I.

This book will prove, if needed, that we can trust his honorability.

However, we often notice in B-V's writings his enormous self-esteem; this is probably a logical consequence of him having successfully joined the elite of the French nation, only by his own merit.

He was an extremely arrogant man, often for a good reason, as proven by this short example from his memoirs: "I should certainly have been bitten by the Stegomya mosquito, which transports yellow fever, but I had in me the element, resistant and protective, which was made more active by the notion that I was indispensable to the life of the great undertaking." (7) What he calls "the great undertaking" is the making of the Panama Canal.

This is why, many times in his memoirs, his aplomb led him to ignore certain facts that would be detrimental to his reputation.

As an example, B-V dealt quite briefly with the period covering 1894, when *Artigue, Sonderegger & Co,* the construction company he had set up with his brother Maurice, where he served as General Manager, was tried for embezzlement. This company brought him and his brother an enormous wealth. Thanks to *Artigue, Sonderegger & Co,* B-V had become a wealthy man.

However, we did not find a single word in his memoirs about the origin of his fortune. Indirectly, he briefly alluded to it, only to serve his reputation, when he pointed out his generosity. Rightly so, as he spent a major part of his fortune to lobby in favor of the Panama Canal and to help giving birth to the future Panamanian Republic.

B-V also feigned to ignore in his memoirs that he was a co-investor in *Le Matin,* which he qualified strangely as: "the newspaper of my brother Maurice."(7) B-V was indeed a partner with his brother and although he was never involved in either managing or editing the newspaper, he surely collected many dividends from this partnership. The profit made by this newspaper from 1900 and 1940 had been more than $ 15 million. B-V received about 30% of it. However, he was certainly ashamed of the newspaper's scandalous policy (see page 286).

B-V also left out his family from his memoirs. His wife and children are mentioned only a couple of times. As he was an extremely proud man, our guess is that he must not have been pleased of his modest origins, of being a fatherless child and of being born poor.

Let us turn for a moment to Maurice, the elder of the two brothers. Although he was as clever as his younger brother was, he did not study successfully. Some sources indicated that Maurice quitted High School when he reached 8th Grade and that he failed the exam to be admitted to Saint Cyr, the French Military Academy for army officers - the equivalent of West Point in the United States. (30)

Maurice did not lack talents, but had a much less egocentric character than his younger brother and was more inclined to socialize.

Seeking power and friendships, Maurice started to work in various jobs related to the Parisian Stock Market and Banks. "It was around 1880 that Jules Maurice Varillat appeared under the peristyle of the French Bourse - the Paris Stock Market . . . He was dealing with matters of banking and stocks." (From Mouthon's book) Maurice was then 24 and the Panama project was about to begin.

These early choices were a presage of Maurice's future career. By being admitted at an early age in the financial circles of the French capital, he was allowed to meet many influent people, who will be useful to his future career. He knew intimately many important men, including Reinach, a malicious banker - whom we shall encounter later.

The brothers were quite different. Philippe had a scientific and logical mind, geared towards his dream: to contribute to the building of the Panama Canal. Maurice had a literary mind, he was astute, philanthropic, wide open to the world, liking money and women.

They complemented each other nicely.

We shall see later how their association worked wonders in running a construction company in Panama and brought them a huge fortune.

They used this fortune to purchase the newspaper *Le Matin*, one of the major Parisian dailies, which exerted an enormous influence on the French political life.

To get into the ambiance of the Parisian world during the brothers' childhood, we need to recall a few dates that have marked the major historical events of the time:

1861-1865: The Civil War raged in America; it will affect the relationship between North and South of the United States forever. To illustrate this, let me quote a personal souvenir. When I worked in Texas in the 1980s, we went to a business meeting in New York City. One of my colleagues, a "true blue" Texan, traveled with me; he had put on his boots and cowboy hat and upon my surprise explained: "I want those Yankees to know where I am from!"

During the Civil War, Napoleon the Third declared that France would remain neutral. However, among his opponents, the liberals substantially backed the Yankees with money and weapons.

On May 10, 1869, the first transcontinental railway was put in service across America, which allowed traveling from New York to California in slightly over a week. Logically, the *Panama Railroad Company* lost some of its customers, but still remained the safest route, as the train traffic was often

interrupted by Indian tribes, struggling for the control of their land in continental America. This problem was quickly solved, as the American railway syndicate, tired of these interferences, compelled the Government to create reservations, where the Indians would be confined. This demonstrates once again the power of the Washington lobbies.

Commenting on the operation of this first intercontinental railway line, Siegfried drew this conclusion: "The United States have reached another state of equilibrium, with a double frontage on the Atlantic and Pacific oceans: they have more than ever to take an interest in a trans-isthmic canal." (13)

On November 18, 1869, the Suez Canal was inaugurated. B-V was ten years old; he was so enthusiastic about this major human endeavor that he vowed to dedicate his future career to achieve something even better. He remembers his mother saying: "You were too young to make Suez, but you still have the Panama Canal left." (7) B-V's dream had begun.

This scene has been turned into a legend, as shown by the text that follows. It is extracted from a French inspirational magazine for children called "Le Messager-École du Dimanche" - *The Messenger-Sunday School* -, published in May 1930 and titled:

"Willpower Does It All!

Philippe is twelve. He listens to a conversation his mother is having with an engineer who had just returned from India.

"What a magnificent trip and how I envy you to have crossed the newly opened Suez Canal."

"Yes, it is truly a world marvel. Did you know that I applied to work on this Canal, but I was not accepted?"

And Philippe's mother concluded:

"In any case, do not get discouraged. There are so many wonderful projects remaining to be built by engineers. There is an isthmus much more important than Suez. It is Panama! You will see, it will be pierced one day, and why not by you?"

The engineer laughed and left.

On the same evening, Philippe rushed to kiss his mother and said:

"I will dig the Panama Canal"

"You darling? Why not? Try to prepare yourself right now by studying well in school, geography, mathematics that give you so much trouble, so that later you will become a talented engineer."

This took place in 1869. Less than twenty years later, Philippe Bunau-Varilla would become the General Manager of the works in Panama.

The dream of the small boy had guided all his life and, at the end, became true.

This 1930 text - written almost fifty years after the facts - contributed to enhance B-V's fame. B-V was in good company. Together with B-V's dream, the magazine told the story of Roald Amundsen, the legendary Norwegian explorer of the poles, of Florence Nightingale, a renowned English nurse, and of many other famous persons who had fulfilled their childhood dreams.

This "nursery tale" shows the extent of B-V's fame in the 1930s, in total contrast with the obscurity in which he has fallen nowadays.

Now that we have mentioned Suez, let us examine its overall economics. The Suez Canal project had attracted a major portion of the French savings and fortunately proved to be very successful. However, at first, the Suez Company did not make a profit for five years and its stock went down.

In 1869, when it started operating, the Suez Canal shares were worth 290 francs, well below their nominal value - they had been sold for 500 francs -, and in the following years, they went further down:

1870: 208 francs
1871: 175 francs
1872: 185 francs.

Fortunately, after a few years, when the Suez Canal generated a profit, its stock came back up and reached 1,327 francs in 1880 - coincidentally, on the same year, the first Panama subscription took place.

The Suez Canal shares reached a peak of more than 6,000 francs in 1912!

It had met all the investors' expectations: its traffic reached 3 million tons in 1879, exactly the figure that had been forecast in 1855.

Suez was a good example of a successful stock market gamble, borne mainly by small investors. Encouraged by such a success, the same small investors would try to repeat this achievement in Panama.

Among other important historical facts happening in France at the time of the Bunau-Varilla brothers' youth - they were born in 1856 and 1859 -, let us mention the 1870 war:

- September 2, 1870. Germany defeated the French army in Sedan.
- September 4, 1870. The Third Republic was proclaimed.
- March 1871. French Civil War raged in Paris, remembered under the name of *La Commune*.
- May 1871. A peace treaty was signed between France and Germany and the French provinces of Alsace and Lorraine (only in part) became German.

The 1870 French defeat was hard to accept. In 1872, obsessed with revenge, France established a five-year military service. High school graduates were limited to a single year. The youngsters who supported families were exempt. B-V, who went to Polytechnique, a military school, was exempt. Maurice was too old to be drafted: he was 26 years old in 1872.

As if France did not have enough misfortunes, on May 8, 1873, the worst economic crisis in a century hit Europe. Caused by the collapse of several Austrian banks in Vienna, it affected most European banks in a domino effect and a few months later most American banks. In Paris, Credit Foncier was seriously hit. All the French industry suffered from this crisis as well. As an example, the cast iron production declined by 20% and only recovered in 1878.

The Vienna crisis started what historians call the "Great Depression" and lasted until 1896. The Panama project could not come at a worse time.

In 1875, France lost control of the Suez Canal when Great Britain bought the Egypt Viceroy's shares. The Rothschild Bank served as the go-between.

But among these misfortunes, France witnessed a few happy events, among which the inauguration of a new Paris Opera on January 5, 1875.

After the military humiliation of 1870 and the 1873 economic crisis, life in France began to re-assert itself. By 1875, two years ahead of schedule, France paid off its war debt to Germany: the huge sum of 5 billion francs in gold. This shows that there still was a lot of gold hidden in the French home mattresses, - as legend has it, it was where the French people hid their savings.

France had lost the war in 1870, but was still a rich country, one of the most powerful nations on earth.

The new Third Republic would now have to prove itself. It would do so in the Panama affair, writing a "sad, but not disgraceful page of history." (7)

3

PANAMA VS. NICARAGUA

Let us turn now to America. We have seen that the United States passion-ately and desperately wanted to have their own Interoceanic Canal in Central America. After Ammen and Menocal recommendations, Nicaragua had become American's favorite and would remain so throughout this story.

This is quite understandable: Nicaragua was a small country, open to American interests. Since its independence in 1840, it had been invaded five times by U. S. troops - 1853, 1854, 1856, 1857, 1867 -, under the alleged reason of protecting U. S. interests there. Walker, an American, had even been President of the country for a few years, when he tried to turn Nicaragua into another United State.

But despite all this, Americans were not free to build their own canal. They were tied by a pact they had signed with Great Britain in 1850 - the *Clayton-Bulwer* treaty -, by which both countries were bound to act together on a Central American canal. Most of the Washington politicians were finding this clause of the pact totally unacceptable and preferred to have a 100% American canal. It would take a long time for the Americans to remove this constraint, through lengthy diplomatic negotiations with Great Britain. Almost half a century!

The French were not tied by any treaty and they took advantage of the situation to display additional activity. They sent explorers to the Central American Isthmus: Godin de Lepinay, Armand Reclus and Lucien Napoleon Bonaparte Wyse, who surveyed several routes in Mexico, Nicaragua and Panama.

These last two countries will ceaselessly compete for having this canal on their land, during the second half of the 19th Century. As we shall see, Philippe Bunau-Varilla (B-V) will play a major part in tilting this rivalry in favor of Panama.

Nicaragua had won the first round of this singular fight, but nothing had concretely happened, as the Americans had not followed suit on the recommendation of the Ammen Commission since it was issued in February 1876.

There were a few reasons for this.

Firstly, the United States were emerging from the Civil War and priority was given to reconstruction at home.

Secondly, the dollar currency was experiencing problems that had not yet been solved - should it be based on gold or on silver? - and this inhibited all investments. See more details of this in chapter 16, page 153.

And finally, the western rush was a major focus for the young nation, concentrating most of its financial efforts. Enormous territories had to be developed west of the Mississippi.

In summary, the Interoceanic canal was not, at the time, one of the highest priorities of Washington politicians. This situation would last for another twenty years.

The contest between Nicaragua and Panama continued actively, with Americans and French engineers supporting their preferred choice. Soon this race would take place in the open, in a public field, where a decisive and vital battle will be held: the International Geography Congresses.

Following the 1871 Congress held in Antwerp and the 1875 Congress held in Paris, the next Congress was planned to take place in Paris in 1879. However, most of the French geographers did not want to wait for this next Congress to act.

They founded the *French Committee for an Interoceanic Canal* in March 1876. It was obviously a move to confiscate the deliberations of the 1879 Congress and establish the idea of a "French Canal". Ferdinand de Lesseps was solicited to become the President of this Committee.

In 1876, the humiliation of the 1870 defeat had been forgotten. The French economy was recovering slowly and the investors thought that the Suez success could be repeated. They were convinced that the future Interoceanic Canal in Central America would be the absolute masterpiece of the French engineers. National glory was at stake.

Encouraged by the surveys brought by the French explorers who had visited Central America, on August 19, 1876, a group of bankers founded the *"Société Civile Internationale pour le Percement du Canal Interocéanique à travers l'Isthme de Darien"*, – International Civil Society for the Piercing of an Interoceanic Canal across the Darien Isthmus[*] –, with the purpose of soliciting a concession from Colombia. Convinced by Godin de Lepinay, they did not even consider Nicaragua, counter to the recommendations of the previous Geography Congresses. The Society's capital was a modest 300,000 francs, divided in 60 parts of 5,000 francs each.

Among the founders were:

- Parisian private bankers, from what French historians call "The High Bank": Reinach and his brother-in-law Kohn, Herz, Camondo, Pereire, Oppenheim, Hirsch,

- Parisian personalities such as: Türr and his brother-in-law Lucien Wyse, and Armand Reclus,

- and a few American investors from New York. (14)

This *Civil Society* was an ordinary financial association, except it had no assets. It has just been created to be a home for future investors. It had its headquarters at the Kohn-Reinach bank. It is believed that the Reinach family, having subscribed several of the 60 founders' parts, was the major supplier of funds to finance the expeditions.

Baron Jacob Adolf - that everybody called "Jacques" - de Reinach can justly be considered as the founder of the Panama Canal. His bank was the leader in outlining the financial transactions that will attract investors in the project. (19) He was ready to gamble his money on a hypothetic canal, with very few data known about the project.

This marked the real beginning of the *Great Adventure of Panama*, as B-V called it in the title of one of his books. (9)

The brothers Elisee and Armand Reclus, together with Lucien Napoleon Bonaparte Wyse, all subsidized by the Reinach family and the *Civil Society*, visited the Central American Isthmus on several occasions. Lucien Napoleon Bonaparte Wyse was the grandson of Lucien Bonaparte, the son of Princess Laetitia, who had married the Irish writer Thomas Wyse. He was also Türr's brother-in-law.

These three explorers had given their preference to Panama over Nicaragua. Wyse had visited Nicaragua and remarked that:

- The port of Greytown was silted up with sands, which was a huge handicap;
- The Rio San Juan had too many rapids - between Machuca and Toro.

---

[*] The Darien Isthmus lies between the province of Panama and South America, where most of the Colombian territory lies.

Their visits in Central America lasted from November 1876 to March 1877 and another from November 1877 to February 1878, when Wyse left his party and went to Bogota with his friend Verbrugghe.

It is worth noting that Sosa, a Colombian engineer, had joined the French team.

The French explorers came back to Paris in March 1879, just two months before the beginning of the International Geographic Congress.

In 1879, ten years after the inauguration of the Suez Canal, Ferdinand de Lesseps was not really involved in the *"milieu des affaires"*. He was reluctant to invest his time in a major project, as he did in Suez. At 74, he wished more than anything to end his life happily, surrounded by his family. He even declared publicly that "I did not think that I could head a new enterprise. My best friends tried to dissuade me from it." (22)

Nicknamed the "Great Frenchman"- by Gambetta -, for his success in Suez, Ferdinand de Lesseps was born in November 19, 1805 in Versailles. He lost his first wife, Agathe Delamalle, in 1853 from scarlet fever, which also took away one of his sons. Two other of his five children had died in their early years. Only two survived: Charles and Victor.

In 1869, he married Helene Autard de Bragard, a 21 years old *demoiselle* from Mauritius Island. She gave birth to twelve children, at the rate of one a year between 1870 and 1885. Eleven would survive their father. (22)

With such a dynasty, Lesseps' family had become his first priority.

Türr, Wyse, Reinach and their associates in the Society were considerably more active than their Honorific President, Ferdinand de Lesseps.

After the Panama visits by the explorers, led by the geographer Godin de Lepinay - alumnus of Polytechnique, class of 1840 -, the Society decided to present a project based on a sea-level canal, with a route following quite closely the PRR railway tract. It should be emphasized that this route is exactly the same one that the Americans will chose in 1904, when they will start building the Panama Canal, after the French project had failed.

Bonaparte Wyse and his friend Verbrugghe went to Bogota to negotiate an agreement with Colombia. It was a tedious task. Access to Bogota was not easy. One possible route was to start from the Atlantic port of Cartagena and then follow the Rio Magdalena: it took three weeks. A better route started from the Pacific port of Buenaventura and took eleven days of difficult mountainous crossing, 500 miles (800 kilometers), on horseback. (3)

In Bogota, the Colombian Government was absorbed in its own internal problems and did not show a lot of interest for its Panama province, which did not provide much revenue - except for the PRR's concession, bringing a year rent of $ 250,000.

However, Wyse's perseverance paid off. On March 20, 1878, Colombia granted the *Société Civile Internationale pour le Percement du Canal Interocéanique à travers l'Isthme de Darien,* a concession for a canal in Panama.

It is interesting to note some of the conditions put forward by the Colombians:

- the Civil Society should be incorporated into a "universal" company, within the next two years;
- once founded, that company had itself a maximum of 12 years to complete the Canal;
- the Canal would remain the property of that company for 99 years;
- Colombia would grant that company a strip of land, not wider than 200 meters on each side – a quarter of a mile in total;
- it also included extensive land – 1.2 million acres - be used as quarries;
- Colombia would receive 5%, 6%, 7% and 8% of the tolls during each period of 25 years.

To finalize this agreement, Colombia voted a law on May 18, 1878, ratifying the concession given to Wyse. This agreement was called *Salgar-Wyse,* from the Colombian of Exterior Relations, Eustorgio Salgar Moreno, who will become President of Colombia in 1880.

This time, Panama has taken a strong advantage over Nicaragua.

The Colombian historian Lemaitre noted that by voting this agreement in just two months, the Colombians showed an "extraordinary example of official velocity and legislative efficiency", a sharp contrast to the events of 1903, when, according to some authors, a "petty, obstructionist and dilatory" spirit hampered the negotiations between Bogota and Washington. (15) Despite Lemaitre's intercession to excuse his compatriots, we shall later witness that every decision taken by the Government of Bogota "could be assimilated to pulling teeth", as B-V wrote, and he was an expert on dealing with Colombians. (7)

Wyse had been extremely convincing. He paid 750,000 francs in gold for the concession. Some authors believed that this success was due to the personality of Wyse, who was a true descendent of Napoleon, the First, a very popular hero in South America.[*]

While the French worked on a Panama project, the Americans continued to pay court to Nicaragua. Initiated by President Grant, a former general and hero of the Civil War, a U. S. expedition visited the country in the early months of 1878. Menocal was refining his first draft, which was already five years old. The number of locks on the Atlantic side was reduced from 12 to 7.

---

[*] Napoleon the First contributed to the liberation from Spain of most countries in South America – except Brazil – by weakening Spain that he invaded during the 1808-1813 war.

Enthusiastic about the project, the Government of Nicaragua granted a new concession to the Americans, the old one having expired.

Meanwhile, Wyse continued to organize the Panama project sponsored by the Civil Society of Türr and Reinach. In May 1878, back from Bogota, he stopped in Panama and crossed Nicaragua, returning to France via San Francisco and New York.

Early in 1879, Wyse returned to New York to finalize a commitment letter, signed on February 24, 1879, with the Executive Committee of the Board of Directors of the Panama RailRoad Company: Trevor Park, G. Francklyn, and Jos. Ogden, making plans for the Civil Society to purchase the PRR.

Wyse came back to Paris in March 1879, just a couple of months before the opening of the Geographic Congress. It had been a well-planned trip. (3)

On May 15, 1879, a sumptuous ceremony marked the opening in Paris of the International Geographic Congress: its goal was to select the route for an Interoceanic Canal in Central America.

98 delegates - 136 had been invited - from 22 nations attended, with a majority of Frenchmen. Also attending were 11 Americans - among them were Ammen and Menocal. Many nationalities were represented: Great Britain, Germany, Italy, Mexico, Russia, China, etc. The young Colombian engineer Pedro Sosa was also there.

Only 5 delegates had ever set foot in Central America: Armand Reclus, Bonaparte Wyse, Aniceto Menocal, Pedro Sosa, and Daniel Ammen.

Menocal was one of the American delegates; Cuban born, he had led many scientific expeditions in Nicaragua, which was his preferred choice for the canal. Despite its technical superiority, Menocal's project did not convince the delegates, who were under the spell of Ferdinand de Lesseps, the man behind Suez. Lesseps' fame would weigh enormously in the final decision.

After two weeks of hard negotiations, during which the technicians revealed the details of their plans, no compromise was reached. Unexpectedly, Lesseps showed up at one of the technical meetings and received a standing ovation, due to his success in Suez.

The delegates acclaimed him as their leader and he was de facto named at the head of the project. At first, he was startled, then he pulled himself together and accepted his mission.

We should not forget that Lesseps' decision had been certainly influenced by the shareholders of the Society of Reinach, Wyse and Türr, Society of which he was the honorific president.

Lesseps immediately took the lead and declared openly his views on the French project. It would be a sea-level canal, "as in Suez, which had been technically proven." (22) Lesseps did not believe in locks.

Emptying Lake Nicaragua being out of the question, it had thus to be Panama. Lesseps's stubbornness was a sign of his senility, but "he carried such an aura that most delegates trusted him." (14)

When they voted, on May 29, 1879, the delegates favored Panama by 74 votes for, 8 against and 12 abstentions. Among the opponents were Godin de Lepinay and Eiffel, who were in favor of a canal with locks - the future will prove them right. Among the other delegates who abstained, were Ammen and Menocal, as instructed by their Government. 38 delegates did not even show up.

It is amazing to notice how Lesseps' passion towards a sea level canal has led many illustrious scientists and engineers to support such an aberration. Some of them even calculated that "such sea level canal is unfeasible", according to the words of Ammen, in his report to Congress, dated June 21, 1879, when he returned home. (L. R. Hamersley in Philadelphia, 1880)

If we believe Armand Reclus' measurements on the Rio Chagres, when torrential rains cause this river to overflow and leave its bed, the amount of water to evacuate - in case of a sea level canal - would require the canal to be 160 meters wide - 500 feet! With its depth of 8 meters - 25 feet - Menocal qualified the project as "impracticable".

To confirm these calculations, let us mention that today, the Panama Canal has been shut down three times since its opening in 1914, because of exceptional rains that caused the Rio Chagres to overflow. The last time was December 8, 2010.

However, nobody would listen to the scientists or civil engineers. Panama won because of Lesseps and despite its higher cost - 1,070 million francs -, for a sea-level canal, compared to only 770 million francs for a canal with locks in Nicaragua. It was almost the same difference - 30% - as in the 1876 Menocal study - 40%. The engineers' objections were not heard.

To be totally honest, we ought to examine briefly some of the advantages of a sea level canal:

- Locks are, by nature, in the way of the maritime traffic; their opening and closing, however diligent, hamper the flow of ships. Given the enormous success of Suez and the consequent increase of international trade, it was feared that the locks would limit such trade;

- Another disadvantage of a canal with locks is that it requires enormous quantities of fresh water; for each crossing of a ship, the amount of water contained in the first and the last lock has to be evacuated to the oceans, which could add up to considerable volumes.

We shall see at the end of this story that the current expansion of the Panama Canal has been designed to specifically avoid those disadvantages - 10% of the investment has been designed to recycle water, in 2014/2015.

Therefore, Nicaragua should have been the favorite, with lower cost and easier land excavation, but the American delegates could not convince their peers. Not only Menocal was not as popular as Lesseps was, but Americans had not yet formed a financial company and lastly, they had no funds to dedicate to the canal.

Lesseps had been very successful in Suez and the delegates thought that such achievement could be reiterated in Panama, so they gave him their confidence.

The Panama Canal's projected route started in Aspinwall, the PRR's terminal on the Atlantic Ocean's side; from there it followed more or less the railway tracks until it reached the Rio Chagres. To get to the Pacific Coast, it then had to cut across the Culebra Hill, at an altitude of 120 meters; it was the major obstacle on the canal's route.

The experts estimated that the volume of ground to be extracted would amount to 45 million cubic meters,* and that the canal could be achieved in 12 years. Wyse had previously estimated only 40 million cubic meters.

Most delegates thought that the Panama job would be much simpler than Suez where 75 million cubic meters had been extracted from the dunes of the African desert. They would later realize their mistake.

More than ever, the maxim : *"Comparison is no Reason"*, will prove to be right.

To be complete about the "locks vs. sea level" canal debate, let us mention that even a sea level canal would necessarily have a lock: this would be a "tide lock", designed to hold the tide on the Pacific Ocean side - the Atlantic Ocean has practically no tide. Without this "tide lock", the 6-meter tidal range would create such a current that ships would have to be delayed and that the canal could operate only a few hours per day.

Lesseps took advantage of his popularity to arrange things his way: without listening to experts or engineers, he declared that the Panama Canal would be built at sea level for 600 million francs. Of the 1,070 million francs, calculated by the experts, he decided that only the amount necessary for the works ought to be mentioned, completely forgetting about settlement costs, administration, interest to the shareholders, and other costs he assumed to be unrelated to the digging of the canal.

Despite many remarks from his staff, Lesseps always refused to quote a different figure than 600 million francs. His Suez experience had taught him not to trust engineers. At that time, a dollar was worth about 5 Francs, more or less what the Euro is worth nowadays: 1 Euro = 6.56/5 = $ 1.3.

---

* The present book uses metric units. One cubic meter is 1.3 cubic yard.

To convert Francs of the 1880s into today's Euros, one has to multiply the Francs by about 5.

Of course, in the 19th Century, the cost of living was much less than today. Around 50 to 100 times less! Panama workers were paid no more than $1.5 per day; a simple meal was only 15 cents. In Europe as well as in the USA, it was a period blessed by the absence of inflation, which would not appear until the First World War (1914-1918).

Soon after the May 1879 decision of the International geographic Congress to dig the Interoceanic Canal in Panama, the project developed quickly. In July 1879, Lesseps created the "*Compagnie Universelle du Canal Interocéanique de Panama*" - Universal Company for an Interoceanic Canal in Panama. We will refer to it as the **Company**.

The name "universal" came from the Colombian concession's obligations. It also was intended to please the Americans, as the Monroe doctrine was clearly opposed to such a construction by any state. A public and universal company was OK.

It is worth quoting the names of a few of the 24 (!) administrators of the Company: 12 were already administrators of Suez, among them four were members of the Lesseps family - the brothers Ferdinand and Jules, Ferdinand's sons: Charles and Victor -, two were French members of the Chamber of Deputies, some were banks' representatives - Drexel, Seligman, Credit Industriel & Commercial, etc. - and there even was a General - Türr.

For the record, we have to notice the absence of Jacques de Reinach. (14)

"This turn of events came as a severe shock to Washington. . . in clear defiance of the Monroe doctrine." (20) The neutrality of the future canal being guaranteed under the *Mallarino-Bidlack* treaty of 1846 with Colombia, the United States "accepted that Panama was out of reach and looked elsewhere for a canal. The obvious alternative was Nicaragua." (20) The American strategy would take almost ten years to come to fruition. (See chapter 11, page 111).

Americans were just following the advice of their best experts: Ammen and Menocal were convinced that a sea level canal in Panama would be "unfeasible" and "impracticable".

In Paris, the newly founded Company went ahead fast. Without any negotiation, it bought the Salgar-Wyse concession for 10 million Francs.

The Society of Reinach, Wyse and Türr had quoted the extravagant figure of 10 million Francs, just to start off the negotiation. There was none!

This is just the first example of Lesseps's carelessness. He was so sure of the success of the project that he did not even bother to negotiate.

It was a great deal of money for a piece of paper. Wyse and his partners of the *Civil Society* got a happy return on their initial investment; they had only made a deposit of only 750,000 francs to get this concession. But Lesseps was a *Grand Monsieur* who would not condescend to negotiate, as we shall see throughout this story. The Company did not possess a cent: Lesseps had to borrow these 10 million Francs to the banks and they were honored to oblige such an illustrious customer.

The Panama Adventure had begun for real.

One month after the creation of the Company, a hasty subscription was set for August 6 and 7, 1879. It called for 800,000 shares, sold at 500 francs each, for a total of 400 million francs. Given an estimated yearly traffic of 6 million tons and a toll of 15 francs per ton, the canal was expected to generate 90 million francs of revenues and after paying operating charges and debt charges, to produce an estimated dividend of 47 million francs. This was 11.75% of the capital and it sounded like a very attractive investment. (14)

But, Lesseps was so sure that if "his name appeared, it would be enough to attract money" (14), that he did not deem necessary to publicize the event or to involve the banks by discussing what commissions they would receive for their services. As a consequence, the banks did not show any active involvement and only 30 million francs were collected. . . and soon reimbursed!

It was a disaster for the Company. This failure can be explained by several facts:

- the press had not shown a very warm support to the project. Some newspapers had nastily pointed out Lesseps' old age - 74 - and even hinted that he could die before the canal could be achieved. (14)

- the subscription had called for an enormous amount, exceeding the Stock Market capability, as it represented about 15% of its annual investment. The French economy had not yet recovered from the 1873 financial crisis and investors were only interested in the most heavily advertized projects.

- the "Major banks" Credit Lyonnais, Societe Generale, Paribas, etc., "accustomed to receiving a sizeable commission, had been ignored by Lesseps, and remained passive during the subscription." (14)

Despite his great fame, Lesseps could not seduce the small investors.

The famous writer, Lamartine, turned him into a joke, saying that: "Even God Himself needs bells." (5)

Lesseps did not get discouraged. Starting all over, he set up a series of conferences around the country. He gave talks in every large city throughout France.

To further increase his audience, he started in September a semi-monthly brochure called the *Bulletin du Canal Interocéanique* - Interoceanic Canal Bulletin -, which would be regularly published on the 1st and 15th of each month, throughout the whole project, until February 1889.

In addition, to be sure to reach the entire world, Lesseps launched a huge campaign intended to involve the global finance. It would be quite a journey!

On December 8, 1879, Ferdinand, his wife and three of his children, aged seven to nine, embarked on the *Lafayette,* in Saint-Nazaire, on the French Atlantic coast and sailed for Panama. This trip was serving a dual purpose. Firstly, it was designed to discourage the adverse reports that said that the climate in Panama was fatal to white people. Additionally, it was intending to obtain the support of rich American investors. Along with Lesseps went bankers, members of Chambers of Commerce, high officials and even members of French and foreign Governments.

After two ports of call in the French Caribbean and in Colombia, the *Lafayette* landed in Aspinwall on December 30, having spent three weeks on sea.

On January 10, **1880**, Lesseps and his group were received with great honors in the City of Panama. Marc de Banville told us about this festivity: "Surrounded by the city's officials and the province's governor, under the applause of all the 14,000 citizens of Panama City, Lesseps enters triumphally. Through the busy streets, lined with saluting soldiers, the Lesseps's carriage stops in front of the Grand Hotel, on the Cathedral's square, where French flags have been placed for the ceremony. This festivity will remain forever in the Panamanian memories." (29) Receptions in honor of Lesseps were held during the whole month of January. Their opulence offended the country officials, as they were not used to the luxury of the Parisian high society. But it was for their good, as Panama was at the time a very poor country and all Panamanians hoped to profit from the canal's construction.

The six-week stay of the French delegation went well. Lesseps had been very lucky. This year 1880, the dry season had arrived early, giving the impression of "an eternal spring", according to Lesseps's words.

During his stay, Lesseps met with Totten, the American engineer who built the PRR - the intercontinental railway line across the Isthmus of Panama -, but he did not listen to Totten's comments about the fevers nor about the unstable ground. Lesseps qualified Panama as "the most beautiful region in the whole world" (22), starting a series of lies which shall continue throughout the project.

In mid-February, the Lesseps party went from Panama to the United States, where Lesseps gave lectures in all the major cities. His purpose was to gather the interest of major American investors and also reassure them about the neutrality of the French built canal. He even went as far as California, where he gave a speech in San Francisco.

Unfortunately, though, everywhere he went he was met with a cold welcome. Americans still believed that Monroe and his doctrine called for a canal of their own in Nicaragua. The defeat they had suffered in the Parisian International Geographic Congress was still in their minds. Also, the nationalists of the young nation were upset by the French project.

On March 7, 1880, Lesseps paid a visit to President Hayes in Washington and confirmed that his Company would be private and without any involvement of the French Government. On the following day, Hayes declared boldly to Congress that : "Our policy is to build a canal under American control." (10)

Would there be a second canal?

After their trip to Panama, an International Commission of experts, who had followed the Lesseps' party in Panama, composed of:
- Totten, the American constructor of the PRR,
- Sosa, a Colombian engineer,
- Alphonse Couvreux, a French contractor,
and many prominent engineers, issued a report on February 12, 1880, indicating that their estimate of the budget was 570 million francs. This figure was close enough to Lesseps' figure of 600, to satisfy him.

At the same time, these international experts declared that it would be necessary to extract 75 million cubic meters. This was bad news. The previous estimate of 45 was outdated. However, the same experts called for a completion in eight years - instead of the original estimate of 12 years. This was exactly what it took to build Suez, same cubage and same duration. With that far-fetched argument, every investor was again optimistic.

It should be noted that nobody dared to object that if the cubage has increased from 45 to 75 million cubic meters, so should have the cost. This lack of common sense will plague the project all along. Or should we call it "lies", as we shall see many examples further on. In justice, it is called "breach of trust" and one could be imprisoned for it.

Lesseps and his group left New York on April 1st. Remained there an "American Committee", chaired by Richard W. Thompson, an ex-Marine Secretary, and with members from prominent banks: J&W Seligman, Drexel, J. P. Morgan, etc. We shall discover later the enormous costs billed to the Company by this Committee, for services that were questionable, such as promoting the canal work to American construction companies.

In the end, the Company would collect very little American money and have only a few shareholders in America.

The enormous disburse to the American Committee would prove to be totally unjustified.

In Europe, Lesseps continued to advertize his project by travelling through Great Britain, the Nederlands and Belgium. In June, during one of his conferences in Ghent - Belgium -, Abel Couvreux, the son of Alphonse, owner of a civil engineering company famous for having successfully worked in Suez, publicly declared that his estimate for Panama was 512 million francs. (2) This was half the estimate of the May 1879 Congress of 1,070 million francs. Couvreux was for this project associated with another civil contractor in *Couvreux & Hersent.*

The *Journal des Débats* wrote: "MM. Couvreux & Hersent made the offer to dig the canal for a fixed cost of 512 million francs; when we add to this sum the 88 millions necessary to pay the interests during construction, to pay for the administration costs, etc. we arrive at a total of 600 millions." (2) This was a journalistic extrapolation of a verbal estimate. But Lesseps did not bother to correct it. He was delighted to have his estimate of 600 million francs confirmed once again, especially when it was confirmed "on a fixed cost basis" by a Suez contractor.

On this basis, Lesseps planned for a subscription of 300 million francs, slightly less ambitious than the subscription that had failed in August 1879 – 400 million francs.

At the end of 1888, when the French Company went bankrupt, it had excavated 55 million cubic meters. The 1888 estimate had climbed to 120 million cubic meters, which made them believe that they had excavated about half of it. In reality, it was only a mere 20%!

When the Americans finally completed the Panama Canal in 1914, the total cubage they had excavated amounted to 260 million cubic meters, about five times more what the French had dug.

Engineering is not an exact science.

Of course, we shall soon examine what caused this inflation of ground cubage.

The basic scope of the project having been defined, the next step would be to collect money from the future shareholders and proceed with the digging.

4
PHILIPPE BUNAU-VARILLA FACED HIS DESTINY

We now return to Philippe Bunau-Varilla (B-V), who, by a happy coinci-dence, was attending one of Lesseps' lectures. In May 1880, the *Grand Français* was concluding his worldwide tour in Paris. One of his lectures took place in the *École Polytechnique's* main auditorium. Invited by General Pourrat, the School Director, Ferdinand de Lesseps addressed the 400 students and B-V was one of them.

B-V was delighted to sit so close to his model. The hero of Suez was ex-tremely popular in France. The shares of Suez had climbed to 2,000 francs - four times their emission price: 500 - and produced a dividend of 9% a year. It was therefore a well-deserved success.

Lesseps was also admired by the popular classes who could read in the Parisian press the detailed reports of his outings from his home on *Avenue Montaigne* to take his beautiful young wife and his many children for a ride in the *Bois de Boulogne*. Ferdinand de Lesseps was often photographed riding a beautiful white horse followed by a large horse drawn coach carrying his family. It made such a delightful picture.

However, this show of happiness did not please everyone. Drumont, a caustic journalist, wrote that: "Nobody could ever imagine that such an illustrious man as Mr. de Lesseps, great officer in the *Légion d'Honneur*, member of the *Académie Française*, could have recourse to such manners, worthy of the Barnum Circus." (4) It was a malicious allusion to the showy manner that Lesseps used in order to run his financial drive campaign for Panama.

Young B-V, a few months away from his graduation from *École Polytechnique*, was delighted to meet such a prestigious man, who represented for him the best example for imitation among illustrious men. He longed to become as famous as Ferdinand de Lesseps himself was. He was anxious to participate in the Panama Canal, his childhood dream. Having lived without a father, he probably considered himself as the spiritual son of the *Grand Français*.

B-V mentioned this conference in his memoirs and wrote with pride: "I sat in the first row of the enthusiastic audience." (7) He must have been mesmerized by the modernity of Lesseps, who embellished his conference with screen projections coming from a modern magic lantern.

This conference, which brought Lesseps and B-V face to face, confirmed B-V into his dream of working in Panama. From there on, he would be galvanized to do everything possible to get there.

In October 1880, B-V was admitted to the National School of *Ponts & Chaussées* - Bridges and Highways -, a School with a much more practical curriculum than Polytechnique and where he would become an expert in civil engineering. It was a standard complement to his theoretical studies. He studied there for three years. His choice of this particular *École d'Application* shows that he graduated from Polytechnique among the best students. Otherwise, he would have had to go through the regular exams to enter one of these *Application Schools*, such as: Artillery, Blasting Powders and Mines. Even today, an *X-Ponts* is considered as the best within the French *élite*.

During the fall of 1880, Lesseps concluded his campaign for the Panama Canal project with another series of conferences throughout France. The 75-year-old man has been campaigning all over the world for a whole year. His efforts would finally soon be rewarded. This time, he had taken good care of every detail and most importantly, he had convinced the bankers to cooperate, not surprisingly by allowing them to collect large money incentives.

Among the bankers approached, we notice *Société Générale, Banque de Paris et des Pays-Bas, Comptoir d'Escompte de Paris, Crédit Lyonnais, Crédit Industriel et Commercial, Société des Dépôts et Comptes Courants, Banque d'Escompte de Paris* and *Séligmann Frères*. Lesseps regrouped them into a "syndicate", set exclusively to cash a commission for each share of the Company that they would sell.

"Given these conditions, success was complete." (14)

On December 6, 1880, the first subscription of the shares of the Company was so successful that instead of the 300 million francs required, it could have brought in close to 600, which meant that demand reached twice the offer.

Having still in mind the 600 million francs estimated investment figure, Lesseps was convinced that he did not need such an enormous sum so early in the project and he refused to sell more shares than the 300 million francs planned by the subscription. His optimism had caused him to make a serious blunder and we shall see that it would not be his last.

In his choice, he had probably thought that it would be too expensive to serve a dividend to these superfluous shares, so early in the development of the project.

It seemed as if old Lesseps had lost his legendary intuition.

Another fact bore witness of Lesseps's optimism. He himself purchased some Panama shares by selling all his Suez shares and by adding his wife's savings, for a total of 1.8 million francs. The unfortunate man would lose it all and, as we shall see later, spend his last years in a provincial retreat, in relative poverty.

The 600,000 shares of the subscription, sold at 500 francs each, would provide a dividend of 5% a year, until the canal would be put into operation. They were considered by the Parisian Stock Market to be an excellent deal, as only 25% - 125 francs - had been called in cash. It was just a marketing gimmick and this advantage would not last. As more funds were needed, earlier than anticipated, the remaining 75% had to be called within a few months.

However, Lesseps had now the financial means to go ahead with his project in Panama. We shall see in chapter 6, page 59, how the project developed.

For the moment, let us continue to follow B-V. Three years had passed and in June 1883 he graduated from the *École des Ponts & Chaussées*, and could now be qualified as "master in civil engineering techniques".

He was ready to test his skills in Panama, but a rule of the *École Polytechnique* prevented him from leaving immediately. All the Polytechnique alumni had to first serve for five years in one of the French Government's services. B-V complained about "an antiquated regulation." (7)

Strangely enough, this rule still exists today. It is designed to compel the students to serve the State, in exchange for having enjoyed a free tuition. As with every rule, there were exemptions. When a student really wanted to join a private company, he could regain his liberty by paying back his tuition - or have his future employer help him in paying it -, a sum equivalent to several years of salary of a young engineer. Unfortunately, B-V's modest family did not have the money to pay for B-V's dream.

Instead of leaving for Panama, B-V reluctantly joined the Corps of Engineers in the National Bridges and Highways Ministry.

He told in his memoirs how he was sent for a mission to Algeria - a French colony since 1843 - and then to its neighboring Tunisia, during the second half of 1883. (7)

Back in Paris at the beginning of 1884, B-V was still looking for a way to join the *Compagnie Universelle du Canal Interocéanique de Panama - CUCIP*, so that he could leave for Panama to fulfill his dream. His good fortune made him discover a ministerial pamphlet encouraging Polytechnique graduates to join the Company's staff. However, regretfully, it was only applicable after the five years service to the State.

Still vexed, he accepted his next mission in Bayeux, a city close to the Normandy's coast, where he worked for six months. He wrote in his memoirs: "I nursed my sorrow, concentrating all my energy on the harbor works of Port en Bessin and of Isigny, and on my tasks of keeping in good repair the *Route Nationale* No. 13 from Paris to Cherbourg, which occupations were not specially fascinating to me." (7)

It is not clear how B-V finally obtained an authorization to go to Panama. It could well be that the rules had been softened to cope with the high demand for engineers by the Company - CUCIP. B-V explained, in his memoirs, what the librarian of the *Ponts & Chaussées* School, told him in autumn 1884: "There is now an excess of engineers in the service of the State. . . Mr. Gouzay, who has charge of this question at the Department of Public Works will soon put you on leave officially for private affairs, with the understanding that you will go and serve on the Panama works." (7)

In any case, B-V could not tolerate to spend any more months repairing roads and was ready to move heaven and earth to leave for Panama.

Whatever the reason for the exemption, his obstinacy was finally rewarded.

We have to praise his courage. The first engineers who worked in Panama, alumni of the French *Grandes Écoles*: Polytechnique, Centrale, Ponts & Chaussées, or other renowned French engineering schools, had been decimated* by fevers and few candidates were willing to enroll. Despite all the efforts of the Company to hide the horrible deaths, rumors of the yellow fever calamity had reached Paris. The Company's Bulletin - *Bulletin du Canal Interocéanique* - had resisted for some time to add an obituary section. However, one cannot prevent people to talk, or gossips to circulate, which resulted in moderating the ardor of the candidates.

---

* "Decimate" means literally kill every tenth man. The mortality in Panama peaked at 10/12% during the first years.

B-V was so anxious to leave that nothing could discourage him. He was determined to go and would not listen to any antagonistic warning.

His decision is really worth of all our admiration.

As a rare coincidence, while B-V was preparing to leave for Panama during the summer of 1884, the Company's General Manager, Jules Dingler and his wife were back in Paris to bury their two children and the fiancé of their daughter. The three young people had been seized by fevers after only a few months in the Isthmus. (16)

As it is easy to imagine, this terrible news was widely commented in the Parisian circles and B-V would have surely been aware of it.

Despite all the dangers menacing the brave engineers working in Panama, B-V was not afraid to leave. On the contrary, he was happy to be able to finally fulfill his dream. He had waited many long years for it.

The Company hired him with the title of "Chief Engineer", in charge of the 3rd Division, which extended from the Culebra Hill to the Pacific Coast. It was the most difficult part of the canal's works, but B-V did not know that yet.

With his adventure in Panama about to begin, B-V was emotionally aroused by the thought of his opportunity to contribute to this great human achievement, a service to humankind. He had waited for it and now he would get it.

He was totally unaware of the great difficulties he was about to experience.

In 1884, Panama was not an ordinary country.

5

PANAMA

The Province of Panama forms a narrow isthmus between South and North America - see map in Appendix 7. After obtaining a federal status from Colombia in 1855, Panama enjoyed a relative independence from the Bogota Government.

In the 1880s, her main resource being agriculture, Panama received some additional revenues from the PRR - the railway line that transported people and goods across the isthmus -, although most of its transit fees were allocated to the American shareowners. The indirect contribution of the PRR did not seem to have been used to improve the towns' infrastructures, which still lacked most of the modern facilities of big cities like Paris, London or New York. In fact, for visitors coming from these large modern cities, the towns of Aspinwall and Panama City appeared like villages from the Middle Ages.

McCullough, described the city of Aspinwall, a port on the Atlantic Coast: "Streets, barely above tide level, were unpaved and strewn from end to end with garbage, bits of broken furniture, dead animals. The entire town reeked of putrefaction. Compared to Aspinwall, the ghettos of Russia, the slums of Toulon or Naples, would appear models of cleanliness." (16)

Ghislain de Diesbach related the reception of Lesseps in Panama City on December 28, 1879: "Due to the calamitous state of the town, Lesseps and his group do not stay long in Aspinwall, located on the Island of Manzanillo, surrounded by unhealthy marshes. It takes a certain dose of courage to ride on the railroad. Set on a ballast regularly softened by the tropical rains, the railroad track tends to sink into the wet ground. A derailed car is lost forever, engulfed by the suction of the swamps. In a country of marshes surrounded by wooded hills so thick that one can only enter with a *machete* - a long curbed knife used to harvest the sugar cane -, the most intriguing factor is the climate. In Panama, there are only two seasons: the rainy season from May to December and the less rainy season, the rest of the year. . ." (22)

Ghislain de Diesbach continued with the description of Panama's climate, somewhat exaggerated for today's seasoned globe trotters, but which must have tremendously impressed the Lesseps group of 1879, as most French people were not familiar with its tropical weather: "The word rain is not proper. The cataracts falling on the Isthmus . . . have the effect of increasing the level of the rivers by several feet in hours. They also bring much humidity, which combined with the extreme heat, covers everything with mold, putrefaction, and decomposes all objects in less than a day. . . At daylight, a thick layer of blue rot is found on the shoes that had been shined in the evening. Everywhere, water is stagnant, releasing a foul smell. Apart from the many diseases that assault the indigenous and degenerated population, the two major plagues . . . are yellow fever and malaria." (22)

Malaria was endemic in the isthmus of Panama, but was not always lethal. As we shall see, the casualties on the Panama Canal works will be mainly due to yellow fever. More details about these terrible diseases can be found in the well-documented and recent book by Fiametta Rocco, who happens to be the great granddaughter of B-V. (28)

Let us listen to Felix-Napoleon Garella, who spent many months on the Isthmus from 1838 to 1843 and brought back a thorough canal project 'see page 11): "It does not seem advisable to expose European workers, without any shield, to the burning sun and to the humidity, both factors of fevers; one necessary condition to achieve the canal would be to hire natives, workers from neighboring republics or even from the South of the United States. . . It would be advantageous to send workers home during the rainy season, when all outdoor work is impossible." (see Garella's book: "Project of a junction canal from the Pacific Ocean to the Atlantic Ocean through the Panama Isthmus." Carilian- Gœury, Paris, 1845)

Given all the above and taking into account the rudimentary state of medicine and prophylaxis during the end of the 19th Century, Panama was not a very friendly country. Apart from yellow fever, there were many more risks threatening the foreign visitors, such as venomous snakes, crocodiles, scorpions, giant ants, mygales, not forgetting sunburns and heat strokes.

About this last danger, Ghislain de Diesbach confirmed Garella's opinion: "During the dry season, one cannot leave his home between 10 a.m. and 3 p.m. without being overwhelmed by the layers of fire falling from the sky like liquid lead." (22)

In conclusion, except for a native, life in Panama was extremely hazardous.

Now let us turn to the beautiful scenery. In Panama, a series of low rolling hills carved by wild rivers are covered with a thick tropical jungle, leaving scarce clearings that were used for agriculture or if extended served as path for communications. At the time, there was no other infrastructure besides the PRR, no paved ways, no means of transportation for heavy freight; it was so arduous to travel by land to the "interior" cities of David or Penonome that people used boats on the Pacific Ocean as their preferred mean of transportation.

For a better understanding of our story, let us give a short description of the projected canal route. It started in the Island of Manzanillo, on the Atlantic coast, where the French would later build the City of Colon - which would no longer be called Aspinwall.

Going southeast - yes, the canal is not oriented north south, as the shape of the Isthmus would indicate, but rather west east - the canal route first crossed an area of thick marshes, produced by the overrunning of the Rio Chagres. Coming from the eastern cordillera, this river was only a small stream during the dry season and turned into a large navigable river when rain came. Each storm caused its level to rise by five meters – 15 feet – in a matter of hours, carrying away everything from its banks, and unfortunately some structures of the railroad. Over the years, the PRR had to replace its wooden bridges with steel ones, as they were damaged every time the Rio Chagres left its banks. Wood proved to be too light to face unharmed the huge floods of the Rio Chagres. The canal route followed the Rio Chagres for a while, until this river turns easterly into the mountain. From this turn, the projected canal route crossed a line of hills, culminating at 120 meters. It was the most difficult part of the route and there laid the major part of the earth to be excavated. The Culebra Hill - in Spanish: Snake Hill - rightly justified its name, as it proved, like a snake, very difficult to grip. From the summit of this Culebra Hill, the projected canal route sloped down nicely towards the Pacific

Ocean, following the beds of the Rio Grande and Obispo rivers, just west of the town and capital of the province: Panama City.

From 1850 and on, the PRR project had the effect of upgrading the entire area. Its terminal cities: Colon and Panama City, where thousands of travelers transited, evolved from small agricultural towns and became fully cosmopolitan, with rows of nightclubs, gambling saloons, brothels and all the facilities necessary to entertain day and night the travelers, while they waited for their train to cross the Isthmus or their ship to sail to California. Most were adventurers looking for gold and profit. By the time they left Panama City, they had lost part of their money to speculators or to thieves, and sometimes had debts to swindlers who had lent them money against their future revenues from an imaginary gold lode. However, they would always remember the good time they had in Panama.

The country's large cities, Aspinwall, Panama City, David, were not yet equipped with modern commodities. They did not have running water, electricity or sewers. The *Forty-Niners* had spent quite a lot of money there, but it all ended in private hands and none of it had been used for any common interests. No police or justice was found in the province and it released a wild atmosphere, similar to that of the American Far West. No wonder that the U. S. marines had to land from time to time to pacify the most violent criminals and ensure the safe transit through the PRR.

The Panama province was too poor to interest Colombian investors. Since 1869, when the New York/California intercontinental railway opened, rare were the American pioneers or gold-seekers that used the Panama route, reducing to almost nil the PRR's profit. In Wall Street, its shares plummeted from $ 370 to $ 50 between 1870 and 1874.

This was what Panama was like, when B-V was en route to work there. Quite a change for a Parisian, used to all the modern commodities!

Since the California gold rush in 1848, very little had changed. The arrival of the French Company in 1880 would bring some significant improvements, but so many were needed that all progress would inevitably be slow.

6
THE PANAMA CANAL BEFORE B-V

We had left the French Company - CUCIP - at the end of 1880 when it had acquired 300 million francs by selling 600,000 shares. Let us examine now the start of the construction work in Panama.

This is quite mnemonic: 1881 was the first year of the canal's construction, 1882 the second year and so on. Easy to remember.

On January 29, **1881**, a group of forty engineers and administrators on board the *Lafayette*, landed in Aspinwall/Colon, on the Atlantic coast of Panama,. This was the first group of administrators, under the command of Armand Reclus, a former vessel lieutenant, who was familiar with Panama, which he had visited in 1875, 1877 and 1878. They will soon be joined by the contractors' team.

On March 3, 1881, in Paris, the Company was formally incorporated. It would later purchase a building at 46, Rue Caumartin, to lodge its headquarters, where three hundred people worked, at a cost of 2 million francs a year. Now that it could dispose of a lot of money, the Company spent it "as if it had too much of it."(2) It allocated the huge sum of 12 million francs to the American Committee, an association of bankers, with the goal of maintaining the neutrality of the project. In 1892, in his report, Vallé commented: "We do not know whether this was strictly necessary."(2) Even more munificent, Richard Thompson, the chairman of this American Committee received 125,000 francs a year, as much as Ferdinand de Lesseps himself did receive.

As for the salaries of the Company's directors, they were absolutely extravagant and consumed a total of 6 million francs of the precious Company's cash. (2)

On March 12, in Paris, the Company signed a construction contract with *Couvreux & Hersent*. Couvreux was a contractor that had acquired a reputation on the Suez Canal works. One article of this contract stated that *Couvreux & Hersent* would have two years to determine "an accurate estimate of the costs involved in the setting of a price per cubic meter." (2) Once this cost established, at the end of the two years, the Company would sign a contract based on a cost per unit - cubic meter - determined from the work already achieved.

The Company advertized - it was another lie - that *Couvreux & Hersent* had committed to an "all included" contract to finish the work for a fixed sum: 512 million francs; it was only their preliminary estimate of the cost.

The earth digging did not start right away. First, the Company had to build some necessary infrastructures, which unexpectedly consumed quite a lot of money, because Panama did not have much in terms of modern facilities. The Company had to build office blocks, warehouses, dwellings for the laborers*, and even hospitals, one in Colon - ready in March 1882 at a cost of 5 million francs - and another in Cerro Ancon - opened in September 1882, which had cost 28 million francs.

Lesseps was reiterating what he did in Suez, where he had built for the laborers three new villages, with all the modern commodities. Here in Panama City, the capital of the province, on the Pacific coast, was the only town close to being called a city. On the Atlantic side, next to the old Aspinwall, the French people would build a totally new city, that they would call Colon. It delighted the Colombians as they had been vexed when Americans had changed its name to Aspinwall.

By May 1881, when the rainy season started, the French engineers had become well accustomed to the torrential tropical rains and were working hard. All was going well, until suddenly an outbreak of yellow fever struck, boosted by the high humidity.

On July 28, Henri Bionne, a geographer, died of that fever attack, onboard the ship that was bringing him back to France. He had been assigned to the position of the Company's General Secretary in Panama. As expected, his death had a negative impact on the Parisian Stock Market. The Lesseps' mythical paradisiacal Panamanian climate began to be questioned.

---

* We shall see later that the Company had great expectations as it constructed dwellings for 26/27,000 laborers, when their number never exceeded 15/20,000. (2)

As the route chosen for the future canal crossed the PRR in many places, it became now manifest that the railroad would be useful to transport men and materials along the canal works. The engineers working in Panama recommended purchasing the PRR.

This finding came in August 1881, about 18 months after the first visit of Lesseps and its group of businessmen. Preliminary calculations had shown that the PRR's toll to transport freight would be an excessive burden for the Company's budget and that it would be better off buying the PRR as soon as possible. Which it did.

This purchase had not been forecast in the canal budget. It now appeared to have become essential for the Company to acquire the PRR. At the time, as a consequence of the opening of the intercontinental railway in North America, in 1869, the PRR was nearly bankrupt. Its shares were worth a mere $ 50 in Wall Street.

It was the right time to purchase the PRR, especially because Wyse had on February 24, 1879, signed a letter of intent with Trenor William Park and his associates, Francklyn and Ogden. But in 1881, Wyse had been excluded from the Company's organization, a dispute having occurred with Ferdinand de Lesseps and, consequently, the letter signed by Wyse was ignored. It could have saved some $ 10 million of cash to the Company. (3)

When rumors were heard in Wall Street about the Company's intent to purchase the PRR, speculators had a ball and the share rocketed to almost $ 300. Consequently, the Company had to purchase most of the shares of the PRR at $ 270, for a total of close to $ 20 million - 93 million francs.

The PRR had been built in 1855 for about $ 7 million. The American shareholders of the PRR were obviously delighted with such an offer, which tripled their assets in only 25 years.

Again, Lesseps acted without a plan, in an unprepared manner, as if the Company's money was unlimited. In one transaction, he spent one third of the 300 million francs he had received during the December 1880 subscription.

Lesseps could only purchase about 68,534 shares of the PRR out of a total of 70,000 – or about 98%. Then, when he wanted to transfer the management to Paris, he was confronted to the charter of the PRR, which stated expressly that: "Directors should be annually chosen in New York City."(History of the PRR, @panamarailroad.org) He thus reluctantly accepted that the PRR continued to be run from its New York City headquarters. The PRR's staff in Panama remained all-American, the Company providing only laborers.

Although the Company paid an exorbitant price, we shall see that the PRR would become the best investment made by the Company.

By mid-1881, serious earth moving work started with some dredging, to better the accesses to the ports of Colon and Panama City. They were too shallow for modern ships, which would bring the materials for the canal works. Huge dredges were brought in from the East Coast.

It was an important and necessary step, but it proved quite frustrating for the French civil engineers who had come to Panama expecting to dig a canal through the Isthmus. About a thousand laborers were now working for the Company. Things started to move, albeit slowly, on the path of the future canal.

Following the death of Bionne, there had been many other victims of the yellow fever. Would the Parisian Stock Market ever get used to these deaths?

Suddenly in November 1881, the Company suffered a very serious blow: Gaston Blanchet, the chief engineer of *Couvreux & Hersent*, died. He had been in the Isthmus for only ten months, but the fever got him down. His death had enormous consequences on *Couvreux & Hersent*, a rather small construction company. Nobody could be found to replace Blanchet, or to be more accurate, nobody volunteered.

All these adverse events did not prevent the Company from making some progress in Panama. In December, it moved its staff to the Grand Hotel, in Panama City, purchased for one million francs. Only 200 people strong at the end of 1881, this staff would grow to more than a thousand by 1884.

Together with the Paris office, the administration costs will amount to 100 million francs, or 7% of the total costs (from 1881 to 1889). (2)

In January **1882**, as the Company began its second year of construction, a huge banquet was given in honor of the staff excavating the Culebra Hill. As it had become customary - this was the third year in a row -, every January would see many festivities given by the French in the City of Panama.

It is surprising that the French expatriates had a heart to rejoice, considering the many funerals they had to attend. In a year, between January 28, 1881, and February 1st, 1882, out of a total of 180 French managers - engineers and administrative staff -, 19 had died from yellow fever, or 11%. This death rate of 10/12% per year had unfortunately become chronic.

This mournful trend would continue during the whole project. As an example, the *École Centrale* Alumni Directory of 1887 sadly regretted that among the 27 engineers sent to Panama during the years 1884-1886, 11 had died. (4) It is easy to imagine the tremendous disorganization that resulted from the sudden disappearance of such important positions in the Company's staff.

However, life went on. The dead were buried and the managers replaced.

During this second year of the Company in Panama, construction continued on the support facilities and orders were placed for the digging equipment, which would be set along the future canal route.

So far, less than a million cubic meters had been extracted - on an estimated total of 75.

Money had been spent without restraint. So sure were Lesseps and his
administrators of their power that they did not even ask for competitive bids
from the suppliers. Contracts were signed through friends or acquaintances,
most of the time involving a commission. Corruption was near.

These methods would be totally unacceptable and unethical in today's
engineering or construction companies.

Lesseps' indefatigable optimism was remarkably explained by Siegfried:
"During these new circumstances, the memories of Suez became an encour-
agement. . . Lesseps knew that certain difficulties would not be encountered again: the opposition of Great Britain, the Turkish interdiction to
requisition the "fellahs". He recalled that ten times he had been right against
the engineers. (13) It is true that, this time, the United States would be
impartial and would only intervene to maintain order in the canal area (an
obligation of the 1846 treaty with Colombia).

By mid 1882, most of the first 300 million francs collected by the Company had been spent in infrastructures, warehouses and purchases of material.
This was half of the 600 million francs advertised by Lesseps as the total cost
of the project.

The Company had once again to call on public savings.

On September 7, 1882, a subscription was prepared for 100 million francs
of bonds. Why did the Company asked for so little money when nothing had
really happened in terms of cubage extracted? Probably, because of bankers'
recommendations, wary about the potentialities of the Stock Market. It should
be noted that from now on, the subscriptions will be for bonds - as the
shareholders had already been called for the entirety of the initial 300 million
francs in 1880, sum that had been already spent.

This first subscription of bonds would be followed by six more, at regular
intervals, one per year from 1882 to 1888. It will become quite a ritual and
little by little the investors will eventually believe that the Panama project was
endless. . . and worthless. A detail of the Company's subscriptions can be
found in Appendix 2.

By an incredible coincidence, on the day following this second subscription, September 8, 1882, Panama was struck by an exceptional earthquake and
a tidal wave - known as a *tsunami* in the western Pacific Ocean area - hit her
shores.

The damages in the Isthmus were spectacular. In Panama City, one of the twin towers of the Cathedral collapsed to the ground. In Colon, the sea pier was destroyed and the city flooded. On top of the damages to the civil structures, the Company's warehouses were hit and a lot of equipment ruined. It is easy to understand why this cataclysm delayed the project by many months.

This event reminds us that Panama is located on the Pacific "ring of fire". Although the country has no active volcanoes, its earth is very unstable, albeit somewhat firmer than in the north - Costa Rica or Nicaragua.

Men have a short memory. In 1903, when Nicaragua would be eliminated from the Interoceanic Canal race on the account of its volcanic activity, nobody recalled that Panama was also lying on capricious grounds.

As the saying goes: *Misfortunes never come singly.*

Only a few months after the earthquake, the Company suffered another setback. *Couvreux & Hersent* relinquished their contract with the Company, as of December 31. After two years, as provided in their contract with the Company, they were to determine the actual cost of excavating a cubic meter. They had encountered so many difficulties, that they were afraid to lose money by quoting a fixed price per cubic meter excavated. Also, they did not have the personnel resources to manage such a large project.

They recommended employing several companies. (2)

True, Couvreux had done well in Suez - on a 13 kilometers long tract (8 miles) - , but here in Panama, things were quite different. Panama's soil proved to be inconsistent, heterogeneous and totally different from Suez.

A contract cancellation fee of $ 1.2 million was paid to *Couvreux & Hersent* by the generous Company.

In December 1882, the list of the Company's misfortunes went on even further. Armand Reclus, the General Manager of the works, resigned for what he called: "a disorder of details". This disorder was, without any doubt, the lack of coordination between Rue Caumartin, the headquarters of the Company in Paris and its offices in Panama City - three weeks away by ship.

After two years of work in Panama - only a year of real excavation work had taken place -, the Company still needed to actually get started. Only a few thousand laborers were at work. Recruiting many more proved to be essential for the Company.

Despite this slow progress, more than half of Lesseps's initial budget - 600 million francs - had been spent and it was hard to see any trench showing the path of the future canal. The General Manager had resigned. The main contractor had given up. Part of the Company's supplies had disappeared in a tidal wave.

What a sinister series of catastrophes!

In Paris, comments and rumors in the press amplified the disaster. Drumont will write later, in 1890: "To understand Panama, it is necessary to imagine chaos, not the chaos of the first days of the world, but a chaos with a semblance of civilization, a chaos of the nineteen Century: engineers, exploiters, innkeepers, owners of disreputable houses, down and outers, beggars, employees who have come from anywhere, workmen from all countries, all these in perpetual agitation without any direction and without any plans, doing over and over the same task." (4) The caustic pen of the journalist Drumont probably exaggerated the matter, but there was some truth in it, as proved by the resignation of such a competent man as Armand Reclus.

To explain what led to Reclus' pessimism and to his resignation, one has to examine the logistical situation in Panama. It was a scarcely populated province of Colombia, with only 25,000 inhabitants living in what is called today the Canal Zone and the adjacent cities of Panama City and Colon. Mathematically, hiring that same amount of laborers would prove to be an impossible task, however hard the Company would try.

Unfortunately, these 1882 disasters would be followed by many others.

As soon as they started digging, the morale of the laborers fell at its lowest, not so much because of the fevers that they endured fairly courageously, but because of a new major obstacle. Although the terrain of the section near Colon, where mostly marshes existed, was easy and soft, in the Culebra Hill, the engineers faced the toughest problem. The soil's geological composition, made of layers of hard stones - mostly volcanic - alternating with soft ones - limestone - was totally unexpected, unique in the world, quite different from the sands of Suez. No engineer had predicted such a difficulty, not even the geographers, who had surveyed Panama in the 1870s.

Geologists recognize today that the hills of Panama are a curious amalgam of all types of soils. B-V called it "the soapy nature of the local clay."(7) To complete the picture, let us add that the Culebra Hill was "one mile long, if we take the part above the altitude of 230 feet - 70 meters." (7)

The first shovels of earth showed the extent of the Culebra Hill problem. The soil was found moist and hard at the same time, very difficult to keep on a slope and form an embankment. It slid under the slightest rain and turned to a rock under the burning sun.

The worst happened during the rainy season when "this soapy clay tended to lose its coherence and suddenly slid away transformed into a mud lake", as B-V would write in his memoirs. (7) And reports of the experts showed that "the swelling of the upper layers spread up to 1,000 yards - 300 meters." (2)

The Company could only hope that all this series of disasters would finally come to an end; and they did, at least partly, at the beginning of **1883**.

As it could not find another contractor to replace *Couvreux & Hersent* and to follow this first contractor's recommendation, the Company's Board decided to hire as many small contractors as it could find. Initially the number reached 100, but was quickly reduced to about 30, for obvious managerial reasons. (2)

Spending continued as if money was plentiful. The Company had no cost control and, worse, it still did not negotiate with the suppliers on the basis of comparative bidding. This careless attitude would later engender dishonesty and corruption.

To set up this new and complex organization, Charles de Lesseps, soon to replace his aging father - he had turned 77 -, traveled to Panama on February 5, 1883. He brought with him the newly appointed General Manager, Jules Isidore Dingler.

Under Dingler, things progressed smoothly. At last, the Company showed some optimism. It was about time that the Company made a real start. Dingler was the third General Manager to run the works in the last two years. First it was Reclus and then Richier, who lasted only a few months each. An engineer from the School of *Ponts & Chaussées*, class of 1849, Dingler showed a lot of skill in running the works. He put together the teams, organized the trenches, had railway tracks put in place to evacuate the earth, used dredges in the marshes near Colon and shattered the harder grounds with steam-driven excavators. All these well-organized activities soon led to some visible progress and boosted the morale of the laborers, as well as of the Company's Board in Paris.

It should be said that the preliminary work, done before the arrival of Dingler, as unproductive as it seemed, was nevertheless quite necessary. It had taken two years - 1881 and 1882 - to build the infrastructures, hospitals, dwellings, harbors, and warehouses, to order the material and ship it from Europe, in summary to prepare everything in order to excavate.

One major task had been to deepen the access to the harbors. Ships had tremendously changed in the last years. They were no longer sailboats made of wood, but steel plated hull vessels, driven by steam engines. Much bigger than before, they needed a deeper draught - about ten meters (30 feet).

When this dredging was done, the large ships could then berth in Colon's harbor and unload their cargo of machinery bought from European factories.

We have to pause here to imagine what a titanic work it was to unload these heavy parts and assemble them with cranes that were sometimes not strong enough or mobile enough. We have also to imagine the poor French engineers, supervising this colossal task under a firing sun, weakened by fevers. Yes, they were hard times and what these hardy laborers had done in the Culebra Hill merits our admiration.

Dingler and his staff were rewarded with a lot of progress. In less than six months, things seemed to be back on track. Even the recruiting went well.

In September 1883, about 10,000 laborers were at work on the canal.

As a French administrative employee, Dingler, the General Manager had the right to a summer vacation in his motherland. In June 1883, he returned to France and declared that "in Panama, the weather is particularly healthy. In the Isthmus, only the drunkards die. There has been a lot of imagination about the sanitary condition in Panama. I just come from there and can testify about the good and healthy status of all the Company's personnel." (4)

Unfortunately, Dingler would soon have to re-think his statement.

In October 1883, he went back to work, full of confidence in the future, taking with him his wife, his son, his daughter and her fiancé. All went well for a while, or at least, better than before. The optimism of the Company climbed to an unseen level. All wished that there could be a favorable period of calm ahead.

Leaving Panama for a while, we need, at this time, to mention some other French accomplishments, which called for the admiration of the whole world. Gustave Eiffel had graduated from the *École Centrale des Arts et Manufactures*, class of 1854, and founded his own company, specializing in steel structures. Very prolific, he constructed bridges in Portugal, Indochina, and all over the world. He has just achieved in Garabit, in the center of France, the world's longest steel viaduct, which took four years to build. He was now busy designing the steel framework for the Statue of Liberty, to be inaugurated in New York harbor in 1886. He would soon become famous in the whole world when he built his 300 meter-high metallic tower in the middle of Paris.

Unfortunately, Eiffel will be caught for having played a dishonorable part in the Panama affair, as we shall explain when we reach the year 1894.

All this meant that the economic climate was bullish at the end of 1883.

We come now into **1884**.

In Panama, work progressed well, more and more earth being extracted every month. It should be noted that the workers had started digging the easiest parts, near Colon, in the marshes.

Elsewhere, many problems still hampered the work and they would delay the project up to its end:
- lack of manpower,
- landslides in the Culebra Hill area,
- floods of the Rio Chagres.

To eliminate this last problem, Dingler planned a dam to control the floods.

This dam is a good example of the lies told by the Company to its share-holders in its *Bulletin du Canal Interocéanique*. This is what the shareholders could read:
- November 1, 1883: "the dam is quite simple, it will cost 8 million francs."
- In May 1884, a huge downpour caused the Rio Chagres' level to rise by 3 meters in a few hours. This caused Dingler to put the dam on top of his priority list,
- In August 1885: "the dam we are building on the Rio Chagres will cost 40 million francs". There was not any construction activity taking place!
- In May 1886: "the supreme difficulty on the canal works is the dam, at a cost of 100 million francs." And still, not a single trace of the dam to be seen.

In fact, it seemed that there was a technological problem to build a concrete dam, as the Company engineers never found the right location with a hard and stable foundation. In 1910, the Americans will go around this difficulty by using a different design - an embankment dam, working as a bookend, its own weight preventing it from being turned over by the water's force. It would be the world largest dam at the time.

As for the lack of manpower, it would continue to slow down the work in Panama. No solution had been found to recruit as many laborers as in Suez - 30,000. It was out of the question to employ native Indians, who considered all kind of manual work to be slavery. As for white Panamanians, mostly poor farmers, their *haciendas* were also looking for manpower. Panama did not have a lot of Black or Indian slaves, as in the Caribbean Islands.

Moreover, Panama was not heavily populated; the City of Panama had only 18,378 inhabitants in 1880 - from Enrique Linares in the *Political History of Panama*. With the canal works, the city would expand and reach 30,000 people.

At the time of the French Company, the whole country had less than 100,000 people.

At first, the company tried to bring mulattos from the French Antilles, convinced that they would not find the Panamanian sun worse than what they had been used to in their islands. But, having been freed in 1848, they were not too prone to toil under the tropical sun and its torrential rains. "They deserted as soon as they arrived in Panama and embraced an easier profession: that of sick workmen." (7)

A solution for this difficult manpower problem was never found. It was not due to the lack of efforts of the Company to recruit them.

Missions were sent as far as Africa - some workers came from Liberia - or Indochina (a French colony). Most workers were finally found in the British West Indies and among them a majority came from the British colony of Jamaica. "So, among the actual laborers, the language was English, not French." (16)

Here we come upon another example of the endemic corruption on the canal works. Just a few days after arriving in the Isthmus, some of the Jamaicans unexpectedly returned home, their trip paid by the agents of the Company. This did not seem to make sense, until it was discovered that these agents received a commission for each worker *arriving* from Jamaica. (1)

B-V explained that "for every eighty employees who survived six months on the Isthmus, one could say that twenty died. The proportion between the number of deaths and the number of arrivals was obviously much smaller, because more than half of the employees left very soon after their arrival." (7)

There are also some references to Chinese laborers, but their grand-fathers who had come to build the PRR - and turned into merchants -, quickly discouraged the new comers. Working in a shop seemed more attractive than digging a hill in full sun. (2) For this reason, the Chinese workers amounted to only a few hundreds.
As for the Europeans, their number never exceeded 1% of the working force. The painter Gauguin and his friend Laval were truly exceptions.

In summary, the labor force will never exceed 19,000, when it would have been necessary for the French Company to have 30,000.
When the United States finished the Panama Canal between 1910 and 1914, the work force reached 40,000, of which many were North Americans.

In 1884, under Dingler, work continued to progress well and the Company's optimism was at the highest. However, its confidence in a bright future had been built through lies, more lies. An internal report from Dingler mentioned that : "Contractors have started excavating on all points of the canal. This work has brought the unpleasant news that we ought to extract 120 million cubic meters and not 75," (2) 45 million more, 60% more!

It was difficult for the Company not to reveal this information to the share-holders and on July 23, 1884, Lesseps reported to the General Assembly, that: "The additional 45 million cubic meters are located in a marshy area, easily excavated with a dredge," (2) which implied that it would cost very little to remove those "soft" lands.

Around the same period of time, at the end of August 1884, only 7,865,666 cubic meters had been extracted. (2) Only 6.5% of the 120 millions quoted above. All this in three and a half years. Doubts arose that the project could not be completed in 8 years, as forecast.

Unfortunately, in the early days of 1884, fate hit again. The three young members of the Dingler family - his son, his daughter and her fiancé - all died in a matter of months. (16)

In July 1884, Dingler and his wife returned to France to bury their children.

At the same time, B-V, our hero, was making preparations to take up his post with the Company in Panama.

7
B-V IN PANAMA

During the summer of 1884, after many applications and much determination, B-V was able to terminate his compulsory contract with the French Government.

Severiano de Heredia, Minister of Public Works, had finally accepted his request. B-V was now free to apply for a job with the Lesseps' Company, where engineers were in great demand. Their number was still being reduced by fevers and logically this situation did not attract many candidates.

B-V must really have been obsessed by his dream of working on the Panama Canal. He knew he would be risking his life, but nothing could deter him from going: "The dream of my childhood was becoming a reality," (7) an exhilarating B-V wrote in his memoirs.

Fever casualties among the French staff in Panama showed no sign of slowing down. Although the Company had done all it could to hide the terrible news, it was now common knowledge in Paris. The burial of the Dingler children had filled pages of the capital's newspapers.

Courageously ignoring danger, full of optimism and his heart filled with joy to be finally able to leave for Panama, on October 6, B-V boarded the *Washington,* a twenty-year-old ship, driven by two paddle wheels.

This type of propulsion, well known on the Mississippi River boats, may seem strange on a transatlantic steamer. When the steam engines were first installed on ships, the right propelling device took time to find. The first screws were quickly abandoned, as they induced heavy vibrations in the hull.

Later, the double screw propeller was found to work satisfactorily, but before they could be installed, paddle wheels had to be used for some years.

By a fortunate coincidence, B-V found himself on the same ship as his boss Jules Dingler and his wife, both returning to Panama after the burial of their poor children. What a privilege B-V had to travel with his new boss!

We shall see that in the future, B-V's life will be filled with such favorable events. Was B-V a particularly lucky person? We think not and rather believe that he was a very bright individual and used every opportunity to his advantage. A more Machiavellian historian would write that B-V was producing these happy meetings in order to fulfill his plans.

All along this book, we shall relate many such encounters. Readers shall appreciate.

On the seas during three long weeks, with only a few stops in:
- Pointe à Pitre - Guadeloupe -,
- Fort de France - Martinique -,
- and La Guaira, the port of Caracas - Venezuela -,

 B-V and his boss had plenty of time to review all the problems that were plaguing the works. B-V could not have dreamed of a better training. He wrote in his memoirs: "During the twenty-one days that I had to spend on board with Mr. Dingler and his documents, I was able to acquire everything that a man can learn outside of that which only actual experience provides." (7)

Not surprisingly, well treated by the Company, Dingler and B-V travelled luxuriously in first class - called *Salon* class –, which was far more comfortable than the *Cabine* class, where penniless travelers were packed in dormitories located at the bottom of the hull. (17)

Once in Panama, B-V began working courageously, as "Chief Engineer of the 3rd Division, which extended from the pacific shores to the Culebra cut, inclusive." (11) His studies at the *École Polytechnique* had trained him to understand problems quickly, to solve them methodically and to maintain a high level of mental concentration for many hours.

He had much to do; the laborers on the work site were slightly more than 19,000, a peak that would never be exceeded. However, sickness and fevers were always present and B-V testified that: "on the morning call, there were rarely more than 13 to 14,000 men able to work." (2)

All seemed to go well on the work site, but unfortunately the past series of misfortunes did not stop. At the end of 1884, death struck again the poor Dingler family: Madame Dingler became ill and died of yellow fever on New Year's Day 1885. Poor Dingler remained courageously at his post and buried his wife in a Panamanian Cemetery.

1885, the fifth year of construction, started on a sad note.

Dingler was devastated. By accepting such a catastrophe-laden job, he had lost his entire family; he had no energy left to continue his work. As a result, he relied heavily on B-V, his young and dynamic assistant.

B-V was still a bachelor. In Paris, Maurice was taking good care of his mother and grandmother. B-V was therefore free to express himself through all his ambitions. Named at the head of the most difficult sector, the Culebra Hill, from kilometers 55 to 57, - the Pacific end of the canal was at the kilometer 70 -, he controlled the Anglo-Dutch company *Cutbill, de Lungo, Watson and Van Hattum*, which had replaced the French firm *Couvreux and Hersent*.

The French *Archives du Travail* - Businesses' Archives - showed us how the contractors worked with the Company. Here, we found the contracts originals, signed by both parties, with all the details.

The Anglo-Dutch contract, dated August 28, 1885, stated that the Company had to supply all the equipment to be used by the contractor: 26 locomotives, 2,200 railcars, 50 kilometers of tracks, 10 excavators and many more pieces of equipment. However, all this was not free; the contractor had to pay an annual lease fee of 8% of the value of the equipment, as stated in the Company's books; such lease fee would later be increased to 10% a year. The only responsibility of the contractor was to pay the workers. They received about $ 1.25 per day at work - the equivalent of 6 francs - about one Euro, paid every week.

By the same contract, the contractor had to follow a monthly excavation program, explicitly stated in cubic meters in the contract. For example, in the Culebra area, the Anglo-Dutch were to receive a sum of 8.38 francs per cubic meter extracted above the altitude of 50 meters, this sum being gradually increased to reach 9.14 francs per cubic meter at sea-level.

The Culebra Hill had an altitude of about 120 meters at its peak.

The total volume of earth to be excavated in the Culebra was estimated at 20 million cubic meters. When and if the contractor met these contractual targets, they received - on top of the 8.38 to 9.14 francs per cubic meter - a variable bonus according to each step of its progress: 2 million francs when they would reach the altitude of 70 meters, another 2 million francs at the altitude of 50 meters and 3.5 million francs at the end, at the bottom of the canal – at an altitude of minus 9 meters. All these incentive bonuses added up to 7.5 million francs.

For the Culebra Hill, the overall contract was estimated at about 200 million francs.

Of course, at his high level of management, B-V had complete knowledge of these contracts. Later on in our story, we shall see how he will take advantage from this knowledge.

At the end of 1884, the Company's spending had already reached the astronomical sum of 700 million francs. This was already higher than the initial Lesseps' budget - 600 million francs. All this money had been spent for a really disappointing result. So far, only 10 million cubic meters had been excavated out of an estimated total of 75 million cubic meters - less than 15%.

In Paris, at the General Assembly of the shareholders, the President of the Company, Ferdinand de Lesseps, announced that the total cost initially estimated at 512 million francs was now revised at 700 million francs. Another blatant lie, when more than 700 had already been spent!

We shall see how this series of lies will finally cause the Company to go out of business.

On September 25, a fourth subscription was called, bringing the total collected to 725 million francs. The detail of the subscriptions is given in Appendix 2.

This fourth subscription did not solve the cash shortage of the Company and it had to borrow from banks. As Lemarquis would write later: "This was not a serious risk for the banks. At the time, Panama still had a good enough credit." (14) But, this optimistic situation will not last. Let us just consider that, according to the statistics of the Paris Stock Market, between 1881 and 1884, the money called for Panama represented about 10% of all the shares and bonds issued.

Would the money supply become a problem just when B-V had finally reached his dream to come to work in Panama? Was he to arrive too late to solve all the problems, including the landslides of the Culebra Hill?

While B-V worked on the Panama Canal, American investors were still very interested in Nicaragua. At the end of 1884, the *Frelinghuysen-Zarala* Treaty was signed between the two countries to prepare for the construction of a canal built in common with Great Britain.

On January 26, 1886, after more than a year of deliberations, the Senate failed to ratify this treaty, as it insisted on having a 100% American canal.

Deliberately ignoring this, some bullish entrepreneurs decided to launch their own company, the *Nicaragua Canal Association,* and investors and bankers cooperated to move the project forward. Considering the "unfeasibility" claimed by the experts, it is quite easy to understand why Americans ignored the French work in Panama and continued to make progress in Nicaragua, as if they had no rival for the Central American Interoceanic Canal. They believed that Panama was doomed to fail!

In Panama, six months after his arrival, B-V recalled in his memoirs how he witnessed a revolution: "Thus there developed before my eyes the para-doxical situation of a revolutionary government protected by American intervention against the attack of an army under the orders of the legal government of Colombia. It was, in fact, the rigorous application of the 1846 treaty . . . I was witnessing the application of the diplomatic theory which, almost twenty years later, was to permit me to establish the Republic of Panama and to rescue the canal undertaking from annihilation." (11)

Early in 1885, the Colombian Government in Bogota had decided to mod-ify the status of the Panama province: federalism would be abandoned and a Governor would be installed in Panama City, reporting directly to the Colombian capital. Fearing for their independence, Panamanians reacted violently: an insurrection started in the City of Panama where Aizpuru led a large group of insurgents, while in Colon, Prestan, an Haitian mulatto, led another group.

This kind of turmoil was recurrent in Panama. In his speech before Con-gress, on December 7, 1903, President Roosevelt mentioned every one of the 53 (sic) insurrections from 1846 to 1903 (see the entire list in Appendix 8).

As usual, when such event occurred, the *Mallarino-Bidlack* treaty entitled the United States forces to restore order. Let us examine in detail how it all happened. This is quite important, as history will repeat itself in 1903.

After the end of 1884 Colombian elections, agitation had filled the entire country. In order to contain insurrections happening in other provinces, Panama's Governor, Pablo Arosemena, had unfortunately sent away 500 of his government troops. So when disorder mounted in Panama in January 1885, the Governor was not in a position to maintain order and called for American troops who - by the 1846 treaty - were given that mission.

Although the number of American citizens crossing the Isthmus - via the PRR - has considerably decreased, maintaining the safety on the PRR, along the future canal path, remained an excuse to use force.

The U. S. war ship *Alliance* brought a battalion of marines; they disem-barked in Colon and order was momentarily restored.

However, during this time, in the City of Panama, Aizpuru had been de-feated by governmental troops. But in March, he regained momentum and proclaimed himself Governor. His troops had vandalized the PRR, arrested its employees, cut telegraphic cables, etc. The situation was serious.

On April 24, marines landed in the City of Panama and captured Aizpuru, who was handed to loyalist Colombian troops, patiently awaiting the end of the insurrection on board a vessel in the bay. Americans had prevented them to land, fearing it could cause more trouble in the City streets. On April 30, Americans handed over the City, at last pacified, to loyal Colombian troops.

In the meantime, in Colon, Prestan had organized a revolt. Colombian troops could not re-establish order and the City was set to fire on April 1st, 1885. American troops finally arrested Prestan and after judgment, he was hanged on August 18. During this revolution, a fire destroyed most of the City of Colon. When things calmed down, B-V regrettably found out that a major part of the Company's equipment, stored in the Colon warehouses had been lost. The Company did not need this new calamity, which added to the previous losses due to the earthquake of September 1882; it was clear that the already ailing Company would experience further delays in completing its work.

In 1903, B-V will look back on the 1885 rebellion, which inspired his actions all along to support the Panamanian revolution. He had remained strongly affected by the political situation of Panama, where revolutions were common place. This would also explain why he eventually modified some articles of the proposed Hay/Herran treaty, in order to give complete sovereignty to the United States in the Canal Zone, (7) and comply with some of the Senators' demands.

In his "Chief Engineer" job, B-V had to solve the same problems as his predecessors. In May 1885, he was faced with a Company's staff shortage. Clavenad, his colleague, in charge of the 1st sector - starting in Colon, on the Atlantic Ocean -, resigned, following a dispute with Dingler. B-V readily took his job, while also keeping his. He was now responsible for two thirds of the canal works. B-V's sectors being at the extremities of the canal, he must have spent quite a lot of time commuting on the PRR. His energy was limitless.

In Colon, he found quite a critical situation. "Profound disorder reigned in Colon. The fire had destroyed the town, its warehouses and its wharves," (7) which slowed down the unloading of the equipment coming from Europe. "It was an unceasing and constant labor, which during five months did not permit me to obtain more than two hours' rest per night," (7) wrote B-V in his memoirs. Among his duties, the Culebra Hill was the most challenging. He observed that to maintain an embankment on the excavated hill, a smaller angle was now necessary. Instead of a 45 degrees angle with the ground level - a slope of 1 over 1 -, a slope of 1 over 4 would have to be maintained. A simple calculation shows that this had the effect to multiply the cubage to be extracted by a factor of 2. B-V, who was an excellent engineer, did find a solution to the Culebra Hill problems. In order to excavate the earth causing the landslides, he developed an original method. He told us in his memoirs that: "I tried to make the dredge excavate the rock after rendering it dredgeable." (11) By first shattering the rock with dynamite, the laborers could then use a dredge to get it out. To achieve this, a floating raft was built, from where holes could be drilled in the bottom of the trench and then filled with dynamite.

After the explosion, the rock, shattered in small debris, could easily be dredged out. B-V's calculations showed that the cost of excavating a cubic meter was much less by this method than by blasting the dry rock.

Later, he would extend this method into a plan. B-V believed that by bringing the dredges above the soil to be excavated, in a series of small lakes, the canal could be built more quickly. But to put his plan into action, he needed to have a canal with locks, which Lesseps had firmly disapproved. Lesseps had decreed it at once when he had been chosen to head the project; he refused to build anything else than a sea-level canal.

In his memoirs, B-V claimed that the use of dynamite was his own invention. In fact, he had most probably seen it in the Cherbourg harbor, not far from Bayeux, - where he served as *Ponts & Chaussées'* engineer in 1883 - where it had first been tested. This method was not easy to use, especially when the dredged material had to be taken out of the bottom of the lake. "Dingler hoped to use pumps to evacuate the dredged soils, but this system failed." (7)

In summary, B-V's plan of a provisional canal was "to first construct a lock canal, then by dredging to turn it into a sea-level canal." (7) His solution would also allow the Company to receive tolls from that provisional canal, before the final project would be completed. B-V believed that his scheme would be a solution to improve the poor cash situation of the Company. He called it: "excavating by dredging". (7)

In July 1885, Dingler went back to France, unwell and overwhelmed by fevers. Fortunately, he recovered, but he never found the courage to return to his job in Panama. He received an indemnity of 100,000 francs and remained a counselor for the Company, with a salary of 30,000 francs a year.

His very unlucky successor, Maurice Hutin, was overcome by yellow fever after only one month in the Isthmus. Alike Dingler, he was lucky to return back to France and to recover.

How did B-V remain healthy when all his bosses disappeared? It is believed that he owed his survival to the daily dose of quinine sulfate that he received regularly from his mother and grandmother. (28)

The Company has already lost four General Managers.

Who will be the fifth?

In Paris, the Company was looking for a successor to Hutin - who did not want to return to his dangerous position -, but candidates were scarce.

After months of procrastination and desperate not to find another option, the Company provisionally named B-V as their General Manager in October 1885. He had just turned twenty-six.

He had met his destiny!

He had remained the only survivor of a staff of four at the head of the works.

He was at the head of a billion-franc project.

Naturally, his youth worried some Company's administrators, especially after they received alarming reports from Mr. Lavieille, the French Consul in Panama, who declared in front of B-V that he was a risk: "How astonished I am to see a man of your age placed at the head of an undertaking of national interest. I might say of universal interest." (7) B-V quickly dealt with this problem by improving his relationship with Lavieille, to such an extent that, during Lesseps's next visit, Lavieille asked why B-V had not yet been proposed for the Legion of Honor.

This is a good example of B-V's magnetic charm. He could rapidly turn situations to his advantage. We shall encounter many other examples of such virtue.

B-V could not be replaced nor helped. He had made himself indispensable. At the end of October 1885, a group of about thirty French engineers arrived; among them, two had been selected to become division heads, under B-V. Unfortunately, both died within two weeks of their arrival. We find here another example of B-V's vanity, as he wrote in his memoirs: "I did not even need them." (7)

Human losses continued. B-V remembered "two ships from New Orleans at anchor in Colon. Nobody remained on board; everyone was dead from yellow fever, from the captain to the last cabin boy." (11)

It was becoming unbearable: "Men die as would flies. Of the thirty engineers landing from the *Washington* on October 29, thirteen had died on November 24. Among them were the two unfortunate Division Engineers," (5) who had been sent to help B-V.

Henri Kuss, an alumnus of Polytechnique, 33 years old, a geology expert, was en route to Chile, through Panama, at the time. His testimony is informative. In a letter to his family, he confirmed B-V's story: "The first thing I saw, was a pair of posters with black borders, announcing the death of two Division Engineers, Petit and Sordoillet. Having left France together, on October 8, both had died on November 24. This is a frightening waste of men." Kuss, also an engineer, gave a faithful and accurate judgment on the progress of the works: "In the central section - Culebra Hill - where the Company is committed to extract 750,000 cubic meters a month, it hardly reaches 30 to 40,000. The reports of the Company have no credibility. It is feared that it would not be able to finish the work. Americans are waiting for the Company's agony and ready to give it the final blow. We would have acted as cat's paws for them."

An admirably prophetic vision, written in 1885.

Not only did the French engineers have to cope with fevers, but they also had to endure natural catastrophes. During the night of December 2, 1885, a very strong hurricane hit the Isthmus. This was an exceptional event, as hurricanes usually follow a more northern route in the Caribbean Sea, avoiding Panama.

In the port of Colon, steamers escaped by reaching the high seas, but twenty sail ships were thrown against the rocky coast and most of their cargo was lost. Yet another loss for the Company, not really needed at that particular time.

While this hurricane struck, the Rio Chagres had its level rising by five meters - 15 feet - in a few hours. B-V made some flow measurements, with the purpose of designing a dam to contain the frequent overflows of the Rio Chagres. It should be noted that, although this dam had been deemed strictly necessary to the future canal, nothing had been started yet on this project. There was not a single preliminary drawing for this dam!

As we enter **1886** and with the beginning of the dry season, despite all the drawbacks, B-V was still optimistic. He was happy to report a lot of progress on the works: about a million cubic meters - 1,068,000 exactly - had been excavated during the month of January. B-V was very proud of it. He was the absolute leader on the works and he could really report what he wanted to.

In fact, these record cubages were for the whole length of the canal. They did not impress the Company in Paris, which was especially interested in the volumes taken out of the Culebra Hill, their main concern. Unfortunately, only a few tens of thousand cubic meters had been extracted from there. Just a scratch on the Hill. These meager results were attributed to the lack of manpower.

The pessimistic reports of Lavieille, the French Consul in Panama, had upset the Parisian financial and governmental spheres.

A book by Wyse - the man who signed the Colombian concession in 1879 - published around the same time, criticized openly the Company. His status report of the works as of October 1885 (3) indicated:

- In the contracts signed by the Company, *Artigue & Sonderegger*, for the Bohio Soldado to Buenavista portion, did not protect the Company's interests;
- The "Anglo-Dutch" lot is poorly organized;
- It would seem appropriate that the General Manager – the names of Dingler and B-V were not mentioned by Wyse - would dedicate more time to the essentials of the task rather than being absorbed by administrative details;
- The errors made by the Company would amount - at the end of the project - to 350 million francs.

Some large shareholders were affected by all these criticisms and, as they had many influential friends, they jointly put some pressure on the French deputies at the Chamber. Was it not one of the major responsibilities of the French Government to protect the interests of all the shareholders, large or small? This led the Chamber of Deputies to commission a special emissary, Armand Rousseau, Secretary of State at the Ministry of Public Works, to produce an official report; he was an alumnus from Polytechnique, class of 1854. His assistant was another alumnus of this prestigious school: "Mr. Luuyt, who had left the "École Polytechnique" in the same year as myself," explained B-V, happy of this coincidence. (11)

By bringing politicians into the picture, the Company hoped to receive the help it needed to survive. It came at the right moment for the Company, which, always short for money, needed to sell more bonds. This time, it had in mind a very large subscription, of a special nature, with prizes distributed by a yearly lottery. Its financial advisor - a banker called Oberndoerffer - had thought that it would be the only way to raise such enormous amounts of money. Such a subscription being banned by a 1836 law, a specific exemption would have to be voted by the Deputies. This was the reason why a favorable report by Rousseau was essential for the Company.

After five years of existence, but only four years of real work, the Company had a catastrophic record, barely revealed to the public. The Company had produced a mountain of lies to its shareholders. It was paying many newspapers to publish false news, the same that would appear in the Company's *Bulletin* and the share-holders believed that they were real news.

The truth was that 700 million francs had been spent and that the Company has absolutely no idea of how many more millions would be needed to complete the canal. Only 10 to 12 million cubic meters had been excavated. Out of how many? Nobody believed that the initial estimate was still holding at 75 million cubic meters. But how many more would it be? Rousseau would have to find out. He landed in Colon in January 1886 and started working on his report.

At the same time, Ferdinand de Lesseps and his son Charles had set up a huge reorganization of the works. It was needed to boost progress. Instead of the 30 small contractors, they divided up the canal in 6 lots, each under contract with a large construction company:

- from Colon (the zero point) to kilometer 23.465: *American Contracting & Dredging Co.* the American firm of the Slaven brothers,
- from 23.465 to 26.350: *Artigue & Sonderegger,*
- from 26.350 to 44: *Vignaud, Barbaud, Blanleuil & Co,*
- from 44 to 53.660: *Société des Travaux Publics et de Construction,*
- from 53.660 to 55.456 : *Cutbill de Longo, Watson & Van Hattum,* also called the "Anglo-Dutch" company; this sector included the Culebra Hill,
- from 55.456 to the Pacific Ocean: *Baratoux, Letellier & Co.*

With these changes, a fierce battle took place in the Parisian spheres, as the Company had decided to increase the contractor's productivity by allowing higher prices per cubic meter excavated. To obtain these very attractive contracts, the construction companies had to call for intermediaries or *arrangeurs* to negotiate with Charles de Lesseps and had to retrocede a commission for each contract. For example, for a contractual price of 6.86 F/m3, the commission to the *arrangeur* was about 0.12 F/m3.

"Such a *laissez-faire* from the Company has led contractors to realize considerable profits and some of them - *Artigue & Sonderegger, Eiffel*, etc - had to pay enormous commissions to obtain their contracts." (2) We shall see later how Maurice, B-V's brother was involved in these commissions.

This system of the commissions would continue without any obstruction from the Company, until the Company died from it.

This new reorganization was materialized by contracts signed at the end of 1885 and by January 1886, with six contractors already actively working on the canal.

Again, following this major and hopeful change, Ferdinand de Lesseps and his son Charles wanted to show to the world that things were progressing well in Panama, and that to complete the work, more money was needed. As they had done in early 1880, the Company organized a trip to Panama for hundreds of bankers, businessmen, and investors from all countries.

On January 30, 1886, the first group of visitors landed in Colon, with Charles de Lesseps, Leon Boyer and Armand Rousseau, the Government's envoy. Leon Boyer had been an associate of Eiffel in the construction of the Garabit viaduct. Boyer had been appointed to be the next General Manager, coming to lend a hand to B-V. The Company had spent six months trying to find B-V's replacement. "Mr. Bunau-Varilla was slightly upset of seeing his successor, Mr. Boyer, arrive," (2) observed Charles de Lesseps. Another sign of B-V's vanity: he was surely expecting to be named General Manager.

During his trip to Panama, Charles de Lesseps had met Emile Arton, a representative of the *Centrale de Dynamite*. Arton successfully convinced Charles to purchase the dynamite - used in blasting the bed rock - from him, at a good price. He would later be prosecuted for corruption in 1893, as an agent of Reinach.

Corruption had now spread through the entire Company and its suppliers.

Charles was slowly taking over the leadership of the Company from his father. Now 80, Ferdinand needed to rely on his successor. But, Charles was not as astute nor as experienced as his father, and in his hands the Company will make many more errors.

There were many more groups visiting Panama, throughout the spring of 1886. B-V hosted them, accommodating some of them in the *Palacio* of the Bishop of Panama City.

On February 17, Ferdinand de Lesseps himself arrived.

During these visits, B-V used all his charm with his prestigious hosts. He flooded them with technical details to persuade them that everything was under control: "The visitors could not sufficiently admire the splendid display of creative force made by these 12 to 14,000 men working in coordinate activity with a countless number of machines of all kinds." (7)

With the Lesseps group, there were many representatives from the Chambers of Commerce of New York, Bordeaux, Marseille, Saint Nazaire and Rouen, "among them were the economist Molinari, the Duke of Sutherland, the English Admiral Carpenter, Colonel Talbot of the English Army." (7)

They were entertained by the many fiestas given at the Company's expense. The Panamanian historian Anguizola, whose grandfather had attended all the banquets, listed the menus served to the guests and even gave some of the recipes used. (18) Of course, all the aristocracy of Panama had been invited.

Many foreign visitors came from Great Britain, Germany and the United States. Among the American delegates was John Bigelow, sent by the New York Chamber of Commerce. He had traveled with one of his daughters, Grace. Arrived on the steamer *Colon*, on February 18, Bigelow preferred to sleep on board during his entire stay. Bigelow was really an important visitor.

Just before he left, William C. Whitney, the Marine Secretary had decided that "in view of your going, I have concluded to order another of our heaviest armed ships there." (1) Following this order, a U. S. war ship was kept berthed alongside the steamer *Colon* for two weeks.

Charles de Lesseps himself boarded the *Colon* to greet Bigelow.

In spite of his enthusiasm, B-V found it difficult to convince the visitors that everything was running smoothly. Bigelow wrote in his diary: "Charles tells me confidentially that more than 800 million francs are still necessary to put it through. . . Grace and the old Baron got on admirably together." (1)

Back home, in full agreement with Wyse's book that had just been published, Bigelow presented a gloomy report to the Engineer's Club of Philadelphia: "Total cubage to be excavated: 120 million cubic meters. 11% done as of February 1st. The remaining 89% will take more than eight years, given the actual rate of progress." (1) It seems that Bigelow had access to the new estimate of 120 million cubic meters - instead of 75.

It was known that the "11% done" represented the easiest part.

Bigelow wrote also in his diary: "There remain four obstacles to the good completion of Panama:
- the Rio Chagres problem is still unsolved,
- cutting through the Culebra Hill is not easy,
- maintaining through dredging the passage between the La Boca and Perico Islands, on the Pacific Ocean side,
- finding manpower at an acceptable cost." (1)

Bigelow was not a civil engineer, but he listened to people and quickly discovered the problems that had hampered the works from the beginning. He knew that none of the above problems had an easy solution.

An agent of the Company, named Connor, confided to Bigelow that: "Of the 13,500 Jamaicans who have arrived in 1885, 11,500 have returned back home. The agents of the Company receive a commission for each worker coming from Jamaica. The end result is disappointing." (1)

Bigelow also reported that the Company's inspectors were corrupted: "Between the contractors, the inspectors and the Cie, the Cie gets only 10% of the work it pays for."(1)

Bigelow had not been very much impressed by the achievements of the Company and would not bet on Panama. We shall see how a year later, having been charmed by B-V, Bigelow would become a fervent supporter of Panama.

B-V wrote in his memoirs: "It is there that began my long friendship with John Bigelow."(7) Bigelow will play a capital role in the future success of the canal. "He never ceased to take an enthusiastic interest in the Panama Canal."

As a matter of fact, in his account, B-V reduced a period of two years to one sentence. In 1886, Bigelow and B-V had met for the first time. However, Bigelow could not even remember his name, as he wrote in his diary: "Before leaving Panama, Mr. Varila - sic - gave me answers."(1) As we shall see later on, their friendship really started a year later, in June 1887.

On March 3, 1886, the French delegates returned home on the *Washington*. Following their visit to the works, Anguizola concluded: "What appeared as a frivolous feast in Panama City, proved to be later on a highly successful marketing rally."(18) In fact, these visits intended to revive temporarily the already moribund Company. So many negative reports circulated that the task proved difficult, if not impossible.

In the meantime, Rousseau had been working on his report, due to be published in April. He certainly was weighing every word of it.

At this time, yet another dramatic event happened. We have seen so many misfortunes that it is hard to imagine what else could now happen in Panama. Really, the poor Company had been through just about everything.

"During this period of visits, that is from the 30th of January to the 3rd of March, Boyer was nominally the only "Directeur", but I continued virtually to exercise the chief authority," wrote B-V. (7)

At the end of March 1886, B-V told us that, just when the new General Manager, Boyer, was "taking the rudder with a firm hand. As soon as the enormous responsibility, which I had long carried with ease, had disappeared, an instantaneous reaction took place within me." (7)

B-V paid for all his efforts and was struck by yellow fever. On April 6, he fell very sick and believed he was about to die. He told us the story of his illness in his memoirs: "Towards the end of March 1886, I was suddenly awakened by a violent vibration of my bed, which I thought due to a seismic movement. I soon discovered that I was really the origin and center of the movement. Yellow fever had just taken hold of my weakened frame . . . The doctor's attention was attracted to this increasing debility. He made me take a quantity of brandy, a wonderful remedy when you are, as I was, an habitual abstainer. The doomed man came back to life for good. . . At last, I could be transported on board a steamer bound for New York." (7)

B-V had spent eighteen months in Panama without taking his annual leave; he was extremely devoted to "his" canal.

He left Colon for New York on a steamer of the *Pacific Mail*, the mother Company of the *Panama RailRoad Company*. He had not felt strong enough to wait for the regular liner heading for France through the much shorter route of the French Antilles. After stopping for a few days in New York, he boarded the *Labrador* on April 17, an old and slow steamer that arrived in Le Havre on May 1st. These 13 days of travel to France must have been quite an ordeal for such a sick man, so pale that one of his friends, Mr. Patenotre, "did not recognize B-V, whose visits to the Hall of Minos*, Eaque* and Radamanthe* had left marks on his face that made it unrecognizable." (11).

When he finally reached Paris, he learned in the newspapers the death of his new boss, Leon Boyer, who had only lasted two months before the Panamanian fevers overcame him. "In the midst of his agony, he wrote: Do not abandon Panama."(7) His assistant, Nouailhac-Pioch, took over. He was the seventh General Manager. A day before Boyer died, another important staff member of a contractor died: Lillaz - an alumnus of École Centrale -; he was an associate of the firm *Baratoux, Letellier, Lillaz,* the only one in the firm who had volunteered to work in Panama.

* The three judges of Hell, according to Greek Mythology.

Before dying, Boyer had sent to the Company's Board a report that was to remain confidential:

- First, it will be impossible to complete the work within the announced budget of 600 million francs, at least another 1,200 will be necessary. Three times more!

- Second, it will be impossible to finish the work in 1889. At least 9 more years are necessary to finish digging the Culebra Hill, which would take until 1895.

- Third and last, the dam on the Rio Chagres is impossible to build. There are no examples of a dam so high (15 meters - 50 feet) in the whole world. (2) A technical impossibility! Such report was a bomb. What a disaster it would be, if such report had been released.

While B-V returned back to France, the conclusions of Rousseau's report had unfortunately leaked to the press, before being formally presented to the Chamber of Deputies on June 26, 1886. The report confirmed what all the experts had already stated in private, including Boyer:

- In the United States, the French project is highly criticized; Americans still do not believe that the Panama Canal is feasible and continue to work on the Menocal project in Nicaragua;

- the Panama project is not going well, "but is beyond a return point," it cannot be abandoned;

- the announced budget is way too short; "the achievement of the canal within the current resources in manpower and in the given time frame, appears more than problematic"; there is the need of 4 times more workers;

- in a few words, Rousseau confirmed Boyer's findings: the canal would cost 1,800 million francs and not the 600 publicized by the Company,

- but Rousseau added: "There are changes and simplifications that could be brought to the project to facilitate its completion."(2)

In this last remark, Rousseau was hinting at, but did not clearly state, that the project could still be saved with the construction of a canal with locks instead of the sea-level canal decreed by Lesseps. It is most probable that Rousseau had been discussing it with B-V, as it was his original idea. But, after reading the report, B-V believed that Rousseau did not make his point strongly enough: "Mr. Rousseau limited himself to a timid indication, instead of to a vigorous impulse towards truth which was needed and which would have sufficed to ensure success. . . If in that year - 1886 - instead of 1887, my solution of a canal with provisional locks had been adopted, everything would have been saved." (11)

At the news of the leak of the Rousseau's report, Ferdinand de Lesseps was furious. He was obstinate to never change his mind about constructing a sea-level canal; he decided that Boyer's report should remain secret.

Thanks to his lies, or rather to his omissions, Ferdinand de Lesseps remained popular within the Parisian financial world; investors backed the August 1886 subscription, bringing an additional 200 million francs - a record amount - to the coffers of the Company. Just enough to keep the works alive for another year.

Having returned home, well attended by his mother and his grandmother, B-V recovered so quickly that he was perfectly well by the end of June and was ready to go back to Panama. While in convalescence, he tried to convince the Lessepses and the administrators of the Company to adopt his clever plan of a canal with provisional locks. Boyer and Rousseau had hinted in that direction with no avail, but B-V thought that the works' salvation needed such a change.

Meanwhile, in Panama, the rainy season was especially fierce and damaged the first cuts made in the Culebra. Rue Caumartin, at the headquarters of the Company, these delays were really taken seriously by members of the board. Pondering the conclusions of Boyer's and Rousseau's reports, they realized that "in the last four years, the average altitude of the Culebra Hill has only been lowered by 3.5 meters, yet more than 100 meters were necessary."

B-V commented the fact in his memoirs: "With the progress made in the last four years, . . . the canal with locks was as unfeasible as the sea-level canal." And B-V added: "It was absolutely vital to forge a new solution to master the Culebra." (7)

He had found the key to the landslides by his clever technical solution - blasting and dredging. He still kept his hope in the project.

In July 1886, another misfortune occurred. The "Anglo-Dutch" denounced their contract with the Company. They declared that they could not meet the contractual price. During the rainy season, landslides had destroyed part of their previous work in the Culebra sector.

The Company's administrators were discouraged. They had no way of replacing soon such an important contractor.

B-V, who had left the works in April, was totally aware of the problem with the Anglo-Dutch, *Cutbill, de Lungo, Watson & Van Hattum*, as he had to control that company, when he was General Manager.

Let us recall the events: in 1882, the first contractor was *Couvreux & Hersent:* they renounced after two years. Now, four years later, another major contractor had left the project, overwhelmed by the Culebra Hill's difficulties.

How would the work be continued now?

8
ARTIGUE, SONDEREGGER & COMPANY

B-V took advantage of these adverse and unfavorable events. As seen before, he had shown to be quite an opportunist and for the time being, he believed strongly in the success of "his" canal. His future actions would demonstrate his tremendous resolve in reaching his goal.

During the summer of 1886, he was, according to his own words, "opportunely convalescing" (7) in his Parisian home. As soon as he felt better, he rushed to visit the offices of the Company, Rue Caumartin. There he met with Charles de Lesseps, whom he tried to convince to send him back to help Nouailhac-Pioch, the new General Manager. However, B-V wanted to change the rules and to supervise the works on a new formula, *a cost basis**, which meant executing the work with a different contract: workers' hours and material used would be charged to the Company on the basis of a pre-agreed price list.

At first, Charles was reluctant, as this formula would require "a supervision and control much more animated - sic." (7) The Board of Directors of the Company was against B-V's idea, not wanting to make an exception for anyone. In France, this type of contract was not at all popular.

As Charles kept looking unsuccessfully for a replacement to the "Anglo-Dutch" contractor, B-V persisted with his idea and they finally found a middle ground. Charles would only accept B-V's suggestion if B-V himself was to head his own firm: "Why should you not put yourself at the head of a

---

* In this formula, the cost was assessed for each elementary task in a schedule described in the contract with the Company.

contracting company, the elements of which you would select according to your judgment? . . . It is the greatest service you can render to the Panama undertaking."(7)

B-V told in his memoirs that he mulled this proposal for some time: "This proposition upset all the conceptions I had formed as regards to my future . . . I was thus led to sacrifice all my personal ambitions to rescue the Panama enterprise from the danger to which it was exposed, and which, if not parried, meant an ignoble death to, and a perpetual condemnation of, the French conception of the Panama Canal." (7) After long discussions with his brother Maurice, they finally decided to go ahead and form their own company.

From that moment, the canal had become B-V's only purpose in life.

This was B-V's side of the story and we do have reasons to doubt his version. Maurice, his brother, had certainly played an important part in B-V's decision. He was an astute investor: "My brother Maurice, member of the Culebra Enterprise, had received some earnings and proposed to assign them to me, as the legitimate reward for renouncing to my career as a State Engineer." (7)

Maurice had earned money in the Culebra sector, when the "Anglo-Dutch" had given up. How was it possible? He knew a lot of people in the Parisian Stock Market, who helped him to be introduced in the "commissions" system of the Company. As explained in Vallé's report (2), Maurice was really one of the *"arrangeurs"*. He received a commission for every cubic meter extracted, whether the contractor made a profit or not. That way, he did not take any risk.

Another possibility could explain the profit made by Maurice: investing in the American Stock Market. Among the 6 large contractors, was a San Francisco based firm, the *American Contacting & Dredging Company,* owned by the Slaven brothers. They had brought gigantic dredges - 300 horsepower, 40 meters long, 20 meters wide - built in Philadelphia. They had signed with the Company a $ 25 million contract to dredge the easier part, in the marshes between Aspinwall - Colon - and Bohio Soldado, a length of 23.465 kilometers (about 15 miles). Since they started the job, their shares had rocketed from $ 30 to $ 400. B-V was a specialist in dredging and it could well be possible that he had tipped his brother off.

Maurice's earnings were probably modest, of the order of several hundred thousand francs. But this relatively small sum allowed the brothers to use it as a leverage towards the future of a new company.

In order to go back to Panama as the head of his brother's new company, B-V had first to resign from his assignment with the *Ponts & Chaussées,* the French Corps of Engineers.

He thought that his resignation would suffice to make him free to leave for Panama after September 1st. But he was caught by Polytechnique's requirement; he had to pay for his tuition.

Fortunately, Severiano de Heredia, the Transport Minister who had exempted him in 1884, before he left for Panama, was still around and testified that he had previously agreed to such a career plan. This meant that B-V had simply to pay a large sum of money, which his brother Maurice lent to him. This system still exists today, the price of this liberty being in 2010: 45,000 €.

B-V was now free to return to Panama. He was convinced that science would solve the Culebra's problems, so that he would find a way to "make Panama. . . From the 1st of September, 1886, he ceased to belong to the staff of the Company in order to take up the direction of the Culebra works."(7)

It was the starting point of the brothers' speculation. Together, they would accumulate an enormous fortune. Maurice had taken advantage of his brother's vanity in order to invest his savings. At only thirty, he was already a seasoned businessman.

To materialize their company, the Bunau-Varilla brothers purchased a majority of the shares of *Artigue & Sonderegger*, which became *Artigue, Sonderegger and Company* - which we will abbreviate as **ASC** -, and acquired its full control.

As we have already seen, *Artigue & Sonderegger* was a small contractor working on the canal. They had signed a contract in May 20, 1883 (2) to excavate 1.4 million cubic meters, between the kilometers 23.465 and 26.350 in Bohio Soldado set in the marshes, near the City of Colon, where kilometer zero was. They had done an excellent job, as B-V was well aware of.

Before being purchased by the brothers, *Artigue & Sonderegger* was quite a small enterprise, happily digging the easiest part of the canal. But soon, the brothers' ambition would turn it into *Artigue, Sonderegger and Company* - ASC - one of the largest contractors working for the Company. According to B-V's account: "The contracting company which I formed to meet the views of Mr. Charles de Lesseps, was to be composed of the elements which would place the success of its difficult task above all commercial considerations. My brother, Maurice Bunau-Varilla, assumed the financial management of it, while two first class canal engineers, MM. Artigue and Sonderegger undertook the technical side on the Isthmus. Both of the latter were sterling products of the severe selection to which Nature subjected men in Panama. Both had shown, first as engineers of the Canal Company, and later on as contractors, the most brilliant moral and technical qualities." (7)

To remunerate the owners of *Artigue, Sonderegger and Co.* (ASC), Maurice negotiated with Charles de Lesseps the extravagant sum of 50,000 francs a month (From Mouthon's book and also from Vallé's report (2)).

At the end of the project in 1889, this remuneration would total 1.75 million francs, or 437,500 francs per person - they were four, counting B-V - for two and a half year, which amounted to 175,000 a year for each of them, when poor Dingler was making only 100,000.

Maurice was the man behind this scheme. B-V had simply followed his brother's advice. Despite his brother's turpitudes, B-V admired him for his success in the Parisian financial circles. "What has brought our success was the unity of our feelings, our mutual and generous affection, combined with the profound duality of our characters and the way we look at things." (Written by B-V in a letter to his brother Maurice, on June 5, 1905)

On July 24, the new partners of *Artigue, Sonderegger and Company* - ASC - were officially registered. The headquarters of the company were set: 30 Rue de Gramont, in the financial center of Paris.

ASC, with Maurice as its new partner, received its authorization to work in Panama on September 14.

Without waiting for this formality, ASC signed its first contact with the Company on July 31, only four days after it had been registered.

We read in such contract that the partners of ASC were: (2)

- Maurice. His name appeared first, as he was the majority partner, taking into account the share owned virtually by B-V. We shall see later that Maurice owned 68% of ASC. He claimed to live: 146 Rue du Faubourg Saint Honoré. Curiously, Maurice changed his residence on every contract he signed between ASC and the Company. (See Appendix 5, which lists all the Parisian *immeubles* owned by Maurice).

- Conrad Sonderegger, with 16% of the shares. Sonderegger was a German-Swiss engineer from San Anton, who he had emigrated to Colombia and set up a civil work company.

- Auguste Artigue, with 16% of the shares. Artigue had joined Sonderegger to work on the French Canal.

B-V could not be one of the partners, as he was still under contract with the Company and could not be employed by a private company until September 1st. He would become ASC's General Manager in Panama.

Maurice logically took all the risks, as he had mostly invested his own money. But the brothers had certainly entered into a verbal agreement to share the prospective profits, as their future investments in the newspaper *Le Matin* would show.

This whole matter had been arranged quite rapidly during the summer of 1886. B-V had now become General Manager of ASC in Panama. We have to realize that it was a much different position than the one he held with the Company, where he had full control of the Panama works.

As we shall see, ASC had only a share of about 25% of the total works, but it was an essential part, the Culebra Hill, of ill repute. Being ASC's General Manager, B-V certainly helped Maurice negotiate the July 31st contract with the Company.

This contract was judged "uniquely advantageous" by:
- the General Secretary of the Company, Étienne Martin, who resigned as a sign of protest,(18)
- the Vallé Report, - October 10, 1892 - indicated that "the price of the cubic meter was increased in a series of wittingly orchestrated contracts,"(2)
- "a pitiable employee of the Company"(7), who will later testify during the trial of the Company on January 13, 1893,
- and last, Mouthon, who wrote that : "the price of the cubic meter was increased in a series of cleverly combined contracts, which allowed this company - Mouthon did not name ASC - to collect remarkable advantages." (*Les Grandes Campagnes du Matin,* Pauwels, Paris, 1910).

It seems that the entire staff of the Company was fully aware of the exceptional advantages obtained by the Bunau-Varilla brothers.

B-V protested in his memoirs: "It was said that I had used my position, as head of the Company in the Isthmus, to sign a scandalous contract with myself."(7)

In any case, this contract' terms were not so easy to meet, as B-V himself explained: "On certain parts of the canal, the cost of excavating a cubic meter, paid 6.95 francs by the Company, would reach as high as 150 francs. But it was this type of sacrifice which ensured the ample reward for taking such risks or dispensing such efforts."(7)

Maurice was utterly convinced of his brother's engineering expertise and believed that B-V's solution, which we recall was: "first blast the rock by dynamite and then dredge", would lower the cost of excavating a cubic meter well below the price paid by the Company and thus generate a hefty profit for ASC.

Actually, ASC, in its July 28, 1886, contract, had been granted an increase from 6.85 to 7.80 francs per cubic meter. But, of this increase of 0.95 francs, 0.85 francs were to be paid to the Anglo-Dutch Company as the indemnity negotiated with the Company; a lawsuit by Colombian law would have been too cumbersome. "The ridiculous Colombian law did not make possible for a contractor to be ejected from any of their works without an interminable lawsuit."(7)

Maurice succeeded in raising this indemnity from 6.85 + 0.85 = 7.70 francs to 7.80 francs. In his memoirs, B-V justified that "the increase was only 10 cents of a franc."(7)

However, the Roubaix Archives (2) show a totally different story: the July 28, 1886, contract mentioned a compensation of 0.40 francs only. In reality, ASC had obtained an increase of 0.55 francs per cubic meter.

Also of great interest are the documents of the "Roubaix Archives" (2), which explained that additionally to the indemnity transiting through ASC, the "Anglo-Dutch" company had also received cash advances. This was current practice. In order to compensate for the contractors' negative cash flow, the Company granted them cash advances.

Before being replaced by ASC, - during the summer of 1886 - the "Anglo-Dutch" had received advances for:

–	setting the discharge tracks	4.3 million francs
–	wells and galleries	3.0
–	reorganizing the works	0.7
		-----
	for a grand total of	8.0 million francs.

This explains the compensation of 0.40 francs per cubic meter: the expected cubage in the Culebra being 20 million cubic meters times 0.40 francs equals 8 millions.

It seems that the Company had been extremely generous with its contractors. The "Anglo-Dutch" left the works, having pocketed 8 million francs, which the Company would never recover, as ASC would never be able to excavate 20 but only 3 (!) million cubic meters.

This is yet another example of mismanagement by the Company.

Maurice, who "was to keep in contact with the Company in Paris, as well as to supply the materials, machinery, explosives, coal, etc., required by ASC",(7) looked efficiently after the interests of ASC and obtained another contract for an additional 8 million cubic meters. This new contract was not part of the original "Anglo-Dutch" contract and was probably added by Maurice on B-V's advice. It brought the total cubage contracted by ASC to 28 million cubic meters.

A further negotiation by Maurice, gave also to ASC the PRR's relocation at kilometer 57 - close to the village of Paraiso. The PRR's route had to be relocated in many places, wherever it crossed the future canal route.

These additions mean that the Bunau-Varilla brothers were wise to hedge their profits by adding some easy parts to the difficult Culebra Hill.

In July 1886, Jacquier replaced the interim manager Nouailhac-Pioch and became the eighth General Manager of the Company in Panama.

During the summer of 1886, Maurice married Sophie de Brunhoff, the sister of one of his college friends. This event has not been confirmed by the Paris Archives, but derives from the fact that their first son, René, was born on July 25, 1887. This date is on the inscriptions engraved on Maurice's burial vault in the Passy cemetery, where his son rests. René unfortunately died when he was only twenty years old - on October 1st, 1907.

We thought interesting to relate a few facts from the life of the Bunau-Varilla family, even though in his memoirs, B-V did not share any information about his family; his book specifically covered the Panama enterprise.

"During the first days of September 1886, I was back in the Isthmus with MM. Artigue and Sonderegger,"(5) wrote B-V. He was no longer an employee of the Company and returned to Panama to manage the works in the Culebra, as General Manager of *Artigue, Sonderegger and Company* (ASC), his brother's company.

This was the starting point of the enormous wealth that the Bunau-Varilla brothers would accumulate in just two and a half years. (see Appendix 5)

Without being fully aware of it, the brothers had become two of the speculators, that Barrès called "the hyenas", who ransacked Lesseps and his ill-fated Company.

Why was ASC so profitable? Having seen how the brothers negotiated the unitary price to their advantage, we have to investigate the possibility of falsifying the cubage itself.

According to the terms of the ASC contract found in Roubaix (2): the Company paid 6.95 francs per each cubic meter excavated out by ASC. But here, we ought to ask ourselves: how many times has a cubic meter been extracted? How were the masses of mud flowing down the slope of the Culebra taken into account? Did the Company hire enough controllers to check the cubage excavated? Were these controllers susceptible of being bribed?

Here is what B-V wrote honestly on this matter: "Why, as soon as the rainy season set in, did we see these regularly disposed masses suddenly collapse from the Culebra Hill and slide away with rails, ties and cars? Only one reason could account for this: the water and the special nature of the soil. . . After a little while, the whole mass tended to lose its coherence and suddenly slid away, transformed into a mud lake."(7)

And again: "There is not a trace of a new favor made to the new Culebra company", wrote B-V. (7)

These questions are appropriate, because the management of the Company was not very diligent and the controls often negligent.

We tend to believe B-V and the conclusions of the Vallé report confirmed his opinion: "As for the cubage measures, the definite figures had been established from the initial and final topography of the land and confirmed by the wagons used to evacuate the rubble. Of course, due to the swelling of the soil, there were disputes between the contractors and the company. For example, with ASC, the difference in the Culebra was 128,000 cubic meters. It was decided jointly to split the difference. This way of solving such a difference did not represent more than 6% of the total cubage." (2)

We could not find here any reprehensible action from ASC; we shall see later on that forging the cubage has not been the major element that caused the brothers to accumulate such an enormous fortune in so little time.

While ASC started digging actively in Panama, the Lesseps Company, at the end of 1886, had collected 300 million francs in shares and 745 million francs in bonds, for a total of more than a billion francs.

Siegfried wrote: "The Company spends money hand over fist." (13)

Bouvier was even more severe: "The Parisian press has been copiously bribed. The commissions of the banks reached the exorbitant amount of 5.67% instead of the usual 2%. All the French Government Ministers required some ransoms." (14)

The Company had begun its activities in 1881 by wasting many millions in the PRR's purchase, then by organizing parties and banquets. Now it wanted to conceal its calamitous results. So, it lied to the shareholders in the *Bulletin of the Interoceanic Canal* and it also distributed generous bribes to the press, to hide the annoying truth.

Some comments from the press, after the General Assembly of the shareholders held on July 29, 1886, are eloquent:

- *Le Figaro:* "Not a single discordant voice. Not a single hand raised against the voted resolutions. A long patriotic acclaim! "

- *L'Événement:* "Our conviction has been strengthened."

- *Le Gaulois:* "The meeting had been adjourned at four and a half, in a euphoria of exuberant joy." (14)

And to make sure that the next bond subscription would be successfully covered by the French investors, the Company paid higher and higher commissions to the banks.

For the subscription of August 2, 1886, the Company spent 3 million francs in publicity.

Corruption advanced through all the levels within the Company.

It was present at the lowest level, such as in the work of the Company's supervisors: "The same tasks were regularly paid twice or three times; the same happened with the materials delivered. The delivery took place and by a bribe to the receiving agent of the Company, the material was taken back and presented again and again."(4)

It was also present at the highest level in the Company. The minutes of the trial against Baïhaut, the transportation Minister who had received a bribe to promote a law in favor of the Company - this trial was held in March 1893 - showed an excellent example of such a sad fact:

« - Charles de Lesseps: "The Transportation Minister, Mr. Baïhaut, asked us for a million francs."

- The General Examining Magistrate: "If this money was being extorted, you should have called the police."

- Charles: "But, here, it was the policeman himself asking for a ransom!" » (14)

This corruption was rampant within all the levels of the Company; it would soon spread to the whole nation, through its representatives in the National Assembly.

We shall see how this corruption became a main factor in the Company's fall.

9

THE PANAMA PROJECT TURNED DISMAL WHILE
THE BUNAU-VARILLA BROTHERS MADE A FORTUNE

As **1887** began, the Company started its seventh year in Panama.

The newly founded construction company of Maurice Bunau-Varilla: *Artigue, Sonderegger and Company* (ASC), had been working for four months. Under the leadership of B-V, it was attempting to tackle the Culebra Hill problem. After having worked two years with the Company, B-V had now his own business and worked as hard as ever. For example, to save in commuting time from Panama City, he settled in a villa close to Culebra Hill.

The Roubaix Archives (2) contain some amendments dated January 12, 1887, to the contract that ASC had signed six months ago with the Company. These documents called for a special indemnity to be paid to ASC in case the Company "suspends the first contract" - these are the exact terms used in the amendment. In fact, rumors had started circulating in the Parisian circles about a possible bankruptcy of the Company and Maurice, always vigilant, had wisely renegotiated the first contract. It is possible that he thought that profits were not coming quickly enough and, in so doing, he was taking an insurance against the Company's bankruptcy, which would annihilate ASC' venture.

All this indicates that the morale of the Lessepses - father and son - and of the members of the Company's Board, was at an all time low. In fact, the Company was about to go under, but just did not realize it yet.

Its agony would last for the next two years.

In March 1887, Charles de Lesseps went once more to Panama - he had traveled there almost every year. This time, the experts he had brought with him recommended unanimously a canal with locks. It was simply the follow-up of Rousseau's report, although a little late. This is another example of the Company's mismanagement; it took almost a year for the Company to accept and adopt Rousseau's conclusions.

It also shows that Ferdinand de Lesseps had finally given up his fight for a sea-level canal. At 82 years old, he had passed all his responsibilities to his son Charles.

About this visit, we have a letter from Sonderegger to Maurice: "The visitors' purpose is not to help in the works, but to collect a rationale of arguments towards future events."(2) Sonderegger really felt that the end of the Company was near.

The Company's Board was now convinced that in order to break the (in)famous Culebra Hill, the only solution was to create an artificial lake, at an altitude of about 30 meters. Ships would be lifted up from sea level to this artificial lake by passing through a series of locks. This scheme* would significantly reduce the cubage to be excavated, as the canal would cross the Culebra Hill at 30 meters above what would be required for a sea-level canal. This new scheme was the only way of completing the canal on time.

This "canal with locks" scheme had been all along the brilliant idea of B-V and it also "offered an honorable alternative to Ferdinand de Lesseps; the old ultimate goal remaining a canal without locks; there need be no promises broken, no semblance of retreat or failure."(13)

B-V lamented that it took so long to convince the Company's Board. However, he was partly to blame for it, as he had left the Company to run his own business with ASC, which drastically modified his priorities. His boss was not any more Charles de Lesseps, but was Maurice, his brother.

Charles absolutely wanted the new scheme to succeed. He knew that the project was ailing and wanted to do everything possible to rescue it. Although he was convinced that the locks would save the project, he knew that this new scheme had to be presented carefully to the investors. It would be disastrous to needlessly worry them, as more bond emissions would still be needed. Once again, it was essential to adopt the right marketing approach. Charles had to find an ingenious way to promote the canal with locks.

In May 1887, as usual, the rainy season started in Panama. It reduced the activity on the canal works and B-V took advantage of it to take a ship back to France. He had now selected the adequate dredging equipment that he would need on Culebra Hill to elaborate his "dynamite and dredge" method. But he still had to find a supplier for those dredges.

---

* This was the same final scheme the Americans adopted to complete the Canal in 1914.

B-V traveled throughout Europe: France, Germany, Belgium and finally, having found what he needed in Holland, he returned to Paris where the Company passed the order for the dredges.

While in Paris, he became aware that the Company had just issued a new allocation for a tract in Paraiso, between the kilometers 55.456 and 57. He and his brother Maurice, swiftly succeeded in winning it for ASC.

It was easy for B-V to determine which portion of the work would make the best profit for ASC. He just had to use his past experience as the Company's General Manager. Meanwhile, Maurice took care of the new contract's negotiation to ASC's advantage.

B-V explained in his memoirs that, during his stay in Paris, he "unofficially" presented to Charles de Lesseps his project of a canal with locks. He also asked Eiffel to design a special type of door for the locks, upon his recommendations, but he was most disappointed when Eiffel later took a patent in his own name for such lock.

Still in Paris, during the spring of 1887, B-V unexpectedly met the man who will remain his best friend for life and one of his most precious allies in defending the Panama Canal. It was their second meeting, but this time, it would forever generate reciprocal warm feelings.

On Saturday June 4, at a dinner given by Charles de Lesseps, B-V was seated near John Bigelow, whom he had briefly met in Panama in February 1886. Bigelow was staying in Paris for a few months, accompanied by his daughter Grace, his eldest son Poultney and Poultney's wife, Edith. He was renting a house at 61 Avenue Marceau, for which he paid a rent of 450 francs per month, plus 30 francs per month for the janitor and the same for the maid.(1)

Charles had certainly arranged this second encounter of B-V with Bigelow, as he knew both of them well. It was nevertheless the product of an extraordinary series of events. Both men had not met since their brief encounter in Panama, at the beginning of 1886. This first meeting had not left any strong memories to any of them, mostly because their interests in Panama were antagonistic. While B-V was working hard on the canal works, Bigelow was presenting to the *Engineer's Club of Philadelphia* a negative report on the ability of the Company to achieve the Panama Canal. At the time, Bigelow was probably, like most Americans, advocating an American-owned canal in Nicaragua.

During this dinner with Charles de Lesseps, B-V listened carefully to Bigelow's arguments and attempted to rally Bigelow to his point of view. Using his extraordinary gift of persuasion, B-V certainly aroused Bigelow's curiosity. In the United States, Bigelow had heard many men of high esteem argue about the advantages of Nicaragua and, here in Paris, he was meeting with a young engineer, young enough to be his son, who was convinced that the

French Company would finish the construction of the Panama Canal. To find out more about all this, Bigelow invited B-V to dine at his home on Monday June 6. This dinner would mark the beginning of their lifetime friendship, as Bigelow explained in his diary. (1)

B-V was not yet a rich man and was probably embarrassed that he could not properly entertain Bigelow. He would remember this encounter and, later, having become a wealthy man, he would entertain Bigelow lavishly during his many future stays in Paris. Bigelow reciprocated with kind invitations for B-V to visit him, in his Highland Falls' manor on the Hudson River, about twenty miles north of New York City.

Following this May 1887 meeting, B-V would spend many summers with his family at Highland Falls.

During the summer of 1887, B-V returned to Panama. ASC had now signed a number of contracts with the Company to excavate the Culebra Hill area and other points along the canal route; this made ASC the second biggest contractor on the canal works. Its share had climbed to 25% of the total.

Since the disappearance of the "Anglo-Dutch", the number of large contractors working in Panama had been reduced from 6 to 4 - Vignaud had renounced, because he was losing money.

For their work, four contractors were receiving payments from the company, as shown below for the 1886-1889 period:

	Sums paid in million francs
– ASC,	50.9
– Baratoux-Letellier-Lillaz,	37.6
– American Contracting & Dredging	16.5
– Société des Travaux Publics	76.2

A few months later, a large contract was signed between the Company and Gustave Eiffel's construction firm: *Eiffel & Cie:* 73.7 million francs. This downgraded ASC to third place.

Meanwhile, the financial situation of the Company deteriorated further. It was now desperate, close to bankruptcy. On July 26, 1887, a very large subscription of 220 million francs was launched: 500,000 bonds worth 1,000 francs each, discounted at 440 francs. It was an excellent deal for the subscribers. Yet, only 260,000 bonds were sold, half of what the Company had hoped for. The Stock Market had shown its reluctance to finance the Panama Canal project. This rejection of the July 1887 subscription marked the "beginning of the end" for the Company. One explanation for the investors' lack of enthusiasm can be found in the economic situation of the period. "The Company asked for a lot of money on a continuous basis at a time (1882-1888) of serious economic depression and decline in the Stock Market."(14)

The failure of the Company's subscription of July 1887 did not have a negative effect on the public, because very few investors were aware of the seriousness of its situation. The bribes paid by the Company to the press were quite effective.

"The newspaper articles on Panama were written with elements supplied by the Company itself. Marius Fontane, its General Secretary, issued documents and information, while Charles de Lesseps was dealing with the press conferences. The end result was that the press was propagating false news."(14)

The *Bulletin of the Interoceanic Canal*, still issued quarterly, supported this clandestine propaganda. However, one could not ignore the staff's movements between Paris and Panama, the letters exchanged, the long conversations on the unsinkable *Lafayette;* so, truth slowly made its way into the well-informed circles of the French capital.

Not surprisingly, the same problems were still plaguing the Company's works in the Isthmus:

- death from fevers. In most of the books quoted in Appendix 4, one can read is a commonly admitted figure of 20,000 casualties. We think that this is way too high as it would correspond to an annual death rate of almost 20%. The Vallé report (2) mentions an annual death rate of 7.2% in 1884 and 1885*, which, if maintained on the entire duration of the project, would give a total of 7,500 deaths. In any case, this was too high a price in human lives.

- landslides in the Culebra area still could not be controlled; despite all his excellent suggestions, B-V could not do much better than his predecessors.

- lack of manpower made progress too slow; the Company had sent missions to recruit workers as far as Africa - Liberia -, Asia - Indochina -, without any notable result.

- lastly, there had been no development of the dam on the Rio Chagres, because its insuperable difficulties discouraged most engineers; a technical solution did not exist.

All these problems reinforced the need for a "canal with locks", to reduce the volume to excavate and speed up the progress of the project. Ferdinand de Lesseps was still attached to the idea of a sea-level canal, as in Suez, but pressed to give a new impetus to his enterprise, he finally agreed with his son Charles on a canal with nine locks, each being 180 meters long and 18 meters wide. (14)

---

* And the Vallé report adds: "this death rate is similar to the 7% found in our marine troops for all our colonies."(2)

By the fall of 1887, it had become an urgent matter to publicly advertise the new scheme. Charles, now the project leader, developed a clever strategic plan, based on the reputation of the future builder of the highest tower in the world, Gustave Eiffel. As if his father's fame did not suffice, Charles chose to collaborate with the prestigious builder.

Eiffel had acquired a huge international celebrity with his light and attractive metallic viaducts - Garabit and Porto, among others. Their arches were over 500 feet long. His most important project was yet to be erected. He had just won the architectural contest to build a 1,000 feet high tower to celebrate the Centennial of the French Revolution. It was already under construction, right in the center of Paris. Parisians could see its progress into the sky and soon it would be visible from 50 kilometers (30 miles) away. Eiffel's fame would soon become celebrated worldwide.

The new canal scheme with locks obviously required a locks specialist. Who else could it be but already famous Gustave Eiffel?

Charles de Lesseps intended to use Eiffel's fame to boost the investors' confidence before the Company called for more funds.

In October 1887, a huge publicity campaign promised the shareholders that Panama would be achieved within four years, thanks to the great engineer Gustave Eiffel. All seemed to be going well again. The Panama enterprise would be salvaged. French engineers could continue to receive praise for their genius around the world. Eiffel was the best of them and he would certainly finish the construction of the Panama Canal.

It had taken more than a year for the Company to recognize the need of a lock canal. Would it save the project?

November 15, 1887, was a special day for the Company. It was considered by some like a real rebirth of the project, but for many others, it was the last sign of life before its final agony and leading to its death.

On that day, Ferdinand de Lesseps sent two letters:

- the first one to ask the French Finance Minister for an authorization to emit a bond subscription with a lottery, the only way recommended by most bankers to collect the large sums of money needed to achieve the works. It was one of the favored financial products at the time; it had been used efficiently to complete the works at Suez in 1868; the investors liked it, because of the lottery, which allotted prizes independently of the success of the venture;

- another letter to all investors and potential bond buyers to officially inform them that Eiffel, the world famous engineer, had been selected by the Company to build the locks.

With these two steps, the French investors recovered some of their lost optimism. The Panama Canal could be completed within the next four years.

B-V was delighted that the Company had finally adopted his "canal with locks" project: "What a magic transformation this meant. Instead of having to excavate 20 million cubic meters in the Culebra saddle, there remained less than 9 to be removed." (7)

This is a proof that B-V was not like his brother, interested just by money, as less cubic meters also meant less profit for ASC. . . except that Maurice found a way to boost ASC's profit in different activities, as we shall see later.

In Panama, ASC, under B-V, continued to work hard. And in Paris, at the end of 1887, Maurice, the majority shareholder of ASC, optimistically took over a "sub-contractor on the same model as ASC's." It was *Erzinger, Dephieux & Galtier,* (5) a firm run by an engineer alumnus from École Centrale, Lefèvre, who would work later with B-V in 1894, in some Spanish railway projects. This company, *Erzinger, Dephieux & Galtier,* had been contracted to "lighten the labors of the general contractor of the locks, Eiffel's company. The particular work at the excavation of the locks was extremely difficult." (7) The fact that ASC was now in charge of the excavation of the locks, could have been a favor from Eiffel to B-V, following their dispute about the patent for the locks' doors. ASC took over only a small part of the work contracted by Eiffel, who "pledged to pay ASC a royalty of 5% on the locks' metallic work and a part of 20% on the profit made on the masonry work." (2)

Eiffel nevertheless kept the steel doors of the locks and their frames, all in steel, which were his specialty.

The capture of *Erzinger, Dephieux & Galtier* by Maurice showed the amazing growth of *ASC,* only a year after it had started working in Panama. It had brought so much money to Maurice, that he was able to invest it into another company.

It should be noted that the locks had not been mentioned in the previous contracts of ASC - nor in any of the other contractors' contracts signed with the Company. Due to this change in scope, all the previous cubic meters figures have now been reduced and would need to be revised. It was a sufficient reason to rewrite all the contracts.

On this basis, ASC, represented in Paris by Maurice, its majority shareholder, amended to his advantage the three contracts it had with the Company:

- one contract dated December 21, 1887: relative to the work in the Culebra area, where: an advance sum of 700,000 francs was changed into a fixed allocation; a new allocation of 3 million francs was designated to reorganize the work sites; another advance of 4.3 million francs was allowed for constructing railways - to evacuate the excavated soil in small wagons.

- another contract dated January 9, 1888: relative to the section around Paraiso, where it was indicated that all advances made up to now - for wells or galleries -, were transformed into fixed allocations.

- and lastly, a contract dated January 12, 1888: relative to the section around Miraflores, from kilometer 57 to 62.2, estimated at 2 million cubic meters, where prices have been increased from 9.9 to 11 francs per cubic meter; an allocation of 1.06 million francs was paid for the reorganization of the work sites. This contract had been "abandoned" by *Baratoux, Letellier & Co* in the Miraflores sector. (2)

As explained in Vallé's report of July 1893: "The new ASC contracts' terms have allowed that company to concentrate its efforts on the construction of rail tracks and accessory work for which it received special allocations." (2)

Flory, the expert named by the Commission investigating the embezzlement of public funds in 1892, was very clear about it: "All the efforts of the contractors were principally geared to build railways, which were much more remunerated than their extraction work. It should be remarked that during the execution of the contracts signed with Artigue & Sonderegger, alone, that is before they modified their company - into ASC, in July 1886 - the Company was absolutely paying only for the work executed, without any special allocation or indemnity." (2)

This shows clearly that Maurice had negotiated directly with Charles de Lesseps. Maurice described with pride to Charles the marvelous work that his brother B-V was doing and negotiated a favorable contract, in which advances became fixed allocations.

This transformation of advances into fixed allocations is worth a word of explanation. It was in no way a favor done by the Company to a contractor, but resulted from its foolish hope that the project would be completed one day and that then, the advances would have been spent. But the contractors' hopes differed widely from those of the Company and thus, the contractors asked for the advances to become fixed allocations.

This embezzlement scheme went even one step further: from January 1888 until the end of the contract that ASC had with the Company - it would end in May 1889 -, a fee of 0.20 francs per cubic meter excavated would go directly to Maurice Bunau-Varilla, as "a compensation for the loss he suffered from abandoning his other businesses in favor of the management of ASC, which consumed all his time." (2)

This meant that if ASC excavated 1 million cubic meters - a close estimate of what the reality was - Maurice had received 200,000 francs, slightly more than his salary of 175,000 francs!

It was so astonishing that B-V, interrogated by the Commission in 1893, "did not deny the allocations allowed to ASC and did not refute Flory's figures." (2) Flory was the Commission's auditor.

In these new contracts, the last that ASC would sign with the Company, the lowest level of the canal had been changed from minus 9 meters to "plus 30 *or* (sic) plus 40 meters"! This showed that the volume to be excavated was still undefined and not guaranteed by the contractor.

To understand these figures, it should be mentioned that the zero level was the reference level of the oceans, while the minus 9 level represented the draught of the ships, which would have transited in a sea level canal.

At the end of 1888, the excavations in the Culebra Hill had lowered its summit from about 120 meters down to 70 meters. One can imagine the tremendous amount of excavation remaining to reach an altitude of 30 *or* 40 meters.

For some, all these changes were heralding the future bankruptcy of the Company. The "hyenas" - Maurice was one of them - had little time left to squeeze whatever cash the Company had left.

In all the newly written contracts, the excavation volumes had to be seriously reduced to become more realistic and to give more chances to the contractors to pocket the premiums.

In the case of ASC, it was determined that the volume excavated in the Culebra Hill would, from now on, have to be 110,000 cubic meters a month, against 600,000 in the previous contract. Quite a radical change!

Even this figure of 110,000 would prove to be too optimistic. During the whole of 1887, B-V only met this target during one single month.

"The changes made to the contracts have led to advantages, difficult to explain . . . ASC has received, when the canal with locks was decided, unjustified advantages in the form of indemnities which they pocketed with no reason," (2) wrote Lemarquis, the lawyer named by the French Government to represent the small shareholders, in his Public Prosecutor's charges of April 1894 – abstracts can be found in Appendix 1.

The Paris financial market took quite well the idea of a canal with locks. However, the Chamber of Deputies was not unanimous about a lottery subscription and the Finance Minister refused Ferdinand de Lesseps' request for a special authorization to launch such a lottery.

The Lessepses were near despair. Their 1888 subscription had to succeed, as the July 1887 subscription did not collect enough to pay the contractors for another year. The enormous sum of 600 million francs was now required!

It should be noted that between 1880 and 1886, the Company had collected an average of 125 million francs a year, amounting to about 10% of the total invested in the Parisian Bourse. This time the 600 million francs were equivalent to half of the yearly Bourse investments. It was an insane gamble!

Contrary to what B-V affirmed, (11) Mollier indicated that most of the bankers expressed their reservations, among them the notorious Henri Germain, founder of the Crédit Lyonnais. (19)

Charles de Lesseps did not listen. He strongly believed that a lottery subscription was the only salvation. For this, each share worth nominally 400 francs, but sold at the reduced price of 360 francs, would be numbered and a lottery drawn six times a year, to distribute premiums worth from 1,000 to 500,000 francs. (14)

Such a "lottery subscription" was the only solution deemed attractive enough to collect this enormous sum of 600 million francs, but this subscription had to be authorized by a vote of the Chamber of Deputies and they were reluctant to give the go ahead.

"The Company has already received negative answers from the governmental authorities, and particularly from Rouvier* in November 1887 and from Tirard* in January 1888. . . While it continued to maintain its pressure on public authorities, by organizing a widespread petition early in 1888, it launched a bond subscription on March 14, 1888 . . . It failed and collected very little." (14) It collected only 35 million francs, enough to keep the contractors working for a quarter.

During a debate in the Bourbon Palace - seat of the French Chamber of Deputies -, Léopold Goirand, a representative, "spoke as an honest citizen: Is it really the purpose of our Chamber? In all our laws, we notice this constant concern, which tries to banish all profit due to hazard, all fortune making through a lottery. We condemn these tendencies." (4)

Most deputies rallied to his opinion. The general climate did not favor this "lottery subscription".

Still willing to obtain a favorable vote from the Chamber of Deputies, Charles convinced his father, the 83 years old Ferdinand de Lesseps, to go back to the campaign trail, as he already did in 1880 and in 1886: "Communications to the Academy of Sciences, a series of conferences with photographic projections about the status of the work in Panama," etc. (14)

The Lessepses' efforts were vain. In their despair, they would make a final mistake. This is really a sad story.

---

* Maurice Rouvier was Prime Minister of France from May 30 to December 11, 1887; and Tirard followed until May 30, 1888.

The banker Jacques de Reinach, later convinced to be a swindler, recommended the Company to bribe the French deputies. He claimed that it was the only remaining solution. Carelessly, the Company wrote him a check for more than 3 million francs to that effect. Reinach distributed most of the amount to a number of the deputies, writing the name of the beneficiaries on a list; such list would be later the subject of a frantic quest.

Was it with the agreement of the Lessepses? They never admitted it.

History is not clear on this matter. But their despair was such that Ferdinand and Charles would have been ready to try almost anything.

This wide spread bribery marked the beginning of the Panama scandal.

104 French representatives received a total of 1.1 million francs. They were, among the 584 members of the Chamber of Deputies, those most drastically opposed to a lottery subscription. They would later all be prosecuted and, after a fake trial, acquitted in 1898. (14)

Finally, after six months of hard lobbying by the Lessepses, the French deputies*, "convinced" that it would save the Panama project, voted on June 9, 1888, a law allowing the Company to organize a lottery subscription.

Hope had returned that the canal would be completed within four years. But would it really happen?

---

* Probably thanks to a change in Prime Minister; Charles Floquet took office on April 2, 1888.

10

THE BANKRUPTCY OF THE FRENCH COMPANY

Having until now faced many unexpected difficulties, the French engineers continued to work courageously and efficiently in Panama. They now had reached a good momentum.

1887 showed encouraging progress: 12 million cubic meters had been extracted, as many as during all the 6 previous years together.

24 million cubic meters had now been excavated since the beginning of the project and there remained to be excavated: 75 – 24 = 51 million cubic meters. Roughly one third of the work had been done.

The Company publicized these good results, predicting that the canal would be completed within four years. This time, it seemed truly logical, as: $51/12 = 4.2$ years.

But such reasoning was highly misleading. The cubage figures for the past 7 years took into account the work completed on soft soils, the easiest to excavate. For example, in the first twenty kilometers of marshy land near the City of Colon, the trace of the future canal could already be seen. However, in the Culebra Hill area, the official documents showed that only 810,472 cubic meters had been extracted by the end of 1887. The initial estimate of earth to be taken out of the Culebra was 20 million cubic meters and it had already been reduced to 9 million cubic meters with the new "canal with locks" scheme. On that basis, only a mere 9% of the work had been achieved!

It was clearly catastrophic.

Could some optimists be found to believe that there was still time to catch up on the original schedule? B-V was one of them.

He forecasted the completion of the project for the end of 1891: "On the first of January 1888, everything was in condition to permit our looking forward to the opening of the canal before the 31st of December 1891." (5) He was miles away from imagining that the Company had already fallen past its recovery stage.

However, in **1888**, work continued as usual in Panama. In February, the foundations of the locks were prepared by ASC. They measured 180 by 18 meters, while the final locks - built by the USA for the canal put in service in 1914 - would be 300 by 33. Panama ended up getting a better canal from the Americans!

In a few years, the commercial ships had shown considerable progress, replacing their old sails by a coal and steam engine; their size had almost doubled, from 500 feet to 1,000. It had to be taken into account and Americans did.

Bribes had finally convinced the Chamber of Deputies to authorize the Company to launch a subscription with a so-called "lottery". Two million shares would be proposed to the Parisian investors, ending on June 26.

The Company was looking forward to the moment it had waited for so long. Its salvation depended on it. It came timely to replenish the Company's funds: on May 14, two banks, Crédit Lyonnais and Société Générale were solicited to loan 30 million francs to the Company, as it was short of cash.

On the first days of the subscription, everything went as predicted. As early as June 18, many investors invaded the banks' counters. On that basis, it was thought that the total amount of the subscription would probably exceed the target of 720 million francs - 600 for the bonds and 120 for the lottery prizes.

It now seemed certain that the Panama project would be saved.

Once again, fate was waiting to destroy this unfortunate project. Quite suddenly, an unexpected event happened.

On June 22, four days before the final closing of the subscription, telegrams were sent to most banks in the major cities of France, falsely announcing the death of Ferdinand de Lesseps. The effect of these telegrams on the subscription was sudden and catastrophic. Without checking the facts, the financial circles immediately advised their customers against subscribing. The investors stopped buying and withdrew their pledges to purchase the bonds.

Who sent these false telegrams? Who wanted to bury the *Grand Français* before his time? This has never been explained.

Most probably, the telegrams were sent by some Stock Market speculators, who never revealed themselves and were not caught.

B-V referred to this event in his memoirs as: "those terrible criminal maneuvers, which wounded mortally the Company." (7)

Some historians claimed that the effect of these telegrams was grossly exaggerated. They believed that, even without the telegrams, the quest of such a large sum of money on the Parisian Bourse would have been an impossible task. To support this view, let it be known that it had also been the advice of many bankers, among whom the Baron Jacques de Reinach and Henri Germain, the head of the Crédit Lyonnais, to split the huge sum into smaller lots. (14)

On June 26, the subscription was closed. Despite the flat denial of Lesseps's death, only a few 800,000 shares - out of the 2,000,000 - had been sold at 360 francs each - for a nominal value of 400 -, only one third of what had been planned. 254 millions had been collected. It should be noted that it was, however, the largest sum ever collected by the Company (see Appendix 2).

Of course, it was a huge disappointment and it marked the end of the hopes to save the Company. After "putting aside the guarantee of the premiums and the interest on the bonds" (2), - 120 million francs -, only 254 – 120 = 134 "useful" millions remained! It was an absolute disaster.

However, the Lessepses did not give up and with a last burst of energy, they left again on a tour of conferences all around France. During the autumn of 1888, the cash situation of the Company had reached a desperate level and, this time, the banks were reluctant to assist.

On December 1st, the Lessepses were compelled to suspend all payments to the contractors working in Panama.

It was the official sign that nobody would support the project any more.

Still, there was a lot of money in France, but it was not destined to help Panama: on December 10, 1888, the first large emission of bonds towards the construction of Russian Railways by a French company was highly successful. This is the proof that investors were still active, but they did not favor Panama any more.

The Lessepses were distressed but did not want to acknowledge that they had been defeated. Against all odds, they launched another subscription that showed that they still were full of hope. On December 12, the banks proposed new bonds of the *Compagnie Universelle du Canal Interocéanique de Panama* – the Company. It would be its last subscription: hardly any of the bonds were sold.

On December 14, 1888, the Company had to declare bankruptcy, as nobody had responded to its last call.

Almost one million* small investors were affected by this terrible news.

The Deputies acted as if nothing had happened. They had been bribed: the rumors of their turpitude were now everywhere. Careful not to get involved, they did not lift one finger to help the Company.

"On the 15ᵗʰ of December 1888, the Chamber of Deputies, by 256 votes against 181, rejected a proposed French Government Bill authorizing the Panama Company to postpone payments for three months." (7) It marked the official end of the Company.

B-V commented: "That rejected proposal was the last that the Government of the French Republic was to make in the interest of the great work of Panama. All the acts of public authorities were thenceforth to be inimical to it." (7)

During the eight years of its life, from 1881 to the end of 1888, the Company had spent almost a billion and a half francs to excavate 37 million cubic meters. With 38 more, the canal would have been completed, as expected by the French engineers. 13 million cubic meters had been extracted from the Panama's land during the year 1888, more than in any past year.

What a tragedy! The final objective had been so close.

Some authors indicated that, at the end of 1888, the Company paid off its debts with its captive shares. This is hard to believe. Firstly, the Company had little debt towards the contractors working in Panama. We have seen how it generously advanced money to the contractors in order to allow them to face the coming expenses. Secondly, the Company had been adjudicated in bankruptcy and did not have the free disposal of its shares.

The Roubaix Archives showed that the Company paid its debts by selling some of its Panama RailRoad shares, (2) because the PRR had remained an American Company and was out of reach of the French tribunals.

These American shares were all that was left of the Company's assets. Among all of Ferdinand de Lesseps's blunders, the fact that he had purchased 98% of the PRR would finally prove extremely useful.

The French Company had failed in Panama.
Now, let us see what happened in Nicaragua.

---

* Historians generally quote figures from 600,000 to 800,000 subscribers. It is difficult to verify such figure, as a given subscriber could have subscribed to several bond issues.
In any case, it represented a high percentage, in a country of 38 million people.

11
AMERICANS IN NICARAGUA

While the French were busy digging in Panama, the Americans continued with their strategy to build a canal in Nicaragua. In 1878, President Grant had decided to send an expedition to prepare for such project.

Despite the fact that, a year later, the French had founded the Universal Company in 1879 and had started digging in 1880, the Americans proceeded wholeheartedly on another canal project.

In March 1880, only a few months after the creation of the French Company and, - as an act of distrust? -, while Ferdinand de Lesseps was touring the United States to promote the French project, President Hayes announced openly his goal for "a canal under American control". (20)

Later on, when the French were digging in Panama, "Franco-American relations remained frigid," noted B-V in his memoirs. Surrounded by American ships, the French activities were indeed protected, but this also caused a climate of mistrust to reign in the Isthmus, as "Americans disapproved the Work carried out by the French, which, in their opinion, concerned only the United States."

As General Manager of the French works, B-V visited the American admirals commanding both fleets - Pacific and Atlantic - and tried "to decry the accusation of impossibility which American engineers had launched against our scheme." (11) Addressed to marine officers, this claim was too feeble to modify American's resolve towards a canal in Nicaragua.

On December 1, 1884, despite the *Clayton-Bulwer* treaty, which prevented them to do so - it called for a British-American jointly built canal - Americans negotiated the *Zavala-Frelinghuysen* agreement with Nicaragua to build the canal jointly. However, the Senate did not ratify the agreement; following their President, who wanted a 100% American canal.

Shortly after the Senate rebuff, President Cleveland confirmed that in his view "a treaty as exclusive as the U.S.-Nicaragua alliance was inconsistent with the principle of a canal neutral and open to all nations, and that he (Cleveland) would have nothing to do with it." (20)

Although very few Americans had invested in the French Company, the financial circles in New York were closely following the progress of the French in Panama. Every time the Company showed some weakness - for example, when Bigelow reported negatively on the progress of the works, after his trip early in 1886 -, Americans' confidence in Nicaragua was strengthened.

Tales of the French misadventures reached New York as soon as they took place, with PRR employees reporting back home when returning home from Panama. Each and every incident encouraged the supporters of an American owned canal in Nicaragua.

In 1886, the American project in Nicaragua entered a new phase of activity. A brigade of marines landed in Nicaragua to protect a delegation of American engineers and experts, under the command of Menocal - who had been one of the American representatives at the 1879 Paris Geographic Congress.

It was an important move, intending to make Nicaragua a strong competitor of Panama.

At the beginning of 1887, Ammen and Menocal gathered some New York financial interests into a company, that they called the *Nicaragua Canal Association*. This *Association* secured a revised concession, signed March 23, 1887, with the Government of Nicaragua, by which the latter would receive a share of 6% of all bonds emitted in the United States. To finance this *Association*, Menocal led a very successful campaign throughout the country and subscribers gathered in great number to buy the *Association's* shares. Possessing a concession and money, the *Association* could begin to work.

This was an amazing accomplishment. One has to realize that, while the French were busy digging in Panama, the Americans had so many doubts about the French success that they themselves started digging another canal in Nicaragua.

The race between the two countries had become more fierce than ever.

It was Menocal himself who headed the American project and in 1888, he established the headquarters of the *Association* in San Juan del Norte, the Atlantic city selected for the canal project's origin, a port that had hosted in the past many *Forty-Niners*, on their way to California.

Joining Menocal, was Robert Edwin Peary, who would become famous later for his explorations of Greenland and the North Pole. Peary was in Nicaragua as special envoy of the National Geographic Magazine, a newly founded publication.

All went well initially, but, within a few months, expenditures proved to be much more than expected and the *Nicaragua Canal Association* quickly ran out of cash. Work continued, although at a reduced pace, throughout the beginning of 1889.

For security, the *Association* obtained another concession - this time from the Government of Costa Rica. This was deemed necessary, as the Rio San Juan, used as the starting line of the future Interoceanic Canal, marked the border between Nicaragua and Costa Rica. In Menocal's project, this *Rio* would be equipped with seven locks and connected with Lake Nicaragua.

In the spring of 1889, the French stopped all work in Panama.
Would Nicaragua win the Interoceanic Canal after all?

B-V was thoroughly aware of the founding of the *Nicaragua Canal Association,* (7) but he was too intelligent to minimize the strength of this competitor. When the French Company went bankrupt, B-V left Panama. His associate Artigue remained there to take care of what was left of ASC. (2)

On his way back to France, B-V stopped in San Juan del Norte and visited the projected canal route in Nicaragua. He wanted to collect all possible information about the outsider, which threatened to replace "his" Panama. He spent some time there, gathering all the information he needed to fight this competitor. B-V mentioned only briefly his trip in his memoirs; it would prove to be extremely useful in the future, allowing him to compare these two potential interoceanic routes better than anyone else could.

Later, on his return journey from Nicaragua, B-V spent some time in New York with John Bigelow. Both men had good reasons to be worried about the future of Panama. Bigelow had certainly been convinced by B-V that Panama was in fact the best route for the Interoceanic Canal, but the bankrupt of the French Company and the American progress in Nicaragua were bringing some doubts in his mind. Surely, B-V and Bigelow spent long hours pondering what they could do about it.

Bigelow suggested to B-V that he should stand for election in the Chamber of Deputies of France. It could be a strategic place to promote the Panama Canal. Bigelow also recommended that B-V would write a book to present the Company's achievements in detail and how the canal could still be completed. It would also be a good way to put forward the advantages of Panama over its competitor, Nicaragua.

B-V would eventually write a book, titled "Past, Present and Future." It was an engineer's report, a description of all the methods he recommended to achieve the work, a guidebook for the completion of the lock canal. It would be published on "the 20th of March 1892."(5)

B-V handed out "Past, Present and Future" to all the members of the Chamber of Deputies, senators, bankers and all influential people in Paris. Filled with many drawings and photographs, maps with foldouts, it was intended to provide a reference for all future engineers working in Panama. (5)

In this book, B-V explained his solution to salvage the French project in Panama. Based on his discovery of first blasting the rock beds with dynamite and then dredging the shattered pieces, he advocated the building of lakes connected by locks. The dredges would be installed on these lakes to enlarge the existing passage. B-V's solution would allow small boats to transit through the canal, with the dredges still in operation, bringing useful tolls to subsidy the completion of the project. Once started, this system would be self-sustaining.

In its first phase, this scheme was very economical, at an estimated cost of only 210 million francs. However, there would also be a second phase costing 500 million francs. B-V believed that his book "was the pivot which turned around the American opinion." (7)

But it came too late to interest the French in salvaging the Panama project. The good faith of small investors had been abused for too long, a trial of the officials of the Company was being planned and they would rather call for punishment of the culprits than support the project any more.

Meanwhile, the main champion of Nicaragua was **John Tyler Morgan**, a Senator from Alabama. Morgan was to Nicaragua what B-V would be later to Panama, a passionate supporter. During the Civil War, young officer in the southern states army - the Confederacy -, Morgan had been distinguished for his actions and promoted to the rank of Brigadier General in the Tennessee Army. He was deeply hurt by the defeat of the Confederacy. After the war, he was ran for election as a democrat Senator for Alabama. Easily elected to the Senate in 1876, Morgan was seen as an active and beloved Senator; he would serve for four more terms, to his death in 1907.

In 1888, as a member of the Senate *Foreign Relations Committee*, Morgan persuaded the Senators to allow the Government to participate in the Nicaragua project.

Coming from the Confederacy that had lost the Civil War, Morgan was a patriot who believed that the Nicaragua Canal would bring many advantages to the South in general and, in particular, to the Port of New Orleans, closer to Nicaragua than to Panama, and which stood as a competitor to New York. Nicaragua had the other advantage of being a more stable and friendlier country, and more open to negotiations than Colombia - a country that had always been plagued by internal troubles (see Appendix 8, page 334).

The strongest argument of Morgan was that the Nicaragua route had been recommended by all the experts since the 1879 Geographic Congress. This idea, supported by Menocal, continued to be unanimously endorsed by all the specialists. The best proof was that Ferdinand de Lesseps had not listened to them and failed.

Menocal had finally been proven right. Demonstration has been made that the Panama Canal was "unfeasible".

On February 20, 1889, after a long lobbying campaign by Morgan, Congress approved the creation of the *Maritime Canal Company of Nicaragua - MCCN -* with assets up to $ 100 million, to be financed by private investors, but which could be later guaranteed by the Government. The MCCN was also authorized to emit up to $ 150 million of bonds, yielding an attractive 5% a year. This was exactly the scheme that Morgan had been advocating. It was deemed to become a great success.

This act of Congress, called a "charter", "had been rarely granted by Congress; only national banks and two transcontinental railways benefitted from such a status. . . This charter granted to the *Maritime Canal Company of Nicaragua -* MCCN - placed it immediately in a unique and powerful position, and was considered as an acceptation of the Nicaragua Canal as the canal of the American people; this canal became popularly known as the "American Canal". (6)

This event took place only two months after the French Company had declared bankruptcy. The MCCN was fortunate to have as its first President James Roosevelt, FDR's father.[*]

---

[*] Franklin Delano Roosevelt (FDR) served as the 32nd President from 1933 to 1945.

To implement this scheme, the *Nicaragua Canal Construction Company* was set up, with a capital of $ 12 million and as its Head Engineer, Menocal.

Menocal was enthusiastic: "It is our opinion that the revenue of the canal will be sufficient to pay 6% on some $ 250 million. As to the technical advantages of this route as compared to the Panama route, they are of the first importance. There is no unsolvable Chagres River problem; there is much less canal in excavation; there is no problem of water supply; there is no rotten, sliding rock; there are no endemic pestilences; there is a stiff trade breeze the year round to maintain health and comfort; there is a prior knowledge from detail surveys of just what is to be done, which was wholly lacking at Panama; there is the experience gained at Panama and of an official "base" on this side of the ocean instead of on the other side; and there is the practicality of far better management. These are enormous advantages and it therefore seems to us that no reasonable man can doubt, first that the canal can be built for $ 100 to $ 150 million at the very most, and, secondly, that it will be exceedingly profitable even at a rate of 6%." (New York Times, September 15, 1889).

With the establishment of the MCCN, work resumed at full speed in June 1889. It would soon become a popular American success.

People were ecstatic when they looked in the newspapers at pictures showing the dredges used by the French Company in Panama. These dredges of the *American Contracting and Dredging Company* were now operating on the Rio San Juan.

Now that the MCCN had money and that the Government was backing it up, it had everything it needed to be successful.

The French Company was ruined. All work had stopped in Panama.

Nicaragua seemed to have won the contest.

Panama seemed defeated and unable to continue the fight.

But B-V did not take it for granted. He wrote in his memoirs: "If the Nicaragua Canal was now on the eve of its completion, and Panama therefore abandoned, this infamous legend* would have been transformed into historical truth. This is why I worked desperately in America for the victory of the Panama canal over its rival, Nicaragua". (7)

Against such a powerful nation as the United States, how could B-V win?

---

* B-V alludes here to the swindling and corruption that brought down the Company, logic that he rejected. He mentioned a "violent political coalition, hostile to Panama." (7)

12

GLOOMY RECORD

As **1889** began, Americans were busy digging in Nicaragua, while in Paris, the French Company had gone bankrupt.

At the same time, "the French Senate, gratified by Ferdinand de Lesseps, loses no time in passing a law concerning bankruptcies, so that this criminal could avoid being blemished . . . But this is not enough and to crown this disposition, a friend of Lesseps, Joseph Brunet, a former Minister, is appointed as the liquidator of the Company."(4) We recognize here Drumont's caustic style; he dared to qualify *Le Grand Français* of "criminal".

Brunet was assisted by three interim administrators, also appointed by the French Government - MM. Baudelot, Denormandie and Hue. The main contractors - ASC, Eiffel, Baratoux, Jacob and Hawen - had agreed to keep working until February 15. Their aim was to salvage whatever they could, to shelter all the equipment before the coming rainy season. Without these conservation measures, rain could damage beyond repair the locomotives, dredges, excavators, and other pieces of equipment. It was also necessary to assign guards to watch over the Company's property.

The interim administrators had a responsibility to protect all the achievements that the Company had made during the past eight years and to keep their equipment in good working order. They believed that work would resume one day, so they needed to ensure that it could happen smoothly.

To cover the contractors' costs, the interim administrators allowed them some cash advances, estimated initially at 5 million francs but finally amounting, when all the tasks would be achieved, to 7.093 million francs. (2)

To pay for this, the interim administrators could not use any cash, because of the insolvency of the Company. They tried to procure a loan, but having failed, they had to dedicate some shares of the PRR - at the time the totality of the shares was worth more than 100 million francs -, because being an American Company it remained out of the French bankruptcy jurisdiction. For some time, these shares would be used to finance the small expenses of the now defunct Company.

Brunet and his assistants wanted to preserve everything in Panama, so that work would resume as quickly as possible. Among these tasks was to ensure of the validity of the concession with Colombia, by complying with all its conditions.

They also named a Commission of French and foreign engineers to take care of all the technical matters.

Between March and May 1889, all work progressively stopped in Panama. At the time, the top of the Culebra Hill had been lowered to 72 meters above sea level. B-V claimed that it was possible to lower it by another 10 meters per year, as he did in the previous year. This would allow completion of the canal with locks within four years, his objective being to reach 42 meters, the level of the internal Gatun lake - with a draft of 10 meters -, created to that effect.

Today, in the existing Panama Canal, the ships reach Gatun Lake through three locks, each lock elevating the ships by about 8 meters. The Lake is thus at a level of 26 meters, about 16 meters lower than what B-V had in mind.

B-V had nevertheless found the right solution.

From September 1, 1886 to February 15, 1889, in about thirty months, ASC, the Company of the brothers Bunau-Varilla, had extracted 2.661 million cubic meters from the Culebra Hill, only 30% of what it had been contracted to dig - 9 million cubic meters.

During the same period, in the sector of Miraflores, between the Culebra Hill and the Pacific Ocean, ASC had extracted 0.1 million cubic meters against a contractual obligation of 0.5. (2)

Clearly, B-V should not have praised his work as he did when he wrote his memoirs in 1913. Of course, he did much better than his predecessors did, but: "ASC never fulfilled its contractual assignments," will write Mr. Lemarquis in April 1894. (see Appendix 1)

This flat judgment will never be contradicted by B-V.

B-V did not mention it in his memoirs, where he claimed that he was the "savior" of the Culebra Hill: "I had since added two brilliant chapters to the history of my Canal services: the victory over the Culebra difficulty and the complete solution of the Canal construction by dredging." (7)

The Technical Commission named by Brunet did not receive B-V's approval, as he was not a member of it: "the greatest part of the members of the Commission . . . preferred a lock canal as perfect as it could be conceived. Their project necessitated seven years and 900 millions."

And B-V concluded: "The result was fatal. All hope of floating the great enterprise was once more at the end." (7)

In its preliminary report, the Commission not only made plans for the future, but they also assessed the value of the work completed to date at 450 million francs. To achieve this, the Company had spent: 1,434 million francs, almost a billion and a half francs! This news had a tremendous impact on the French public: it was a recognition of the fraud!

Their project involved a canal with locks - of course -, with a lake at 25 meters above sea level. B-V believed it should be at 40 meters above sea level, while the Commission put it at about half this altitude.

The Commission envisaged a traffic of 4.1 million tons a year, again lower than the 7.25 million tons endorsed by the Geographic Congress of 1879.

As the Commission's report was not especially encouraging, Brunet asked its members to revise their judgment. The Commission went back to work and came back eight years later (!) with their final report, not without having asked for complementary work to be done in Panama.

For the small investors who had subscribed to the Panama Bonds - about a million of them -, the preliminary Committee's report proved to what extent Lesseps had cheated them. The value of the work achieved was estimated at 450 million francs - for 1,434 spent - and it would require another 900 million francs to complete the canal. They had really been cheated.

Lesseps had told them in 1879 that the canal would cost 600 million francs and after spending more than twice this sum since 1881, they were now told that another 900 million francs would be necessary. Ferdinand de Lesseps appeared to be an impostor!

The mere revelation of these figures called for full abandonment of the project. Who would invest again in such a canal when its profitability would be ruined by such an enormous final cost?

For the rest of 1889, the Panama project was forgotten, while the interest of the Parisian people was diverted to other matters.

This was good news for Nicaragua, where the Americans continued to dig with no major problem to report.

It is interesting to describe the event that contributed to help the Parisians forget their losses in Panama. De Diesbach wrote: "In Paris, external events divert people's attention from the misadventures of Panama." (22)

On May 6, 1889, as the Universal Exhibition was about to open its gates, the Eiffel Tower was inaugurated. It celebrated the Centennial of the 1789 French Revolution. Millions of visitors from around the world came for this anniversary. Paris was named "the City of Lights". During the Exhibition, two million people climbed to the top of the Eiffel Tower.

This quickly replaced Panama "in taking up the attention of the masses". (22)

Drumont, in his exasperating and caustic style, commented this mass amnesia: "Panama has no interest for the French public. Thirty thousand people dying in a corner of the world to facilitate the subscriptions, this does not exist for the Parisian reading newspapers. Such reader is filled with an immense emotion when he reads that a man from Austria has traveled in a horse pulled carriage to come and visit the Exhibition. This reader says to his family: Children, he really did come in a carriage! How all Europe should admire us!" (4)

Panama had been completely erased from the memories of the French people.

Soon after his return from Panama, on February 20, 1889, B-V married his sister-in-law, Ida de Brunhoff. (2) She was the youngest sister of Sophie de Brunhoff, Maurice's wife. The brothers, already associated in ASC's business, will become even closer.

On September 22, 1889, B-V, who had turned 30, campaigned in Mantes for a seat in the Chamber of Deputies. He was following Bigelow's advice, hoping to have a voice on a national scale to defend Panama. He was defeated by a 10% margin - he obtained 6,000 votes against 6,600 to his competitor. (7)

This is highly surprising, as B-V had certainly invested heavily in this fight. Thanks to his success in ASC, B-V was now a rich man.

It is also surprising that B-V, newlywed, would leave his wife to try to enter the political world. B-V's daughter, Giselle, would later explain that Ida had accepted that her husband be "bigamous" from the very beginning of their marriage.(18) B-V's marriage had not changed his passion for the Panama Canal and his wife Ida would have to live with it.

In fact, the private matters of his marriage would remain a well-kept secret. B-V dedicated his 1913 memoirs to his children Giselle and Etienne, but had only a few words for his wife Ida. The exception was when he mentioned that: "Madame Bunau-Varilla remained in her rooms in the greatest secrecy the whole day making the flag of liberation" in 1903. (7)

To conclude this chapter, let us mention that on October 14, 1889, the company *Artigue, Sonderegger & Compagnie* was dissolved, by Pierre Dominique Parodi, who would become later a great friend of Maurice.

This "liquidation" of ASC would not spare its three shareholders from being prosecuted in 1894.

The investigation would last almost five years before a trial could take place. Rendering justice is a slow process.

13

HOW THE BROTHERS BECAME WELL-OFF

While in Nicaragua the Americans were working hard, in Paris justice was investigating the complaints of the small shareholders of the Company. It would engender the greatest scandal of the new Third French Republic, today recalled in the History books as the *Panama Scandal*.

For the reader interested in this s*candal*, the most recommended books are by Jean-Yves Mollier (19) and Jean Bouvier (14). The first one deals mainly with the political scandal, the consequence of the "pressures" exerted by the Company on the French Deputies. The second book brings to light another kind of scandal: the enormous commissions - 10% instead of the regular 2 % - collected by the banks selling the Company's bonds to the small investors.

These books also relate interesting facts about the corruption that was rampant within the various categories of the Republic: politicians, newspaper editors, construction companies, etc.

Since the Company had declared bankruptcy at the end of 1888, and despite the disclosure of some facts by the press, French justice had been slow to act on the case. This is understandable, as most people in high places had received bribes from the Company and were keeping a low profile.

Some of these crooks were fully indebted to the Company: the press, Deputies, bankers, etc. The Company had asked them to:

- conceal the deaths from yellow fever in Panama,

- promote the Company's bonds subscriptions, once a year,

- lie about the real progress of the work in Panama and lie about its completion date,

- write frequently that the work is progressing well, that everything is under control and that the canal would be finished on time as scheduled,

- vote the law allowing the Company to emit lottery bonds, etc. (2)

However, "in a country where was published, only in Paris, 1,573 newspapers, newsletters or periodical magazines"(4), statistically, a few honest journalists must have to be found. On February 9, 1890, a full year after all work had been stopped in Panama, Edouard Drumont, who would found later his own newspaper - *La Libre Parole* -, published a book about Panama, - "*La Dernière Bataille*" The Last Battle - where he wrote the now famous "it was a gigantic swindle, for the purpose of their political ballyhoo."(7)

It is worth quoting from this book, written in the caustic and sharp-witted style, characteristic of Drumont, the following sentences found in the third chapter, titled: "An Enterprise in the Nineteen Century. Panama."

"A whole small world lived on Panama, like they used to live on the Revolutionary Tribunal under the Terror Regime. The big shots came first, with enormous demands, then followed the average guy, and lastly the very small caps as little as children's. And, at the end of this line, came an unknown news reporter, who would receive a thin check, 200 or 250 francs to have inserted in his article a few lines on the "Great Frenchman", on Tototte or on Ismael. Some had not written anything, but just said: "I am sympathetic to the enterprise" and they received a check like the others, so that they would not become unfriendly. The Company wanted to thank you just for not mentioning Panama . . ." (4)

Tototte and Ismael were the nicknames of two of Ferdinand de Lesseps' eleven small children.

Drumont was proud to have invented the word "checkards" - as were called those who received bribes on a check. His newspaper, "*La Libre Parole*", was the leader of the anti-Semitic press. Considering that many among the major bankers supporting the Company were Jews, who were not in high esteem in the popular newspapers, Drumont condemned violently the bankrupt that had ruined a lot of French underprivileged people.

B-V was especially sensitive to any criticism addressed to Lesseps, his mentor and the hero of Suez. He wrote in his memoirs a lengthy tribute attempting to justify Lesseps's honesty. He had such a high image of the "Great Frenchman" that he would not allow some "hysterical man" to attack the name of "glorious and unfortunate Lesseps." (11) He was extremely upset of Drumont's expression "a swindler's trick", used to describe the embezzlement of the small investors' money.

B-V was intimate: "The inquiry demonstrated the absolute lack of any shadow of foundation for this cynical assertion." (7) As usual, B-V was considering only his own self. Although this was true when applied to himself or his company ASC, the Company's trial demonstrated clearly the responsibility of the Lessepses. Let us read what B-V had to say to exculpate Lesseps: "Has the Company paid for imaginary volumes of earth because of false agreements with the contractors? Answer: All the cubic meters have been paid according to contracts and in view of the measured inventories made under the order and the responsibility of the directors of the Company, all registered engineers from the French Republic." (7). Again, B-V was inclined to consider things on a technical point of view.

Adding to the pessimism of Brunet's Technical Commission, Drumont's book came at a bad time and forever buried the hopes of the small investors, the shareholders of the Company.

However, a few large investors were still hopeful. On March 11, 1889, they created the *Société Internationale d'Etudes du Canal Interocéanique de Panama* - International Society for the study of the Interoceanic Canal of Panama -, registered 3, Rue Louis le Grand in Paris. It delivered 20,000 ownership tittles, assigned to the bearer, without any nominal value. This society had 200 members, each owning a maximum of 200 titles. Its members pledged to invest in the completion of the Panama Canal, under the guidelines of Brunet's Technical Commission.

Wisely, the Bunau-Varilla brothers did not take part in it. When the Technical Commission's report was issued by Brunet, its recommendations were so frightening that most of the members of the *International Society* opted out and the *Society* was dissolved at the end of 1889.

We have mentioned this episode to show that there were still in Paris a few believers in the Panama project, but they were not very enthusiastic about it.

To see where laid the heart of the scandal, we should now examine in detail the expenditures of the Company. The list below is quoted by B-V (7) and confirmed by Bouvier (14) and Vallé's report. (2) For once, all agreed on the money spent by the Company. Figures are in million francs:

-	Payments to contractors and workmen	443
-	Cost of administration and verification of works	83
	Houses of employees and workmen, workshops, storehouses, offices, wharves, etc	47
-	Purchase of equipment and its transportation cost	119
-	Erection and repair of equipment	30
-	Coal, oils, grease and miscellaneous consumables	29
-	Workers transportation and housing maintenance	16
-	Cost of hospitals and chapels	9
-	Expropriation of properties and land purchases	5
-	Boreholes, soundings, etc.	2

	TOTAL SPENT FOR THE WORKS	783

– Purchase of the Panama RailRoad Cy (PRR) 68,500 shares at 1,350 francs each	93	
– Purchase of the concession to the Wyse Syndicate	10	
– Subscription costs - publicity, banks' commissions, etc.	135	
– Interests or amortization paid to the shareholders	250	
– Accessible Assets of which 77 in back payments	163	

TOTAL SPENT ALTOGETHER	**1434**	
The resources of the Company were:		
– cash collected through the subscriptions *see Appendix 2*	1335	
– miscellaneous products	99	

Total in million francs	1434	million

From the above figures, we deduce that the sums allocated to the works, excluding the administration and verification costs represented only:
(783-83) = 700/1434 = 49 % of the total expenses.

Every contractor knows that for such a large project, the overhead charges represent usually about 15% of the total spent. Lesseps had spent almost 50% in overhead, more than three times the standard figure.
Where had it been spent? What was all this money wasted on?

The 135 million francs spent in publicity and subscriptions paid to the banks are the subject of Bouvier's book. (14) They were not the interests paid to the banks, but only the commissions they received from the Company to sell its bonds.

The banks' services were quite expensive. On a sale of 1,335 million francs in bonds and shares, their commission was: 135/1335 = 10% !

Bouvier noted that the "usual rate, customary, of such a commission varied around 1.5% to 2%, no more. There laid evidently the second scandal of Panama." (14) The banks had taken advantage of Ferdinand de Lesseps' absence of negotiation to load up the bill.

B-V was well aware of these figures! He wrote in his memoirs that: "out of the cash box of the Company, only 400 million francs could be traced in the works and nobody knew where vanished the rest of the billion and a quarter francs." (7)

It is not the purpose of this book to dwell upon the double scandal, political and financial, but to show how the Bunau-Varilla brothers made their fortune in Panama in working with *Artigue, Sonderegger & Co.*

Up to now, this has remained a mystery. To date, no historian had been able to unveil this secret.

The documents found in the French Archives in Roubaix (2), together with Vallé's report (2) reveal clearly the secret of the brothers' fortune. There we find the sums paid by the Company to various contractors. The investigating commission - headed by Mr. Vallé - had also audited the contractors' books, which showed how much has been paid by the Company to each of the contractors and also the profit made by each of the 5 contractors remaining at work until May 1889. Unfortunately, the profit of the contractors working before 1886 could not be determined because:

- the Commission did not ask to audit the small contractors,
- the Commission did not have access to the books of foreign contractors.

The sums shown below are for the contractors working from 1886 to May 1889:

In million francs	Paid by the Company	Profit	%
Companies regrouped	187.8	?	
Eiffel	73.7	33.0	45
Baratoux	37.6	12.5	33
Jacob	16.5	8.0	48
Société Travaux Publics	76.2	20.7	27
ASC	50.9	11.4	22
Total in million francs	442.7 (total payments to contractors)		

We notice that ASC's profit was moderate - in fact ASC had the smallest ratio - while Eiffel and Jacob made a hefty profit.

We shall give later the detail of ASC's profit of 11.4 million francs.

Lemarquis, the representative of the small shareholders, declared that he believed that ASC had made a fraudulent profit of 5 million francs. If it were true, this would reduce ASC's profit to : 11.4 – 5 = 6.4 million francs and its profit ratio to : 6.4/50.9 = 12.6%.

This profit was certainly well below reality. We have seen that, at this time, a simple bank commission was 10%. An industrialist who had to pay a dividend of 5 to 10% to his shareholders would need to realize a profit of at least 15% and typically achieved a profit close to 20%. This has been a universal rule, valid ever since.

Qui ne dit mot consent - whoever keeps quiet, agrees -, as the French proverb goes.

Not only did the Bunau-Varilla brothers not disagree with what Lemarquis was asking, but they acknowledged the 5 million figure. However, as they were good managers, they dragged their feet and attempted to negotiate.

At this point, we conclude that the Bunau-Varilla brothers had made a fortune of at least 6 million francs. We shall reveal the details of this sum in chapter 15. This sum was absolutely colossal for the time. It represented many times the lifetime paycheck of a high official as the General Manager of the Company - Dingler's salary was 100,000 francs a year, thus 6 million francs would have been his payroll if he had worked 60 years!

Some typical salaries of the time will show us the sheer size of these sums. An ordinary French worker earned 5 to 10 francs a day, or about 2,000 francs a year. An unimportant employee in a Ministry earned from 4,000 to 10,000 francs a year. Maurice, once he had acquired *Le Matin,* would pay to his office clerks a yearly salary of 3,000 francs, while his General Secretary, a key position in *Le Matin,* would make yearly about 40,000 francs .

Within the Lesseps Company, some of the salaries were:
-Division Head in Panama - B-V occupied the function from Sept. 1, 1884 to July 1885 - 70,000 francs per year,
- Head of the Titles Department: 12,000 francs per year,
- Office Supervisor: 6,000 francs per year,
- Assistant Supervisor: 3,600 francs per year.
- For every 50 office clerks, there were 15 office supervisors.

In the Titles Department, there were 3 supervisors for every 5 office clerks. (2)

In little less than three years - from the end of 1886 to the beginning of 1889 -, the Bunau-Varilla brothers had accumulated an enormous fortune. Their future and their heirs' future had been assured, unless some misfortune may befall on them.

As we shall see, nothing is certain in our world.

Although nobody could refute that their fortune was made in earnest, it certainly attracted some criticism. We have seen how B-V contributed to spread the lies that ruined the small shareholders of the Company. His foolproof optimism, which, in particular, strongly influenced the Rousseau's report, had unquestionably been fatal to the Company. For Drumont, B-V was one of those "civil engineers from the *Ponts & Chaussées,* eaten up in self-conceit, exclusives, thinking of themselves as no small beer, looking at themselves as the first escorts of the pope" (4) and thinking that the financial resources of the Company were infinite.

B-V was aware of this criticism when he wrote, in his usual arrogant style: "The Canal Company, whose enterprise I had saved from a technical point of view, was wrecked at the end of 1888 on a financial shoal." (7)

Coming back to the Panama Scandal, on May 5, 1890, Brunet, the liquidator, released his Technical Commission's report to his successor Monchicourt. (7) On June 21, as if the Drumont's book and the Commission's report were not enough, some members of the Chamber of Deputies - le Provost de Launay and Jules Delahaye - testified in front of a Justice Court having a "high technical authority".

B-V commented that: "it was the most absurd and ridiculous confusion of names and figures ever imagined." (7) Clearly, some of the Deputies wanted to denounce their colleagues, while others wanted to hide the bribes they received from the Company.

In his memoirs, B-V told a funny story, regarding this deposition, perhaps the only example of humor in his books: "The forged paper which Mr. Delahaye read at the tribune - of the Chamber of Deputies - was published once again, but a long time afterwards. It was in New York in 1904. The *Evening Post*, a paper of high standing, undertook a violent campaign against me in order to prevent the ratification of the "Hay/Bunau-Varilla" treaty by the American Senate. Challenged by my lawyer to assert the veracity of the document, the *Evening Post* brandished triumphantly the *Journal Officiel de la République Française* with the reproduction of Delahaye's speech in its issue of June 22, 1890, page 1142." (7)

It is well known that the *Official* Journal of the French Republic is just a faithful record of what was said and does not in any way points out what is true or not.

On December 10, 1890, Monchicourt, the recently named liquidator of the Company, successfully renewed the old concession with the Colombians - *Roldan-Wyse*, which specified that specified that work would have to resume before February 28, 1893. This new concession also required the Company to pay for the salaries of the 250 Colombian soldiers stationed in Panama City.

It is believed that the influential dignitaries of the Panama Province, who were worried about the economic crisis brought about by the cessation of the works, had also campaigned for the renewal of the concession.

In December 1890, the Kohn-Reinach bank, leader of the cohort of High Banks that got involved in the Panama subscriptions, declared bankruptcy. The financial climate was extremely competitive. Another large bank, *Société des Dépôts* ceased its activities in March 1891.

On June 11, **1891**, after more than a year of debates, the investigation against the members of the Board of the Company was finally opened by order of Armand Fallières, the Minister of Justice. Many complaints had been filed at the Paris Tribunal and could not be ignored any longer.

This investigation was headed by the general Prosecutor, Quesnay de Beaurepaire. Some months later, he would issue an indictment report, which can be summarized as follows: "Lesseps did not show any honesty in defending or respecting other people's money, the small investors' savings; he had been their methodical pilferer." (14)

However, despite such serious accusations, Ferdinand de Lesseps, "the Great Frenchman", Officer of the Legion of Honor, had maintained some of his old fame. The old man was now 86 and the French Republic was reluctant to send him to jail.

Following Drumont's book, rumors circulated about the beneficiaries of the "bribes". Emile Loubet, who headed the French Government, did not want to open up a Pandora Box, highlighting some of his friends. Everybody in Paris knew now that certain members of the Chamber of Deputies had benefited from the Company.

For obvious political reasons, the investigation dragged along.

In January **1892**, the Minister of Internal Affairs received a list of the members of the Chamber of Deputies who had benefited from the Company.

Despite all these turpitudes, some people still remained firm believers that the completion of the Panama Canal would be feasible. On May 9, 1892, they established the *Société d'Etudes et de Publications pour favoriser l'Achèvement du Canal de Panama* - Society for Studying and Publishing to Promote the Achievement of the Canal of Panama.

It was mostly endorsed by celebrities from the newspapers - Maurice Bunau-Varilla was not yet one of them. This Society issued 30,000 shares, payable to the bearers, and with no nominal value.

It was the second attempt of a Society founded with the objective of salvaging the idea of the Panama Canal.

Unfortunately, by the end of 1892, the members of the Society had become concerned by the enormous sums necessary for their enterprise and did not follow through. This was a sign that some hope remained, however.

We shall see that a third attempt would be successful, but with a less ambitious goal: to maintain in good condition all the work done by the Company in Panama.

Many high placed people were involved in the scandal and this obviously delayed a necessary trial. The investigation had lasted a couple of years and more than three years had elapsed since the Company had been declared in bankruptcy.

Fortunately, democracy was still at work in the new French Republic and it was the press which finally brought the Company to trial.

From September 6 to 18, 1892, a provincial banker, named Ferdinand Martin, an ex-employee of the Company, who had been involved in the marketing campaigns of the Company's bond subscriptions, published a series of articles in the newly founded newspaper of Drumont, *La Libre Parole*, under the title: "The shady side of Panama". He signed under an assumed name of *Micros*: "During the period of construction of the Panama Canal by the Company, the press was mastered. Lesseps distributed bounties, not to bondholders or shareholders, but to a band of vultures, starting with French Government members, bankers, etc. The right wing was in favor of it, but it was hard to convince the leftists." (14) Without naming him explicitly, Martin accused Baron Jacques de Reinach to be the mastermind behind the bribes' distribution.

After these articles had been published, public agitation was such that Quesnay de Beaurepaire, the General Investigator, was compelled to send a report to the Justice Minister, asking that the members of the Board of the Company be prosecuted for "breach of trust and swindle".

The deceived bond holders have been waiting for such a long time. Would they finally see the criminals jailed for their wrong doings?

14

THE LESSEPS' COMPANY'S TRIAL

Before dealing with the trial of *Artigue, Sonderegger & Co*, we have to explain briefly how leniently the Company Board members had been dealt with by the French Justice, as it would show the same clemency later on, towards ASC and its owners.

On November 19, 1892, just when the defendants were about to testify in court, Baron Jacques de Reinach was found dead in his *Hotel Particulier* in Paris. He was the key banker who had instigated the first concession with the Colombians in 1878 and who had formed a bank syndicate to promote the various subscriptions of the Company's bonds. He was later named Director of the Company, in charge of its publicity. As such, he was one of the *"arrangeurs"* and pocketed many million francs in commissions from the canal construction contractors.

As Reinach had ordered his personal files to be destroyed before his death, it was assumed that he committed suicide, but the motives remain a mystery. Reinach was a well known figure of the Parisian high society and the press quickly associated his death with the rumors about corruption. For B-V: "It seemed an auspicious moment to fight the political battle." (7)

This happened in November 1892. Almost three years had elapsed since the Company had declared bankruptcy. At last, the culprits would be finally judged. The Justice Minister announced to the Chamber of Deputies that Ferdinand de Lesseps and his son Charles, Eiffel, Fontane and Cottu - those last two being members of the Board of the Company - were called to appear before the Court of Appeal.

As Ferdinand de Lesseps was *Grand Croix de la Légion d'Honneur*, he could only be judged by a Court of Appeal - that is without a jury -, and all the other defendants had to be tried in the same court. The charges were:

- fraud and maladministration,
- fraudulent maneuvers to induce belief in unreal schemes,
- raising imaginary hopes for the realization of chimerical events. (16)

The major event that precipitated the scandal happened on November 21, 1892, two days after Reinach's death, when Delahaye, a member of the Chamber of Deputies, publicly accused some of his peers of receiving bribes. Called "checkards" - receivers of checks - 104 had accepted money and, of them, 26 had seen their names disclosed. Among them was Georges Clemenceau, the founding father and president of the Radical-Socialist party, owner of the newspaper *La Justice*, regrettably sponsored by Cornelius Herz, a major swindler.

B-V commented that: "Delahaye had unchained an enormous cyclone." (11)

Following Delahaye's speech at the Chamber, what was a financial scandal became a political one. In the turbulence that ensued, Emile Loubet, the President of the Republic was compelled to name an investigating commission of 33 members; a few days later, his government fell.

B-V refuted the bribery gossip and wrote naively in his memoirs: "The alleged corruption of 150 Deputies was a fiction." (7) He was clearly mistaken and demonstrated here his great naiveté.

Today, we have full evidence that the charges were justified. The books of Jean-Yves Mollier (19) and of Jean Bouvier (14) are crystal clear on this.

B-V's comment stemmed from his blind admiration and his endless defense of Ferdinand de Lesseps, *Le Grand Français,* his model of excellence in life.

As usual, B-V is at the same time right and wrong.

On one hand, Delahaye, interrogated by the investigating Commission on November 25, declared: "I am totally unable to obtain a material proof, because the proofs are in the checks", (2) and , of course, nobody would admit to receiving one. Delahaye refused to tell the names of his informants; he only mentioned Reinach, suicided, and Arton, a broker who had fled to England. As the saying goes: "To dead man and absent, there are no friends left."

On the other hand, there was no trace of a 5 million francs check - mentioned by Delahaye - in the accounts of the Company.

Without proof, would the culprits be condemned to jail?

On January 7, **1893**, Charles Baïhaut, the former Minister of Public works was arrested; he had been the only one to publicly admit to having received a bribe. All the others had denied the accusation and there was no proof left since Reinach, who had distributed the money, had died without leaving any evidence. Reinach's accomplice, Emile Arton could not be found anywhere in England.

Three days later, the trial began at the Court of Appeal of Paris.

The above charges were obvious for Ferdinand and Charles de Lesseps and the administrators of the Company.

But what about Eiffel? Eiffel had received unwarranted sums, related to the locks' contract he signed with the Company: "to thank his intermediaries, he would pay them 10% of these sums, 2% to a hidden financier, 3% to Jacques de Reinach, 5% to Adrien Hébrard and also 2% to Maurice Bunau-Varilla." (19) Hébrard was a French Senator, accomplice of Eiffel, to whom he procured contracts, in exchange of a commission.

The main charge was a list of "false claims:
- announcing that the *Couvreux & Hersent* contract was "fixed cost";
- lowering all cost estimates of the project;
- fact concealment in annual reports;
- magnifying work achieved and covering up difficulties;
- claiming that new work organizations would be successful." (2)

In a few words, the public has been abused, but it was found that "none of the administrators of the Company had directly benefitted from expenses for work and accessories, charged to the Company." (2) It thus appeared that – except Eiffel - none of the accused had personally profited financially from the situation.

B-V tells us that on January 13, during the trial, a former employee of the Company gave evidence that he had heard "rumors being circulated" and that consequently he had given his resignation. Those rumors were about a commission of 1.4 francs per cubic meter, given to Baron Reinach, for a total of 20 million cubic meters - adding up to the tidy sum of 28 million francs. This was allegedly for the transfer of the Anglo-Dutch contract to ASC in the summer of 1886.

This was correct, but we have to mention that although this commission was paid by ASC to Reinach, he received only 383,256 francs (2), as ASC excavated far less than the 20 million cubic meters, which were its contractual obligation with the Company.

Here, B-V was wrongly indignant; he could not be aware of all his brother Maurice's tricks, while he was working for the Company in Panama.

The most unbelievable rumors were being circulated about everyone and, as it is often the case, most of the rumors had some truth in them. The trial had created an unprecedented witch hunt by the press.

On February 9, 1893, the Court of Appeal delivered its judgment.

Found guilty, Ferdinand and Charles de Lesseps were sentenced each to 5 years in jail - the maximum penalty for embezzlement.

Cottu and Fontane, the Company's administrators, and the constructor Gustave Eiffel were sentenced to 2 years - the maximum penalty for breach of trust.

On March 21, the Court sentenced Baïhaut - the former Minister of Transportation - and Arton - the handy-man of Reinach, who had fled to England - to 5 years imprisonment.

Ferdinand de Lesseps could not be sent to jail, he was too famous and too old - he was 88 -, so he was assigned to house arrest.

Charles de Lesseps, Cottu, Fontane and Eiffel would only remain in jail until June 15, when the Supreme Court of Appeal canceled the indictment for a flaw in the trial paperwork, "for a point in the law that was so obscure that various analyses were plausible." (19)

Justice had certainly shown here a great clemency.

Panama had been the greatest scandal of the Third French Republic. People started questioning the Republic itself:
- Had Lesseps not built the Suez Canal during the Second Empire, under a nephew of Napoleon? Why would he fail under the Republic? People began to wonder.
- Was corruption a fact of life in the new Republic? To crown it all, this Republic that people had called for so long, had not been able to establish the freedom of the press and the democratic process. It was not even able to punish the criminals involved in the Panama scandal. Doubt was everywhere.

Poor Eiffel was devastated by his conviction. He would never recover from such a blemish. After the scandal, he abandoned his structural steel building company and started a new career as a scientist. Setting up an office at the top of his Tower, he kept making experiments in meteorology, aerodynamics and calibration of pressure measuring devices.

These activities, combined with using the Tower for a radio antenna during World War I, would save the Tower from being dismantled in 1919.

Initially built as a temporary attraction for the 1889 Paris International Fair, the Tower had become permanent.

With Eiffel and Clemenceau, two of the most famous men in France, the Panama scandal had also affected many distinguished people of the Republic.

Clemenceau, the head of the Radical party, was forced to quit his political career for almost twenty years. He had been - although indirectly - one of the "checkards", as well "political men who had been compromised in the "Panama Scandal": Floquet, Freycinet, Thevenet, Rouvier, Jules Roche, Yves Guyot, Burdeau, Ranc, . . . (14)

In the Chamber of Deputies' elections of September 1893, Jules Delahaye was not re-elected in Chinon, even though he had been denouncing the scandal by publishing the list of representatives involved in the bribes.

Most of the Deputies have lost their seats; the "checkards" were rightly sanctioned.

We must quote here an additional proof that the French Deputies wanted to totally and definitely forget Panama.

B-V had asked the new elected Chamber to make a gesture in favor of "the 600,000 French families, ruined by Panama. The Government was asked to express a word of solidarity with the efforts made for the rescue, a pure moral solidarity. . . . They refused to raise their voices."(11)

To end this despicable affair, let us quote once again B-V, who summed up the scandal: "They had succeeded in making the most glorious enterprise of our nation a symbol of shame and breach of trust," and: "It is necessary to have passed through this curious phase of political hysteria to believe it to have been possible." (7)

15

THE TRIAL OF ARTIGUE, SONDEREGGER & COMPANY

After the trial of the Company Board's members, the court examined other complaints filed by the small investors. The charge was "embezzlement against all the parties concerned".

On July 1st 1893, the Chamber of Deputies voted a law naming a legal representative of the small investors, Mr. Lemarquis, and a "co-liquidator", Mr. Gautron. (19) This law allowed them to investigate once more the responsibility of the members of the Board of the Company, as well as the responsibility of the banks - *Crédit Lyonnais, Société Générale, Crédit Industriel & Commercial* and other private banks -, not forgetting the major construction contractors.

Georges Émile Lemarquis was reputed to be an honest man; expert in banking matters, he came from a neutral bank - the *Banque de France*. He would later - in 1900 - be administrator of the *Crédit Lyonnais*.

This was more than four years after the work had stopped in Panama. It is often difficult for us, citizens of a Republic, to understand how slowly justice works.

On July 4, 1893, Vallé presented the Chamber of Deputies with his report: "Report by the Enquiry Commission to shed light on the allegations made in the Chamber of Deputies about the Panama affair." (2)

It had requested 18 months of inquiry. It contained all the figures relevant to the contractors, the interviews of more than 100 witnesses, the expenses and payments made by the Company to the contractors, the audit of their books by Flory, a chartered accountant, the profit of the contractors according to their books, etc. In more than 2,000 pages, the whole scandal provoked by the embezzlement of some contractors was fully explained.

In this report, were found a great deal of facts that would unnecessarily burden this book. A reading of this report is highly recommended to understand how the embezzlement took place within the Universal Company (go to www:gallica.bnf.fr).

We shall only reveal here the information that is strictly essential to understand how the Bunau-Varilla brothers made their fortune: ASC's revenues and profit figures.

Once again, B-V deprecated in his memoirs what had been the investigation of other engineers; he trusted only what he had done himself; he saw "errors so flagrant that some of them had to be accepted by Vallée (sic) and corrected before the report would be printed." (7) B-V showed so little esteem for Vallé that he misspelled his name - unconsciously ? - on various occasions in his memoirs.

Vallé's report contained the proof of the unjustified enrichment of the Bunau-Varilla brothers: "It is true that the successors of *Cutbill, de Longo, Watson & Van Hattum,* the company *Artigue, Sonderegger & Cie,* did not work more efficiently and yet had benefitted from a higher price per cubic meter and from large grants." (2)

It would take another year for Lemarquis to analyze all the information released in the Vallé's report and to prepare his charges against the contractors.
All contractors were concerned: Eiffel, Baratoux-Letellier, Jacob, Hawen and especially the Bunau-Varilla brothers, with their company: *Artigue, Sonderegger & Co.,* ASC, founded, as one may recall, in the summer of 1886. Maurice had been managing the finances of ASC in Paris and B-V, assisted by the engineers Auguste Artigue and Conrad Sonderegger, had been the director in charge of the canal works in Panama.

For some time, Panama had disappeared from the Parisian conversations. At the end of 1893, the Republic had a new Chamber of Deputies, mostly right-wing. A major concern of the Deputies was the threat of anarchists' bomb explosions; there had never been so many bombs in such a short period of time
They were intended to destabilize the Republic.
On December 9, 1893, one of these anarchists, Auguste Vaillant, threw a bomb inside the Palace housing the Chamber of Deputies. Nobody was killed, but 50 people were wounded. Vaillant was arrested and executed on February 5, 1894.

On February 12, **1894**, as a protest against this execution, another anarchist, Emile Henry - who had already killed four people on November 5, 1892, without being caught - , set a bomb at the Café Terminus of the Saint Lazare Railway Station. Here, there was one fatality and 20 wounded. Henry was captured and executed on May 21, 1894.

The Deputies prepared a series of laws against the anarchists, who called them the "wicked laws"; these laws were intended to punish an association of evil-doers – *Association de Malfaiteurs.*

In this agitated climate, a bomb of a totally different nature exploded at Maurice's home. In the morning of April 24, 1894, he was surprised to receive a subpoena, simultaneously addressed to:
- Maurice Bunau-Varilla, 22 Avenue du Trocadero ;
- Auguste Artigue, 12 Place Vendome;
- Conrad Sonderegger, 30 rue de Gramont, where the headquarters of ASC were established;
They were the three shareholders of *Artigue, Sonderegger & Co.* - that we abbreviate ASC.
The letter asked for a devolution of the embezzled money, of which: "a provisional sum of 5 million francs should be paid up within 48 hours." (2) Nothing less!
The letter was signed by Mr. Lemarquis, representative of the small investors, and demanded that ASC reimbursed the money improperly received from the Company, for "unjustified profits and aimless collection of funds".
Lemarquis' logic was unquestionable. He was asking for five million francs, but how many more millions had been embezzled?

Appendix 1 provides the full detail of the indictment of Lemarquis, which we have found during our research in the National Archives in Roubaix - North of France - in the file numbered 7 AQ 22. (2) Here are a few of Lemarquis' charges against ASC:

- lost equipment	800,000 francs
- unjustified payments by the Company	697,249 francs
- unjustified move of one of the works' yard	1,105,000 francs
- advances for laying rail tracks - not done -	1,531,330 francs
- and many other charges - not detailed here,	1,414,691 francs
	--------------
all fully documented for a total of:	5,548,270 francs.

Lemarquis' letter surely caused quite a shock to Maurice!

Of course, B-V was not involved, because at the date of registration of ASC – summer of 1886 –, he was still an employee of the Lesseps Company and, as such, could not become one of the partners of the firm.

He had an indisputable alibi: when ASC started to work in Panama, B-V was their General Manager and had no financial responsibility.

As Lemarquis' letter stated rightly, only Maurice and his two associates, MM. Artigue and Sonderegger were suspects of embezzlement.

However, B-V felt as if he had been also accused and he could not accept the tarnishing of his reputation. He felt that he was equally responsible with his brother. After all, he was the father of the idea that led to the creation of ASC, at the suggestion of Charles de Lesseps. He had certainly contributed to set up the whole thing.

In his memoirs, written twenty years later, he mentioned: "the offer which my brother had repeatedly and generously made to share with me the profits he earned from the *Culebra Company* and that he largely attributed, perhaps not without any reason, to my technical knowledge." (7) Before they set up ASC, Maurice had invested his savings and made a large profit thanks to his brother's recommendations. They thought that such success could be duplicated with ASC.

We believe that the understanding that had always existed between the two brothers had just been extended when they had started their association in ASC. B-V had been very useful to his brother when he was General Manager of the Company in Panama and had logically received the fruit of his efforts. The millions earned by the Bunau-Varilla brothers in ASC represented certainly much more than B-V's remuneration as the head of the Company - 70,000 francs annually.

It is believed that B-V was so anxious to complete the Panama Canal and to dedicate this work to future generations, that he never imagined he would end up with such an enormous fortune, thanks to the efforts of Maurice, his brother, who managed the finances of ASC in Paris.

He must have had quite a surprise when he first realized the size of ASC's profit.

It is not necessary to comment in detail all the charges of Lemarquis against ASC, but let us just mention how some of these charges particularly offended B-V: "Monsieur Philippe Bunau-Varilla, former Division Engineer and Director of the Works, had filled many positions in the high management of the Company, which had allowed him to be fully informed on the conditions of execution of the task he was about to perform."(2) In a way, Lemarquis accused B-V of having been dishonest.

For B-V, it seemed a periphrasis meant to accuse him of cheating, of embezzlement, and we know that he hated this kind of accusations.

B-V considered himself as the most ethical of all engineers and to some extent, we are inclined to believe him.

He took personally Lemarquis' charges and reacted with the passion that we are already familiar with.

One day, called as a witness before the Commission of Enquiry, named by the French Parliament - chaired by Vallé -, B-V threatened to jump out of the window if anyone could bring him the evidence of the accusation: "Sir, we are here, if I am not mistaken on the third floor of the building. You may well believe that I have no intention whatever of committing suicide. Now, if you will produce the proof you speak of . . . I will undertake to leave this room by the window instead of by the door . . . When my examiner came back, his face was haggard." (7) There was no such proof.

B-V was not a liar, he was scrupulously honest and did not allow anyone to question it.

In his memoirs of 1913, B-V occulted his brother Maurice's reaction to Lemarquis' letter. We easily believe the revelations of Mouthon concerning Maurice's reaction at the receipt of Lemarquis' letter: he left for London to escape being interrogated by the Parliamentary Commission and delegated his defense to his brother.

This was confirmed by Vallé's report, which stated that : "In the absence of Maurice Bunau-Varilla, Philippe Bunau-Varilla will not answer to any question relative to the financial or political aspect of the contracts." (2)

B-V could have called an army of lawyers to defend ASC. He could easily have afforded it. But, he did not need to. He himself was worth more than all the lawyers of the world. Honored with a huge prestige as the young General Manager of the Company from 1885 to 1886, he himself dictated the response to the subpoena letter and attempted to negotiate with Lemarquis.

B-V was on good terms with Lemarquis, who recognized his reputation as an engineer, even in writing: "The technical skills and qualities of the directors of *Artigue, Sonderegger & Co.*, cannot be disputed, and so is their devotion to duty." (See Appendix 1)

However, without Maurice's presence in Paris, it was indeed difficult for B-V to defend his honorability.

We are left to imagine how lengthy and animated the negotiation between B-V and Lemarquis could have been, as there is no record of them. Four months had elapsed since Maurice received Lemarquis' letter and all parties remained anchored to their initial positions.

B-V denied all irregularity. "There is no trace of payments to the contractors outside of what was due on account of excavations made and of the stipulations contained in the contracts. There is no trace of any fraudulent understanding between contractors and members of the Board of the Company." (7)

He took the accusations very seriously and denied all of them by showing a great deal of arrogance. We encounter here another example of B-V's high self-esteem. He criticized the "frenzied search for culprits which was to besmear many of the most eminent citizens of France." (7)

As for Lemarquis, he claimed that his experts were correct. He explained that Flory - a member of Vallé's team - had audited all the Company's books and that his integrity could not be questioned.

Bouvier agreed that Flory's audit had been honest: "In a long and scrupulous analysis of the expenses allocated to the construction activities - 592 million francs - Flory had audited the sums spent by the Company and the sums received by the contractors in the Isthmus. The excess money paid to the contractors and remaining in their books as profit, amounted for five contractors to 85.6 million francs; the company of Gustave Eiffel had kept an illicit profit of 33 million francs," (14) and (2).

We found confirmation of the Bunau-Varilla brothers' fortune in the French Chamber of Deputies' report by Ernest Vallé, page 494, main report (2), which details ASC's and its associates' profits, composed of (quoted to the last "centime"):

- ASC's profit,
according to its balance sheet as of October 7, 1889: 7,390,668.92 francs
- fee by Eiffel Company for "common studies"   1,842,327.22 francs
                                                 ----
Consolidated profit of ASC   9,232,996.14 francs

- fee of 0.02 francs per cubic meter,
in favor of Maurice Bunau-Varilla: 594,336.95 francs
- salaries of the ASC associates: 1,750,000.00 francs

For a total of: 11,577,333.09 francs

It is difficult to assess with certainty the origin of the 0.02 franc per cubic meter fee received by Maurice. Vallé's report mentioned that Jacques de Reinach and the Senator/contractor Adrien Hébrard had each received 1.8 million francs from Eiffel. Reinach had "favored" Eiffel in the choice of a contractor to build the locks; Hébrard had "favored" Eiffel in contracts obtained before the canal - before 1880. It could well be that Maurice was receiving his share for a favor he did to Eiffel - for example, in preparing the locks' masonry.

B-V had full knowledge of Vallé's report, which is mentioned in his memoirs: "On the 4th of July 1893, the Commission of Inquiry of the Chamber of Deputies presented its report signed by Mr. Vallée (sic)." (7)

For obvious reasons, nothing else is mentioned in B-V's memoirs about the contents of Vallé's report. The origin and amount of the brothers' fortune was to remain confidential, . . . until today.

As we shall see later on, Maurice's share in ASC was 68%. We are now able to substantiate the exact figure of the Bunau-Varilla brothers' profit in ASC:

- 68% of 9.233 million francs:	6.278 million francs
- Fee in favor of Maurice:	0.594
- Salary of the Bunau-Varilla brothers: half of the 1.75 million francs (the Vallé report mentions erroneously 4 "associates")	0.875

For a total of:	7.747 million francs

It was extremely difficult for Lemarquis and his experts to prove the embezzlement, to demonstrate that the allocations did not correspond to any real excavation, but rather were related to the construction of useless railway tracks.

Would the increases in francs per cubic meter paid to the contractor ASC and re-negotiated by Maurice Bunau-Varilla suffice to explain the enormous profit?

Had B-V worked so efficiently that he managed to excavate a cubic meter in the Culebra Hill for only 60% of what the Company paid to ASC?

And what about the advances made to the contractors; did Maurice invest these sums wisely and made a huge profit?

Of course, none of these questions will ever have an answer.

B-V asked: "Has the company paid imaginary volumes? The answer is: all the excavated volumes had been compensated according to the existing contracts and according to the statements calculated under the orders and supervision of the directors of the Company, all registered French State engineers. These volumes had been controlled by the engineers of the Company."

And again: "The sincerity and scientific value of the documents established by the engineers and corroborated by the land surveys, are beyond reproach." (7)

We have already dealt with this question of cubic meters measurement. Technically, this was absolutely incontrovertible.

We are convinced that there never was any embezzlement, because B-V was too clever to stoop to fraud. He had only taken advantage of the situation to negotiate some contractual obligations that he would easily fulfill.

His brother Maurice was an experienced financial manager and transformed in a timely manner the advances received by ASC into fixed allocations. We have also to remember that he hedged the Culebra's contract, the most difficult part of the canal, with additional contracts in easier sectors.

As expected, Lemarquis could not find any transgression of the Company rules by B-V and ASC. Furthermore, it should be remembered that all the individual prices for the cubic meters had been set by the Company.

Did Maurice have enough influence on Charles de Lesseps to renegotiate them in favor of ASC?

B-V had been through a lot of calculations when he worked for the Company. He had certainly mastered well the contractual price figures.

However, Lemarquis insisted that: *"Artigue, Sonderegger & Co.* had received, when it amended its initial contracts with the Company, on the occasion of the change from a sea level to a lock canal, unjustified advantages, under the form of a contract termination indemnity, which advantages should not have been paid by the Company to ASC." (See text in Appendix 1)

Additionally, there had been a few unexplained errors: 800,000 francs in lost equipment; 1,105,000 francs in unjustified payments to a subcontractor, etc.

Whatever B-V may argue, the charges made by Lemarquis were unambiguous and overwhelming.

Lemarquis expressed some doubts about the regularity of ASC's work in Panama. These doubts came from the report issued by General Vallé - investigator for the Commission of Inquiry of the Chamber of Deputies - which indicated that: "The cubic meter price had been raised through a series of new contracts cleverly designed to allow ASC to reap serious advantages . . . Cash Advances had been converted into firm allocations for 8 million francs and indemnities for installation costs for 1.5 million francs. The Company thus spent 9.5 million francs, outside of written contracts and without any work in return." (2)

We know that Maurice could not be interrogated during the investigation of ASC, because he had fled to London. (Mouthon's book of 1910: "From Bluff to Blackmail", page 149.) Maurice - B-V's brother - had abandoned him, but the stratagem worked, as Maurice would not be interrogated at all.

After months of intense debate with Lemarquis, B-V and his brother Maurice were afraid that a possible condemnation could be near. They had no more high-placed supporters to defend them, as all their accomplices in the political scandal had been forced into retirement and the newly elected politicians had no desire to become involved into a "reborn" Panama affair.

B-V's memoirs, written in 1913, were completely silent about the origin of his fortune. This silence would prove very detrimental to B-V in the future, as everyone would wrongly assume that he was a "poor" civil engineer. In 1903, he would be accused of promoting the sale of the assets of the New Company to the United States, in order to sell his personal shares and make a profit out of it.

In most History books, B-V is represented as a "wicked speculator". This is inaccurate and unfair; however, without the knowledge of the origin of the Bunau-Varilla brothers, it was the historians' only possible explanation.

But it was obviously an incorrect reasoning, as the authors overlooked the fact that B-V had been a rich man since 1890.

Before revealing the results of ASC's trial, we should explain how the Bunau-Varilla brothers acquired some shares of what would be called the New Company.

B-V owned 0.8% of the capital of this New Company, while Maurice owned 2.3%.

Their involvements differed, because their shares came from two different transactions with Lemarquis.

Of the two brothers, it was Maurice who first became a shareholder of the New Company.

According to the trial, ASC was found guilty and convicted, but its punishment was lenient.

On August 14, 1894, a settlement was reached with Lemarquis, who "called for their financial assistance to revive the Company." (2)

It seems, from the documents found in the French Archives, that B-V himself had suggested such a compromise, - a letter from B-V to Lemarquis indicated such possible solution - (2) which seemed logical, as B-V would continue to show his persistence and never abandoned his childhood dream.

The settlement demanded that all the parties involved in the trial: contractors, bankers, syndicates of subscribers, and so on, subscribe shares in a New Company. This would have the effect of gathering funds, which would allow the work of the old Company to resume after eight years of idleness. It would enable the digging to continue in Panama and maybe help salvaging the canal.

Lemarquis reasoning was clever and simple. As the accused had received too much money from the Company, they had to give it back under the form of shares to found the New Company. It was a brilliant solution and it was unanimously adopted by the culprits, who would become share holders of the New Company..

There was no record that any of the people condemned ever went into appeal. All things considered, Maurice, the main shareholder of ASC and his associates Conrad and Sonderegger, were happy with the settlement.

The judgment asked the shareholders of ASC: "Maurice Bunau-Varilla, Auguste Artigue and Conrad Sonderegger to subscribe 22,000 shares worth 100 francs each in the capital of the New Company, for a total of 2.2 million francs, sum which shall be divided among the above named persons as ASC will decide." (2)

This was not a big enough sum to make a dent in the fortune of the Bunau-Varilla brothers. They managed to get out of trouble with a very small penalty, because their fine would be invested into the New Company.

Maurice had to subscribe to 15,000 shares of the New Company, at 100 francs each. He had to pay 1.5 million francs. (2)

We have here confirmation that the share owned by Maurice in ASC was: $1.5/2.2 = 68\%$.

The other partners, Artigue and Sonderegger must probably have owned 16% each.

Among the other contractors, we have to point out that Gustave Eiffel was condemned to "pay back" 5 million francs that he had supposedly received in excessive advances. Additionally Eiffel was asked to subscribe 10 million francs worth of shares of the New Company, which he did without difficulty, as he had pocketed a profit of 33 millions.

The New Company was created by the sum of such settlements. All parties involved were asked to contribute: Colombia - the country -, the banks, the members of the Board of the old Company, the contractors, the syndicate of investors and many others. The reader will recognize most of them.

Just a word about Hugo Oberndoerffer, a banker who had counseled Lesseps about the "lottery" scheme in 1887 and received 3.8 million francs, as his commission. He admitted having received such enormous sum for just a verbal advice. (2) It was another sign of the blind generosity of the Company.

The other parties, "subject to penalty", had been condemned to subscribe to the New Company with only a portion of their profits.

By such agreements, on October 24, 1894, the *Compagnie Nouvelle du Canal Interocéanique* - New Company for the Interoceanic Canal - was born. It received the assets of the old Company - *Compagnie Universelle du Canal Interocéanique de Panama*. It inherited a capital of 65 million francs, made of 650,000 shares of 100 francs each, the major part of this capital being brought by the "profiteers." (14)

Here is a list of the shareholders of this New Company: (14)

Colombia, the country	5 million francs
Crédit Lyonnais, Société Générale and CIC	10
Former Administrators of the Company:	
Demormandie, Blandelot and Hue -	8
Former Contractors working in Panama	
of which Artigue, Sonderegger and Co.	
for 2.2 and Eiffel for 10 -	15.6
Subscribers of the New Company	15.9
New subscribers, called the "optimists"	
- among them was B-V for 500,000 francs -	3.5
Hugo Oberndoerffer	3.8
Other syndicates	3.2

Capital of the New Company	65.0

It should be noted that the assets of the New Company did not include the shares of the Panama Railway Cy (PRR), still operating in Panama, but remaining under its New York administration.

Concerning the shareholders of the New Company, Bouvier commented that: "These subscriptions to the New Company shares, due to the settlements with Lemarquis, give an idea of the magnitude of the second scandal of Panama." (14) The banks, penalized for a sum of 10 million francs, had pocketed - according to Bouvier - 135 million francs in commission fees, just for having helped the Company to sell its bonds and shares.

Together with the former administrators of the Company, the banks and the contractors are what most English authors call the "penalty stockholders".

This settlement is quite surprising, considering that Lemarquis was supposed to represent the small investors. His remarkable stratagem had the effect of annihilating the 1,335 million francs subscribed by the small investors in the Company. These unlucky investors were replaced by a New Company owned by shareholders who had robbed the old Company.

This was totally unethical and unscrupulous!

The shares of the New Company were of course quoted in the Paris Bourse - from a low of 65 to a high of 150 francs. They would be the object of a huge speculation in 1903, when the New Company would be purchased by the United States.

One has surely noted with surprise that Eiffel and ASC shares added up to: 12.2 / 15.6 = 78% of the total of the contractors. Only 22% had been asked from the others: Baratoux, Jacob or Hawen, probably judged unworthy of a severe condemnation.

This proves that ASC was in the same boat than Eiffel, who had been condemned to two years in jail for breach of trust - although his sentence was thereafter overturned.

The company created by Maurice Bunau-Varilla was not completely free from guilt. We understand now why this was a good enough reason for B-V to omit this period from his memoirs.

Among the shareholders of the New Company, 3.5 million francs had been gathered spontaneously from various subscribers, called by B-V the "optimists", the few investors who still believed in the Panama Canal. Their detailed list is still unknown, but B-V told us in his memoirs that he had participated for a sum of half a million francs. He was more than ever convinced that the Interoceanic Canal would be completed in Panama, as he was well aware of the problems encountered by Americans in Nicaragua.

We shall find out about this in the next chapter.

Having subscribed voluntarily to the New Company, B-V explained that these 500,000 francs were the only shares he ever owned and that he, or any member of his family, never thought of speculating by reselling those shares. We can certainly believe him, as he did not need the money.

B-V believed that the canal could be "resurrected" - it was the title of a chapter in his 1913 memoirs. He wanted to help by investing this half million francs. This was the first time, but - as we shall see later - it would not be the last time that B-V invested part of his own fortune to help the Panama Canal.

To conclude on the subject of the Bunau-Varilla brothers' fortune, we have to add that it is quite easy to confirm the extent of B-V's personal fortune by a careful reading of his 1913 memoirs.

In 1903, the Panamanian insurgents asked him to provide 30 million francs ($ 6 million), which he found unnecessary and reduced back to a half million francs ($ 100,000).

B-V explained in his memoirs: "The idea that I could risk $ 100,000 from my private means to save the work of Panama. . . It is a small sum (sic) that I shall probably be able to borrow in a New York bank. . . I can make such a sacrifice as that, but I could not give $ 6 million." (7)

To sum up this chapter, which is the essence of this book, we can conclude that **the Bunau-Varilla brothers had earned a profit of about 8 million francs** between 1886 and 1889.

How much of these 8 million francs had Maurice allocated to his brother? This has remained the secret of the brothers and it certainly disappeared with them.

However a letter written by B-V to his brother indicates that: "The project you nourished offered me a participation with equal advantages to yours," (letter of June 5, 1905, (2)) and, although it was related to their participation in the newspaper *Le Matin,* it could imply that logically the brothers had always shared their earnings on a 50/50 basis.

It is very likely that B-V, who could not become a shareholder of ASC - because he still was employed by the Lesseps Company at the time ASC was founded -, had benefited from a tacit agreement with his brother.

B-V was not penniless. He had earned as Section Manager and General Manager of the Company between October 1884 and August 1886 a salary of 70,000 to 100,000 francs per year. It is more likely that he had trusted his brother to invest this money into ASC.

Their huge earnings can also be confirmed by looking at the expenses of the brothers during the years following 1889.

B-V bought for his family a luxurious mansion near the Arc de Triomphe de l'Etoile in a newly developed part of Paris: 53 Avenue d'Iéna, which was worth about a million francs. He would lead the life of a rich man, with servants, his own secretary - Ms. Dallet, hired in 1894 and who served B-V up to his death in 1940 -, extensive traveling, etc. His travel expenses, mostly related to his lobbying in the Panama Canal, are detailed in Appendix 3 and amounted to a million francs.

The brothers purchased shares in a newspaper called *Le Matin,* for about 3 million francs. Why? Pinsolle explained that : "Nothing predestined Maurice to manage a newspaper. He was not an editor, nor was he involved in politics, nor was he a writer; he came from behind the scenes - the outer market; Maurice clearly saw an interest in owning a newspaper, a vector for defense and attack, in order to preserve a fortune made too quickly." (30) Pinsolle also believed that Maurice needed to invest his money as an insurance against the accusations that he feared would be generated by ASC's huge profit. We shall see that there were other motivations.

Additionally, the brothers bought innumerable real estate properties.

As it would be too long to quote them here, a detailed list of the expenses/acquisitions of the two brothers is shown in Appendix 5.

The lawsuit against ASC was finally closed on November 19, 1894.

A document of the Roubaix Archives indicates that:

Pierre Dominique Parodi - whose widow was buried in Maurice's burial vault; he was certainly one of his intimate friends -, residing 95 Av. Kléber, liquidator of ASC, declared that he received from the Company a sum of 1,921,004 francs in settlement of all accounts.

This was, according to the August 14, 1894 deal with Lemarquis, the sum being represented by 15,576 lottery bonds, worth 122.68 francs each. (2)

These bonds had been purchased in 1888 at 360 francs each. Their value was 122.68 francs at the end of 1894, a sign that there was still hope for the investors when the New Company was formed.

Finally, we observe that ASC has been treated quite generously in this trial.

Instead of paying back the 5.5 million francs requested by Lemarquis, the settlement had cost ASC:

Shares of the New Company:	2.2 million francs
Settlement of all accounts	-1.9 million francs
a bottom line of only	300.000 francs ! !

ASC had been treated with much clemency. Its fine was low compared to the embezzlement described in Lemarquis' letter.

Would this be the subject of a third scandal? That of the pillaging of the Company by its contractors. We have described in detail the case of ASC. It would be interesting to investigate Eiffel's case.

Bouvier concluded rightly: "The Panama scandal could not have led to the condemnation of the free enterprise . . . Governments never die from their scandals. They die from their inconsistencies." (14)

16

MEANWHILE IN NICARAGUA . . .

While the French had failed to complete the work in Panama and were busy bringing the culprits to trial and punishing them for their crimes, the Americans were still focused on their enterprise, which was to build a canal in Nicaragua.

Curiously, they acted as if the French had never done any work in Panama. It was not difficult to explain why: the French failure had totally discredited Panama in the American public opinion.

We have seen how the MCCN - Maritime Canal Company of Nicaragua -, with a capital of $ 100 million, had been created at the beginning of 1889. Its major shareholder was J. P. Morgan - not related to John Tyler Morgan, the Alabama Senator -, a banker, who was so rich that he often loaned money to the Government.

We notice that the MCCN budget, initially calculated for the canal in Nicaragua, was significantly higher than that of the French New Company ($ 100 million = 500 million francs, almost ten times the 65 million francs of the New Company).

Some references indicated that the MCCN had been authorized to collect up to $ 150 million in bonds. (21) It was the sign that Americans had made a good start and had launched their project without any delay.

In June 1889, the MCCN revised its original studies and made important changes. In particular, they planned to build several artificial lakes on the Atlantic Ocean side and added the Flor lock (on the Isthmus of Rivas, on the Pacific Ocean side), designed to flood the Rio Grande valley.

This looked very much like the scheme recommended by B-V for Panama: first, a series of lakes would be established and second, floating dredges would operate on these lakes. B-V had visited Nicaragua at the beginning of 1889. Could he have suggested this scheme to the Americans?

The initial planning stage went well. Therefore, everything was ready to start effectively. Work began on October 9, 1889 and in a few months, saw the completion of an impressive list of achievements:
- a seawall was built in San Juan del Norte on the Atlantic Ocean, a shallow harbor, which needed to be equipped to receive dredges and ships carrying heavy materials,
- the access to San Juan del Norte's harbor was enlarged by dredging,
- warehouses were erected in San Juan del Norte,
- dwellings for the workers were constructed, along the mouth of the Rio San Juan,
- a telegraph line was laid between San Juan del Norte and the North American continent,
- the Macucha rapids on the Rio San Juan were split by dynamite to mark the trace of the future canal,
- an 11-mile long railroad was built along the proposed route. (21)

Americans were active on all fronts.
There were few problems reported and, unlike in Panama, there was absolutely no mention of any casualty caused by deadly fevers.
It seems possible that Jamaican workers – idle since mid-89 – had come to Nicaragua, looking for work. In addition, we have already mentioned (page 116) that many of the dredges came from Panama, where the New Company did not need them. With all these resources dedicated to Nicaragua, the project looked well launched. All the efforts that once were put in Panama had been shifted to Nicaragua.

All went so well in Nicaragua that President Benjamin Harrison, in his annual message to Congress, on December 9, 1889, mentioned with pleasure a report from the *Maritime Canal Company of Nicaragua* indicating that during the first year of construction, a costly but necessary preparation work has been successfully started: warehouses, railroads, harbors, excavations, and so on.

Harrison praised Senator John Tyler Morgan who supported the project in Washington. He also indicated that Congress should consider giving the Government's guarantee to the MCCN's stocks.

The following year, 1890, went almost in euphoria. Excavations had started and progressed well. The country was spared by fevers and workers were working happily.

However, towards the end of the year, the MCCN would be slowly running out of money; the Government had been reluctant to give its guarantee, which chilled the investors' enthusiasm.

In January 1891, Ohio Senator, John Sherman, who was also the President of the *Foreign Relations Committee*, tried to untie the deadlock by proposing a new law to give the Government's guarantee to MCCN's assets. But, a consensus could not be reached within the Senate, because the *Clayton-Bulwer* treaty still obliged the United States to act jointly with Great Britain, which deterred some Senators from endorsing such a law.

On the other hand, despite the Senate's procrastination, the American public was showing its enthusiasm for the project. In December 1891, the New York Chamber of Commerce passed a resolution exhorting the Government to approve Sherman's proposal. The MCCN stockholders held various meetings across the country: in Saint Louis - June 1892 - and in New Orleans - November 1892. This last meeting gathered a crowd of 600 delegates from all States, proof that the MCCN project generated a lot of enthusiasm.

Such fervor of the American public for Nicaragua put some pressure on Congress, where Senator Morgan remained the active leader of the project.
But again, Congress was slow to act: in December 1892, Sherman finalized his bill, which provided for the Government to give its guarantee to the capital invested in the MCCN, up to $ 80 million.

Hiram Hitchcock, the new President of the Maritime Canal Company of Nicaragua - he had replaced James Roosevelt -, wrote in his annual report for 1892 that the MCCN had already spent a sum of $ 4.8 million (25 million francs) for the work it did in Nicaragua and that it had sold bonds for an amount of $ 6.9 million. The campaign of the MCCN across the United States had borne some fruit.

Of course, these amounts were not as large as the Lesseps' spending in Panama - they had been of the order of 125 million francs a year -, but they represented some visible progress on the ground of Nicaragua.

Unfortunately, these efforts were not to last.

It indeed seemed that bad luck was plaguing all the canal projects in Central America.

Just when the MCCN would get near to gathering enough capital to continue working in Nicaragua, a huge monetary crisis stopped the Senate from voting Sherman's proposal.

On May 3, 1893, the most severe economic crisis since the birth of the United States hit the New York Stock Exchange. This crisis, known as the "1893 Panic", was like an anticipation of what would happen in 1929 - or even in 2008.

Thousand of banks were forced to closed their doors; unemployment rocketed from 4 to 12% and remained high for the following 5 years, even causing the western states expansion to slow down. It was indeed a very serious economic downturn in the United States.

Consequently, all the activities of the MCCN came to a sudden stop.

The 1893 Panic, as this financial crash was called, was caused by the combined effects of speculation, ignorance and rigid laws, which seems worth to be related here in some detail.

At the beginning of the 19th Century, the American currency, the dollar, was backed by the Government with gold and silver reserves. For decades, this twofold system functioned quite well, with a ratio between gold and silver set at 15. Little by little, with the abundant production in the silver mines, this ratio turned to the advantage of gold, and rose to 15½. It thus became tempting to sell silver, because the Government was purchasing it at a fixed price, above its market value.

In 1834, Congress decreed a ratio of 16, thinking it would quench the speculation on silver. However, this ratio proved a little too high and caused people to sell their gold to Uncle Sam. After 1870, the silver's market price went further down, at times reaching 18¼ times less than gold.

Consequently, people were again happy to sell their silver to the Government for 1/16th of the price of gold.

Despite the *Sherman Silver Purchase Act* of 1890, which allowed the Government to purchase the entire production of the silver mines, things deteriorated again.

Isn't it a curious coincidence that it was the same John Sherman who pushed for the Nicaragua project and, who, by his Act, caused its collapse?

While the United States hesitated between silver and gold, to back up their dollar currency, most European countries had already adopted the gold standard.

To crown this series of misfortunes, the balance between gold and silver continued to remain very unstable. An abundant supply of silver caused its price to go down even further with respect to gold. The Government could not buy back all that silver and its gold reserves became almost exhausted.

The Banks had to call back their loans in gold and the weakest companies declared bankrupt, followed by the strongest ones. This caused a complete collapse of the banking system.

On May 3, 1893, a financial crash occurred.

On August 28, the *Sherman Silver Purchase Act* was repealed.

On August 30, the MCCN declared itself bankrupt.

The end of the MCCN also meant the end of all contractors' work in Nicaragua.

Some warehouses, railroads, sea jetties and accesses to the harbors were really noticeable in the scenery, but very little had been done in terms of earth excavation.

However, one source mentioned a trench, 1,000 meters long, 6 meters deep and 100 meters wide, the start of a canal.

Another source mentioned that deforestation had been done along a 12-kilometer tract and that an eighteen-kilometer long railway and a jetty in San Juan del Norte had been built. (21)

We shall see later that the budget estimates for the Nicaraguan canal would be around $ 120 to 200 million. At this stage, the MCCN has thus done about 5% of the task.

Despite this setback, Senator John Tyler Morgan - a Democrat - did not stop his lobbying action. This proved increasingly difficult, as the Democrats were thought to be responsible for the 1893 crisis and had lost most of their political influence.

The Republicans, headed by William McKinley would later win the 1896 elections, but John Tyler Morgan would nevertheless be re-elected, despite being a Democrat. He was extremely popular in Alabama and his fame as a former general of the Confederacy was still attracting him much respect.

The failure of the MCCN in 1893 did not discourage the American investors. On the contrary, it bolstered their determination and they were soon ready to start again.

In the meantime, in 1894, President Zelaya of Nicaragua took control of the Mosquito Coast by force, dismantling the British protectorate. At the time, Great Britain did not wish to go to war for such a small territory, so much distant from the British Isles, and it soon recognized Nicaragua's sovereignty over the area.

This move simplified the access to the future American Canal, its entry port on the Atlantic Ocean, San Juan del Norte, the main city of this Mosquito Coast; it had now escaped from British control.

However, the Americans had to wait until April 1895, when President Cleveland gave the project a new start by creating the *Nicaragua Canal Board*, under the authority of Colonel William Ludlow, with the assistance of two engineers, one being a specialist in sea projects - Mordecai Endicott - and the other in civil works - Alfred Noble.

This Board was designated as the *Ludlow Commission*.

In October 1895, the *Ludlow Commission* issued a report in which the choice of Nicaragua was not questioned, but Menocal's proposed route had been slightly modified to take into account several options.

On the Atlantic side, from the Ocean to Lake Nicaragua, 32 meters in elevation, the Commission recommended three possibilities:
  – Bluefields to Rio Escondido,
  – Punta Gorda to Rio Punta Gorda,
  – San Juan del Norte to Rio San Juan - this had been the route recommended by Menocal.

On the Pacific side, the canal would cross the Isthmus of Rivas at an altitude of 50 meters above sea level - much easier to dig than the 120 meters of the Culebra Hill in Panama.

The Commission estimated the cost of the canal at $ 133 million.

In its report, the *Ludlow Commission* did not mention Panama at all.

The *Ludlow Commission's* report was not followed by any quick action. Although the United States were slowly recovering from 1893 crisis, investors could not be found and the Government preferred to continue improving the studies.

After two years of abandonment, newly elected President William McKinley gave a new momentum to the project.

In July 1897, he created the *Nicaragua Canal Commission*, often designated by the name of his President John Walker. Its members were eminent engineers: Professor Aupt, University of Pennsylvania, Carter and Hains, Heads of the Corps of Army Engineers.

This "first" *Walker Commission* worked from December 1897 to February 1899.

Its report, issued in March 1899, finalized the route for the canal and estimated its cost to $ 118 million, slightly less than the *Ludlow Commission's* estimate.

It is remarkable that still nowadays more studies often lead to a lesser cost.

As in the earlier projects, the canal route followed the Rio San Juan that would be dredged and equipped with 6 locks. Crossing Lake Nicaragua, the route sloped down to the Pacific Ocean.

The total length of the canal would be 220 kilometers, its depth 10 meters and its width from 50 to 100 meters.

We have to stop here to note that the estimates of the Nicaragua Canal quoted above - $ 133 for Ludlow and $ 118 million for Walker -, were equivalent to about 550/650 million francs, about half of what the French had already spent in Panama.

By design, Nicaragua was coming out much cheaper than Panama.

While the *Walker Commission* was busy, in May 1898, the Senate voted a resolution authorizing the MCCN - out of business since the 1893 crisis - to sell its assets, which consisted of the concession from the Nicaraguan Government and the preliminary work done. In June, the MCCN asked for a selling price of $ 5.5 million. John Tyler Morgan immediately posted a motion before the Senate, recommending that the Government be the buyer.

Morgan was very perseverant, as his proposals had been adjourned many times. However, it would not be the case for this particular one.

Suddenly, the Government was ready to act and providentially a favorable event would help. This was an extraordinary occurrence, which took place while the *Walker Commission* was still elaborating its studies.

This event would forever embed in American minds the idea of their own Interoceanic Canal. It would accelerate the Nicaragua project and compel the Government to take action.

This event would "resuscitate" Nicaragua.

In Cuba, an intensive war of independence against the Spanish rule had started in 1895 and would cause 200,000 casualties. Suddenly, on February 1898, this war took a complete new turn.

The U. S. cruiser *Maine,* brought in Havana's harbor to protect American interests on the Island, was blown up by a mine and sunk.

260 marines were killed. This loss was unacceptable for the young American nation, which was on the verge of becoming a world power. On April 25, 1898, the United States declared war to Spain, the owner of the Island since 1492, when it was discovered by Christopher Columbus.

In 1898, the American war fleet was only six ships strong. The war against Spain had the effect of calling most of them away from Cuba - except for the *Maine* -, to the Philippines, Guam, or elsewhere in the Pacific Ocean.

There was no other American ship than the *USS Maine* in the Atlantic Ocean, the closest available ship being the *USS Oregon,* moored in San Francisco.

To reach Cuba, the *Oregon* sailed for 67 days, around Cape Horn, about 12,130 nautical miles between San Francisco and Cuba. This fight against time was exacerbated by the American press.

The newspapers explained that the *Oregon* 's voyage through Panama - 5,260 nautical miles - or through Nicaragua - 4,660 nautical miles -, if they had been built at that time, would have reduced its travel time by 60 to 65%, bringing it from 65-70 days to 20-25 days.

At about the same period in time, another incident would catch the attention of the Government and a strategy of having a U.S. war fleet in both oceans with a canal joining them would start to make sense. During this Spanish/American war, "the Spanish flotilla dispatched from Spain to the Philippines, . . . was held up by the Suez Canal authorities for several days. Ten years earlier, Britain had signed the Constantinople Convention, declaring Suez open to ships of all nations in war and in peace, but it had shown that a powerful nation could bend such a promise, if it chose. The lesson was not lost in Washington." (20)

The sinking of the *Maine* convinced the Government to quickly build a war fleet worthy of its ambitions of becoming a major world power.

Which it did: from 6 in 1898, the number of U.S. Navy cruisers rose to 25 in 1910 and 45 in 1920.

To complement this strategy, it would also be necessary to also build an Interoceanic Canal in Central America, in order to optimize the war fleet distribution in both Oceans.

This general idea had already been active for some time, but the French failure in Panama and the 1893 crisis had prevented it from materializing. The Havana disaster happened *à propos* to make the Canal of Nicaragua a national priority.

The war against Spain absorbed all the attention of Congress. As a consequence, Nicaragua was momentarily put on the back burner.

The United States won the war and a treaty of peace was signed with Spain on December 10, 1898.

President McKinley, in his annual address to Congress in December 1898 declared: "A question of the highest importance for our country is to build a large scale commercial route between the Atlantic and the Pacific Oceans, known as the Nicaragua Canal." (16)

A year after the Cuban incident, in January 1899, the Senate approved - by 48 votes against 6 - Morgan's proposal to have the Government acquire the MCCN for $ 5.5 million.
Again, this time, Panama was not mentioned at all.

At the beginning of 1899, at the dawn of the 20th Century, Morgan and Walker still believed that their canal project would be built in Nicaragua.

Meanwhile in France, a 41 year old civil engineer still believed that the Panama venture, although abandoned by all, was not dead.
Thanks to B-V's determination, the struggle between Nicaragua and Panama would continue, fiercer than ever.

17

WHO WANTED TO PURCHASE THE FRENCH ASSETS ?

We have seen that in 1894, B-V became an "optimist" shareholder of the New Company, founded thanks to Lemarquis - the representative of the small shareholders. B-V had invested half a million francs in the New Company (see page 145). He had not lost the hope to revive Panama and still wanted to salvage what was left of the excavations of the French Company in the Isthmus.

Naturally, for this purpose, he needed to find some rich investors that he was confident to find in the United States, a fast developing country, soon to become the first world power. How could he find them? The only American B-V knew was John Bigelow.

We have already seen in which circumstances B-V had met John Bigelow, in Panama, in 1886. Since that time, he had cultivated this "American connection". Both men met again, unexpectedly at a dinner given by Charles de Lesseps, in Paris in 1887, and they had become very close. The relationship between these two men, both exceptional personalities, would become crucial in shaping up the victory of Panama.

They got along so well that during the winter 1888/1889, when B-V traveled back from Panama to France, he stopped in New York to visit his friend. They discussed the fate of the moribund French Canal.

With his usual strength of conviction, B-V persuaded Bigelow that Panama would be worth being achieved. Bigelow was glad that B-V was eager to continue promoting Panama and advised him to write a book to express his ideas in full detail. As we have already mentioned, B-V published "Panama. Past. Present. Future", (4) in 1892.

But, who was exactly John Bigelow?

John Bigelow held an eminent place in the American society.

Born near New York on January 25, 1817, of a wealthy family, he would live to be 84 years old and remained active until his death on December 19, 1911. After studying law, he joined the New York bar and from 1848 to 1861 worked with the *New York Evening Post*, of which he became a major stockholder. There, he held assets of $ 175,000 and received a salary of $ 25,000 a year. Quite a wealthy man!

In 1861, President Abraham Lincoln named him General Consul in Paris and, four years later, still in Paris, he served as the American Plenipotentiary Ambassador until 1867. While he filled these functions, Bigelow met most of the influential people in France and in Europe. He was said to have played an important role in avoiding a formal French support for the Southern Confederacy and to have advised Napoleon the Third in his Mexican venture.

Bigelow was also a man of *belles-lettres*; having found the original manuscript of the diary of Benjamin Franklin in a Paris bookshop, he published in New York in 1868, the *Autobiography of Benjamin Franklin*.

Another of his books, *France and the Confederate Navy*, published in 1888, exhibited a significant historical work.

In 1850, he married Jane Tunis Poultney. They had four children: two sons John and Poultney and two daughters Grace and Jenny. B-V was about the same age as Bigelow's children and became like another son to him.

While Bigelow was ambassador in Paris, his secretary was John Hay, who had been President Lincoln's personal assistant-secretary. Hay would remain very close to Bigelow and when he became Secretary of State, he would naturally welcome B-V as a friend.

No wonder that they signed the *Hay/Bunau-Varilla* treaty in only four days!

When B-V returned from Panama on February 20, 1889, he married Anne Gisèle Sonia de Brunhoff, (2) that everybody called "Ida". Maurice had certainly much to do with this marriage. Did he arrange it? Most probably, as Ida was the young sister of Sophie, Maurice's wife!

Philippe and Ida had a son, Etienne, born in May 1890 and a daughter, Giselle born in 1892.

In July 1890, B-V visited once more his friend Bigelow in New York, the first of what would become a series of regular summer visits. In 1890, at 73, Bigelow had no longer an official status. His major occupation was the development of the New York Public Library, which would be decided in 1902 and inaugurated in 1911. He also continued to write history books, which were well received.

By the end of century, in his seventies, Bigelow had become "an eminent man; he was termed "grand old man of America" or "first citizen of New York". (6) Although Bigelow was out of the political mainstream, he remained an extremely influential person and his many contacts in the political circles would help B-V convince Americans to continue the work started by Ferdinand de Lesseps in Panama and to discard the Nicaragua project.

Convinced of Panama's superiority over Nicaragua, Bigelow encouraged B-V to ardently pursue all matters concerning the Panama Canal.

B-V did that, but it was not a full time job. Laden with energy, but also compassionate, B-V wanted to keep busy "his engineers" (7), the survivors of the Panama ordeal. He created a kind of engineering office to provide a job to the engineers he had met in Panama or to those who helped him in running ASC and who had become idle since the failure of the Company. These engineers worked on different projects, in which the Bunau-Varilla brothers had invested. Some of these projects are worth being mentioned here.

One of these projects took place between 1890 and 1894. B-V was "President and Chief Engineer of the company building the Western Spanish Railroad. This was the line which permitted . . . to establish a railroad communication between Seville and Salamanca." (11) B-V was one of the major shareholders, with his brother Maurice, Antonio Blasto and Alfred Charles Edwards.

B-V also was General Manager of the *Compagnie des Chemins de Fer de Galicie*, while Lefèvre, a graduate from *École Centrale des Arts et Manufactures*, was Operations Manager.

Later, in 1902, the Bunau-Varilla brothers would manage the railroad they had built, under the *Compañia de Explotación de los Ferrocarriles de Madrid a Caceres y Portugal*.

In 1891, B-V was also a Member of the Board of the *Compagnie du Katanga*, where he had "an interest, as Director of the Belgian Congo Railway, in the building of the first railway from the ocean to the heart of Equatorial Africa," (11) position that brought him yearly the nice salary of 30,000 francs. His assistant was Georges Espanet, a graduate of Polytechnique, who would later build the Congo RailRoad, "the great creation of Colonel Thys". (7)

In 1902, his brother Maurice became a major shareholder and member of the Board of the *Compagnie du Katanga*, where he sat with B-V's Belgian friends: Despret, de Decker, Thys, d'Oultremont, Goffinet, Oppenheim, Philippson, Lambert, etc. (From Mouthon's book: "The Great Campaigns of *Le Matin*", 1910, where is also related the scandal caused by Maurice's blackmailing the King of Belgium, Léopold the Second.)

At the time, the brothers were still closely associated in the same businesses.

About those projects, B-V thought that "those two enterprises - he meant Spain and Congo - were not linked, as the other chapters of my career were, to facts of national and international importance." (11) He seemed to regret that he could not dedicate his entire time to Panama.

To evaluate potential investments, B-V traveled extensively: Mexico, Portugal, Russia, Venezuela and others.

He was lucky to escape the accidents, which plagued the modern passenger ships. The Panamanian engineer, Pedro Sosa - and his son -, disappeared in the shipwreck of the *Bourgogne* - 500 casualties - when it hit another transatlantic liner, the *Cromartyshire,* a few miles offshore of New York City, on July 2, 1898.

In addition to all this, B-V's engineering office probably participated in the construction of the Paris *Metropolitain* - the subway. His friend Bienvenüe, a graduate of Polytechnique may have asked for his help. The Metro construction started in October 1898, a couple of years before B-V became - once again - absorbed full time by the Panama project.

While he was busy running his engineering projects, B-V still had time to get involved in other matters. Among these unusual events, which were quite foreign to the Panama Canal matter, B-V's involvement in the Dreyfus' affair is worth being briefly mentioned here.

At the end of 1890, when B-V was a busy international contractor/investor, he unexpectedly met, walking "one day, on the Avenue Montaigne" (11) Alfred Dreyfus, an old companion from Polytechnique, now a Captain in the French Artillery. He recalled him as: "a Hebrew, one of those that Mother Nature has loaded with the ugly features of the race. . . he was a comrade who had nothing bad about him to distinguish him from the others, apart from his features. . . Our relations were not close at the École Polytechnique and ceased together when we left it." (11) Dreyfus wanted to leave the French Army and took advantage of his meeting with B-V to solicit a job in his engineering office. Soon after their meeting, he wrote to B-V to ask him a series of question about "the exploitation of the French Congo simultaneously with that of the Belgian Congo". Unfortunately, B-V "was obliged to go suddenly to Mexico. . . . and that is why the letter slipped from his memory." (11)

Having completely "forgotten" Dreyfus' letter, B-V would make up for this, six years later, in 1896, when he exhibited Dreyfus' hand-written letter, to prove him not guilty of spying. His accuser had forged his handwriting.

B-V concluded that "Dreyfus had been a victim of his very Semitic features and of the anti-Semitic fury that had been unchained in France."(11)

Although the role played by the Bunau-Varilla brothers in the Dreyfus affair was never decisive, they contributed somewhat to Dreyfus' rehabilitation. Maurice published on November 10, 1896, in his newspaper *Le Matin*, a facsimile of the *bordereau* that was wrongly attributed to Dreyfus and had condemned him to be deported to Guyana Devil's Island, on motive of spying for the account of the Germans. By comparing the handwriting of this *bordereau* with Dreyfus' letter to B-V, the evidence was out that: "the two documents had not been written by the same man." (11)

B-V seemed here to capture some of the glory from all those who contributed to clear Dreyfus of his charges. Indeed, Dreyfus' letter to B-V was not the only evidence that cleared Dreyfus of his accusations, but "its publication caused a series of events, which shook the world and which ended with the rehabilitation of Captain Dreyfus in July 1906." (11)

B-V treated the subject extensively in his memoirs - the entire chapter 8, nine pages long - and believed that "all the credit for this great act of justice was due to my brother."(11)

This was another example of B-V manipulating events to make them appear in sync with his narration.

On March 20, 1892, B-V published: *Panama, Le Passé, Le Présent, L'Avenir*, (5) (Panama. Past. Present. Future.), a book laden with drawings and pictures - in color! It was the masterpiece of a civil engineer, describing in detail how the Panama Canal should be completed. Published at a time when the trial of the Company occupied all the minds in Paris, it did not receive much attention. Very few copies were sold. In the mind of the people, Panama was dead and it was out of the question to invest in it again.

B-V sent copies of his book to all the eminent members of the Parisian political and financial circles. Unfortunately, it did not raise their interest.

However, in the future, this book would prove a useful reference to B-V in his campaigns to promote the Canal of Panama. He would give a copy to all prospective lobbyists or buyers.

After trying to convince people to revive the Panama project by publishing a book, B-V looked for some further support among the French politicians. He found it in Auguste Laurent Burdeau, a graduate of the *École Normale Supérieure*, eight years older than B-V, "intellectually superior", who flattered B-V, when he saw in him "the Bonaparte of the engineers". (7)

Unfortunately, B-V did not make the perfect choice in recruiting the services of Burdeau, because, as many of his colleagues of the Chamber of Deputies, he would later be accused to have been a "checkard".

Drumont, who was still seething in his newspaper *La Libre Parole*, claimed that Burdeau was an insignificant person who did not even write the report he published about the *Banque de France*, "but only did reproduce the opinion of the banker Mr. de Rothschild." (4)

To please B-V, Burdeau quitted his political career - he had been Minister and produced reports for the Government about social subjects. He now worked for B-V towards the revival of the Panama project. When he started his new assignment, Burdeau looked for support from the members of the French Government, but Panama had had such bad press that he could not find any backers in the political world.

Let us turn now to Maurice's activities during this time.

One can read in the Roubaix Archives a document from the Paris Mortgage Service (2), dated October 13, 1893, indicating that Maurice Jules Bunau-Varilla, owner of various properties in the 16th ward of Paris, had subscribed a mortgage worth 420,000 francs. This document showed two things:

- Firstly, that Maurice had invested in the Parisian real estate the profit he had made with ASC in Panama. He had mainly bought properties in the 16th ward of Paris, which was in full development (see the list of Maurice's real estate properties in Appendix 5). Apart from the Stock Market - Bourse -, investing in real estate was extremely popular because it produced steady rents.
- Secondly, this document was a proof of Maurice's diversification of his investments. By mortgaging his properties, he could purchase shares in the well-known Parisian newspaper *Le Matin*, which had been founded as a limited liability society on June 21, 1884. He had been convinced to invest in *Le Matin* by his friend Pierre-Dominique Parodi - whom we have already met as being the liquidator of ASC -, who was a member of the newspaper's board. Maurice at first purchased 300,000 francs worth of shares, which was really a small sum compared to the millions he had pocketed with ASC.

Would Maurice have imagined, at the time, where this small investment would lead him? We shall see how he brought *Le Matin* to be the second largest Parisian newspapers, although he never wrote one line in it. (30)

In one of B-V's books, we can read that a newspaper like *L'Eclair* was worth at the time 1.5 million francs. (7) *Le Matin* was worth even more because it had a larger circulation. Its owner, Poidatz - who owned 58% of the shares - estimated the total value of the newspaper to 6 million francs in 1897. (2)

We shall see later that Maurice will invest a total of more than 3 million francs in shares of *Le Matin*.

Le Matin's format had been modified in 1890, when it went from two to six pages and tried to imitate the American newspapers by publishing many sensational events, inquiries, investigations and extensive reports on exotic subjects. In addition, it sold cheaply at 5 centimes of a franc, the price of all popular newspapers, because its major source of revenues came from publicity.

Now that he had won a fortune in Panama, Maurice was hungry for more power. Purchasing additional shares in *Le Matin* would be his next move.

As for B-V, he followed his brother by investing on an equal basis, but he never took - or was never allowed to take - any part in running the newspaper's business. This is confirmed in his memoirs, where he wrote: "The newspaper of my brother Maurice." (7)

It is certain, however, that when Maurice started buying shares of *Le Matin* in 1894, he had found his aim in life, and would continue to pursue it by purchasing more shares, until he would take total control of the newspaper. In 1896, Maurice was "Political Director" of *Le Matin* and Poidatz was "Chief Editor". (30)

On December 28, 1899, Maurice was admitted as a member of the Board of *Le Matin*. Aside from being one of the most successful editors of the newspaper, Maurice - together with his brother B-V - was an important shareholder.

On December 23, 1901, he would be elected President of the Board, but Maurice Poidatz was still at the time the majority owner.

Under Maurice's strong hand, *Le Matin's* circulation climbed from a few 50,000 in 1890 to 285,000 in 1902 and reached a peak of 1.6 million copies during WWI (1914 to 1918).

Le Matin would become the second largest of France's newspapers, smaller than *Le Petit Parisien*, but larger than *Le Petit Journal* or *Le Journal*.

In 1905, the major shareholder of *Le Matin,* Henry Poidatz, died. Maurice - together with B-V, on a 50/50 basis - , had previously concluded a deal to purchase his shares, in a timely manner. The brothers progressively increased their ownership from 30 to 92 percent - Maurice would own 62% and B-V 30%. (30)

It is not easy - for us, common people - to imagine the enormous fortune that Maurice accumulated. He had wisely invested his profit made in Panama - the 8 million francs, which he shared with his brother B-V-, and had become a major player in the Parisian press. In 1910, Mouthon estimated that Maurice had a wealth of 50 million francs. Later, in the 1920s, his fortune probably peaked in the hundreds of million francs, one of the largest in France.

Maurice's increase in power and domination of the Parisian social life did not go without a fall into the depravity of the time: corruption. During the period between World Wars, 1919 to 1939, the French press was considered by all serious authors as the most venal in Europe. *Le Matin* made no exception; it was considered the most venal of all Parisian newspapers.

Which did not go without lawsuits and condemnations, but it did not stop the paper from being extremely aggressive towards its enemies.

It unearthed many scandals, among which was a crusade against King Leopold of Belgium, who owned the Belgian Congo - yes, the King personally owned the entire Congo territory. In 1904, the King wanted to change the rules governing the concession of the Belgian Congo Railroad, where the Bunau-Varilla brothers had invested. A few articles in *Le Matin*, some of them extremely offensive, similar to a blackmailing endeavor, were successful in stopping the King's initiative and in salvaging the brother's money.

Many celebrities worked for *Le Matin*. Maurice was an influent man in the French politics. He was a close friend of Aristide Briand - who served as French Prime Minister eleven times from 1909 to 1929 - and of Raymond Poincaré - the French Republic's President from 1913 to 1920.

His power was enormous and, consequently, he had many enemies.

To emphasize Maurice's important role in the spirit of the *Belle Epoque*, as the turn of the 19th Century was named, here are a few of the titles that used to qualify Maurice in the Parisian spheres:

- The wealthy owner of *Le Matin*, one of the richest citizens of France,
- Magnate of the press, a strong personality, at the edge of megalomania,
- A tyrant, swelling with the gold he brought from the works of Panama,
- "He had some influence on the awarding of prizes and decorations connected with the Paris Exposition", noted an American visitor from Ohio.
- And finally, the sentences attributed to Maurice himself, which shows his enormous self-complacency: "my chair is worth three thrones; I do not have any other political enticement than mine; one works in my newspaper as in a religion." (30)

Such was B-V's brother: Maurice was a man of considerable influence on his times. He managed *Le Matin* "with an iron hand", from 1905 to 1944.

Meanwhile, on the other side of the Atlantic Ocean, the unfortunate Panamanians were devastated by the failure of the French Company. Their economy had gone to the pits since 1889 and the American 1893 monetary crisis had brought it further down.

A Panamanian delegation, concerned about the future of the province, traveled to Bogota; Amador, Sosa, Arango and others asked the Colombian

Government for economical help. However, Colombians were still plagued by internal problems and had not developed any internal wealth. All they could do was to renew the French concession, replacing *Roldan-Wyse* of 1890, by *Suarez-Mange* dated April 4, 1893.

Helped by French envoys, the Panamanians succeeded in extending the concession for ten years, until October 31, 1904.

Let us keep this date on mind, as it will play an important role in the future negotiation between Americans and Colombians.

As one would have guessed, none of this was free, the Colombians having asked and obtained 10 million francs from the New Company, which was founded a few months later.

This new *Suarez-Mange* concession provided for the New Company to show some activity on the canal site, in order to maintain the PRR's concession active. (12)

We have seen that B-V's book of 1892 did not meet the success he expected. In France, for obvious reasons, nobody wanted to be reminded of Panama. At this time, the saying "it is a Panama" was frequently used to imply a bitter disappointment.

Truly, a swindle of such a magnitude was not common. It defies one's imagination! About a million of small shareholders had lost altogether 1.3 billion francs - more than 6 billion Euros in today's value. This amounted to more than a thousand francs per person - or one half-year salary for a laborer. For many, this sum represented their lifetime savings.

To add to this disaster, the highly paid individuals who organized this swindle had not been caught or punished. Among all those responsible, only a few ended up in jail: Minister Baïhaut, who naively admitted to having received bribes and his colleague Blondin, who was caught with him.

The other swindlers were still at large. Arton had gone to England. A defaulter, he would finally be arrested in London on November 16, 1895, and sent to jail, where he committed suicide.

The main swindler, Herz, who was blackmailing Reinach, was still at large in England where he died, without being caught, in 1898.

As for the banker Jacques de Reinach, he had killed himself, giving proof of his guilt to the whole world.

The French people were revolted; trials had been conducted for six years for a pitiable result.

The Third Republic had indeed disappointed its supporters.

B-V was lucky not to be among the investors who lost money. On the contrary, he had made a huge fortune by working with ASC in Panama.

He did not desire punishment for the criminals. He was not really interested by the scandal that lingered around the Panama affair, but was obsessed by its technical aspects, a remainder of his childhood dream. What he wanted more than anything was to finish the work that he had contributed to start.

He was convinced that the future of the Panama Canal was no longer in France.

The administrators of the New Company disagreed with this. They still hoped to save the project and to maintain it into French hands. This looked like an impossible task. To show their interest, they sent a delegation of engineers to Panama, where it reached Colon on December 9, 1894. Its mission was to investigate the status of the works and then recommend how work could be resumed in the Culebra. Taming this difficult hill had become an obsession.

B-V took no part in this mission; he had not been asked to participate. He was quite busy running his engineering firm, traveling extensively.

His attitude contrasted with the investment he had made in 1894: half-million francs of shares in the New Company.

Had B-V lost all hope to revive Panama?

Maybe he thought that the actions of the New Company were not worth of being supported. Maybe he had other plans.

In 1895, the New Company decided to resume digging the Panama Canal. It had a capital of 65 million francs, but, of it, only 40.595 million francs had been "recovered from the profit makers." (14) This sum could pay for thousands of workers during years. The New Company did not have any more overheads; it did not have to pay for any marketing expenses, did not have to distribute bribes; it did not need to organize large gatherings of important people from all over the world to publicize the project. Most important of all, its capital was totally available and it did not need to pay any dividends or interests to anyone.

It just had to pay the Jamaican workers, those who had not defected to work on the Nicaragua Canal. Given that the workers were paid 10 francs a day, the New Company's capital (about 30 million francs, once one deducts the 10 million francs for the Colombian concession and the Parisian staff's salaries) represented 3 million days of work, or about 5 years with 3,000 workers.

Little by little, the work resumed and during the fall of 1895, about 2,000 to 3,000 laborers were working in the Culebra area. This was a ridiculously small number, in view of the enormous task that remained to be done.

However, the New Company left its mark: "A long-needed railroad wharf had been built at Panama City," (2) a good start to dispose of the soil excavated from the Culebra Hill, which would later form the "Amador Causeway".

The New Company hoped that in the future, when French opinion would be ready and once the scandal had been forgotten, work could be resumed at full speed. These extravagant hopes never materialized.

The number of laborers was increased somewhat and reached 4,000 in 1897. The New Company had probably decided to allocate more workers to the maintenance of the equipment and machines, hoping it could one day resell them.

As for B-V, he believed that the solution to finish the work in Panama would necessarily come from a foreign country, but he did not know where to start. Americans had not yet called for him.

Five years had now elapsed since B-V stopped working in Panama. It is surprising that he had not returned to the Isthmus, even though his fortune allowed him to travel in luxurious conditions. He had probably been too busy running his engineering company, building railways in Spain or in Africa.

He had little time to dedicate to Panama. It was probably the only period in his life where Panama had not been his highest priority. He often thought that something needed to be done, without delay - he knew how corrosive the tropical weather could be on the equipment, infrastructures, railways and retaining walls.

Fortunately, for the Panama project, a series of lucky events would help launch B-V into a new career: promoter of the Panama Canal.

In March 1894, when B-V was traveling for his own business, "in Dortmund, Westphalia, in order to examine certain new processes for washing coal, in order to separate the schist from the useful matter," (11) he met unexpectedly with Russian Prince Tatischeff, on the train, as he was returning from Germany. As always, superbly convincing when he talked about Panama, B-V explained that it could be of interest to Russia in its strategy of global development to access the waterways on the Pacific Ocean. Flamboyant, as usual, B-V described Panama as an extension of the Trans-Siberia railway, which had recently commenced operating. It was a quite a clever suggestion.

B-V was so convincing that, on his return, he looked for and found several supporters of this idea within the French Government. It is believed that this new interest for Russia laid in continuation with the success of the French financial subscription for Russian railways. His friend Burdeau set up a meeting with Casimir-Périer, the President of the French Cabinet, who suggested a visit to Russia.

Despite his work in the Spanish railways, B-V made himself available to leave as soon as possible.

On March 24, 1894, he reached Saint Petersburg by train, after a four-day long journey. There he met with Serge de Witte, the Finance Minister of the Russian Tsar, Alexander the Third, who declared that "His majesty would gladly accept your suggestion, if it was proposed by the French Government." And B-V added: "Nothing remained but to persuade the French Government to adopt my idea." (11)

On April 20 *, back in Paris, B-V met again with President Casimir-Périer, who was seemed keen to proceed.

However, this time, B-V was quite unlucky, as the following facts prove.

The Cabinet of Casimir-Périer fell on May 22.

On June 25, the French President Sadi Carnot was killed by an anarchist.

B-V concluded: "It was my checkmate for my Franco-Russian solution for the salvage of Panama." (11)

Misfortune struck again on November 1st of the same year with the assassination of the Russian Tsar by another anarchist.

His most fervent supporters having disappeared, B-V did not know where to turn. This incredible series of fatalities ended B-V's hopes of selling the New Company's assets to Russia.

This possibility would never be mentioned again in B-V's memoirs, where he concluded this sad episode by writing: "A terrible fatality seemed to have wiped out all the men - with the exception of Mr. de Witte - who could have helped to resurrect Panama in France." (7)

As for his friend and former Deputy Auguste Burdeau, unfortunately, he fell sick and died prematurely in December 1894. He was only 43.

To end this sad and unfortunate period, on December 7, 1894, Ferdinand de Lesseps died. Since the bankruptcy of his company in 1889 and his conviction in the 1893 trial, he had lived as a recluse in his castle of *La Chesnaie,* in the center of France, confined in his bedroom.

This series of sad events definitely marked the end of B-V's hopes to revive the Panama project in France.

---

* April 1894 has not been a clement period of time for the Bunau-Varilla brothers. Let us remember that the subpoena from Lemarquis had been presented to Maurice and his associates on April 24.

18

CROMWELL, GENERAL COUNSEL OF THE COMPANY

After the failure of the MCCN on August 30, 1893 and the birth of the French New Company on October 24, 1894, the coming period would be rather unproductive for both routes - Panama and Nicaragua.

Investors decided to "wait and see".

Of course, Congress was still interested in Nicaragua, but the 1893 financial crash had chilled the investors' bullishness.

Of course, the French New Company was still active on the Panama works, but just for the bare minimum required to keep active the Colombian concession - it was a requirement of the original Wyse's concession.

B-V mentioned that "after four years of efforts, the New Company had excavated 3 million cubic meters." (7) This probably took place from 1895 to 1899. This digging was just a "drop in the bucket" when one remembers that about 35 million cubic meters remained to be excavated, according to the estimates of the New Company.

Overall, none of the two routes had taken the advantage over the other. The contest was still on and supporters of the routes remained busy.

At the end of 1894, soon after its birth, the New Company organized the management of its American asset - the PRR -, which had been wisely kept out of reach of Lemarquis, the French liquidator of the Lesseps Company. The American committee, chaired by Thompson, had been dissolved and the New Company was in need of a "serious" correspondent, to take care of its interests in America.

Well inspired, it selected the New York firm of *Sullivan & Cromwell* for this important mission, which was to "represent, defend, protect and advance the interests of the New Company". (6) This mission was vague enough to allow *Sullivan & Cromwell* to launch any initiative if saw fit, which would cause later brisk debates with the Company's directors, even to the point that they cancelled - temporarily - the mandate.

Among the employees of *Sullivan & Cromwell*, the New Company had a special regard for William Nelson Cromwell, who had been lawyer of the PRR for the last two years and had performed in the United States achievements that brought him international fame in the business world.

Born in Brooklyn in 1854, **William Nelson Cromwell** lost his father at eleven, when he was killed during the Civil War - 1861-1865. Coming from a poor family, Cromwell had to work as a clerk with Algernon Sullivan, a lawyer specialized in financial matters. He proved to be such a brilliant employee that Sullivan paid for his tuition at Columbia Law School. Having graduated *cum laude,* Cromwell came back to work with Sullivan, this time not as a clerk but as a lawyer, and at only twenty-five, became a Partner of the firm. In 1887, after Sullivan's death, he became Senior Partner.

Cromwell is considered the founding father of *Sullivan & Cromwell,* a law firm that would become America's largest in the 1930s.

Cromwell's specialty was to "facilitate" alliances between large industrial groups, some of his accomplishments being the creation of the United Steel Company, of Edison's General Electric and many other industrial empires. He was also talented in "manipulating" the books of bankrupt companies to make them more attractive to prospective buyers. "He would restructure their balance sheet, convert their debt to equity, cut deals with their creditors, control the press, look out for new fresh venture capital, and in the process take a hefty fee." (16) He was called the "fox", because he was very tricky and was - almost - never caught. He planned all his actions with the highest care, sending his messages three different ways: by mail, by telegraph and by a messenger.

In 1893, Cromwell made his debut in the matters of Panama, as lawyer and member of the Board of the PRR, which was managed as an American company, headquartered in the State of New York.

Cromwell soon became one of the strongest supporters of the Panama project and would later work towards its success.

In January 1896, the shareholders of the French New Company named Cromwell their *General Counsel,* perhaps because they had been impressed by his performance within the PRR, or because they wanted to make use of his many contacts in the New York financial spheres.

As Cromwell would explain later - in 1907 - : "Not have only the members of *Sullivan & Cromwell* established close and intimate professional relations with their most distinguished colleagues throughout the United States, but they have also come to know and be in a position to influence a considerable number of public men in political life, in financial circles and on the press, and all these influences and relations were of great and sometimes decisive utility in the Panama matter." (6)

B-V, who never had any attraction towards Cromwell, believed that: "The influence said to have been exercised by *Sullivan & Cromwell* was grossly and enormously exaggerated." (6)

As their *General Counsel,* Cromwell then felt mandated to save the New Company and endorsed the seemingly impossible mission of selling its assets to the United States Government. He was certainly attracted by the hefty commission that he could pocket from this sale. He liked wealth as a proof of his success and would die with a multimillion-dollar fortune - some say $ 19 million -, at the age of 94.

Once nominated by the New Company, Cromwell took his mission very seriously. This was the beginning of a long and difficult path, which would eventually see the United States buy the French interests. Cromwell would be behind all the dirty tricks involved in this process. "He was a 'behind the scenes man', who did not care about publicity." (16)

When Cromwell was named in January 1896, he encountered a difficult situation. According to his own words: "The menace against the New Company was the pronounced tendency of the people of the United States to realize their long cherished plan, to support the building of a canal in Nicaragua, under American control. . . The platform of the Republican Party at the time of the presidential election in 1896 formally endorsed the construction of the Nicaragua canal." (6)

During 1896, Cromwell and his assistant - Curtis - became familiarized with their mission, interviewing number of Senators and Representatives in Washington, meeting with the New Company directors in Paris, inviting them to New York. Georges Emile Lemarquis, representative of the small shareholders, would also come into the United States, expenses paid by Cromwell.

In Paris, the New Company had revived its *International Technical Commission* (ITC), with fourteen experts from all countries: France, Germany, Great Britain, Belgium, United States and Colombia. Their mission was to evaluate the work done to date in Panama and to recommend a plan for the achievement of the canal. They left for Panama in February 1896.

B-V did not trust their capability: "Their experience was European and not American, and still less Isthmian. Their work was disastrous." (11)

In November 1896, McKinley, a Republican, was elected. Cromwell was confronted with the difficult mission to have McKinley change his mind over Panama. Morgan, a Democrat, had been for many years a supporter of Nicaragua. As his opponent, would it not be logical for McKinley to support Panama?

"When Congress met in Washington in December 1896, everything was ready, except that the session ended on March 4, 1897, - fortunately for Panama - without Nicaragua being put on the agenda." (6)

All along 1897, Cromwell followed the Congress' debates about Nicaragua. He did not succeed in drawing the attention of the Representatives to Panama, lacking relevant information. To fill this deficiency, he asked his assistants to develop a compilation of all historical documents relative to the Interoceanic Canal, which occupied three books, 1,840 pages long. A sterile task, because it contained only contractual information. It could have been substantially improved by adding a translation of B-V's 1892 book, which contained all the necessary technical information about Panama.

Not sparing any effort, in June 1898, during one of his stays in the French capital, Cromwell met with every one of the fourteen members of the *International Technical Commission* (ITC), and pressed them to issue their report, which would be an essential document to present to President McKinley.

Cromwell worked on all fronts; his main idea was to inform and convince the American people about the advantages of Panama and abandon their prejudiced idea in favor of Nicaragua.

During the summer of 1898, he set up a press bureau in New York; its task would be to produce articles praising the merits of Panama. Several canal specialists had been approached to write those articles: General Henry Larcom Abbott, a member of the ITC, whom Cromwell had met in Paris; Civil Engineer Elmer Lawrence Corthell also helped in the writing. At first, these articles were rejected by most newspapers, judging them contrary to their readers' opinion.

Abbott published in November 1898 a booklet comparing Nicaragua and Panama, which showed a strong preference for Panama. (6)

At this stage, we ought to ask ourselves: why didn't B-V and Cromwell collaborate? It seemed so logical to unite the expertise of an engineer and of a lawyer. Was B-V's egotistic character responsible for such a misfit?

On November 16, 1898, the unofficial conclusions of the New Company's International Technical Commission (ITC) were published. After having met 97 times (!) during four long years, the ITC rendered its verdict.

B-V had not attended any of these meetings, although he was a shareholder of the New Company. Firstly, as we know B-V, he would have found unbearable for him to sit as a simple member of this Commission.

He was too accustomed to be the only one to take decisions. Secondly, as we have seen, during the years 1895-98, he was busy running his own engineering and consulting company. His failure in Russia had led B-V to abandon all hope to save Panama with a purely French solution and he began to believe that the only salvation would come from the United States.

The recommendation of the ITC was a canal with locks, costing 500 million francs for the first phase, estimated to take ten years, which consisted in building temporary locks. B-V was delighted, as this was the exact scheme he had recommended in his 1892 book, now six years old. He would recommend the same scheme again when Americans started building the canal in September 1908. However, the French Commission was silent on the fact that the project had now lost all profitability. At the beginning of the project, in 1880, the first estimate to dig the canal was 600 million francs and today, after spending more than 1.4 billion, another 500 million francs were required. This added up to almost two billion francs. It was truly excessive and the French investors had lost all interest. They had already been ruined by investing into the Panama project and did not want to hear any more about Panama.

B-V was right: in France, the Panama project was therefore unquestionably dead.

The New Company shareholders - among them was Colombia - became worried about the American preference towards Nicaragua and were looking for a way to stop this in its tracks.

On November 18, 1898, two days after the ITC had issued its final report, the New Company Directors - under the recommendation of Cromwell - decided to make an offer to sell the new Company's assets, in a letter to President McKinley. However, it was not a formal commercial offer, as there had been no agreement of the shareholders on its terms. It was just informative. It estimated the work already achieved by the French in Panama at $ 120 million. Although it was a curious move, rather resembling a desperate one, to draw the President's attention on Panama, it proved nevertheless to be useful in starting the dialogue with the Americans.

To explicit their offer, some New Company's representatives traveled to New York, where they arrived on November 28, 1898. A few days later, they went to Washington, where they met with John Hay, the Secretary of State of President McKinley; a formal proposal was handed out to Hay.

Let us pause here to examine the personal history of John Hay, as he will play a major role in the negotiation of the future canal. **John Milton Hay** was born on October 8, 1838, in Indiana. After studying law, he started working as a lawyer in 1861 in Springfield, Illinois. Luckily, he met and became friend with the future President Abraham Lincoln. Once elected President, Lincoln called him to be his personal assistant-secretary.

Just before Lincoln's assassination, Hay was sent to the Paris Embassy where he worked under John Bigelow, to whom "he remained modestly subordinated." (11) B-V was a good friend of Bigelow and would later become friend with Hay too.

Back in Cleveland, Ohio, Hay occupied several positions, as a journalist, a writer and briefly in 1879, as the Assistant-Secretary of State, under President Hayes - the 19th President who had been formerly Governor of Ohio. For a time, Hay abandoned politics to write some books and returned to Cleveland in 1897 when McKinley - another former Ohio Governor -, sent him as Ambassador to London. In 1898, he was appointed Secretary of State, replacing Sherman, whose famous "Monetary Act" of 1893 had been mentioned earlier. Hay would play an important role in negotiating a peace treaty with Spain following the Spanish/American War of 1898.

It is generally recognized that Hay, in his position of Secretary of State, convinced by Bigelow, greatly influenced President McKinley, who would later ask not only for the Nicaraguan route to be studied, but also for the Panamanian route to be evaluated "impartially", on equal grounds as Nicaragua.

Cromwell attended the meeting of the representatives of the New Company with Hay in Washington, on December 2, 1898. The $ 120 million offer did not meet any interest. This was not surprising as it was too close to the cost estimate for the Canal of Nicaragua ($ 133 million, revised down to $ 118 million). However, there was another important point left pending before a valid offer could be made by the New Company: Colombia had to agree to the sale. We already know that the country was poor and needed money. Of course, this would become a major problem later on.

Panama was not at all in a competitive situation.

Three days later, in his annual address to Congress, President McKinley asked that the Interoceanic Canal be built urgently. He declared himself in favor of the project of Senator Morgan in Nicaragua. Yet Hay had not come up with a strong reason to convince the President of the interest to include Panama in the study.

While in Washington, Cromwell tried to pay a visit to Senator John Tyler Morgan - a Democrat -, who not only refused to receive Cromwell, but had his secretary show him to the door, in a most cavalier manner. Morgan had no time to dedicate to Panama. He was a fervent supporter of Nicaragua.

Unaffected by these disappointments, Cromwell did not abandon the fight and continued to act in favor of Panama. At about the same time, he donated $ 60,000 to Senator Hanna, the Chairman of the Republican Party and a close friend of President McKinley, for the Presidential campaign of 1900.

This was quite a hefty sum: as a reference, Cromwell's family mansion, a summer residence in Monmouth Beach, Virginia, had been purchased for $ 65,000.

Marcus Alonzo Hanna, Senator from Ohio, would be a prominent figure among the men who composed B-V's "American connection", most of them coming from Ohio. Not to make exception to that lucky link, Hanna was born on September 24, 1837, in Lisbon, Ohio. He was not a particularly good student and worked in the wholesale grocery business of his father. However, he was capable of much more than being a grocery clerk. In 1867, he set up an oil refinery business and after a few setbacks, made a fortune out of it. Later, he founded a newspaper and then started a career in politics.

Around 1885, he had become one of the most influential Republicans in Ohio. He donated so much money for the election of McKinley to the Ohio Governorship that in 1896 he was rewarded by being appointed President of the *National Republican Committee*. Later, he contributed $ 100,000 to the presidential campaign, which saw the election of McKinley.

Elected Senator in 1898, Hanna became the most faithful ally of McKinley. He had, not without reason, the reputation of being very unscrupulous and corrupt. The press called him "Dollar Mark", witness the "gift" of $ 60,000 made by Cromwell to the Republican Party, through his chairman: Hanna.

B-V was kept aware of all this through the many letters he received from Bigelow, who at 82 was still a very active man. On November 15, Bigelow had written to Hay, who, 30 years ago, had been his assistant in the French Embassy in Paris and who was now Secretary of State. He had begged him "not to commit himself to the Nicaragua route until he had taken the same measures to investigate the Panama route that he had taken to investigate Nicaragua." (7)

While the New Company representatives were visiting Hay in Washington, B-V received a letter from Bigelow, pressing B-V to join him there: "I persist in the opinion that no one, that I know of, could do more than you to enlighten our legislators in regard to the superior advantages of Panama over Nicaragua."(7)

However, unfortunately, B-V was not in a position to leave for Washington. He had already left for Caracas where he intended to check the contractual relationship with the Colombians.

He was not acting on behalf of the New Company. He had been called there by a friend, Francis Loomis, the American Ambassador to Venezuela. That was at the end of 1898.

B-V did not mention this trip in his memoirs, but his daughter Giselle positively recorded it and had told Anguizola that: "he decided to investigate the situation in Colombia from neighboring Venezuela. He accepted an invitation from Loomis, the American envoy to Caracas, to visit that country."

It was during his post in Caracas - from July 8, 1897 to April 8, 1901 - that Loomis, who reported to Washington about the British activities in the region, started a friendship with Theodore Roosevelt. At the time, "Teddy", the future President, was Under-Secretary of State in the Department of the Navy. (18)

In Caracas, B-V met with the Colombian politician, Pedro Nel Ospina, who would be involved later in the American-Colombian negotiation. B-V's major concern was the fact that the Colombian Government had indicated that it would not allow the assets - and the concession - of the French New Company to be sold to a foreign country without its agreement.

B-V willingly accepted Loomis' invitation. Both men had already met when Loomis was the American Consul in Saint-Etienne, France, from 1890 to 1893. B-V must have had a high regard for Loomis, as he dedicated the American version of his memoirs to "Lesseps, Roosevelt, Hay and Francis B. Loomis, the resurrectors of the Panama Canal, whose work has been the cradle of the Victory won." (9) This surely showed that B-V remembered Loomis as a great friend of Panama.

Born in Marietta (Ohio!) in 1861, Loomis had first started a career as a journalist, and then became an ardent militant for the Republican Party.

By a happy coincidence (yet another one!), Loomis would become later Hay's assistant in the State Department.

During the meetings in Caracas, B-V realized that the Colombians were only mildly enthusiastic about the Panama project. In fact, the country's internal troubles took priority over the problems of Panama. These troubles would later evolve into a civil war, called the "Thousand Days" War.

B-V understood that the fate of the canal would not depend upon the Colombians. He recorded in his memoirs that his idea of a revolution in Panama leading to its independence was born during this period, because he had to find a way of getting around the indifference of the Colombians. Yet, he did not want to acknowledge the idea of a revolution in Panama and would later deny that he was one of the instigators of the 1903 revolution.

On his return journey to France, B-V stopped in New York, where he met with his friends Bigelow and Asher Baker and reviewed a plan of action to promote Panama. B-V's strong friendship with Bigelow led him to expect his support as a lobbyist for the Panama cause in the United States, as he explained in his memoirs: "the propaganda made by my friends Mr. Bigelow and Lieutenant Baker advanced rapidly." (7)

Asher Baker had been B-V's friend since 1896, when he was given responsibility for the American pavilion at the Universal Exhibition of 1900, in Paris. They had been introduced by a common friend, Percy Peixoto, the director of an American insurance company in Paris.

"Baker's mind was alert, active, and keenly interested in the public welfare. He soon grasped the great importance for the United States of not persisting in the prodigious error of Nicaragua. . . He started resolved to devote his spare time to enlightening his friends in Congress as to the real situation of the Panama Canal," (7) wrote B-V, quite an extraordinary compliment. Asher Baker would play an important role in the events to follow.

Some sources pretend that Asher Baker, who traveled often between Paris and Washington after 1898, was acting as a "paid lobbyist" of B-V, who wrote that: "Lieutenant Commander Baker had backed with a lot of conviction the Panama Canal in Washington and in Chicago." (7)

There is no evidence that Baker ever received any money from B-V. Of course, B-V was always active in persuading his friends of the superiority of the Panama Canal and he could have successfully done so with Baker.

B-V had already installed Bigelow as a supporter of Panama in New York. Baker would be his main contact in Washington. B-V had masterly planned his future moves, as all major decisions in American politics originated from those two metropolis.

At this stage in our story, all the main actors in the triumph of the Panamanian cause have been introduced:
- President McKinley,
- Hay, the Secretary of State,
- Hanna, a Senator from Ohio,
- Loomis and Baker.

B-V will soon become their expert and the most active promoter in defending the noble cause of Panama.

In parallel with B-V and his friends, another influential group would be at work, under the leadership of Cromwell.

It is interesting to clarify here the relationship between the two champions of Panama: B-V and Cromwell. Both men were very active in favor of the Panama Canal, however for different reasons:

- B-V desired strongly to realize his childhood dream; having worked in Panama with the Lesseps company, having almost died in the Isthmus, but having returned with his construction company to collect a huge fortune, he wanted to "resurrect" the work of the "Great Frenchman";

- Cromwell, a lawyer, was working for prestige and money; aspiring for the prosperity of his firm *Sullivan & Cromwell*, he casted an envious eye on the commission promised for the sale of the New Company to Americans.

Their efforts, turned towards the same goal, were never coordinated, combined nor deliberately programmed. Proof is that they did meet only a few times:

- On February 23, 1902, when Cromwell, suspended by the New Company, needed B-V's intervention to be reinstated as *General Counsel*;
- On March 26, 1902, when Concha, the Colombian negotiator, asked for such "impossible" conditions, that they requested a combined effort to bring Concha to propose new "reasonable" contractual terms;
- From June 9 to 11, 1902, during Hanna's speech in the Senate, where he was defending the advantages of Panama; Both B-V and Cromwell had helped Hanna by supplying him with useful information;
- On November 19, 1903, the day after the signature of the Hay/Bunau-Varilla treaty, to congratulate B-V (?);
- Finally, on February 23, 1904, by luck, in the hall of a Washington's hotel.

Of course, we shall cover those encounters in more detail later on.

Both men ignored each other, politely:

- In his "letter" of 1907, Cromwell justified the disbursements of *Sullivan & Cromwell* during their mission as *General Counsel* of the New Company; in 100 pages, B-V was not even mentioned once!
- As for B-V, he thought that this "letter", which he called a "plea for fees", was "a tissue of erroneous and misleading assertions." (6)

Obviously, both men could not have worked together.

In his memoirs, B-V went a step further in dealing with Cromwell, qualifying all lawyers – without naming Cromwell, but the hint was obvious – of being "impostors".

We think that Panama was the lifetime achievement of both men and the reader shall to judge whose part - of B-V or Cromwell - had been the most influential in selecting Panama.

At the end of 1898, both lobbies were ready to work and endeavor to change the public opinion in favor of Panama.

It would take another four years for the Panama project to prevail, through very unusual circumstances, worthy of a thriller.

19
THE SENATE PROCRASTINATED
1899-1900

Since the Monroe's doctrine proclamation in 1823, the United States had struggled to eliminate Great Britain's influence on the American continent, on their "hemisphere". The 1850 *Bulwer-Clayton* treaty was still an obstacle. However, due to the friendly British neutrality during the Spanish-American war in 1898, a renegotiation of the treaty appeared possible.

After many conferences, on February 5, 1899, Secretary Hay agreed and signed with British Minister Pauncefote, a new treaty. This *Hay-Pauncefote I* agreement allowed the United States to build a canal in Nicaragua, however under the control of both parties. It had taken some time for Great Britain to accept the United States' ambitions in this part of the world. The signature by the United States of the Constantinople Convention on October 29, 1888, which allowed free navigation in all international waterways, as in Suez, had clarified their intent.

However, the "expansionists", Theodore Roosevelt, Henry Cabot Lodge, Alfred Thayer Mahan, among others, were opposed to any deal with Great Britain. They accepted that the canal be their own "American" canal, but asked for a complete freedom of action. Bolstered by the opposition of the "expansionists", the Senate refused to ratify the *Hay-Pauncefote I* agreement and proposed some amendments.

Mortified to see his efforts reduced to nil, on March 13, 1899, Hay handed out his resignation letter; President McKinley refused it.

Secretary of State Hay did not give up and, we shall see that after almost three (!) more years of negotiations, he finally worked out an acceptable version, called *Hay-Pauncefote II*, on November 18, 1901.

We have seen how in December 1898, the New Company could not produce a credible offer and had a cold reception in Washington. Vexed by the adverse results of its negotiations with the Americans, things remained at a standstill for the New Company.

On their side, the Americans felt that they had failed to convince the French to lower their selling price, so they continued with their project in Nicaragua. We have seen that in June 1898, Senator Morgan had proposed a law recommending that the Government purchased the assets of the MCCN. However, the agenda of the Senate was overbooked; the Spanish-American war had occupied most of the debates in the second half of 1898; the debate was delayed, and Morgan's resolution was submitted to the vote six months later, on January 21, 1899. The Senate approved it by 48 votes for and 6 against.

After the Senate's vote, the House had to examine Morgan's resolution. It was thought to be a mere formality: "In the House, an enthusiastic and large majority was openly pledged for Nicaragua.   .   . If the vote could not been deferred, the fate of Panama was sealed." (6)

However, in the House of Representatives, there was a minority showing strong antagonism; it was led by a Republican representative from Ohio (!), William Peter Hepburn, the powerful Chairman of the *Interstate and Foreign Commerce Commission*. He had been a member of the House since 1880 - except from 1888 to 1892. He was of the opinion that Morgan had "disguised" his project, under a real "masquerade" - the word is from B-V. (6) He felt that, under Morgan's proposal, it would be the MCCN, a private company, although supported by the Government, which would build the canal.

Hepburn absolutely wanted the Government itself, as a nation, to build the canal. It was a question of politics: for him, the United States ought to have complete control of the canal, including its construction and fortification.

Hepburn and Morgan had diametrically opposed positions.

Of course, as many authors claimed, they also wanted their name to be attached to such a project, which was ready to be approved. However, the dispute was more profound that a mere fight for precedence.

In the House, Hepburn introduced a bill of his own, with provisions slightly different from Morgan's Senate law. More time passed in sterile discussions. Apart from the differences pointed out in the above, Hepburn and his friends had legitimate concerns about Morgan's plans.

Firstly, they had some legal doubts about the validity of the concession owned by the MCCN, which according to some would expire on October 9, 1899 - 10 years after the beginning of the works - and which according to others would continue after this date, because Nicaragua had accepted that Edward F. Cragin and Edward Eyre, two American contractors, could take over. They represented a syndicate called "Grace-Eyre-Cragin" and had the financial support of bankers and business men such as William R. Grace, John A. McCall, Warner Miller, John Jacob Astor, George Westinghouse, Darius O. Mills, Levi P. Morton or G. T. Bliss, who had deposited $ 100,000 at the *Ministerio de Hacienda* - Finance Ministry - in Nicaragua and had promised to deposit another $ 400,000 before August 9, 1900. (21) But this syndicate would remain a private enterprise and Hepburn was against it.

The second argument of Hepburn and his friends was well known. If the United States were to go ahead by themselves in this project, it could provoke a conflict with Great Britain; the signed *Hay/Pauncefote I* did not meet their approval.

With these strong arguments, Hepburn militated in the House to oppose the Senate project "which called for a change in the status of the MCCN, to serve as the agent of the United States in the construction and the operation of the future canal. If we gave $ 5 million to the MCCN, $ 6 million to Nicaragua and $1.5 million to Costa Rica, we will not open the doors of the Grace-Eyre-Cragin syndicate, nor those of the Atlas Company, nor those of all the speculators who have obtained concessions during the last fifty years. The best way is that the United States negotiate directly with Nicaragua and Costa Rica." (21)

It should be noted here that the lobbying of Cromwell and of B-V's friends would be decisive in the House vote.

Cromwell claimed that he convinced Reed, the Speaker of the House, Cannon, leader of the Republican Party and Burton, Chairman of the *Rivers & harbors Committee*, three very influential members of the House that the only way out was to name a joint Commission of Representatives of the House and the Senate.

Curiously, B-V claimed that his friends had also intervened: "Lieutenant Asher Baker had become a fervent partisan of Panama. . . . His conviction passed, thanks to his friend Deering to Reed and Cannon. The cumulative result of these two influences was a dramatic turn of events." (7)

We have to note that simultaneous pressures on the House by Cromwell and B-V's friends led to a resolution to name a joint Commission.

President McKinley was favorable to such a Commission, because he had "been troubled by Hutin's letter of February, 28, 1899." (16)

This letter found its origin in December 1898, when the French delegation, led by Cromwell, did not receive a warm welcome in Washington. Cromwell, always active, suggested that Hutin write a letter detailing the French proposal. This letter, in very vague terms, "offered to incorporate the New Company in the State of New York and to head it with American Board members." (10)

A second letter, dated March 11, offered the help of experts to perform further studies.

Of course, both letters, addressed to President McKinley, had been copied to Walker, the President of the *Nicaragua Canal Commission*.

With the President and Congress' agreement, this Commission was named on March 3, 1899 : *The Isthmian Canal Commission*, still chaired by the Vice Admiral John G. Walker. It is often called the "Second Walker Commission".

However, it should be noted that its name was *Isthmian* and not *Nicaragua* any more. Panama had been put back into the race. It was, in part, due to Cromwell's efforts; B-V, who did not really appreciate Cromwell, did not mention it in his memoirs!

This "Second Walker Commission" had nine members. Three were already members of the first Commission: John G. Walker, Professor Lewis M. Aupt and Colonel Oswald H. Ernst. There were also civil engineers: Alfred Noble, William H. Burr, Peter C. Hains and George S. Morison, from the U. S. Corps of Engineers; ex-Senator Samuel Pasco and economist Emory R. Johnson.

Initially, this Commission functioned quite smoothly. Most of its members were in favor of Nicaragua, influenced by the last report of the *Nicaragua Canal Commission*, which recommended this route. However, with time, some members would become favorable to Panama.

The Bigelow-Baker lobby, independently of Cromwell, but pressing towards the same goal, developed its influence in the Washington circles. Hay probably intervened too in convincing President McKinley.

On June 10, 1899, McKinley sent a letter to the Commission asking that Panama be included in its mission, which was "to investigate all possible routes for the Interoceanic Canal, in particular Nicaragua and Panama." (7)

Panama had unexpectedly come back into the picture!

In so doing, the President required formally a full comparison between Nicaragua and Panama.

B-V was convinced that this change, vital in the attitude of the United States towards the Interoceanic Canal, was the fruit of the efforts of Hay, the Secretary of State, and of Bigelow, his friend of thirty years, supported by Asher Baker. They had certainly used the arguments listed in B-V's book of 1892, which had generously been distributed in the circles of Washington.

It should be noted that B-V, after his trip to Venezuela, returned directly to Paris, and did not take part in the lobbying in Washington. He was confident that his friends, Bigelow and Baker had everything under control.

B-V was right. Thanks to this new Commission nomination, Congress turned away from the Interoceanic Canal matters. The Commission would work for about three years and would remit its conclusion in November 1901. Of course, Cromwell, B-V and their friends continued their lobbying for Panama, although in a slightly less persistent manner.

In France, on June 30, 1899, the New Company issued a report about its activity in Panama. Work had resumed there, although at a very slow rate since 1895, and after spending 35 million francs, about 4 million cubic meters have been excavated plus about another 3.5 million cubic meters in the area of La Boca, the port of Panama City.

This was quite an achievement, completed since the creation of the New Company in 1894. The statutes of the New Company had required such a report: it stipulated that when the expenses would reach half of the capital of the Company (65 million francs), a Committee of five civil engineering experts would issue a report.

Now, the big decision was whether the work should be continued. The members of the Board of the New Company were split. They had hoped that the negotiations in Washington would help them in that decision.

As Americans were close to formally decide in favor of Nicaragua, the New Company would have to wait for better conditions in which they could call for new French public funds. In such a difficult situation, the best was probably to wait and see, and not to venture a deceiving move.

The five experts also indicated in their report that the achievement of the Panama Canal would cost 525 million francs ($ 105 million) and would take another 10 years. It was a clear message to the *Walker Commission.*

In order to fulfill President McKinley's request, the *Second Walker Commission* left New York for France on August 9. Why did they choose to go to Paris when their mission was to study an Interoceanic Canal in Central America? This was probably due to Cromwell's lobbying, and also to the convincing powers of the B-V's "connection" in America.

Cromwell boasted in his "plea for fees" that he had met everyone in the Commission and convinced them to begin by meeting the ITC.

As most of the ITC members were still in Paris, the nine members of the Walker Commission headed for Paris. There, some of those members were about to change their mind in favor of Panama: "my friends Morison, Burr and Ernst", wrote B-V in his memoirs. (7)

As *General Counsel* of the New Company, Cromwell organized this trip to Paris and, once there, he entertained lavishly the members of the "Walker Commission" in the Inter-Continental Hotel. (26)

B-V explained in his memoirs that he spent a lot of his time, during the Parisian stay of the Commission, multiplying his lobbying actions with the still undecided members. Of course, he could only do it in secret, as he was in no way representing the New Company.

Ernst, a member of the Commission, was a friend of Bigelow.

Frank Dunlap Pavey, a lawyer, former Senator of the State of New York, also a friend of both Bigelow and B-V, "was the connecting link" (5) for B-V to meet Morison and Burr. Pavey was luckily in Paris at that same time.

"Our conferences were long and frequent," wrote B-V. (5) Which Pavey confirmed: "The first time I dined in B-V's house, I stayed until two o'clock the next morning, listening to his picturesque and fascinating argument in favor of Panama and against Nicaragua.   .   . He was doing that in the firm belief that sooner or later the United States would come to adopt the Panama Canal route and he was contributing his efforts in that direction." (6)

Some authors pretended that B-V would later use the Pavey's law firm - Pavey & Higgins - on a retainer contract, which explained why Pavey himself was called to review the treaty's draft on November 16, 1903 (see chapter 25, page 254).

"Among the gentlemen of the Commission, was a man characterized by a great energy of conviction. It was George Morison.   .   . He played, in the formation of the opinion of the technicians, a part similar to which Senator Hanna played in the formation of the opinion of the politicians. When the Walker Commission left Paris, the scales had fallen from the eyes of three of their members." (7)

This proves that with some entertainment, good arguments and strong conviction, one can easily turn around an opinion.

Would it be enough to have a majority in the Commission?

Following the visit to Paris, three members out of a total of nine seemed to have rallied the cause of Panama.

Curiously, B-V and Cromwell never met during the Commission's visit to Paris. Each man had his own strategy and each wanted to claim the glory of his personal achievements.

During his visit to Paris, Walker, the Chairman of the Commission, was unable to obtain from Bonnardel, the Chairman of the New Company, an offer to purchase its assets. It seemed that the members of the Board had not yet reached a consensus. It was necessary, according to the rules of the New Company that this offer be agreed by a majority of its members, which was not the case.

This did not discourage Cromwell from acting. He wanted to have a plan for action. After the Commission members had returned to America, at the end of September, Cromwell extended his stay in Paris and had numerous meetings with Bonnardel and the board members of the New Company. On October 19, 1898, they agreed to Cromwell's idea: "Americanize the New Company" in order to seduce the American investors. (6)

On December 5, 1899, in his annual address to the Congress, President William McKinley declared: "The contract between the MCCN (Maritime Canal Company of Nicaragua) and the state of Nicaragua has expired on October 10, because ten years had elapsed without any work having been undertaken. It is our wish that negotiations resume quickly with the Government of Nicaragua." (16)

McKinley did not mention that in Colombia, on October 20, 1899, had started a civil war called "The Thousand Days' war", between liberals and conservatives, which would ruin the whole region and cause about 100,000 casualties. This war would be catastrophic for the Colombian Government: President San Clemente - who would be ousted in July 31, 1900 - declared martial law and as a consequence, all laws could be signed by Ministers, without Congress ratification. Congress had lost all power.

This generated many disputes, among which the extension of the concession of the New Company from 1904 to 1910, which could never be validated. (12) The deadline for the New Company thus remained October 1904.

Morgan and the supporters of Nicaragua rejoiced about this hectic situation in Panama, a province of Colombia; Nicaragua, their favorite, was much more peaceful.

It seemed that the slight advantage acquired by Panama when the Walker Commission had travelled to Paris had been lost.

Refusing to have lost the battle, Cromwell continued to apply the plan decided together with the New Company directors and that he qualified of "Napoleonic". He took the initiative, on December 27, 1899, to create the *Panama Canal Company of America* with a capital of $ 30 million, of which only $ 5,000 had been collected in cash. This financial structure was supposed to shelter the assets of the New Company, before they could be sold to the United States Government.

Participating in this *Company* was all the upper crust of the New York banking society, mostly friends or customers of Cromwell: J.P. Morgan – not a relative of Senator Morgan -, J. E. Simmons, Kuhn, Loeb and Co, Levi Morton, Charles Flint, Isaac Seligman, E. C. Converse, George Sheldon, etc. (6 and 12)

In his memoirs, B-V recalled a different story: "The imaginary *Panama Canal Company of America*, with its paper capital of $ 30 million and its cash capital of $ 5,000, seemed to have been conceived in order to secure at the cost of the real owners a large part of the proceeds of the sale of the Panama Canal Company to the United States, if this sale was ever to become a reality. The Board of Directors of the New Company had accepted to transfer all their holdings to this airy nothing calling itself a Company. . . This scheme was outwitted by the vigilance of the representative of the French Courts: Mr. Gautron, the receiver of the Old company and Mr. Lemarquis, the representative of its bondholders. . . The New Company's Board was forced to resign on December 30, just three days after this questionable company was incorporated in New Jersey. A new Board was elected and Mr. Navarre, a judicial administrator, was appointed by the tribunal. There was no further talk of Cromwell's fake company. . . Navarre, the judicial administrator acted as the temporary Director. Nobody ever heard of the famous Society. " (7)

Cromwell never explained why he created the *Panama Canal Company of America*. In 1906, sitting in a Senate hearing - investigating the possibility of a plot to emancipate Panama from Colombia in 1903 -, Cromwell declined to talk about his intentions: "It would be a violation of the secrecy of my profession. I was the representative lawyer of the New Company and cannot divulge anything of its matters." (6)

And later, it was found that he intentionally destroyed all evidence: "Cromwell appears to have purposely created one of the larger gaps in the historical record. For in the otherwise complete file of his business dealings, still in possession of *Sullivan & Cromwell*, there is not a paper relating to his Panama operations, all correspondence, cables, documents, expense vouchers, and the like are mysteriously missing." (16)

All this contributed to increase B-V's natural distrust of Cromwell.

This event has been the subject, fostered by their imagination, of a few novelists who imagined that Cromwell had founded a syndicate, together with his friends, the New York bankers, in order to take control of the New Company by purchasing its shares at a discount.

Some authors indicated that they had successfully purchased an amount of about 3.5 million francs worth of shares, which represented about 5% of the New Company's capital.

This episode concerns only the Panamanians who want to believe that "Wall Street Created a Nation", according to the title of Diaz Espino's book. (22) In Panama, it is called the "black legend".

Through the many cables exchanged between the Washington's and Paris' offices, negotiations continued, represented on the Parisian side by Navarre, the newly appointed Chairman of the Board of the New Company and on the American side by Walker, who headed the American Commission.

"A lengthy correspondence, filled with a lot of empty terminology", was how historian Anguizola qualified the exchange. (18)

Having seen its proposal rejected once, "the New Company's Board had adopted the attitude of not answering to the Walker Commission's question: do you want to sell and for how much?" (7)

A question remained: how could Colombia's agreement to the sale be obtained?

In the December 1899/January 1900 period, there still existed a majority of the Walker Commission's members in favor of Nicaragua and they sought to discourage those who were still pushing in favor of Panama. Following their visit to Paris, they had gone to Panama and Nicaragua, but their convictions remained unchanged. Without a sale offer from the French New Company, no real comparison between the two selected routes could be made.

President McKinley understood this and to remain impartial, he required the Commission to send a clear message to the French New Company, asking: "Do you wish to sell? And for how much do you wish to sell?" (7) This was done by Walker on April 10, 1900.

At this point, we should remember that the concession with Colombia did not allow the New Company to sell its assets to a foreign country without a formal permission. B-V had been to Caracas to check this condition; he had met with some Colombian dignitaries to see whether they would allow the sale to the United States. Of course, he could not get a positive answer, because the Colombian law prevented it and to change the law was not on the agenda of the Bogota Congress; Colombians were too absorbed in their internal troubles - the thousand days' war.

This prevented the New Company from responding to the Walker Commission's request.

In April 1900, a Republican Convention took place. It was intended to agree upon the platform and chose the candidates for the November 1900

Presidential election. Unexpectedly, it changed its 1896 platform, which was explicitly in favor of Nicaragua and modified it to: "favor the construction, control and protection of an isthmic canal by the Government of the United States." (20)

It was a major change, opening the door to Panama.

Some authors recognized that the $ 60,000 gift from Cromwell to the Republican Party had certainly much to do with this platform change. It has also to be mentioned that Cromwell had logically charged this amount to the New Company, which did not fully appreciate the usefulness of this donation.

During the summer of 1900, Paris received 50 million visitors, from all over Europe and the United States, coming to admire the Universal Exhibition pavilions spread along the banks of the River Seine. It was a unique opportunity for B-V to strengthen his "American connection" with the men whom we shall call the *Ohio clique*. (18) We have already mentioned that this state had produced a great number of distinguished politicians: Sherman, McKinley, Hay, Hanna, Loomis, among others.

Another auspicious coincidence!

B-V told us in his memoirs that, dining alone *Chez Foyot,* a restaurant close to the Garden of Luxembourg, in Paris, he "providentially" met with Asher Baker. It is difficult for us to believe that this meeting was totally unforeseen and once more, we find B-V re-arranging the facts when writing his memoirs. Of course, their meeting of that particular day at that particular place could have been unexpected, but both men had known each other well for some time; Baker would never have visited Paris without notifying B-V.

This was another of B-V's omissions, giving credit to the story of Giselle about her father's trip to Caracas.

What was not unexpected was the great number of Americans visiting Paris during this summer of 1900. At the restaurant where B-V was dining, Baker sat with two wealthy industrialists from Cincinnati (Ohio again!): Harley Thomas Procter and William Watts Taylor, who were prominent in this State.

Procter will later start the multinational company *Procter & Gamble*.

Taylor was the General Manager of the *Rookwood Pottery Factory*.

Soon after this dinner, B-V invited them in his mansion, 53 Avenue d'Iéna.

And, this not being enough, a few days later, they had another dinner together, this time with another of their friends, Lucien Wulsin, maker of the *Baldwin* grand pianos. B-V's brother, Maurice, used his Parisian connections to obtain Baldwin a 1900 Paris Universal Exhibition Honor Medal. This showed that the brothers still worked closely together.

All these important American businessmen were convinced that the Interoceanic Canal would be built by the American Government in Nicaragua. But, once they had met B-V, it proved difficult for them not to be in favor of Panama, so strong were B-V's arguments. At least, the men from Cincinnati were so stirred by B-V's rationale that they decided to investigate the matter further.

It took some time for them to establish B-V's credibility, but eventually once the momentum of the *Ohio clique* was up and running, these men would become the most significant lobbying force for the Panama Canal.

On November 30, 1900, as expected, the *Walker Commission* recommended the Nicaragua Canal in a provisional report. This time, they produced a few figures, served to demonstrate their choice.

As asked by President McKinley, the Commission had studied two possible routes:
-    Nicaragua: $ 200 million and ten years of works;
-    Panama: $ 142 million, with no indication of a time period, as the United States did not have a concession from Colombia. The Commission regretted that no agreement could have been found with Colombia.

The Commission added, to be precise, that "the yearly estimated cost of maintenance and operations is $ 1.3 million greater in Nicaragua than in Panama." (25)

The estimate for Nicaragua had surprisingly gone up significantly from previous estimates: $ 200 million, when before it was only $ 133 million in October 1895 and $ 118 million in February 1899.

The Walker Commission now found a difference between Nicaragua and Panama of: 200 – 142 = $ 58 million.

A few days later, on December 3, McKinley declared in his annual message to Congress that he: "awaited Congress' views about the Walker Commission's report." (16)

Although the Panama route came out cheaper, B-V was nevertheless disappointed by the conclusions of the Walker Commission's report. B-V's friends in the Commission, Morison, Burr and Ernst had not been able to plead victoriously the cause of Panama, despite its advantages. B-V had expected them to produce a minority report.

To finalize its decision in favor of Nicaragua once for all, the Commission still had to formally eliminate Panama. It thus asked once more the New Company for an offer.

Aware that its assets were losing value, but unable to act without the Colombians' agreement, the New Company replied that one solution could be that the United States become one of their stockholders. It would be the only way the French Canal could be rescued by the Americans. But, as Americans had never considered this possibility, it was an exchange of ideas that did not lead to any progress in bringing together the negotiators' positions.

As usual, B-V found in this set back the necessary arguments for a rebound. He noticed that there were only $ 200 million minus $ 142 million or: "$ 58 million between the total cost of constructing the Nicaragua Canal and that of finishing Panama". (7)

This caused B-V to transform this fact positively into a strong argument in favor of Panama. He wrote that: "this report opened an admirable opportunity for an offer of sale of $ 58 million." (7)

Of course, B-V was also happy to note that "my friends had marked their imprint and for the first time in a public American document, there is mention of the advantages of Panama."(7) It was a naive confession by B-V of his Washington's lobby.

Would B-V and his American friends succeed in altering the Commission's recommendation?

Not immediately. As time went by, B-V became quite nervous, wondering whether he should step in. "It was now the proper moment to intervene to support the efforts of the friends of Panama within the Commission itself by creating a current of opinion outside of it."(7)

It had been about six months since he had met with his friends from Ohio, during the 1900 Exhibition in Paris, and yet the *Ohio clique* was not giving signs of life. What was taking them so long?

Good ideas take sometimes a long time to become embedded in one's mind.

As B-V pondered the means of reversing the American public opinion, a cable arrived from Wulsin and Taylor on December 11, asking him to make a presentation at the Commercial Club of Cincinnati, comparing Panama and Nicaragua. He was delighted and he replied that he would leave immediately after the holidays.

Crossing the Atlantic Ocean took twelve days and B-V did not wish to be away from his family for Christmas. He wished to spend this time with his wife Ida and his young children: Etienne, ten, and Giselle, six.

20
HOW B-V RESCUED PANAMA
1901

Fulfilling the promise made to his Ohio friends, B-V sailed to New York on the ocean liner *Champagne* on January 5, **1901**. 2,000 passengers were on board, of which 390 in first class. The liner belonged to the *Compagnie Générale Transatlantique,* launched in 1885 and renovated in 1896, a most modern steamer. Obviously, B-V traveled in first class.

B-V still believed that, despite the *Walker Commission*'s decision in favor of Nicaragua, the Interoceanic Canal could still be in Panama. He was convinced that only Americans had the money and the interest to purchase the assets of the New Company. He was ready to fight and reverse the American public opinion. The optimism of his Ohio friends had boosted his fading hope.

"As soon as I arrived on board of the *Champagne,* the series of favorable chances again became manifest," (7) wrote B-V, always optimistic about his encounters. On board, he met with a Roman prelate, who had an important position in the Vatican, and was - another coincidence - a very close friend of Myron T. Herrick, a businessman from Cleveland (Ohio), himself a friend of President McKinley. It was due to this connection that B-V "met Colonel Myron T. Herrick. He was the friend, not only of President McKinley, but he also knew intimately a man far more important for B-V's purpose, Senator Marcus Alonzo Hanna." (7) B-V would soon become acquainted with Herrick, Hanna and their friends, who would be tremendous allies to support the Panama's cause. The *Ohio Clique* was growing every day.

One question is often asked about B-V's travels. Who paid for them?

A New York banker, Jesse Seligman affirmed that he financed them. He had a brother, also banker in Paris, who had been involved in the Panama scandal. His name was on the list of the "penalized" shareholders of the New Company. Annoyed to have been mistaken for his brother and to show that he was totally innocent, Jesse Seligman declared that he had indemnified B-V - an independent consulting engineer - for his travel expenses. B-V flatly denied it. He would not have tolerated that anybody but himself paid his travel expenses; Panama was "his dream, his ideal", it belonged entirely to him. (16)

Apart from his family and a few friends, nobody knew about the origin of B-V's wealth. This obviously led to the most ridiculous rumors. One of them was to assume that B-V was working for his own interests and for the interests of his brother Maurice, as they both owned shares of the New Company. However, the authors, who support this story, forget to mention that together they owned only 3% of the New Company shares.

People imagined that B-V wanted to maximize the profit of his shares and that he was an opportunist or a speculator.

It was known that Maurice, his brother, had made a fortune and purchased *Le Matin*, but B-V's money was not as conspicuous and his wealth had remained hidden, as his name never appeared in managing *Le Matin*.

B-V was certainly paying for all his travel expenses, as he was able to afford them. However, some authors believe that the strong lobby of businessmen, which supported Panama, led by Bigelow, had helped in "preparing" his trips.

We will not mention this controversy any longer, as it has little interest for the continuation of our story.

B-V arrived in New York on January 16, 1901. His confidence was infinite: "I was embarking on an apparently impossible enterprise. It was nothing more than to change the settled opinion of 80 million Americans." (7)

Asher Baker punctually met him on the New York wharf and together they headed for Cincinnati, 600 miles from New York. It was a long journey, one day and one night by train; B-V and Baker found plenty of time to talk. They decided that it would be best to approach Myron T. Herrick, a leading figure in the Republican Party and friend of President McKinley. Herrick would be able to arrange a meeting with Mark Hanna, the Ohio Senator, and perhaps later with the President himself.

B-V's luck continued. "Every time I was in need of a man, he appeared, of an event, it took place." (7) We have already mentioned how B-V explained his luck, in various ways. We do not believe one single word of it; what he called luck was nothing else than opportunism.

Once in Cincinnati, B-V met again with his American friends, acquainted in Paris, during the summer of 1900: Procter, Taylor and Wulsin. They arranged for him to give a talk at the Chamber of Commerce. His success was absolute. "Before I had finished (the lecture), the opinion of my audience had totally changed," (7) wrote B-V in his memoirs.

After his speech, Taylor introduced B-V to Jacob Schmidlapp, an intimate friend of Myron T. Herrick - the man B-V absolutely wanted to meet. To oblige, Schmidlapp called on the telephone his friend Herrick, who accepted willingly to set up such a meeting.

Herrick was in Cleveland, at the other end of the state of Ohio, 200 miles away. B-V jumped again on a train and after having travelled the whole night, arrived in Cleveland on January 20. Eagerly, B-V gave his speech in front of Myron Herrick and his friends.

However, on that day, Hanna, the Ohio Senator, was out of town. When he returned to Cleveland, he found all his friends praising B-V, who had turned around their opinion in favor of Panama. Hanna reportedly said: "A fortnight ago, everybody here was for Nicaragua. I come back and now Cleveland is solid for Panama." (16)

Ohio was the starting point of B-V's endeavor to rehabilitate Panama. He did not stop there and continued giving talk after talk in all the major cities of the country. "The impact of his whirlwind tour was unmistakable. He was a novelty. American audiences had simply not encountered an authority on Panama before, let alone an engineer who had the experience of actually attempting to dig a canal there. The engineering argument of building at Panama rather than at Nicaragua had never been set forth publicly and with conviction."

B-V emphasized that he was not working for the New Company and was totally independent. "He stressed basically what was in the Walker Commission's report: a Panama canal would be a third the length of a canal at Nicaragua, it would have fewer curves, would require less excavation in total, fewer locks, would cost less in operating costs." (16) The details of B-V's comparison between Panama and Nicaragua are in Appendix 6.

As we describe B-V's trip, we cannot help to recall that Ferdinand de Lesseps made the same tour in 1880; however, this time success would be met.

Throughout January and February 1901, B-V journeyed throughout the country. First to Boston, where he met with Lucius Tuttle, the President of the *Boston & Maine RailRoad Company*. Thereafter, he went west, to Chicago where Asher Baker greeted him with John Deering, the farming machine magnate, who would also become a fervent supporter of Panama.

Informed of his support, Maurice managed to obtain Deering the French Agricultural Medal. This shows how closely the brothers still were.

Despite Bigelow's help, when B-V arrived in New York, to give another series of speeches at the Chamber of Commerce, he found the doors closed.

Thanks to his friend Pavey, who knew Gustave Schwab of the New York branch of the Lloyd Bank, they took advantage of the absence of the President of the Chamber of Commerce, Mr. Jesup, to set up the first conference on March 7.

In New York, B-V stayed at the Waldorf Astoria Hotel, located on number 33 of the 34th Street, at the corner of Ustor Court, with a cable address: "BOLDT" New York. This hotel would be his headquarters during all his visits to New York. It is interesting to note that this hotel was close to the Bigelow's residence in the Gramercy Park area. Bigelow had probably recommended it to B-V.

Later, B-V gave another speech at the Chamber of Commerce of Philadelphia. There, his success was even more immense.

B-V's series of conferences were now in their third month and, logically, his enthusiastic listeners had spread the good news about Panama. The press had reported at length about B-V's talks and had published eulogistic reports.

On March 13, 1901, the *New York Herald* titled its front page: "Resurrection of the Panama project," and on March 18: "Defenders of Nicaragua Are Alarmed", which delighted B-V.

On March 20, at the suggestion of his friends, B-V finished writing a short leaflet, titled: "Panama or Nicaragua?", which listed the main features of the rival projects. It was irresistibly in favor of Panama, because B-V (wisely) had omitted to mention the cost estimates for both projects.

According to the last Walker Commission's report, Panama had an advantage of $ 58 million over Nicaragua (142 against 200), but we should not forget that this was still subject to the agreement of the Colombians and did not include the cost that they would ask to transfer the concession from the French New Company to the American Government. For the moment, Colombians were as silent as the New Company and neither had released any figure.

B-V's brochure brought a new element in the Nicaragua vs. Panama comparison. It mentioned the seismic and volcanic activity in Nicaragua: "In 1835, one of the volcanoes of Nicaragua, the Cosigüina, had, during forty eight hours, ejected every six minutes a volume of lava and ashes equal to the total volume of the prism of the Nicaragua Canal." A footnote mentioned: "What have the Nicaraguans on their coat of arms? Volcanoes!" (7)

The leaflet was intended to kill the arguments of those who still supported Nicaragua. B-V "waited for the document to be printed to leave New York for Washington." (6)

B-V claimed everywhere in America that he did not act in the interests of the French new Company, but for the sake of Panama: "I am a soldier of the "Idea of the Canal" and have no connection near nor afar with the New Company." (7)

B-V tried to distance himself from the New Company. As we recall, the recent visit of the French envoys to Washington had not made any impact on Americans. But, B-V had not cut off all his links with the New Company. Maurice, aware of all the Parisian events through his newspaper *Le Matin*, was keeping his brother acquainted.

On March 26, 1901, events suddenly began to accelerate. B-V unexpectedly met with Senator Hanna in New York, who was in the company of Mr. and Mrs. Herrick. Soon after, he met, also by coincidence, Benjamin Duryea Woodward, a Columbia Professor of Romance languages, who had been Asher Baker's assistant during the 1900 Paris "Exposition". Woodward was with Charles G. Dawes, the *Controller of the Currency*, and a close friend of President Roosevelt.

Thanks to his speeches across the United States, the eulogistic reports in the press, his leaflet showing the advantages of Panama and his new influential friends, B-V was getting closer to meeting President McKinley himself.

McCullough noted that:"The impact of his whirlwind tour was unmistakable. He was a novelty. American audiences had simply not encountered an authority on Panama before, let alone an engineer who had had the experience of actually attempting to dig a canal there. The engineering argument for building at Panama rather than at Nicaragua had never been set forth publicly and with conviction." (16)

B-V's series of speeches, from Ohio to New York rallied the interest of the American industrial and banking spheres in favor of Panama. This was the starting point of the movement, which will culminate with the June 1902 Senate's vote in favor of Panama.

Most of these supporters of Panama were wealthy people, who finally believed that America should have the best possible canal. They did not understand why Washington had a preference for Nicaragua. B-V had explained to them that Panama had many more advantages. They believed the logical arguments that B-V had presented at length and started lobbying for Panama within the Republican Party.

We have already met most of these men:
- Lucien Wulsin, maker of the *Baldwin* grand-pianos,
- Harley T. Procter, son of the founder of *Procter & Gamble*,
- William Watts Taylor, owner of the *Rookwood Pottery Manufacturing Company*,
- James Parmelee, owner of the *National Carbon Company*, a firm which became later part of *Union Carbide*, the gigantic chemical complex,
- Jacob G. Schmidlapp, of the *Union Savings Bank*,
- Edward Goepper, industrialist,
- Major William Henry Bixby,
- And the politicians we have already mentioned: Hanna, Herrick, Loomis and Baker.

All these men will be active supporters of the cause of Panama and will help convincing their friends in Congress and in the Republican Party.

B-V converted the President's close friends to the cause of the Panama Canal: Milton Herrick, who had been the President's assistant, when he was Ohio Governor, and Mark Hanna, Ohio Senator. They managed to get B-V an appointment with President McKinley, on April 7. Charles Dawes was there too. It was a very brief visit, during which B-V handed out his leaflet, although preliminary - it will be completed later and widely distributed in the Washington circles.

This visit had the effect of boosting B-V's confidence towards the victory of Panama.

While he was in Washington, B-V paid a visit to Senator Morgan, "the veteran of the Nicaragua campaign." (7) We have to recall that a year ago, Cromwell could not be received by Morgan. However, Morgan accepted to meet B-V, but the conference did not go well at all. As expected, Morgan showed to B-V his contempt for the supporters of Panama. B-V could not utter a single word and this irritated him tremendously. Morgan kept talking, to such extent that he provoked B-V when he said: "Between ourselves, you would not put one dollar of your own money in this absurd project, in this rotten project of Panama." (7)

Morgan talked imprudently as he ignored that B-V had already invested half a million francs in shares of the New Company. We can easily imagine that B-V had a hard time to keep his nerves. B-V left Morgan without shaking his hand. "If ever in my life, I was near the point of slapping an American Senator's in the face, it was at this instant." (7) Hopefully, nothing of the kind happened. It could have been a serious incident, which would probably have killed the Panama Canal, by making B-V unwelcome in America.

This meeting had shown the very unusual conduct of B-V, who was always described by his peers as an extremely courteous man, able to contain his anger. With Morgan, his mortal enemy, he had been carried away in a rare moment of fury.

This was certainly not the only sudden outbreak of anger on B-V's part.

We read in his memoirs that in July 1885, when he found himself alone at the head of the Company in Panama, he believed that, in the offices of the "Central Administration in Panama City, reigned a spirit of criticism, a sense of defeatism. I decided to make two dismissals. . . One was a chief of section . . . the second was a British gentleman and his sinecure was the reward to facts anterior to Panama." (11) These were at the time exceptional punishments. B-V could sometimes show a "quick-tempered" state of mind.

At this point of our story, after his visit with President McKinley, B-V's optimism was at the highest.

On April 9, 1901, he cabled to Charles de Lesseps: "Nicaragua is dead". (7) Having ended his lectures, he went back to Paris, where he certainly needed to take care of his engineering and investment business. It was the first time since his stays in Panama (1884-1888) that B-V had been away from Paris for such a long time. Maurice certainly missed B-V's investment advices.

B-V left New York on April 11.

Back in Paris, he was upset by the comments from some of his friends who still believed that the Panama Canal could remain French. They criticized him for having forgotten this possibility and for spending too much time and effort in America. Although most French investors had lost all faith, B-V did not want to abandon his friends. He did not want to arbitrarily exclude any opportunity for France to save Panama. He affirmed that he would "attempt even the impossible to secure its completion (the Panama Canal) by the French." (7)

He did not hesitate to dedicate part of his wealth to the cause of the Panama Canal.

On April 25, 1901, he published a two page appeal in 27 Parisian newspapers and 212 outside of Paris, stating that "before accomplishing this act (the sale to America), it is necessary that those interested in it, namely the share and bond holders, should be put into a position to judge whether they prefer the solution, entailing the disappearance of a strip of the national flag, to the virile solution, which consists in courageously resuming the task and in completing it for the credit of France and for the honor of her name." (7)

B-V involved himself personally by informing the press that he had written a letter to the Director of the *Crédit Lyonnais* to subscribe an amount of 2 million francs, in the eventuality that the New Company would decide to emit new shares.

This seemed like a marketing campaign designed by B-V for the New Company. He had returned from the United States with a re-born optimism. He was ready to "speculate" with his own money, perhaps because his consulting engineering company was bringing him large profits.

A second appeal to the French public was published by B-V on May 10, 1901. A third one would be issued at the end of the year.

All these efforts to save Panama had cost him 140, 000 francs ($ 28,000).

They touched a wide audience and generated many letters to B-V. Hundreds of subscribers who had been ruined by the Lesseps' Company wrote to him to express their hope of some salvation of the Panama Canal project.

B-V had given false hopes to those poor investors, but he acted in his self-centered way, because all he wanted was to receive gratitude from the New Company shareholders for his accomplishment in the United States.

Maurice, as a shareholder of the New Company, had certainly some influence on his brother's behavior. He certainly wanted to save his shares in the Company's if they could still be.

Drumont's newspaper, *La Libre Parole*, described B-V's appeals as "the phantom brought on from the wings, which was supposed to be forever dead and buried." (4)

The *Times* of London wrote that "B-V's attempt tried to bring back to life the inert body of the Panama canal which everybody supposed to be dead and interred forever." (11)

Despite B-V's efforts and all the letters he has received, the French public opinion had already buried Panama. The idea of the *Grand Français* was really dead.

"Even *Le Matin* itself did not help me," complained B-V. (7)

It should be recalled that, in 1901, Maurice had not yet conquered the head of *Le Matin* with full powers; Henry Poidatz, a journalist, remained the major shareholder and decision maker at *Le Matin*; in 1901, Poidatz had about 50%, the Bunau-Varilla brothers about 30% and others 20%.

Poidatz proposed his help to B-V, but "it was but a transitory emotion and the offer was not renewed." (7) It could imply that B-V, strengthened by his recent American trip, did not persevere on an action in France.

B-V wrote in his memoirs: "When no echo of any substantial effort answered to the sound of my two appeals, I understood that the idea of Panama was indeed dead in France."(7)

And again, B-V regretted this failure to resurrect Panama in his own country: "This resurrection was not the one I had dreamed. Why did it not take place in France and by France?" (7)

It was clear now that all hopes to have the Panama Canal completed by the French had been abandoned.

B-V concluded that: "There was nothing left to do except save the honor of France by obtaining the adoption by America of the French Conception." (11)

Meanwhile, in America, the *Walker Commission* was anxious to issue a final recommendation and asked once again the New Company by letter of May 8, 1901, for an official sale offer for the French assets. The Commission's last letter, dated April 10, 1900 - a year ago! - had still not been answered.

On May 14, B-V, his impatience growing too, wrote to Bigelow to express his concern, as he did not know what to do next. He had given a series of lectures and speeches all around the United States during four months and he now lamented that his supporters had not yet acted accordingly.

Finally, on June 2, B-V's American friends published the leaflet titled: "Panama or Nicaragua?" 30,000 copies were printed and distributed in an enormous mailing. His friends had supplied all the addresses: "Taylor of the Commercial Club and Elzner of the Engineers Club had supplied him with membership lists." (History of Ohio by Charles D. Ameringer).

On the American side of the Atlantic, it was Cromwell's job to communicate officially with the New Company in Paris. On June 25, Walker, the Chairman of the Commission, concerned that he had not received an answer from the French Company, paid a visit to Cromwell in New York, to reiterate his appeal. Walker said: "The work of the Commission in connection with the preparation of the final report has made such progress that it expected to submit to the President, according to his request, in the first part of July a semi-official report. . . I promise to delay this report until July 20, if Pananovo (The French New Company) come here and fix a definite sum." (6)

Cromwell was caught off guard by Walker's visit. He reacted furiously and admonished the New Company, in such a "pressing" manner that the New Company "informed him by return cable that his services were no longer desired. Apparently, they had enough of his high-pressure methods and his liberal use of their money." (16)

In fact, it was not only this event, which caused Cromwell to be discharged, but also his $ 60,000 "gift" to Senator Hanna, which had not been fully appreciated. And, to top it all, the new Directors of the French Company had not really understood the reason behind the creation of the "Panama Canal Company of America", at the end of 1899.

One last reason could have been that the New Company wanted to lead the negotiation and mistrusted Cromwell's initiatives.

Learning all this, B-V was furious. Although he had little esteem for Cromwell, he believed that his help was not to be neglected. Cromwell had many friends, who were dedicated to the cause of Panama. It was even patent that "Cromwell had spies in Bogota, paid agents in Colon and Panama City, political supporters in Washington and financial backers in Paris and New York." (25)

However, B-V had very little influence on the New Company and did not succeed in changing their decision to "take over the management of the affair, relieving Cromwell of all responsibility." (6) The New Company would remain without an American representative for six months, until January 1902. We shall see later how Cromwell had been reinstated, thanks to Maurice's intercession.

Let us turn now towards Colombia, entangled, since October 1899, in a nasty civil war. This unfortunate country had not maintained her legation in Washington. The New York Consul, Arturo de Brigard, acted as the official contact in America and was keeping Bogota informed of the Interoceanic Canal race developments.

At the beginning of 1901, Brigard strongly recommended that a plenipotentiary ambassador be sent to Washington. The destiny of the Panama Canal depended on it. His appeal was heard.

Carlos Martinez Silva, Ministry of Foreign Affairs, a friend of President Marroquin, whom he helped set up the *coup d'état* that brought him to power in July 1900, arrived in America in February 1901.

As soon as he arrived, Cromwell took good care of Silva and updated him with all the stories behind the negotiations. He was totally acquainted with the facts when he presented his credential letters to Hay on March 13. Hay immediately asked Silva to propose a *Memorandum* of Colombian requirements, to serve as a starting point in the negotiation.

However, Silva was so much convinced of Panama's superiority, that he did nothing of the sort. He knew that the New Company would not be able to complete the Canal and that a transfer of the concession to the United States was inevitable. On the other hand, he also knew that without a signed and acceptable *Hay/Pauncefote* agreement, the Nicaragua project could not go ahead.

In July 1901, just when Cromwell had been discharged, Silva thought appropriate to take up the negotiator's lead. Writing to Bogota, he proposed to use the *Hay/Pauncefote* terms that the Washington Senate had wished to incorporate: a canal neutral and fortified, under the United States' control. In Silva's mind, what was required for Nicaragua ought to be acceptable for Panama; Panama was to remain in a competitive situation. (10)

Unfortunately, the Bogota Government, misinformed and absorbed by the civil war, had a very vague idea of what Washington required. Silva would not get any answer to his proposal until early in 1902, six months later. This would cause Silva to believe that his help was not valuable; displeased, he offered his resignation.

By autumn 1901, B-V's efforts to sell the assets of the New Company had taken a favorable turn and were close to be rewarded.

Unexpectedly, a new event turned the tide of our story. This time it was a crime, an assassination attempt. We have already seen tempests, revolutions, earthquakes, bankruptcies, but never a crime!

It is a sad story. A son of Polish immigrants, Leon Franz Czolgosz was a laborer who lived in Cleveland - Ohio, yet again -, where so many events of this story took place. Czolgosz, unemployed, was seduced by the anarchist theories of Emma Goldman, who had been for some time exhorting her followers by preaching around the United States. Czolgosz proved to be a good disciple and tried to act consequently.

On September 6, 1901, Czolgosz visited the Latin America International Fair in Buffalo - in the North of New York State. Carrying a gun, which had not been detected by the guards, he shot President McKinley, who, badly wounded would die a week later, on September 14. "He was interred on Friday, September 20, 1901." (25)

As per the Constitution of the United States, President McKinley was re-placed by Theodore - "Teddy" - Roosevelt, the acting Vice President.

Born in a wealthy New-Yorker family, **Theodore Roosevelt** had studied Natural History at Harvard and Law at Columbia. He had an exuberant personality, loved to hunt and was a fervent naturalist. Owning a ranch in North Dakota, he had spent many sabbatical years there, before starting a brilliant career as a Republican politician. Having served in 1898 in the Spanish-American war as a hero, at the head of his *Rough Riders,* he was elected Governor of New York state in 1899, until November 1900, when he took office as Vice President of McKinley.

At 42, Roosevelt became the youngest President. Although he was a Re-publican, like McKinley, he had a totally different circle of friends. With the death of McKinley, the *Ohio clique* had lost their main spokesman.

Cromwell and B-V were in shock. They had to start their lobbying in fa-vor of Panama all over again!

It should be noted that with the change in the President's staff, Hay, an important ally, had remained faithful to the Panama lobby. When Roosevelt took over, John Hay had first wanted to resign as Secretary of State, due to his past antagonism with the new President, but Roosevelt ordered him to stay: Hay "could not decline or even reconsider." (25)

In the middle of these adverse events to the Panama cause, we find an-other minor reason to rejoice.

Finally, Cromwell's efforts to obtain a bid from the New Company proved successful. The New Company had finally obtained the consensus of its members to send a proposal to the Americans.

On October 17, after more than a year of procrastination, President Hutin went to Washington to present a new proposal to the *Walker Commission*. It was a letter offering a base for negotiation. But, it was still not a detailed offer. B-V commented in his memoirs: "The answer, so long waited for, so long deferred, was not an answer at all." (7)

As a matter of fact, this offer was just a plain declaration of intentions, restating the terms of the February 1899 letter - two and a half years ago! - and indicating that the dialogue could now begin. It was not much, but it indicated that hope remained for a real negotiation.

The concession from Colombia would expire in three years, in October 1904. Time was of essence, it should not be wasted.

On November 13, 1901, as he was very concerned with a possible President Roosevelt's preference for Nicaragua, B-V left Paris for New York, having reserved the now famous suite # 1162 of the Waldorf Astoria Hotel. As he stayed always in the same suite, we can infer that he had settled there, with his business papers and clothes, renting that suite on a monthly or even on a yearly basis.

This time, B-V had decided to be the head-lobbyist. He would attend all sessions of the Chamber or of the Senate, concerning Panama. For this purpose, he would often have to take the train from New York to Washington and, in this city, he lodged at the *New Willard* Hotel.

Before B-V reached New York, on November 16, the *Walker Commission* issued its official and final report to President Roosevelt, recommending Nicaragua. A leak had occurred and a summary of the conclusions of the Commission had been published by November 22, the exact day when B-V arrived in New York.

Also published was the full text of the "minority report" by George Morison, the only member of the Commission having remained faithful to the cause of Panama, thanks to B-V's pressure. His two other friends, Burr and Ernst had abandoned him.

McKinley's assassination had completely changed the deal. The wind had turned again in favor of Nicaragua. "The new President - Roosevelt - was the most vivid expression of popular sentiment and was in direct touch with it. This sentiment had always been obstinately turned towards the idea of Nicaragua, and the new President was its decided partisan." (7)

Among the faithful supporters to Panama, Senator Hanna, a good friend of McKinley, was ready to militate in favor of Panama for another year, with such zeal that he would be nicknamed "Hanama Canal". In 1903, he would barely be active, as he would campaign for President against Roosevelt.

He would not carry out his ambition, dying of typhoid fever on February 15, 1904.

With McKinley's assassination, started a black period for Panama.

To further blacken the picture, Hay announced that he had finally and successfully concluded his negotiation with Pauncefote. A treaty was signed with Great Britain on November 18, 1901. The clauses of *Hay-Pauncefote II* were, among others:

- The old *Bulwer-Clayton* treaty was repealed;
- The United States obtained the right to build and control their own canal in Nicaragua;
- They also obtained the right to fortify such canal.

On December 16, the Senate ratified the treaty by 72 votes against 6.

This led to put the vote of Hepburn's resolution on the Senate agenda for the January session.

It seemed that the fight for Panama was over: the treaty with Great Britain had removed the last obstacle for the Nicaragua Canal to be built by the Government.

The Holiday season was near. Congress left on recess.

B-V could do no more for "his" canal.

On December 12, 1901, he left New -York and went back to Paris, more pessimistic than ever before.

Congress would to resume its sessions on January 7 and, following the recommendation of the *Walker Commission,* it would most probably vote in favor of Nicaragua.

This was only four weeks away and B-V had to act quickly, as Maurice Hutin, Chairman of the New Company, still hesitated to send a formal offer to the Americans. B-V thought that : "The New Company again eluded the frank, clear and precise answer which could alone save Panama and that the Commission had asked for so long." (7)

B-V thought how he could help the New Company to emit an offer.

B-V arrived in Paris just in time to attend the meeting of the General and Extraordinary Assembly of the shareholders of the New Company, set for December 21. He hoped to exert some influence. He begged the shareholders to send an offer for $ 40 million for the sale of their assets. But they would not listen.

Those $ 40 million were a reasonable sum, according to B-V, who had been informed by Morison of the frame of mind of the members of the Commission. B-V had also checked this amount among his many American friends.

On December 23, B-V received a cable from Hanna, who confirmed that: "the Republican members of the Canal Committee (Senatorial) are ready to re-examine the question of adapting the route via Panama, should the owners of the French works be disposed to sell their enterprise for $ 40 million."(7)

On Christmas day, this cable was reproduced in *Le Matin* and again on December 27. Nothing happened. Business was at a standstill. All countries were celebrating the holiday season and most people were at home with their families.

To awake people during this respite, "in order to force action on the New Company", attempting an ultimate effort, B-V had the $ 40 million proposal published in all the Parisian newspapers of December 27. He also declared in the same article that the Company's President, Hutin, was incompetent.

This brought an unexpectedly quick result. On the next day, December 28, Maurice Hutin was dismissed by the shareholders and replaced by Marius Bô. However, it was still the holiday period and nothing would happen until December 31, which would be the last day on which one could take a ship from France to New York in order to attend the Senate vote, set for January 7, in Washington.

Fortunately, at the last possible moment, on January 4, 1902, President Bô, recently appointed by the shareholders at the head of the New Company, cabled to Washington an official offer from the New Company for $ 40 million. (16)

This offer came as a shock to the Americans. In the past, they had experienced only apathy from the French Company, and so, they wondered if this time they had received a serious offer.

Therefore, they ignored this hasty proposal and continued to move ahead towards a canal in Nicaragua.

All of B-V's work of the past two years seemed lost, once again.

Panama had been defeated. The Interoceanic Canal would certainly be built in Nicaragua.

21

NEGOTIATING WITH COLOMBIA FAVORED NICARAGUA JANUARY-APRIL 1902

As expected, on January 9, **1902**, the House of Representatives voted the Hepburn Law. This law authorized the construction of a canal in Nicaragua at an estimated cost of $ 200 million. "In spite of the New Company's telegram, offering its properties for $ 40 million, the law selecting Nicaragua was approved by an almost unanimous decision," with 308 votes for and 2 against. This was the conclusion of the *Walker Commission's* two year-long investigation.

We note here that this action by the House contradicted Hanna's theory by which the "Isthmian Commission, impressed with the superior advantages of the Panama route, had recommended Nicaragua just to bring the French to terms." (25)

After the House, it would be the Senate's turn to vote the Hepburn Law. The vote was set for January 14.

Thanks to Senator Hanna, the vote was postponed. He convinced President Roosevelt to ask for additional information from the *Walker Commission*. "Roosevelt called the members of the Commission to the White House, one by one, for private consultation, . . . Walker and the others were told to get together and issue a supplementary report. Roosevelt wanted to get the French offer to be accepted," narrated McCullough. (16)

The lobbying efforts of Panama's fervent supporters, Hay, Hanna, Bigelow and Baker, had made an impact.

This marked an important phase in the Interoceanic Canal race.

Now that the French New Company had officially announced a sale price of $ 40 million, the overall comparison achieved by the *Walker Commission* had to be reconsidered. This important turn of events was due to President Roosevelt, who followed the matter closely.

The Commission met again and could only come up with an evident calculation: with the new French offer at $ 40 million, Panama could be built for: 142 + 40 = $ 182 million, against Nicaragua unchanged at $ 200 million.

To this small difference of $ 18 million in favor of Panama, ought to be added the general inventory of the French New Company, "an immense amount of machinery" (16), and of course the PRR, but it was certainly something else that carried the decision. McCullough continued: "Clearly, something or somebody had caused him (Roosevelt) to conclude that Panama was the better alternative." (16) We have a good example here of President Roosevelt's determination, enhanced by Hanna's convincing arguments, to build the Interoceanic Canal at the lowest possible cost - therefore in Panama - ignoring that the threat of a veto from the Colombians could block the sale.

This was the first important decision of Roosevelt, who would become the irreplaceable leader in the Panama negotiation.

So, the Walker Commission weighed carefully the terms of the French offer for $ 40 million, and unanimously recommended Panama in a new report, issued on January 18.

During those ten days - January 9 to 18 – the whole picture had changed.

Why did the members of the Commission change their minds so rapidly?

The lobby, led by Hanna, had most probably convinced the President that the offer was very attractive: the United States could purchase the French works for $ 40 million. The French Company had already spent $ 160 million in effective work in Panama. It really was a bargain.

As a bonus, the United States would get the Panama RailRoad - worth $ 25 million in August 1881, but somewhat less in 1902 as the New Company had been compelled to sell some of its capital to pay back its debts.

The Commission acted immediately to take up the purchase option offered by the French. Panama was again back in the race, thanks to the help of Roosevelt and Hanna.

Hanna's efforts did not stop there. Pursuing his action in favor of Panama, he thought appropriate to call back Cromwell. But how would he convince the new company to re-hire his *General Counsel*?

B-V told us how it happened: "After the unanimous recommendation of the Panama route by the *Isthmian Canal Commission*, Senator Hanna requested me to do him the service of urging the New Company to take again Mr. Cromwell. I answered: "I have never seen Mr. Cromwell. I know he had been dismissed by the New Company." A short time after, Mr. Cromwell came to see me at the New Willard Hotel and engaged in a conversation of terrible length rather in the form of a monologue. After he had gone, at 2 am, on January 23, I sent a cablegram to Mrs. Bunau-Varilla (B-V's wife) in Paris, requesting her to inform a certain Mr. Dolot, who was the intimate friend of an important member of the Board of Directors, Mr. Terrier. They refused to listen to the suggestion. . . I cabled again to inform my brother, Maurice, proprietor of the greater part and directing editor of *Le Matin*. He acted personally on the Board and carried their decision the following day in favor of the reinstatement of Mr. Cromwell." (6)

This episode in our story tells us that :
- Hanna was right to ask for the return of Cromwell, as he would prove of great help for preparing the June 1902 Senate debate;
- Maurice's reputation as the most influential man in Paris had clearly been demonstrated.

On January 27, Cromwell was reinstated in his mission of *General Counsel* of the New Company, but under the following conditions: "We require most expressly that no donations be made now or later, nor promises to anyone whomsoever which might bind the New Company. . . It should be clearly understood that results must be sought only by the most legitimate means." (letter from Bô to Cromwell of January 27).

Ironically, B-V commented : "In plainer words, it clearly meant: no corruption." (6)

Now that the deal was about to be concluded, Cromwell would be strongly needed to follow the negotiation in its minute detail.

This purchase had yet to be finalized. At the end of January, Senator Spooner presented a proposal indicating the Senate's preference for Panama, with the condition that the United States could find an agreement with Colombia and that the French New Company could deliver a property title.

This latter condition was easy.

As for the first condition, it was complicated by the *Salgar-Wyse* agreement, continued by the *Suarez-Mange* concession, which prevented the sale of the French assets to a foreign country. Colombia was therefore becoming an essential partner in the deal - without her nothing could happen.

Despite the fact that Carlos Martinez Silva, the Colombian Ambassador in Washington, had declared it a simple matter, politicians in Bogota were of a different opinion.

B-V was ready to act as an intermediate between Washington and Bogota. For this, he would be helped by his friend Loomis, who had just been appointed to be Hay's assistant in Washington.

The Panama lobby had entered the State Department!

On February 15, B-V visited Carlos Martinez Silva in Washington and found him in favor of a swift negotiation.

But, unfortunately, Silva had no support in Bogota, where the Government accused him of having authorized the negotiation between the United States and the New Company. After a year in Washington, Silva resigned.

On March 9, he was replaced by **Jose Vicente Concha**, who declared that he would follow all of Bogota's instructions to the letter. The Colombian politicians had decided to supervise closely the negotiation.

As he did for Silva, Cromwell took care of Concha and acquainted him with the recent developments in the Interoceanic Canal race.

Alike his predecessor, Concha was an ex-Minister of Foreign Affairs, under the ex-President San Clemente, who was ousted by Marroquin. "Although brilliant and very intellectual, he was not only without knowledge of the English language, but entirely without experience of the world outside of Colombia." (6) Fortunately, his assistant, Tomas Herran was a graduate of Georgetown and American customs had no secret for him.

Moreover, Concha had no leeway to negotiate, and had to wait for further instructions from Bogota. When he left for Washington, "he was instructed to obtain the final adoption of Panama for opening of the Interoceanic Canal, on the best terms for Colombia, without affecting the integrity of her territory or her national sovereignty." (10) Concha's assignment was rather vague.

Poor Silva died of pneumonia soon after his return to Colombia on February 10, 1903. B-V pretended erroneously that: "Silva died in a mysterious manner, on his way back to Bogota. A rumor got aboard, without, however, material confirmation, that he had fallen a victim to the hatred generation by his devotion to the cause of the Canal." (7) B-V, who was very disappointment by Silva's removal, was close to accusing Bogota of assassinating her Minister.

B-V seemed to become especially nervous in his dealings with the Colombians. Was this due to his bad memories of the time spent in Panama?

Were Panamanians just the same as Colombians?

B-V had developed a good working relationship with Silva and hoped to resume the same kind of rapport with Concha. Unfortunately, he quickly discovered that it was impossible to work with Concha.

Concha had received firm instructions from Bogota to block the negotiation. This greatly upset B-V, who was keen to see the negotiation succeed.

Many authors believe that the Colombians had wanted to "play for time". This comes from the fact that the French New Company's concession was due to expire in October 1904, in two and a half years.

Another treaty, called *Calderon-Mancini,* extending the concession for 6 years, until October, 1910, had been obtained, from the Colombian Government in December 1899, but the Colombian Congress was dissolved in the *coup d'état* of July 1900 and could never ratify it. The Colombians probably thought that they could make some money by selling another concession. Their coffers were empty following the savage and seemingly endless *Thousand-Day War,* which consumed all the country's resources.

B-V had a different opinion; he believed that Bogota's hesitations were simply a consequence of that war. Internal affairs had become a first priority and the political chaos engendered by such war had made the provisional Government of Marroquin unable to deal with important decisions on the international scene.

Before we rush to blame the Colombians, let us not forget that the United States still had to be "formally" released from the treaty they had signed in 1850 with Great Britain, requiring the Interoceanic Canal to be built in common.

Fortunately, after months of bargaining, the United States and Great Britain signed the *Hay-Pauncefote II* agreement on February 21, 1902. It granted the United States "exclusive rights to build an interoceanic waterway in Central America." (12)

Hay had certainly been motivated to please the President who desired to redraft the first Pauncefote Treaty. Roosevelt had been a strong opponent of the first treaty - his strong nationalism could not accept to share the canal with Albion.

This new treaty finally allowed the United States to build the canal, the other nations keeping an "equal access in peacetime." (12) Americans were now free to build their own canal. All they had left to do was to convince Bogota to negotiate.

This proved an impossible task as they could not find anyone in Bogota with the authorization to deal with the United States.

The uncertainty in Colombia brought Nicaragua back on the stage. Morgan and his supporters had been watching carefully the situation and were ready to push the vote in the Senate in favor of Nicaragua.

As we have seen, Senator Hanna had asked President Roosevelt to postpone the vote *sine die.* But this situation could not be maintained for too long.

B-V needed to act quickly in Bogota and he did so most effectively. On February 23, still dwelling in the Waldorf Astoria Hotel in New York, he sent a long cable directly to Marroquin, the President of Colombia. B-V implored Marroquin to let him lead the transaction, as he was the "uncompromising defender enterprise Panama and faithful friend of Colombia". (7)

This long telegram costs him $ 304.38 (1,521.90 francs), half of what an employee of *Le Matin* would earn in a year!

Was this move a presage of B-V's future leadership in the negotiation?

It took some nerve, for a complete stranger like B-V, to write directly to Marroquin, the President of Colombia. It was thought that General Nel Ospina, whom B-V had met, acted as his intermediary. Of course, there was no answer, as, at that time, Marroquin had no idea who B-V was.

On his part, Cromwell continued to meet with Concha, the newly appointed Colombian Ambassador in Washington. His efforts were rewarded by a project of agreement, proposed by Concha, which started with: "The Government of Colombia authorizes the New Company to sell and transfer her rights to the United States" but reserved this agreement to one condition: "provided that a mutual satisfactory convention be concluded between the parties." (12)

Such proposal was considered by Cromwell to be a good starting point, as it contained "Colombia's consent to the transfer."(6)

However, Hay found the proposed terms totally unacceptable:
- Concha wanted 99 years and Hay perpetuity;
- Concha wanted a yearly rent of $ 600,000, a sum of $ 7 million paid by the United States and another of $ 10 million paid by the New Company.

Hay found these terms "absolutely exorbitant, excessive and impossible".

After many meetings, Concha did not change a word from his proposal.

Cromwell thought that "Concha was bound by the imperative instructions of his Government. The matter had reached an impasse." (6)

On March 22, it would be B-V's turn to try his luck with Concha. He tried to see him in Washington, but met a wall of resistance. However, he did not yield. He then wrote to Concha to suggest an agreement between Colombia and the United States, based on a payment of $ 10 million and a rent of $ 250,000 - representing the lease of the PRR's concession. This proposal was strictly a suggestion by B-V and although it did not have the formal approval of Hay, B-V had certainly discussed the matter with his friend Loomis.

B-V was so strongly supporting the cause of Panama that he assumed with aplomb the position of lead negotiator. Despite his efforts, there was no positive answer from Concha. The situation had become extremely serious.

It took the combined effort of B-V and Cromwell to solve the problem. "Cromwell called to see me on the morning of March 26, 1902", wrote B-V in his memoirs. "He indicated that a crisis has been reached, because Concha refused to yield. . . It meant the rupture of negotiations, as Nicaragua was contented with only one-fourth of the indemnity asked by Colombia." (7)

Cromwell saw no issue and was extremely pessimistic.

B-V, still impatient to keep things moving, used a stratagem to force the Colombians to come to the negotiation table. On the same day, March 26, he divulged his course of action to the Panamanian newspaper *Panama Star & Herald*, which immediately printed the entire story of Bogota's obstruction in the negotiation. This paper was owned by a certain Jose Gabriel Duque, a Cuban, naturalized American, whom we shall meet again later on.

B-V hoped, in this way, to encourage indirectly those of the Colombians who were still in favor of Panama. Concha was aware of all this, but he had received strict orders and he reacted by indicating to B-V that this was "an affair touching high interests, which cannot be discussed on a mere commercial basis or superficially." (7)

This was a strange way to say that the Colombians still wanted to wait.

But B-V was obstinate. He wrote to Concha: "Your conception is absolutely just, the essential point is not that of money.   . The triumph of Nicaragua was prevented through my action in Paris, not more than three months ago, . . . when I recommended the sale of the New Company for $ 40 million. Today, for a paltry question of some millions, Colombia is nigh throwing away the marvelous privilege that Nature gave to her people." (7)

As a matter of fact, the difficulties met in negotiating with Bogota worked in favor of Nicaragua. Morgan and his supporters insisted that this route was more patriotic, more "American". It was true that Nicaragua had been for decades a very friendly country. "By 1894, thanks to the establishment of the first banana plantation, the United States had become by far the most influential foreign presence in Nicaragua, controlling over 90% of wealth, enterprise and commerce on the Mosquito Coast – on the Atlantic side –, in what could be said to have remained for some years a model of American economic penetration in Central America."(20)

The Colombian's attitude was exactly the opposite; they were not even grateful for the United States to intervene to maintain order in their territories, in Panama.

A reason for this could be found in the isolation of Bogota. Communications from Washington to Bogota were extremely lengthy and difficult. From New York, one had first to spend a week on a ship to reach Cartagena. Then, "to travel from the Atlantic Coast to Bogota, took twelve days, in a canoe and on horseback." (5) Of course, one could use the telegraph line, but it would not replace the face-to-face contact needed for efficient diplomatic conferences.

In total, traveling from New York to Bogota, took almost a month.

This isolation caused a lack of good understanding on both sides. The current and endless negotiation was just one example of this.

Nicaragua was in a much better position, as it had already signed with the United States, over a year ago – December 1st, 1900. Rumors started in Washington that because the Colombians were unable to negotiate, Nicaragua should be again the favorite.

During the entire month of March 1902, B-V and Cromwell, although separately, spent long meetings with Concha to try to find a solution to the stalled negotiation, but no progress was made.

By insisting once and again, on March 31, 1902, B-V received what he had been expecting, the counter-proposal from Concha: $ 7 million for the concession of a Canal Zone, 10 kilometer wide, plus an annual allocation - Concha did not quote any figure - to be renegotiated every 100 years (sic).

This was an important event, as it was the first time that the Colombians had made a move towards the American position in the negotiation. Of course, B-V immediately sent the Colombian proposal to Hay, the Secretary of State.

After a few changes, this proposal was transformed into a *Memorandum*, dated April 18 (quoted in its entirety in 12), which provided that:
- "The Government of Colombia authorizes the New Panama Canal Company to sell and transfer to the United States its rights, privileges, properties and concessions, as well as the PRR;
- The United States shall have the exclusive right to excavate, construct, maintain, operate, control and protect a maritime canal;
- To enable the United States to exercise their rights and privileges, Colombia grants the use of a territory along the route of the canal, 5 kilometers in width on either side (about 3 miles), for the term of one hundred years, renewable at their option (Note of the author: this was equivalent to perpetuity!);
- The rights and privileges granted to the United States shall not affect the sovereignty of Colombia over the conceded territory;
- As a price for the right to use the zone granted in this convention, the United States pledges to pay to Colombia the amount of $ 7 million and an annuity of $ 250,000.

Hanna had now all the arguments he needed to defend his "minority report" in the Senate.

In Paris, going back to the first days of April, when the *Memorandum* had not yet reached the offices of the New Company, President Bô did not understand what was happening. In December 1901, the directors of the New Company had agreed on the sale of its assets for $ 40 million. The offer had been sent to the Americans and an emissary, Edouard Lampré had traveled to Washington to answer questions about it.

Then Spooner had introduced his amendment in which he had asked the shareholders of the New Company - and not only its Directors - to approve the $ 40 million offer, which they had done in a meeting on February 28, 1902.

Nobody in Paris understood the situation. Three months ago, the *Walker Commission* had recommended Panama. Practically all demands from the Americans had been satisfied and nothing had happened. The Spooner Law had not yet been voted by the Senate; the supporters of Nicaragua had the upper hand again.

B-V was accused by some Parisian newspapers - except of course by *Le Matin* - of being out of his mind, as he was still defending Panama, which was judged to be a lost cause, with no impending result.

These criticisms were unfair. During the whole month of April, B-V had spent long working days in Washington trying to find a solution acceptable to the Colombians, and such solution was now expressed by the April 18, *Memorandum*.

In Paris, people grew very impatient. Without even waiting for the *Memorandum* to be made public - it would be on May 15, when President Roosevelt would officially receive it – indignation mounted against B-V.

In early April, Maurice, B-V's brother, left Paris for New York.
Would Maurice become involved in the Panama matter?

22

MAURICE ARRIVED IN NEW YORK

Unexpectedly, by mid-April 1902, Maurice Bunau-Varilla, B-V's brother, arrived in New York.

Maurice had no major interest in Panama, except for his shares in the New Company, valued at one and a half million francs, a trifle compared to his huge wealth (see his many possessions in Appendix 5).

As one may recall, Maurice had started purchasing shares of *Le Matin* in October 1893, with the money he had made with ASC, the company digging the Culebra in Panama.

As "Political Director" of *Le Matin*, Maurice was obviously well informed of the race for the Interoceanic Canal in Central America. He socially frequented the Directors of the New Company and was even in good terms with some of them (as demonstrated with the rehabilitation of Cromwell, pages 208-209). However, we have not found any evidence of Maurice playing any part in the Panama matter. Some authors thought that he was involved in the *Panama Canal Company of America,* set by Cromwell at the end of 1899, but we could not find any evidence for this thesis.

We have mentioned earlier that *Le Matin* was owned by Alfred Edwards, the son of a rich banker. In June 1895, Pierre-Dominique Parodi - whom we have already met as ASC's liquidator - a close friend of Maurice, entered the Board of the newspaper and with Poidatz - another owner of *Le Matin* -, they were compelled to vote an increase in the paper's capital. This was dictated by the poor financial condition of the finances of *Le Matin.*

According to Pinsolle, Maurice was already a large investor. "He was an astute businessman and had invested in three sectors: mines, transportation and banking." (30)

Pinsolle thought that Maurice was approached by Poidatz, who needed help. We rather believe that it was Parodi, a closer friend of Maurice, who convinced him to make such investment. Or maybe both of them?

Maurice probably thought it over for some time; *Le Matin* was losing money, but his friends were insistent. Maurice was a cautious investor and he decided to subscribe shares for only 300,000 francs - this invalidates the theory according to which Maurice needed a newspaper to protect his fortune. For such a small amount - about 5% of Maurice's estimated fortune - it was clearly only a diversification of his investments.

Edwards and Maurice ran the paper together; they named Poidatz, their common friend, "Chief Editor" of *Le Matin*.

From January 1896, Maurice developed such a liking in running the newspaper that, later on, he decided to become the majority owner and consequently the only one in charge. Gradually, he purchased shares of the paper - 50/50 with his brother B-V - to achieve his goal.

When Maurice arrived in New York to visit his brother in April 1902, Henry Poidatz was still the majority owner of *Le Matin*, but he had decided to sell his shares and Maurice had signed with him an agreement to become the preferred purchaser. It was an important transaction; Poidatz had set a selling price of 3 million francs, to be paid in three installments; the first was be due soon.

We believe that this was the main reason for Maurice's trip to New York. B-V had been busy negotiating with Concha; he had left Paris in November 1901 and apart from a few days spent in Paris for Christmas 1901, had not returned home. Maurice needed some serious talk with his brother.

On the other hand, being a major investor, his fortune still growing, Maurice certainly needed to have his brother's advice on potential new investments. One of them was dealing with *Le Matin*.

Our evidence for one of the purposes of Maurice's trip was a long letter from B-V to his brother Maurice, dated June 5, 1905, a monument of circumspection. (2)

In this letter, B-V mentioned that: "as we are about to conclude our agreements of 1903," - which means that it had taken a year to negotiate these agreements; the spring of 1902 was probably when Maurice and Poidatz had started negotiating their deal.

The same letter revealed the agreements passed by the brothers: "You have offered to me an equal participation to the titles sold by Poidatz . . . the first payment amounted to 500,000 francs for each one of us." (2)

Except for the 300,000 francs invested by Maurice in June 1895, the brothers had decided to invest jointly.

Such was the situation when Maurice landed in New York. Maurice worked in Paris. B-V was absorbed in the affairs of Panama in America.

Communication between the brothers proved difficult to sort out such an important matter. The future of Maurice's newspaper was at stake, so he came to New York to consult with his brother.

Poidatz's death in 1905 was the occasion for B-V to confirm in writing to his brother Maurice that: "he will always abstain from any interference in the newspaper's financial strategy" and "formally forever relinquish his voting rights to his brother". Again, B-V was very clear to Maurice: "50% of the newspaper's shares should always remain in your hands." (2)

Maurice had been since 1895 an exceptionally able editor of *Le Matin*. He had worked hard and brought this newspaper to the top of the Parisian press. He had been among the first journalists to introduce modern features: various advertisements filled two pages and a novel published in daily series occupied the bottom of the second page - the newspaper had 6 pages and sold for 5 cents. Huge popular gatherings were organized: marches, a world tour in 63 days (1901), an automobile long-distance run (Paris-Beijing in 1903), etc.

Maurice took, as we have already mentioned, a major part in the Dreyfus' affair, publishing the letter written by Dreyfus and which B-V had luckily found at the right moment.

Le Matin adopted a radical and laical policy. It claimed to be the only Parisian newspaper to publish exclusive news; its sub-title was: "The only French paper receiving by wire the ultimate news" and another title below claimed: "Last wires of tonight".

Maurice was rich, but also generous; he loved his country and in January 1899, he launched a subscription in favor of modernizing the French army and navy. The funds collected had been used to build the first French submarines: *Le Français* and *L'Algérien*.

Le Matin, devoted an important part of its profits to encourage artists, to subsidize scientific research (the wireless communications of Marconi, the medical work of Finlay on yellow fever), polar expeditions (Charcot in Antarctica), etc.

As a consequence of Maurice's efforts, the distribution of *Le Matin* climbed from a meager 30,000 in 1895 to 285,000 in 1902 and would reach a million copies in 1914 and a record 1.6 million by the end of the war in 1918.

Boosted by his success, Maurice was co-opted to join the Board of Directors of *Le Matin* in 1899. A few months before coming to New York, on December 23, 1901, Maurice had been elected President of the Board.

He now was the powerful manager of *Le Matin* and will remain at this position until his death in 1944.

Maurice Bunau-Varilla had really been a celebrity in the Parisian press, but this achievement would not be remembered. We shall see why later on.

Coming back to Maurice's arrival in New York, an additional - although secondary - reason to visit his brother could be the interest that B-V was taking in *Le Matin*'s technology. B-V had contacted Richard M. Hoe in New York, a manufacturer of rotary printing presses that were widely used by American newspapers. Apart from dealing with his Panama obsession, it seems that B-V was collaborating in solving the technical problems of his brother Maurice. This is another proof that - up to now - the brothers had always remained close.

"*Le Matin* was printed according to the latest technical developments of the modern science. It was printed five times day and night, from a factory equipped with the best equipment that the current civilization has produced." (30) B-V must have been proud of the success of his brother's newspaper.

So, Maurice arrived in New York. B-V wrote in his memoirs: "The information transmitted by the French Embassy in Washington to the Department of Foreign Affairs on the Canal question was so hopeless that the rumor was current in Paris that I had gone crazy. My brother, much disquieted, crossed the ocean to comfort me. I tranquillized him." (7)

What was behind this sentence?

We see here another example of B-V's discretion concerning his familial affairs.

Could Maurice's trip had been about the Panama vs. Nicaragua contest?

Did Maurice carry a secret message from Bô, the President of the New Company? This was possible, although the telegraph would have been quite appropriate in such a case.

Could it be that the Parisian rumors had led Maurice to believe that B-V was losing control of the situation in the United States?

Or that Cromwell could have criticized B-V's course of action with the New Company and that its president Bô could have mandated Maurice to discover the truth about it? After all, four months had elapsed since the Americans had received the $ 40 million offer and nothing had happened. The Senate was procrastinating. All the New Company shareholders, who wanted the sale to go ahead, became nervous.

We estimate that none of these above assumptions are credible.

B-V had such an independent character that he would never have allowed his brother to interfere with his Panama affairs. It was in pure reciprocity with his attitude towards his brother's newspaper, where he never intervened.

We think that it was extremely unlikely that B-V could have asked for his brother's help in the Panama's issue. We are inclined to think that Maurice had come to discuss with his brother B-V, the terms of the *Le Matin's* purchase that he was going to sign with Poidatz – or perhaps some other investments.

B-V had not spent a lot of time in Paris in the last months and was not expected to be in Paris soon, as the Panama negotiation was dragging on. The brothers had probably decided to equally invest in *Le Matin* and they had great difficulty to communicate being each on one side of the Atlantic Ocean.

After the April 18 *Memorandum* had been agreed by Concha and Hay, there was not much going on in Washington; everybody was awaiting the Senate debate of Hanna's minority report, planned for June.

B-V was thus ready to spend some leisurely time with his brother Maurice. Only a week after his arrival in New York, at the end of April 1902, the brothers sailed to Havana, Cuba.

Here is what B-V wrote about this trip: "As nothing remained to be done in Washington, I proposed to go with him (Maurice) to Cuba. It was at the moment when the first statistics were being obtained as to the results of the campaign against yellow fever. We went to see Major Gorgas." (7)

According to Anguizola, Maurice had already traveled to Cuba in 1901, on his way to Central America, "to investigate progress made in fighting malaria and yellow fever." (18)

In Havana, Maurice - maybe associated with his brother B-V - could have been subsidizing the research of Carlos Juan Finlay, a Cuban born doctor, of French-Scottish origin, who had been jointly working with a U. S. Army scientist, William Crawford Gorgas. (28)

Finlay had discovered in 1881 the link between the mosquitoes and the yellow fever. Unfortunately, the French workers in Panama could not take advantage of this recent discovery.

Maurice's philanthropy had met his brother's altruistic concern; B-V had almost died of yellow fever when he was in Panama in 1886. B-V had taken the sanitary problem of Panama very seriously and believed that finding a cure to this horrible sickness would also save "his" canal.

When the United States took control of Cuba in 1899, they were faced with a serious health problem caused by yellow fever and were keen to solve it. Carlos Finlay had suggested a few years ago that a mosquito was the cause of the propagation of the disease, but no action followed. As epidemics burst out in Cuba for no reason, the Americans summoned Major Gorgas, a specialist in tropical diseases, medicine doctor in the U. S. Army, stationed in the South. He was named Head of the Cuban Health Department.

Working together, Finlay and Gorgas were able to solve the enigma, and "early in 1901, the Army Medical Board was able to state categorically that yellow fever was transmitted by the *Aedes* mosquito." (28)

This would prove later to be of extreme importance in the completion of the Panama Canal by the Americans. We shall see how Gorgas, hired by the Americans to cleanse the Canal Zone, in 1905, will eradicate the yellow fever epidemics and allow the laborers to work in a much safer environment.

In the 1880s, the French were ignorant of the effect of the mosquitoes.

In 1901, the mosquito was found to transmit yellow fever to humans.

Work could now start safely on an Interoceanic Canal in Central America: but will it be in Nicaragua or in Panama?

23
HOW A VOLCANO SAVED PANAMA
1902

After their short visit to Cuba, the brothers were back in New York on May 8, just in time to read in the newspapers all the details of the horrible calamity that had just struck the Island of Martinique.

On May 6, the *Montagne Pelée* volcano had entirely exploded, blown up to pieces. The city of Saint Pierre had been pulverized. There were 31,000 casualties. It was a terrible catastrophe and everybody in New York commented about it.

At about the same time, in the Island of Saint Vincent, close to Martinique, the volcano called *La Soufrière* killed 1,500 people. This incited commentators to think that there could be subterraneous connections between volcanoes. This conjecture would be confirmed by seismology, years later.

We have to recall that almost twenty years ago, on September 8, 1882, an earthquake had struck the Isthmus of Panama. At this time, it did not cause any casualties and nobody had worried about such a risk during the construction of the canal. Once the material damages had been repaired, the Company resumed its work as if it had never happened. And no other major earthquake hit had hit Panama ever since.

This time, it was much more serious. God was reminding His people that any volcano, even one tagged as dormant, could become active one day.

The members of the *Walker Commission* became worried. They quickly met and decided to appoint some experts to assess the risks in Nicaragua and in Panama.

It was easy enough to look at the maps and observe that those two countries were located right on the famous "fire belt" of volcanoes running along the Pacific Ocean shore of the American continent. While they were investigating further, God sent them another sign.

One week after Martinique, on May 13, the *Momotombo*, a volcano close to the northern edge of Lake Managua, north of lake Nicaragua, sent fumes and ashes into the atmosphere. It had also been dormant for years. Although its eruption was much less serious than in Martinique, because there were no casualties, it was nevertheless spectacular. A dock was destroyed and a coffee warehouse was burned down.

This came as a favorable event for Panama, where newspapers reminded their readers that the Arco Chato, an arch built by the Spaniards in the 17th Century within the Convent of Santo Domingo in the City of Panama was still intact. It had strongly resisted all earthquakes and other aggressions of time. It was a genuine example of the ground stability in the Panama Isthmus.

This Arco was thin, almost horizontal, fifty feet wide and was an insult to the law of gravity, a proof of the extreme stability of the ground.

B-V was ecstatic when he learned about the *Momotombo*: "What an unexpected turn of the wheel of fortune", he wrote in his memoirs. (7) "It is a curious thing to remark that in my book of 1892, I had written: The explosions of the volcanoes of this country, Nicaragua, occupy the front rank in the history of seismic movements. One of them, Momotombo, has won a place in literature: *The Reasons of Momotombo,* by famous French writer Victor Hugo." (7) This certainly carried more than a grain of truth.

In New York, the Bunau-Varilla brothers met with their friends Bigelow and Pavey. During one of these reunions, an event happened which proved once again the enormous persuasive power of B-V, who had become an expert in making his luck work to his advantage. During a dinner given by John Bigelow, B-V lectured the guests at length on the danger of living close to a volcano. Among the diners was Dana, the owner of the *Sun,* a New York newspaper. On the next day, May 12, the *Sun* published an interview of B-V, "ranking the *Sun*, hitherto neutral, definitely on the side of Panama." (7) (Here B-V's memory was somewhat deficient, as Dana died in 1897! It was probably Edward Mitchell or William Laffan, Dana's successors)

Two days later, the news of the *Momotombo*'s volcanic blast reached New York. The newspapers other than the *Sun*, which had been campaigning for the "American" solution, were taken by surprise.

However, Nicaragua supporters were determined to do anything to win the decision. Senator Morgan went as far as obtaining from the President of the Republic of Nicaragua, Zelaya*, a flat denial of the event in a telegram: "News published about recent eruptions of volcanoes and earthquakes in Nicaragua are entirely false." (7)

Furthermore, Corea, the Ambassador of Nicaragua in Washington added: "Nicaragua has had no volcanic eruptions since 1835 and, at that moment, the Cosigüina emitted smoke and ashes but no lava." (7)

Partisans of Panama had to react. During the following days, the walls of the hallways inside the Senate became covered with maps highlighting the volcanoes. "When Senators reconvened on June 5, they were surprised to find the chamber festooned with maps and diagrams. A twenty-foot projection, hanging from the visitors' gallery, showed red and black dots splotching Central America. Active volcanoes were marked in red, and the extinct volcanoes in black. Nicaragua had eight active sites, Panama was dot free." (25)

It should be noted that the Momotombo is located northwest of Lake Managua, about 20 miles from the capital city of Managua. In any case, its eruption would not have affected the future canal, as it would have been about 100 miles north of the planned route for the Interoceanic Canal.

As for the other volcano, the Cosigüina, it is even further away, 180 miles northwest of the future canal.

Obviously, none of these volcanoes could have been a threat to the future Nicaragua Canal.

Two other volcanoes stand in the Island of Ometepe, in the middle of Lake Nicaragua, right on the path of the future Interoceanic Canal, as recommended by Menocal. These volcanoes, Concepcion and Madera, have not emitted a single plume of smoke for centuries.

B-V did not mention in his memoirs these elementary facts. He was not interested by the location of the volcanoes in Nicaragua, but only by the psychological effect that these volcanic blasts would have on the Senators' vote.

Only a fortnight after these events, on June 4, the debate on the Spooner amendment, about the future Interoceanic Canal, started in the Senate. B-V was confident that the conclusion would be favorable to Panama, as he had deluged the Senators with his leaflet comparing both routes: "It was printed on the 2nd of June, two days before the opening of the debate before Congress. Senator Hanna had a copy of it immediately distributed to every Senator." (7)

---

* José Santos Zelaya (1853-1919) took power in 1893 in Nicaragua and was later elected President until 1909. When the United States shifted their canal interests to Panama, he negotiated with Germany who happened to be in the middle of a cold war with the United States over the Caribbean ports.

Again, we notice B-V's extreme self-esteem; he was confident that the vote would favor Panama: "Having in hand this brief, limpid and incisive summary of the whole matter, summed up in thirteen sketches, the Senators heard . . . Hanna's speech." (7)

On Friday June 6, "even as he spoke, *Montagne Pelée* was erupting again." (25)

On June 12, after staying almost two months in America, Maurice returned to France, on *La Lorraine* - a new transatlantic liner, launched in 1900. During his stay in New York, he had visited most of the large newspapers' printing factories. B-V explained that : "The director of the *Star* had invited my brother and myself to visit his printing office." (7) The *Star* had printing presses made by Hoe: *Le Matin* would purchase six of them. (30)

Meanwhile in the Senate, despite all Hanna's efforts - his speech lasted two days -, the debate was not showing any advantage to any of the parties. Surprisingly, two weeks of speeches had not been successful in convincing the supporters of Nicaragua. B-V was confident that, after the blatant lies of the Nicaraguan officials, "it was absolutely necessary to reply with emphasis and to refute the false statement by an explicit and undeniable answer." (7)

Then an unusual set of circumstances occurred, which has since been turned into a legend.

B-V had a brilliant idea. He had remembered very opportunely having seen some postage stamps from Nicaragua, which represented "a beautiful volcano belching forth in magnificent eruption." (7) Having purchased many of these stamps, he proceeded to send them on June 6 to all the Senators, each stamp pasted on a single page of paper, where under the title: "Postal Stamp of the Republic of Nicaragua. An official witness of the volcanic activity of the Isthmus of Nicaragua." was written the short sentence: "On account of the earthquake consecutive to the eruption of the Momotombo volcano (to be seen in the background with its cloud of smoke), the greater part of the wharf (to be seen in the foreground), went to the bottom of the lake with a large quantity of bags of coffee, on March 24, 1902, at 1:55 p. m. (*Iris de la Tarde de Granada* and *Democracia de Managua*, two newspapers from Nicaragua; see also *New York Sun* of June 12, 1902)." (7 and 11)

All this was true, except that the lake shown on the stamp was not Lake Nicaragua, which the proposed canal would cross, but it was Lake Managua, located 100 miles away!

A curious reader could ask why such an important eruption had been known in New York almost two months after the facts (March 24 - April 14).

The factual truth was of no real interest to those involved at the time. B-V had wished to create a psychological impact and he did so. The effect of the stamps on the Senators was immediate.

On June 19, only three days after receiving the famous stamp - showing a volcano in eruption - the Senators adopted the *Spooner Act*.

This *Act* gave preference to Panama for the Interoceanic Canal. One condition of the *Act* was that the assets of the French Company were to be bought for a maximum of $ 40 million. Another requirement was that an agreement with Colombia would be reached within a reasonable time.

It was a tight vote: 42 for, 34 against and 12 abstentions.

McCullough wrote: "So, had there been a difference of just five votes, the result would have been a Nicaragua canal." (16)

After the Senate, the bill had to be ratified by the House. To lobby in favor of this vote, B-V put together a new mailing of a letter with the stamp of Nicaragua glued on it. He wrote in his memoirs: "I spent some time hunting for about 500 odd Nicaraguan stamps." (7)

His stratagem worked a second time and even better. On June 26, the House of Representatives voted the *Spooner Act* by a huge margin: 260 votes for and 8 against:

- The President of the United states is authorized to acquire at a cost not exceeding $ 40 million, the rights, privileges, franchises, concessions, grants of land, right of way, unfinished work, plants, and other property owned by the New Panama Canal Company, including the PRR;
- The President is authorized to acquire from Colombia, upon such terms as he may deem reasonable, perpetual control of a strip of land not less than six miles in width;
- Should the President be unable to obtain a satisfactory title of the New Company or a treaty providing control of the necessary territory from Colombia, then the President, having first obtained perpetual control by treaty of the necessary territory from Costa Rica and Nicaragua, shall cause to be executed a canal from Greytown to Brito, by way of lake Nicaragua." (12)

Clearly, the ball was in Roosevelt's hands.
The President ratified the bill on June 29.

At the beginning of July 1902, B-V returned to France, satisfied with his work. His happiness was extreme: "the joy which I felt at this victory, so improbable and so long and so ardently desired, was intense", he wrote in his memoirs. (7) But he also added: "The question of the treaty with Colombia, the second condition of the *Spooner Act*, did not go so easily."(7)

He was right, the agreement with Colombia – "upon terms that President Roosevelt would deem acceptable" - would take quite many more efforts.

In Paris, during the summer break, Charles Russell, the Under-Secretary of State to the Justice Department met with the French Company's officials to review the detailed conditions of the sale. Mr. Knox, the Attorney General, convinced that the property title of the New Company was valid, arrived later for the formal signature ceremony.

The first condition of the *Spooner Act* was fulfilled. All was well.

It should be noted that many Senators, who had voted in favor of the *Spooner Act*, because they favored Panama, had other requisite conditions:
- First, wait that Panama, now in full civil war, be pacified;
- Second, that the *Memorandum* of April 18 be modified to extend American jurisdiction on the Canal Zone: they asked for police, justice and salubrity to be totally under American control;
- Last: wait for a new Congress to be elected in Bogota.,

During that 1902 summer, negotiations with Bogota were at standstill. Concha had hoped to have a positive reaction from his Government, but was disappointed when orders came to wait. Now that Panama was accepted by Congress, Concha was asked to delay all negotiation until October 1904, which would mark the end of the French concession. How could he procrastinate for another two years ? It was an impossible mission, as the civil war, which extended throughout all of Colombia did not allow a serene negotiation.

In Central America, more trouble were brewing.

The civil war in Colombia had engulfed all its territories, including Panama. There, General Benjamin Herrera, had proclaimed himself Governor of the Province in February 1902. He had been victorious against the conservative Carlos Alban. The situation became so chaotic that in June, Marroquin, the President of Colombia, asked the United States to intervene to restore order to the Canal Zone. He believed that the PRR's safety was jeopardized by Herrera's actions.

"That reluctant appendix to Colombia was having one of its annual rebellions against the authority of Bogota." (25) Admiral Silas Casey, commanding the U. S. fleet off the coasts of Panama, declared a ban on all transit of armed forces on the interoceanic railway (PRR), as he was authorized under the 1846 *Mallarino-Bidlack* treaty.

As the revolution remained on going in Panama, the United States responded favorably to Marroquin's request and sent their warship *Cincinnati*, which arrived in Colon's harbor on September 26. Marines landed and took control of the main cities: Colon and Panama City. Revolutionaries left those cities. Calm had been restored.

It was clear that no one in Washington was ready to invest in such an unsettled country. This agitation had been started in 1899 - it was called the *Thousand-Day War*.

Nicaragua proved to be far more peaceful than Colombia and especially than her remote Province of Panama.

Everybody in Washington recalled the terms of the "Spooner Amendment, now enshrined in law, which required to revert to Nicaragua in the event of a failure to negotiate a satisfactory agreement with Colombia." (25)

"Towards the middle of November, a rupture was again imminent" commented B-V. "The newspapers which had unwillingly abandoned the cause of Nicaragua saw their hopes revive." (7)

B-V volunteered once again to help the cause of Panama: "I resorted again to the method of direct intervention, and I cabled to President Marroquin. I did not hesitate to make him face the terrible danger of a possible secession of Panama." (7)

In October 1902, B-V was back in New York, in his usual *Waldorf Astoria* hotel, suite # 1162. This time, nobody had called for him and no one can accuse him of having his trip ticket purchased by the partisans of Panama.

Altogether, in a few years (1899-1904) B-V had been spending an enormous sum of money out of his personal fortune to defend the Panama Canal project. A curious reader may turn to Appendix 3, where we have estimated his expenses for that period of time to reach almost a million francs, equivalent to $ 200,000.

Quite a huge sum of money for the time!

However, B-V did not spend as much as Cromwell and his many assistants – Farnham, Hill, Curtis, etc.

On October 24, in Colombia, the parties involved in the *Thousand Days* civil war signed a peace treaty - in Neerlandia, near Barranquilla, in the north of the country.

On November 21, the head of the liberal opposition in Panama, General Herrera, abandoned the fight and surrendered onboard the *Wisconsin*, a U. S. war ship.

This event announced a period of stability in the Isthmus and B-V took advantage of it by sending on November 23 another cable to President Marroquin of Colombia: "Extremely perilous situation. Loss of all results when towards the end of next February, present Congress adjourns. The only hope is in a decisive radical action of the Supreme Government of the Republic." (7) This time, B-V's call was heard in Bogota, "as Mr. Concha was immediately recalled on December 1st." (7)

Marroquin declared that he was ready to abandon Colombia's sovereignty on the land along the Canal in Panama, but he remained inflexible on the question of money.

We recall that eight months ago, in March 1902, Concha had proposed to Hay that he was ready to waive the non-transferable clause in the contract with the French Company for a sum of $ 7 million. During the summer, the Colombian Congress had declared its intent to increase this sum to $ 10 million. This was the first obstacle.

Another obstacle was that Concha had not included in the "territory" the ports of Colon and La Boca, near Panama City. These ports were included in the *Spooner Act*.

A third obstacle was that Concha had proposed a concession for 100 years renewable, in order to disguise the concept of perpetuity. In the *Spooner Act*, the perpetuity of the concession was spelled out explicitly.

It was clear that the *Spooner Act* was more favorable to Americans than was the *Memorandum* presented by Concha on last April 18.

All these obstacles - we have no room here to mention them all - announced a difficult negotiation.

Today, the whole world is well aware of the negotiation tactics of the United States of America. Conscious of their position as a powerful nation, they ask first for the most favorable conditions, until the discussions are about to break off, with the purpose of testing their adversaries' resolve.

So, the Americans camped on the conditions spelled out by the Senators in the *Spooner Act*.

Concha's conditions, dictated by Bogota, were quite different.

It thus seemed extremely improbable that an agreement be reached soon.

Marroquin, the Colombian President, was too busy with internal affairs to pursue further the negotiation. Now up for re-election, he could not help Concha in the negotiation.

Panama was still in a state of chaos, following Herrera's capitulation.

On November 22, Hay cabled to Hart, the American Ambassador in Bogota: "We have made all possible concessions to Colombia in canal matter; have ceded question of perpetuity and several minor concessions, but can go no farther." (12)

At the end of November 1902, Concha, "heartbroken and discouraged", went back to Bogota. He was sick, according to some authors. Undeniably, the climate in Washington was not suitable to Colombian diplomats. First Silva had to go back home, now it was Concha.

In the absence of a replacement, **Tomas Herran**, the First Secretary of the Embassy of Colombia, took over on December 1ˢᵗ. At 58, "his long diplomatic career had carried him to posts in London, Paris, Lima and Hamburg. He was a master of four languages and highly regarded in Colombia for his intellectual refinement." (12) He had been very helpful in assisting Concha and Hay had much esteem for him.

Wisely, he started by obtaining some very precise orders from Bogota and, having received an agreement, he proposed: a payment of $ 10 million and a $ 500.000 rent annually.

It seemed almost impossible to believe. After months of impatient expectation, the promise of an accord came from Colombia. "I was persuaded that the solution was equitable. I was resolved to force it through," (7) wrote B-V, who was hopeful again.

Hay was ready to accept a lump sum of $ 10 million, but he refused to pay an annual rent of more than $ 100,000. The difference between the two positions was enormous: calculated for the duration of the contract, 100 years, it amounted to $ 40 million.

It was understandable that the United States were reluctant to satisfy Colombia's demand, because they were undertaking an expensive project, with an uncertain profitability.

On December 19, 1902, B-V persisted once again and sent another cable to Marroquin, urging him to find a compromise: "I believe that a firm, final decision of Colombian Government to accept $ 10 million plus annual rental of $ 250,000 would have much chance of saving the situation if the offer of signing immediately the Panama Canal treaty accompanies the said proposition." (7)

It seemed that after so many cables to Marroquin, B-V had managed to establish a dialogue.

B-V sent another letter to Hay to beg him to accept a conciliatory agreement. It seemed that Hay would accept up to $ 250,000 for the annual payment. Like B-V, Hay would be ready to make concessions to save the Panama project.

On December 25, Christmas Day 1902, B-V believed that an agreement was within reach. He set sail for France, where he would arrive too late to spend the holiday season with his family. Sadly, he celebrated alone on board his luxurious transatlantic liner. B-V's devotion to the cause of the Panama Canal called for many sacrifices on his part.

We shall encounter many more of these sacrifices in the next chapters.

24
HOW COLOMBIANS FAILED TO NEGOTIATE
1903

On January 21, 1903, "anxious of not seeing the acquiescence of Bogota to my proposition of December 19, 1902,", (7) B-V re-embarked once again back to reach New York. On board, he met with General Nel Ospina, whom he had met before in Venezuela in 1900. The ex-Minister of War of Colombia would soon become Vice-President of the Senate in Bogota. Our hero was happy to cultivate such relationship, which might become useful in the future.

In Washington, B-V's proposal had unexpectedly been considered by both the United States and Colombia. He had waited so long for this moment to happen that he had a hard time believing it could finally be there.

He had worked on the negotiations for the last three years!

While B-V was still on board, crossing the Atlantic Ocean, on January 22, the *Hay-Herran* Treaty was signed between the United States and Colombia. Colombia would receive $ 10 million and an annual payment of $ 250,000. This would amount to $ 35 million compounded over the 100 years of the contract.

However, In Bogota, the provisional Government thought that better conditions could be obtained by further negotiations. On January 25 - three days after Herran had signed - President Marroquin cabled his Minister "not to sign but to await new instructions." To which Herran replied that he had signed with all required credentials and that "President Marroquin had no constitutional authority to enter into a convention." (12) Such a strange dialogue between a President and his Ambassador!

Unfortunately, B-V landed in New York on January 31, a week too late to witness the treaty's signature. He was, of course, immensely delighted with this happy ending.

Cromwell was too; he claimed in his "plea for fees" that "thanks to the strongest pressure, we succeeded to have the treaty concluded." (6)

We can imagine that B-V celebrated this event with his faithful friends, Hay, Baker, Bigelow, Loomis, Pavey, etc.

Having reached his objective, he sailed back to Paris on February 24. He had remained in America less than a month.

Despite the strong opposition of Senator Morgan - he proposed sixty (!) amendments and detailed them in a series of speeches from March 9 to 14 - on March 17, the Senate ratified the *Hay-Herran* Treaty by 73 votes for and 5 against.

All was well that ended well.

But was it really over?

Hell, no, not yet! We were only in the early days of a year, which would see more surprises than in all the past years combined.

1903 would prove to be rich with unexpected events.

The ratification of the *Hay-Herran* Treaty by Colombia was the last step necessary to enforce the Treaty. This was expected to be just a matter of time. In Bogota, the election of the representatives had taken place in the last months of 1902.

A new Congress had been elected and soon will have the power to ratify the Treaty. It had been expected that the Colombian electors would keep in power the government officials, who were so passionately negotiating the Treaty. They had fought to obtain the Interoceanic Canal in Panama and to defeat Nicaragua; this canal would bring them immediately a large lump sum and a considerable annual rent for a hundred years.

Yet, it did not happen as expected: "the elections were an incredible surprise," (15) wrote the Colombian historian Lemaitre. And what a surprise!

Unexpectedly, the Colombian elections brought a majority of opponents to the *Hay-Herran* Treaty to the Congress in Bogota.

"The country sincerely loathed to have surrendered its full sovereignty in the Isthmus," (15) continued Lemaitre.

This matter of the Canal Zone's sovereignty was so significant and over-sensitive that it will later corrupt the relations between the United States and Panama during an entire century.

Having an unfriendly Congress in Bogota was not a good sign for the conclusion of the *Hay-Herran* Treaty, recently signed by the ambassadors and ratified in Washington. One single last step remained; that the treaty be signed by the Colombian Congress. It would be a shame to have to return to the negotiation table once again.

The Bogota Congress was to meet again on June 20. B-V was ready to take action. He was extremely concerned about this situation. On June 10, in Paris, he received a Colombian "distinguished personage" in his villa of Avenue d'Iéna - B-V did not reveal his name in his memoirs; it could have been General Nel Ospina or one of his friends. This Colombian told B-V that "a formidable opposition was being organized against the Treaty." (7) B-V could not accept easily that his work of the past three years be lost in such a formality. He was so angry that he first threatened everybody, without realizing where his passion would lead him. It was a trait of his character to fly off the handle and thereafter to find calmly a solution to the problem.

"After thinking the matter over, I decided to put him (President Marroquin) face to face with the possible secession of the Isthmus." (7)

On June 13, B-V sent another cable to Bogota - in Spanish -, where he showed a much more incisive tone: "it will either be Nicaragua, or Panama, but after its secession and its declaration of independence, under protection of the United States." (7)

B-V's actions were now manifest: he was favoring the independence of the Panama province, if this could yet save "his" canal.

This cable marked an important step in our story. For the first time, appeared the idea that the United States could as well negotiate with an independent Panama.

In Bogota, for a private reason, the American Ambassador, Charles Burdett Hart, was called back to Washington. He was replaced by the Secretary of the American Embassy, Arthur Beaupré, to whom Hay sent the following telegram on June 9: "The Colombian Government apparently does not appreciate the gravity of the situation. . . If Colombia should reject the treaty, . . . action might be taken by the Congress which every friend of Colombia might regret." (25) sadly, it did not have any effect.

It goes without saying that Colombians were completely opposed to the independence of their Panama province, but they did not yet realize that this independence was already being plotted.

On June 13, "Roosevelt sat in a private conference with Cromwell. It was not in the President's habits to receive lobbyists, but Mark Hanna had strongly required the meeting." (25) Hanna believed that Cromwell's connections could be of some use to the President. It was said that he maintained paid connections in Bogota and Panama City.

"Roosevelt considered that with the *Hay-Herran* Treaty now signed, all the conditions required by the *Spooner Act* had been met and that he wanted a firm decision to build the canal in Panama." (12) As next year, 1904, would be an election year, the President was determined to act quickly.

Cromwell would act on behalf of the President.

On the following day, Cromwell wrote an article for the *New York World*, with "an uncannily prophetic title: *The State of Panama Ready to Secede*, if the treaty was to be rejected by the Colombian Congress." (25)

It is strange that Cromwell used almost the exact same words that B-V put in his cable to Marroquin, except that Cromwell went as far as predicting the date for such secession of Panama, on November 3, 1903! (6)

On June 20, the Colombian Congress, which had not met throughout the Thousand Days War, was ready to convene again. Of course, the formal approval of the *Hay-Herran* Treaty was on the agenda. The Colombian Senate appointed a Committee to study the treaty; towards the end of July, it recommended that nine amendments be added to the treaty. "The presentation of the Committee's report marked the real crisis in the Colombian Senate's consideration of the treaty." (12)   What the Committee tacitly recommended, by asking for so many amendments, was to start the negotiation from scratch.

In Panama, although there had been a cease-fire at the end of 1902, peace was still uncertain and some effervescence remained. Many people would not readily accept the conservative rule in Bogota and thus, a liberal opposition was actively working to achieve the independence of the province.

Panamanians must have been aware of the mood reigning in Washington, which encouraged their sedition.

On July 28, an important meeting of some Panamanian "conspirators" took place.

At the origin of this movement, set up at the initiative of Jose Agustin Arango - Land Agent and Attorney of the PRR, Senator for Panama - with his four sons and some of his best friends - Lewis, Lefevre, Orillac and Arosemena. To these first members, were added later those who shall become later the founding fathers of the Republic of Panama (the *Proceres*, in Spanish): Manuel Amador Guerrero - Medical Officer of the PRR -, Federico Boyd, Espinosa Batista, Tomas and Ricardo Arias, Nicanor de Obarrio, Pablo Arosemena, etc.

They had instigated a secret alliance. All these men, belonging to the high society of Panama, were obsessed by the idea of getting their independence.

It should be noted that many of the "conspirators" belonged to the management of the PRR; this would lead later to the false conclusion that Cromwell - Attorney of the PRR - was the leader of the conspiration.

During the July 28 meeting, not the first of its kind, the "conspirators" decided to delegate Manuel Amador to New York, in order to find funds in America to subsidize their independence. Money was the essence of the revolution. The Colombian garrison in Panama City was sounded and found to be easily corruptible. The troops had remained in Panama for a long time, mostly underpaid and were ready to accept a financial relief.

However, a few days later, in Bogota, the opponents to the *Hay-Herran* Treaty celebrated their victory. On August 12, the 24 Colombian Senators rejected the treaty unanimously; only one Senator was absent, José Domingo de Obaldia, the representative from Panama, with the excuse of being ill, when the vote took place. (15)

"Desperate to keep Colombia intact, President Marroquin ignored Obaldia's open rebelliousness and appointed him Governor of Panama." (25)

A Congressman, Perez y Soto, considered that: "The ignominy that Herran has cast upon Colombia's good name will never be obliterated. The gallows would be a very light penalty for such a criminal." (15) This sounds strange, as Herran always claimed that he had followed Bogota's orders.

General Veléz, a Colombian army official, explained the vote by saying: "This Treaty - *Hay-Herran* - is a violation of our fundamental institutions, a breach of our sovereignty. The canal has to be Colombian or not to be at all." (15) There were rumors "of mysterious commissions from some North-American railway companies, intended for preventing the vote of the treaty; and of the secret influence of Germany, ready to carry through the canal work for its own account. Anyway, the Colombian Congress had officially rejected the Treaty, bringing stupefaction in Bogota, Washington and Paris." (25)

"It can be seen here that the prejudiced Colombians have themselves called for an "external" solution", concluded rightly B-V, having still in mind Panama's victory. (7)

B-V was dismayed by the vote in Bogota, but he did not give up. On August 17, he wrote to General Nel Ospina, who had been elected Vice-President of the Colombian Senate, urging him to hark back to the vote which, if not overturned, "would be equivalent to stabbing your country to the heart, destroying its prosperity and its interests, whereas ratification insures a glorious future." (7) As usual, B-V tried everything to reverse the Senate decision, but it would prove to be an impossible task. The Colombian Senate had cast its vote unanimously.

In Washington, the Colombian vote was perceived as a request to renegotiate. It was understandable that after all the efforts it took for the Americans to sign and ratify the *Hay-Herran* Treaty, they were quite reluctant to start the process all over again. The *Spooner Act* had been voted more than a year ago.

Logically, American politicians were utterly discouraged.

On their part, the Colombians were still willing to go ahead with a canal in Panama. Their arrogance was in their proposition: Panama would be a source of revenues, which they badly needed. It was now their turn to use the American way to renegotiate, to find out where laid the rupture point.

On August 29, General Nel Ospina and other Senators - Manuel Rodriguez and José Maria Campo Serrano - intended to restart the negotiation by moving a resolution setting the new conditions for a treaty: $ 20 million and an annual payment of $ 400,000. Obviously, B-V's letter had absolutely no effect on General Nel Ospina. B-V qualified this new motion of "immoral proposal . . . and extortion," (7) which was absolutely true because the figures were twice the amounts of the *Hay-Herran* Treaty. Accumulated during the hundred years of the contract, this new proposal amounted to $ 60 million, or $ 25 million more than the *Hay-Herran* Treaty - $ 35 million.

But the Colombians did not stop here. The rest of their proposal was quite surprising; it stipulated that: "Colombia authorizes the French New Company to transfer its rights (Note: under the concession purchased to Colombia) to the United States in consideration of a payment of 50 million francs."($ 12.5 million)

When we examine the figures closely, we find that they added up to a total of: 25 + 12.5 = $ 37.5 million over the *Hay-Herran* Treaty, more than doubling its amount, which was $ 35 million!

Again, this proved that the sovereignty matter, once the main argument of Marroquin, had been put aside and that greed had become the primary issue for the Colombians. The negotiation could not start on these premises. Logically, American Senators categorically refused to amend a treaty they had already approved.

It is interesting to note that during all these events, nobody ever mentioned Nicaragua. Did this imply that the Americans already knew their way out of this deadlock? Would they dare to force the issue?

It was said that President Roosevelt, very irritated by the Colombian veto, had his spokesman declare: "we might make another treaty, not with Colombia, but with Panama." (16)

All historians agreed that this was, as B-V qualified it: "a confiscation through stagnation". The Colombian officials had decided to "drag along until the expiry date " (7) of the concession belonging to the French New Company (October 1904), to seize its assets and have the canal achieved by the United States.

It made sense; October 1904 was only a year away and the prize for Colombia would then be the $ 40 million value of the French New Company..

B-V was, once again, flabbergasted. He considered the situation as extremely critical and unsalvageable. He had worked almost four years to have Panama selected against Nicaragua and all his work would be in danger to be lost.

We had seen that B-V was a man of emotions. Quick to become angry, he later calmly decided on a plan of action. This time, we shall see the same scenario.

To break the deadlock, B-V met with his American friends to find a legal solution. After many meetings and long discussions, B-V endorsed an original idea which, by chance, coincided with that of President Roosevelt, and would in the end result in Panama's victory.

By reading all the texts and treaties relative to the matters of Central America, B-V discovered in the *Mallarino-Bidlack* treaty of 1846, an interesting clause by which Colombia granted the United States the right to have its citizens and goods transit freely across the Isthmus of Panama by using "any transportation mode, existing or to be built in the future."

This same idea was being examined by President Roosevelt's counselors. The President wrote to Hay, his Secretary of State, in a cowboy like style: "It seems that the great bulk of the best engineers have agreed that the route (of Panama) is the best; and I do not think that the Bogota lot of jack-rabbits should be allowed permanently to bar one of the future highways of civilization." (16)

Not a word of this transpired, and it was really necessary, because the President was also considering the use of armed forces to achieve his goal.

Roosevelt was still in command of the Panama matter, as he had been since the beginning of 1902, when he forced Walker and his Commission to alter their report and include the New Company's sale offer.

Would B-V accept to be left on the side?
How could he come back into the action?

25

A REVOLUTION IN PANAMA

In Panama, the "conspirators" were restless. The Colombian Senate's veto had strengthened their resolve to work hard towards the independence of Panama. Their plan was to corrupt the Colombian garrison assigned to the Province of Panama. Those poor soldiers had not been paid for many months, as the money provided by the French New Company - under its concession agreement with Colombia - had been delayed (or perhaps stolen?) when transiting through Bogota.

To bribe the Colombian soldiers, the "conspirators" needed money. This was a rare commodity in Panama since the departure of the French Company. The expenses of the French Company had been the only resource of the province, apart from the PRR, which no longer carried hordes of passengers.

A month ago, Amador and his friends had sent to New York a trustworthy envoy, Captain James R. Beers - erroneously called George by some authors; George was his father's name -, the Freight and Port Captain of the PRR. As already mentioned, PRR officials would play an important part in the coming revolution:
- Jose Agustin Arango, Land Agent and Attorney,
- James R. Shaler, Superintendent,
- Herbert G. Prescott, Assistant Superintendent,
- Manuel Amador Guerrero, Medical officer. (12)

Once in New York, Beers met with Cromwell, who showed much enthusiasm for Panama's independence and promised the moon to Beers, who passed his enthusiasm back to the "conspirators". Cromwell had so many friends in *Wall Street* that money would not be a problem.

Reassured about the success of their quest for funds, the "conspirators" mandated Amador to elaborate their mission in New York.

Manuel Amador Guerrero, a Colombian doctor, born in Cartagena, moved to Panama where he became an employee of the PRR in 1855. Politically active, member of the Conservative Party, in 1867, he was elected President of the Federal State of Panama, but a riot prevented him from taking office. In 1886, he was the Civil and Military Head of the Province for a few months. After retiring from the PRR, he dedicated himself to an humanitarian mission in a large hospital in the City of Panama. However, he always remained in contact with his political friends. In 1893, he traveled to Bogota with Arango and Sosa to beg for the extension of the French New Company's concession.

On board the ship from Panama to New York, Amador met Gabriel Duque, a Cuban, naturalized American, who owned an important import/export business as well as the *Star & Herald*, a large newspaper in Panama City. Duque "was aware of all that was going on and appeared entirely sympathetic." (12)

Amador and Duque did not team up when arriving in New York on September 1st. Amador had been officially sent by the "conspirators" and Duque was just a businessman.

On his side, Amador "trailed off uptown to find an inexpensive hotel" (12) and visited Lindo, the New York correspondent of a large Panamanian bank, to negotiate a loan. These visits took time and when he arrived at Cromwell's offices, he was told that Cromwell was out - which was not true.

In fact, Duque had promptly visited Cromwell, who was still hoping to pocket a hefty commission in case Bogota would authorize the sale of the French Company. Cromwell renewed his offer of good offices to Duque, whom he took as a "conspirator". He, therefore, ignored Amador, that he knew from the PRR.

By coincidence, Duque was a good friend of Hart, the former American Ambassador to Bogota. Their sons were partners in a business set in Bogota. Hart easily obtained an appointment for Duque to see Secretary of State Hay the next morning.

Leaving Amador in New York, on September 3, Duque traveled to Washington - overnight, not to leave any trace of his passage. This visit to Hay, marked an important step forward for the "conspirators", - although Duque was not one of them - as his visit would now render their movement official.

Boosting their hope, Hay confirmed to Duque that the United States were determined to build the Interoceanic Canal in Panama, even if the Government of Bogota disagreed with the terms of the treaty. All was clear now. The United States had decided to force the issue, or in a more diplomatic language had judged that the 1846 Treaty allowed them to intervene to maintain order in Panama. Alluding to the 1846 Treaty, Hay tacitly confirmed to Duque that the U. S. Fleet would be used to guarantee the free transit across the Isthmus and would not allow any Colombian troops - coming from Cartagena - to disembark in Colon. In fact, this would protect the "conspirators" from an external attack. (6)

We notice here Roosevelt's influence. The President will later comment this action: "Panama declared itself independent and opened the negotiations with us. I had two courses open. I might have taken the matter before the Senate, in which case we should have had a number of most able speeches on the subject and the Panama Canal would be in the dim future yet. We would have had a half a century of discussion afterward."(25) Roosevelt did not detail his second course, but it would be easy to recognize on what followed.

Of course, the President could not appear to be involved.

B-V would find himself in the right place to serve as a catalyst to Roosevelt's plans.

As he could not remain idle, he published a long article explaining the subtleties of the 1846 Treaty in *Le Matin*, - the newspaper of his brother Maurice -, on September 2, 1903, just a day before Duque's trip to Washington. This article explained in detail how the United States had the right to maintain open the traffic to people and to goods across the Isthmus. B-V added a complete update of the Panama Canal's matter. Always sure of his views, he sent a copy of the article to all his friends in America and in Panama.

The article reached President Roosevelt who was totally surprised to find his own views printed in a French newspaper. It was such an obvious solution to use the 1846 Treaty that everybody involved in the Panama negotiation had the same thought. As B-V wrote naively: "It is possible that similar views had been uttered before the publication of the article." (7)

Let us return to New York, where dispirited Amador had not found the financial help he hoped for, in the offices of Lindo and Cromwell in New York City. On September 4, he cabled to his Panamanian friends: "disappointed, esperen cartas" (wait for my letters).(18) He was preparing to return back home, empty handed.

The plan of his friends, the "conspirators", was now in jeopardy. How would they convince the Colombian garrison to remain friendly, when they had no money to bribe them? Money was the essential ingredient and Amador, about to turn 70, lacked the energy to fight any longer. Discouraged, without any money, he was preparing to return home.

To make things more complex, Amador's and Duque's outings had been discovered. Unfortunately, on September 5, Amador's telegram ("disappointed") had been reproduced in the American press.

Worse, when Duque was on September 3 in Washington, he could not resist to pay a visit to his good friend Herran, now Colombian Ambassador. Both men had met a long time ago, around the 1870s in the City of Panama. Duque informed Herran of his meeting with Hay and that "Amador was in New York with the intent to meet with Cromwell and to organize the separatist movement. " (27) Although he had been informed of that movement, Herran had now the evidence of its reality and he clearly foresaw the threat of a secession of the Province of Panama.

Immediately, Herran complained to Hay and made him promise to receive only authorized delegations from Panama. He also warned Cromwell, who had organized the visit of Duque to Hay, that he would hold him responsible for it and that Bogota could ask that he be dismissed from the Panama RailRoad Company (PRR) and eventually cancel her concession.

Cromwell was enraged to have failed in his enterprise to help the Panamanians. We have already seen that he generally acted in secret. This setback directly affected his pride. Overwhelmed, having lost his control of the situation, he decided not to meet any more with Amador or Duque. He would now keep a low profile. This is confirmed by Arango (one of the "conspirators", in Panama) who wrote to Cromwell on September 14, asking him not to use the cable any more, as it was not safe enough.

To avoid any more suspicion of connivance with the conspirators, Cromwell would leave later - October 15 - on a trip to France, pretending he had matters to clarify with his employer, the New Company.

In doing so, Cromwell - knowingly? - would abandon the lead negotiator position to B-V.

At this point in time, would object a vigilant reader, wasn't B-V still in Paris? He was not. On September 10, he took a steamer leaving from France to New York. Who had called him?

Some authors believed that Cromwell had sent him a cable, probably around September 5 to 8, - just a few days after the scandalous Duque visit to Herran - explaining the intricacies of the situation and stating that, because he had been discovered by Herran, he could no longer remain involved.

We do not share that belief, because Cromwell and B-V always had a very chilly relationship and were not really working together.

Some other authors, whom we are more inclined to believe, stated that it was Loomis who sent the cable to B-V. Both men had met for the first time in 1890, when Loomis was the American Consul in Saint-Etienne - in the center of France - and they had become good friends; they met again in Caracas in 1899. Now Loomis was Hay's Assistant Secretary State.

It seemed absolutely impossible that Loomis had not informed B-V of Duque's visit to his boss - Hay - and of the consequences of that visit (Herran's furry and Cromwell being threatened).

B-V knew Herran well and was very concerned about this *faux pas*.

He was also convinced that he would be able to help Amador in his negotiation.

B-V's memoirs, written in 1913, seemed to give the right perspective of the event, probably as a result of the ten years that have elapsed. Time often helps historians in unraveling the unimportant facts. We extract here only a few sentences from B-V's book:

"During the summer of 1903, my venerable friend John Bigelow had come, with his daughter, (Note: it was most probably Grace, as the other three daughters were married) to spend some days under my roof in Paris. My young son, then thirteen years old (Etienne), was suffering at the time from hay fever. . . When Miss Bigelow . . . was on the point of sailing for America, she proposed to take him back with her. She was persuaded that he would soon recover, thanks to the sea voyage and his stay on the coast of Maine. . . My wife, . . . reluctantly consented to be separated from her child, and agreed only on the understanding that she was to join him in September. The kind offer of Miss Bigelow was accordingly accepted under these conditions. My plan was to join my family in America about six weeks later. When my wife was ready to start in the middle of September, she was somewhat afraid to take the trip alone with her little daughter (Note: Giselle was 9 years old) and she pressed me to accompany her. At the last moment, I decided to yield to her request. But, as I did not see that there was anything to be done at that moment in America, I decided simply to make the sea voyage to New York, and then to come back by the first boat to France with the intention of again sailing some weeks later to sojourn in America as long as events should make it necessary. It is owing to these quite fortuitous circumstances, that I arrived in New York on September 22, 1903." (7)

We witness here again another voluntary omission by B-V.

All this was false and true at the same time.

While it was true to write that Congress cessions would resume within six weeks in Washington (the 1st Session of the 58th Congress was to begin on November 9), it was erroneous to pretend that Congress was the only key to Panama's rescue.

B-V omitted parts of the story.

The Congressmen still had at their disposal the Nicaragua solution. It could be easily retrieved from the files and implemented at any time. This was allowed by the *Spooner Act*.

This was a danger that B-V knew too well. To avoid such a catastrophe, he decided at once to take advantage of his wife going to New York to travel with her. On a timing point of view, the arrival of B-V appears quasi-miraculous. He came at the right time to set the whole conspiracy in motion again.

B-V would also explain in his *Statement on Behalf of Historical Truth* that: "Upon my word of honor, I do state that no hint or indication came to me from any quarter whatever which prompted me to go. . . . When I arrived, I did not have the slightest hint as to a revolution being started." (6) We had already commented on B-V's omissions on page 30-31.

Landing in New York, Ida and Giselle (B-V's wife and daughter), went directly to Bigelow's summer residence in Maine, where they found again Etienne, B-V's young son. Soon thereafter, they moved to Bigelow's villa in Highland Falls (New Jersey), about fifteen miles north of New York City, on the Hudson River, next to West Point. Later, the whole group (the Bigelows and the Bunau-Varillas) took residence for the cold autumn months in Manhattan, in the New York Bigelow mansion, close to Gramercy Park.

Once in New York, B-V did not stay with his family. He had better things to do. He had reserved his usual suite #1162 in the Waldorf Astoria Hotel, very conveniently located at walking distance from Bigelow's Gramercy Park address.

As a further proof that he had been informed by his friend Loomis, B-V went directly to visit the banker Joshua Lindo, who was "at the head of one of the oldest banking firms on the Isthmus. . . I had known him nearly twenty years before," wrote B-V. (7) Lindo had already met with Amador and gave B-V a full account of the complex situation. He informed B-V that Amador lodged at the Endicott Hotel. B-V set an appointment to meet with Amador the following day.

On September 23, Amador came to visit B-V at the Waldorf Astoria Hotel. He had been in New York for three weeks and was utterly discouraged about finding money. Both men recalled with emotion the French Canal years, when they had worked together for the same goal. They probably had kept a decent opinion of one another, because Amador quickly accepted B-V's help.

It is not known whether Amador had read the article published in *Le Matin*, but their common goal was now to achieve the independence of the Province of Panama. B-V had joined the "conspirators".

At first, B-V recommended to Amador to wait for "a few days, maybe up to a few weeks, as at this moment there is nobody in New York, nor in Washington". (7) Congressmen were still enjoying their summer break. Logically, after visiting with Amador, B-V went to see his American friends. Through the intervention of Professor William Burr, a former member of the *Walker Commission*, on September 29, B-V had the privilege to meet with the eminent Professor John Bassett Moore. Both Burr and Bassett Moore were members of Colombia University's staff.

Having served briefly as Secretary of State, in 1898, just before Hay, Bassett Moore occupied at that time a chair of International Law and Diplomacy at the University of Columbia, in Manhattan. Bassett Moore was a close friend and counselor of President Roosevelt. They had worked together during the Cuban crisis, an episode of the American-Spanish war, when Roosevelt had set up the "Rough Riders". This was the 1st Cavalry Regiment, formed with volunteers, which won fame in July 1898 in Cuba, with "Teddy" Roosevelt in command.

Professor Bassett Moore revealed to B-V that the President had been very interested to read the September 2 article in *Le Matin* and had expressed his surprise to find his own views, so well explicated. He told B-V confidentially that Roosevelt had also contemplated using the 1846 treaty and that "he was ready even to employ coercion," (7) against Colombia. It was certainly not a coincidence that all the major players involved in solving Colombia's deadlock were moving towards the same solution.

Bassett Moore explained to B-V that, as soon as he heard about the negative vote of the Bogota's Senate, Francis Loomis, Hay's assistant, had contacted him to check the relevance of using the 1846 treaty. Bassett Moore had confirmed to Hay and Loomis that Colombia had no right to oppose to the building of the Canal in Panama. After this interview with Bassett Moore, B-V was reassured in his view: only the secession of Panama from Colombia could insure the completion of the Panama Canal.

This goal became B-V's primary focus. He would help the conspirators in their negotiation with the Americans. With his background, his personal relationships with Hay and Loomis and the three years of dedication he had spent to this cause, he was surely much more experienced and better positioned that Amador or Boyd, who had absolutely no understanding of the political environment in Washington.

Last and not least, B-V was totally independent of: 1. The American Government, 2. Colombia, 3. The Panamanian "conspirators".

He would be the ideal "collaborator" of the President.

On October 3rd, having consulted with all his friends in New York and anxious to meet with his Washington friends, B-V left New York for the American capital and rented a suite in the *New Willard* Hotel.

Once there, he was lucky to find that, despite the Congress' recess, his friend Loomis was still in his office. Loomis managed to get B-V an appointment with President Roosevelt within a few days.

On October 9, B-V was received by the President, escorted by Loomis, and eagerly suggested that only a revolution could be the solution to Panama's problems in the current circumstances: "If Colombia wants to ruin the Isthmus, the conspirators will not permit it," B-V said. (7) Roosevelt remained totally quiet when he heard this, - as his position required -, but B-V clearly understood that the idea of a revolution had made its way into the President's strategy. B-V declared later: "His look was enough for me. I took the gamble."

Roosevelt later wrote about this meeting: "B-V was a very able fellow and it was his business to find out what he thought our Government would do. I have no doubts that he was able to make a very accurate guess, and to advise his people accordingly."(From Sevareid: "The Man who invented Panama".)

President Roosevelt was reported to have declared in a private conversation: "I took Panama because B-V brought it to me on a silver platter." (16)

In his memoirs, B-V told us that his idea of a revolution was born in April 1885 - only six months after he had arrived in Panama -, when he witnessed the insurrection led by Prestan: "I had seen with my own eyes, in 1885, the Revolutionists protected from the aggression of the Governmental Colombian troops by the American military authorities." (7)

This foreseen revolution would not be an exceptional event. Riots and insurrections had been endemic in Panama since 1850: once per year, on average, as shown on Appendix 8.

A few days later, on October 16, President Roosevelt confidentially received two high ranked U. S. Army officials, Captain Chauncey B. Humphrey and Lieutenant Grayson M. P. Murphy, "who had just returned from a four months' military intelligence tour of the northern portions of Venezuela and Colombia. . . . Reports had already reached him (Roosevelt) from a variety of sources that a revolution was imminent, but here was evidence of a kind which might fairly be relied upon." (12)

Encouraged by President Roosevelt in his idea of a revolution, B-V was ready to proceed along the same line.

Back in New York, on October 13, B-V met again with Amador. The "conspirator" was still debating the idea of bribing the garrison of Panama City, but had not yet found the funds to do so.

Amador had certainly consulted some war experts; he now asked B-V for a sum of $ 6 million to "acquire a fleet to prevent Colombia from overwhelming with troops the Province of Panama." (7) In the long discussion that followed, B-V tried to convince Amador that his plan would take too long to implement and that bribing the garrison would be good enough. Having met with Roosevelt, he knew for sure that the American Government would block any Colombian ship approaching Panama.

Having convinced Amador, B-V volunteered to personally advance the money necessary to pay for the salary arrears of the Colombian troops based in the City of Panama, which they estimated to $ 100,000. "I shall give it out of my own pocket. I can make such a sacrifice as that, but I could not give $ 6 million." (7)

At first, Amador refused, sticking to his own idea of a war fleet.

But the next morning, Amador came back to B-V and agreed with his proposal. Lindo, the banker, had not been able to find any money for the conspirators and Amador had no other choice than to take B-V's money.

This sum of $ 100,000 represented about six months of pay for the 500 Colombian soldiers, who were receiving annually $ 400 each.

B-V detailed in his memoirs how he transferred the funds from Paris to New York. He told us that he first contacted "without saying for what purpose" American bankers Pierpont Morgan and Isaac Seligman. However, B-V "saw obstacles", (7) using American banks and asked for this sum to be taken from his personal accounts with:
- Banque Balser et Cie, Brussels
- Banque Crédit Lyonnais, Paris.

"This branch office was accustomed to make cable transfers for me during my sojourns in America, when I needed money for my travel expenses."(7)

In fact, B-V wanted an absolute discretion and was worried about leaks, which would have provoked a wave of speculation on the shares of the New Company, easily detected by the Colombians.

We witness here another proof that B-V was not a speculator.

B-V's money was sent to Heidelbach Ickelheimer, a New York bank, on Thursday 22, only nine days after B-V had made his proposal to Amador. It was a record for this time.

In the meantime, on October 15, 1903, B-V had returned to Washington to meet with Hay, who, concerned about confidentiality, received him at his private residence. Hay informed B-V that the President had decided to support the revolution and had ordered some units of the U. S. fleet to head for Panama. The President's plan was into its first phase of being executed. "The interview with Mr. Hay removed my last hesitations", remarked B-V. (7)

When B-V reunited with his family on October 17, at the home of John Bigelow in Highland Falls, he was so convinced that all will end well for Panama that he asked his wife Ida to manufacture the future flag of the new Republic (a picture of the flag proposed by B-V is given in reference 29).

We see here again that B-V took care of every detail in this matter. Although Panamanians did not accept the B-V's flag suggestion, his memoirs do not mention any resentment on his part.

On October 19, B-V assured Amador of the American support to the conspirators and confirmed that the money he had asked for was en route. He also reported his conversation with Hay: "I give you the assurance that you will be protected by the American forces forty-eight hours after you have proclaimed the new Republic in the whole Isthmus." (7)

Amador was so happy to see his plans fulfilled that he was ready to accept any request from B-V, who wanted to collect the fruits of his successes. Satisfied with his conversations with Hay, B-V convinced Amador that, while he was away in Panama, he would be most qualified to represent the "conspirators". Indeed, the "conspirators" could not be received by Hay, without upsetting the Colombian delegation. "It will be necessary to entrust me with the diplomatic representation of the new Republic in Washington." (7) It is not impossible that this idea came from Secretary of State Hay himself, who had seen his negotiations with Herran drag on for months, with no result. Hay was certainly not keen to repeat this experience with Amador or any other "Colombian".

Amador was trusting B-V that he had known for a long time. After some discussion, he accepted that, in his absence and until the independence of Panama was proclaimed, B-V be "entrusted with the diplomatic representation (Plenipotentiary) of the new Republic in Washington." (7) Having returned to his country, Amador would be severely reprimanded by his friends, but it would be too late for changing B-V's plan.

Some "caustic" historians accused B-V of having bought his nomination in exchange of the half million francs - $ 100,000 - lent to Amador.

All was well. Amador "at 70, was an honest man, but with absolutely no sense of politics. His background was absolutely valueless for taking the complex and urgent decisions required by the creation and recognition of the new State," (18) wrote Anguizola, not without some exaggeration.

It was true that Amador lacked experience on international negotiations, while B-V had already played an important role in the *Hay-Herran* Treaty and had many friends to support him in America (Bigelow, Loomis, Burr, Bassett Moore, Pavey, etc.) as they also happened to be ardent supporters of the Panama Canal project.

B-V had planned everything for Amador to the most minute detail. All should now happen smoothly in Panama.

On the following day, both men met again to seal their agreement. B-V handed out to Amador the text of the message he would have to send him once the "conspirators" had proclaimed the independence of the province: "The Government has just been formed by popular acclamation. . . . I request you to accept the mission of Minister Plenipotentiary in order to obtain the recognition of the Republic and signature of Canal Treaty." (7)

He had also prepared, as a reference, a copy of "the constitution of Cuba, which has just been written by American and Cuban jurisconsults of high legal talent and was to be the model for the Panama constitution." (7)

B-V had taken control of every matter relating to the future country "as I was well acquainted with the hesitating temperament of Spanish Americans" (7), he explained. He would follow every detail closely, until the treaty would be signed.

Amador left for Panama on October 20 and arrived in Colon on the 27. Duque was on the same steamer.

Hay had not bluffed. On October 22, American newspapers announced that two small U. S. war boats, the SS* *Marblehead* and the SS *Mohican* had left San Francisco. Given their speed, they should be in sight of Panama City by November 3.

A few days later, on October 25, "Governor Obaldia, assured that the "conspirators" could count on American support, sent away to Penonome, a town of the interior - 100 miles west of Panama City -, on the pretext of an invasion from Nicaragua, that never occurred and was purely a pretext, a detachment of Colombian troops that the conspirators believed would remain loyal and whose officers it had not been possible to bribe." (6)

Little by little the rebellion was getting organized.

On October 26, B-V received a cable from the conspirators informing him that a Colombian ship, the *Cartagena*, would soon sail for Colon with troops.

Lemaitre told us that an order had been sent from Bogota to the *Cartagena*, asking the ship to head towards the port of La Guaïra, where some smugglers had been unveiled. But, as the ship's captain will be learning later, this order was coded (communications were unsecured) and it really meant for the *Cartagena* to head for Colon.

Following the order to the letter, the Colombian troops, on board the vessel, headed east, in the opposite direction of Panama, which delayed them by a few precious days. (15) They would finally reach Colon, but too late to be of any use.

* SS stands for "steam-ship".

Amador, now in Panama, informed B-V on October 29, by a coded cable that: "more than 200 Colombian troops arriving on Atlantic side in five days. Press steamer Colon." (7)

This meant that he was asking for the help of a U. S. war ship in Colon to oppose any landing of the Colombian troops.

Roosevelt had already taken care of it: the U. S. cruiser *Nashville*, based in Jamaica (Kingston), had been mobilized and was planning to reach Colon on November 2. It would be followed by many other ships: *Dixie, Atlanta, Mayflower, Prairie* and *Olympia*.

On the Pacific side, a huge deployment of U. S. war ships was observed too: *Marble head, Concord, Boston, Nero* and *Wyoming*.

Finally, on November 3rd, exactly as Amador had informed B-V, after a detour via La Guaïra, the 500 soldiers aboard the *Cartagena*, landed in Colon, under the command of General Tovar. It happened just a few hours after the arrival of the *Nashville*.

Colombian troops occupied the city, but could not proceed further to Panama City, because the employees of the PRR blocked them from boarding on the train. They only allowed Tovar, their General, to travel unarmed. It was the standard procedure, according to the 1846 Treaty, which had been used many times before and especially during the Thousand-Day War.

As he reached Panama City, Tovar was placed under arrest by the garrison under the command of General Huertas, whose troops had taken the conspirators' side. Historians told us that the troops that had remained in the capital of the province had been for some time on the side of the conspirators. Amador had promised them to pay off their arrears of the past year and this definitely "tipped" them in favor of the conspiracy.

Bogota had lost the province.

On the same day, **November 3rd, 1903**, Amador and his friends proclaimed the independence of Panama.

Six weeks had elapsed since B-V arrived in New York "by a fortuitous incident which had incalculable consequences." (7)

On November 4, B-V who had received the cable promised by Amador, sent him $ 50,000, which was half of the amount they had agreed upon.

In Colon, under the command of Colonel Torres, the Colombian troops were still occupying Colon. This was not tolerated by the U. S. Navy command. It ordered marines from the *Nashville* to land. Torres surrendered, convinced that he had in front of him the overwhelming power of the U. S. Navy.

The U. S. war fleet was truly impressive: up to ten ships were now close to the coasts of the Panamanian Isthmus. To be truthful, it should be noted that most of these units were just small armor-plated boats, but they had the back up of some cruisers like the *Nashville* or the *Wyoming*.

Two days later, after a harsh negotiation, the 500 Colombian soldiers were "persuaded" to leave Colon. They embarked on a *Royal Mail* steamer chartered for the occasion by the provisional Government of Panama. Their return to Cartagena had been paid by the provisional government of Panama.

All this revolution had happened in a relative calm, although one single casualty had to be reported. There were accounts of a cannon shot, fired by the Colombian war ship *Bogota* towards the City of Panama, which hit an unfortunate Chinese man by the name of Wong Kon Yee.

Siegfried commented the coup by writing: "Whatever the opinion one has about this revolution, on the technical point of view, it was a masterpiece." (13)

Lemaitre agreed: "It is impossible to believe that so many coincidences, combined with complex events, could have been totally fortuitous." (15)

There is no better homage to pay to the work of Philippe Bunau-Varilla, who was ready to put a final touch to his accomplishment.

26
PANAMA WAS INDEPENDENT !

A Panamanian Government was rapidly formed. Three consuls were named: Arango, Arias and Boyd.

On November 6, B-V received a cable from them, informing him that "the authority of the Republic of Panama was established on all her inhabited territory." (7)

On the same day, the United States recognized the new Government of Panama. Hay happily confirmed this by cable to Bogota.

Most countries recognized Panama in the following days.

As he had asked, B-V received another telegram from the new Government: "The Junta of Provisional Government of Republic of Panama appoints you Envoy Extraordinary and Minister Plenipotentiary near the Government of the United States of America with full powers for political and financial negotiations." (7)

As he had agreed with Amador, he sent him the other half of the sum he had promised: $ 50,000.

B-V felt now free to negotiate the treaty, which would seal the future of Panama and of "his" Canal. Without any delay, he informed Hay of his visit to Washington with the purpose of settling all the terms of the treaty between the American Government and Panama; such treaty would replace the *Hay-Herran* agreement.

Less than a week after the proclamation of Panama's independence, on November 8, B-V and his family took residence in the *New Willard* hotel in Washington. B-V's objective was to promptly formalize the treaty, before the new Panama Government's delegates would arrive. He knew that he could act effectively and reach a fast conclusion with Hay.

In Bogota, obviously, the news of the independence of the province of Panama had caused some turmoil. Beaupré, the American representative, informed Hay that Bogota had declared martial law and was preparing to send 1,000 soldiers to Colon and the same force to Panama City.

Hay was not impressed. What could a few Colombians do against the powerful U. S. fleet?

Once in Washington, B-V immediately solicited an appointment from Hay.

The Secretary of State had sized up B-V when they had met and had developed a real confidence towards the Frenchman. He accepted to receive B-V on the following day, Monday November 9, at his residence. During lunch, without any other witnesses, Hay mentioned that the newspapers announced the imminent departure from Panama of a delegation, coming to Washington with the purpose of negotiating the new contract. B-V confirmed to Hay that he had been named Minister Plenipotentiary and that he would be the unique negotiator in the name of the new country - until the Panamanian delegation would arrive.

According to the newspapers' information, on Wednesday November 11, Amador and Boyd embarked from Colon on a steamer bound for New York. In a week, they would reach New York.

Time was of essence, as B-V wanted by all means to avoid any interference from the Panamanian delegation. He had less than a week to complete his task. The treaty must therefore be signed before Wednesday November 18.

B-V's first move was to visit President Roosevelt to present his credentials. Despite the fact that Roosevelt and B-V had already met, the agenda of the President did not allow this to happen before Friday November 13.

B-V went to the White House, with his son Etienne, who witnessed the ceremony. It is interesting to note that B-V's speech was in French, the diplomatic language of the time - although his English was quite good.

After the ceremony, B-V said to Hay: "For two years, you have had difficulties in renegotiating the Canal Treaty with the Colombians. Remember that ten days ago, the Panamanians were still Colombians and brought up to use the hair-splitting dialectic of Bogota. You have now before you a Frenchman. If you wish to take advantage of a period of clearness in Panamanian diplomacy, do it now! When I go out, the spirit of Bogota will return." (11) Hay agreed totally as he could himself have made exactly the same speech.

On Sunday November 15, only three days before the expected arrival of the Panamanian delegation, B-V received a draft of a treaty from Hay. It bore much resemblance with the *Hay-Herran* Treaty; "with insignificant modifications", noted B-V. (7) However, B-V would bring significant changes to *Hay-Herran* in the course of his conferences with Hay.

Pressed to conclude, B-V spent the whole night rewriting Hay's project. "The indispensable condition of success was to draft a new treaty, so well adapted to American exigencies, that it could challenge any criticism in the Senate. The only things that I resolved to defend were:

- the principle of neutrality of the interoceanic passage,

- the rigorous equality and perfect justice in the treatment of all flags, whether American or non-American,

- the attribution to Panama of an indemnity equal to that agreed upon with Colombia, ($ 10 million),

- the protection of Panama by the United States.

By way of compensation, I had decided to extend widely the share of sovereignty attributed to the United States in the Canal Zone by the *Hay-Herran* Treaty. I recognized that if I enumerated in succession the various attributes of sovereignty granted, I ran the risk of seeing, in the Senate, some other attributes asked for. To cut short any possible debate, I decided to grant a concession of sovereignty *en bloc.* " (7)

There we find the heart of the matter; it explains why Panamanians could never "swallow" the article III of the new Treaty, which read as follows:
"The Republic of Panama grants to the United States - in the Canal Zone - all the rights power and authority which the United States would possess and exercise, if it were the Sovereign of the territory. . . to the entire exclusion of the exercise by the Republic of Panama of any such sovereign rights, power or authority." (the whole text of the treaty is quoted on page 482 of reference 10).

The *Hay-Herran* Treaty was not so demanding on the matter of sovereignty; it only stated that justice and police within the Canal Zone would be shared between the United States and Colombia.

"The formula stood as the center-piece of B-V's counter-proposal." It was a major change instigated by B-V.

B-V added the notion of absolute sovereignty by the USA in the Canal Zone, 10 miles wide (16 kilometers). In the *Hay-Herran* Treaty, this width was in kilometers. Thus, B-V added 60% to the Canal Zone, although the blame could well be put on others, as the Spooner Act had already mentioned these "10 miles".

Panamanians will execrate him forever for having added this sovereignty clause.

After all the time, effort and money that B-V had spent on this project, this came really as a terrible and unfair indictment that B-V never really understood.

In his memoirs, B-V explained his motivations: "I decided to avoid in the Canal Zone any conflict about sovereignty, a concept that is always debatable, from one party or the other. This sharing of power was the weakness of the

Hay-Herran Treaty. I introduced then a radical innovation in the international law."(11)

He also explained that this change would make it easier for the Senate to ratify the Treaty. Some senators, favoring Panama, had asked for this change.

Apart from the sovereignty clause, B-V brought a few minor changes to Hay's project. Later, Panamanians would also blame him on the perpetuity matter. Wrongly, because this notion was already present in the *Hay-Herran* Treaty (not necessarily endorsed by Panamanians), although in a quite hypocritical manner (the *Hay-Herran* Treaty mentioned: 100 years, renewable at the option of the USA!).

It should be noted, to B-V's credit, that he "negotiated harshly to keep the cities of Panama and Colon out of the Canal Zone under the North-American authority, recognizing however to the United States a right of intervention in both of these cities for reasons of public health or police." (25) After all, B-V could not remain insensitive to these problems, which were due to happen in the Canal Zone, as he had already experienced them during the French Canal years.

After a long night spent at re-writing the contract, on Monday November 16, 1903, before showing his prose to Hay, B-V had his friend, the famous New York lawyer Frank D. Pavey, travel from New York to "correct the literary imperfections, polish the formulas and gave them an irreproachable academic form." (7) With the help of Pavey, B-V "did indeed set his personal mark on the treaty in his response to Hay's draft." (20)

On Tuesday October 17, B-V showed the new project to Hay. They discussed a few points and agreed that it was a good draft, although "one significant change* was made." Major also commented that: "B-V conceded even more than Hay demanded." (20)

In the afternoon of the same day, Boyd and Amador landed in New York. They informed B-V of their arrival by cable. They were welcomed by Farnham, an employee from the Cromwell's law firm. Quite opportunely, Cromwell himself was returning from France on the same evening on a German steamer. Logically, Farnham suggested that the Panamanians wait for his arrival, "to confer with him." (6)

---

* "In article 2, B-V had proposed the perpetual lease of a Canal Zone to the United States. Hay, however, preferred the phraseology of his own draft, which had followed *Hay-Herran*, in stipulating a grant in perpetuity of the use and control of the zone. Hay added "occupation" for good measure, though this was a marginal alteration beside his insistence on a grant rather than a lease. " (20)

"This obviously was what kept the delegates in New York." (7) B-V would have an extra day to achieve his task with Hay.

B-V grew anxious. Since he agreed with Hay on a final text, "Hay did not give a sign of life for the entire day." (7)

At 10 p.m., B-V called Hay on the telephone and, in spite of the late hour, obtained an immediate appointment. Hay had an obvious interest to deal with B-V rather than with Amador. Together, they reviewed once again the text of the Treaty.

Hay proposed to share the indemnity of $ 10 million equally between Panama and Colombia, but B-V disagreed because it would mean the recognition by the United States of their interference in the Panamanian revolution. They left the text unchanged: all the indemnity would be paid to Panama.

After agreeing on all stipulations, Hay and B-V kept the last version of the treaty unchanged. The race against time continued.

Will B-V sign before the Panamanians arrive in Washington?

On the following day, Wednesday November 18, Hay invited B-V to come to his office at 6 p.m. At 6:40 p.m., both men signed the document that would hence be known as the **Hay/Bunau-Varilla Treaty**.

It was just about time!

On the same evening, only two hours after the signature took place, the Panamanian delegation, led by Amador and Boyd, arrived in Washington.

B-V went to meet them at the train station, as he wanted to inform them that he had just signed with Hay. It was too late for their intervention!

They were absolutely furious. It was reported that on the station's platform, one of the Panamanians had a bad gesture - he allegedly spat on B-V's face or slapped him. This fact was not corroborated, but it was obvious that the encounter must have been tumultuous: "Amador was positively overcome by the ordeal. He nearly swooned on the platform of the station. His consternation, as well as that of Mr. Boyd. . .", wrote B-V. (7)

B-V handed them a copy of the signed Treaty. Boyd was surprised and asked: "Will the land of Manzanillo Island, on which the town of Colon is built continue to belong to the Panama RailRoad?" To which, B-V admonished him almost rudely: "The point you raise is a question of secondary importance and does not belong to a treaty." (7)

B-V was convinced that the Panamanian delegation would never have successfully negotiated in such a short time: "A delay of several hours would have sufficed to involve the difficult enterprise in the danger zone of personal ambitions and intrigues," (7) wrote B-V, happy to have concluded the treaty with his friend Hay.

Once more: all was well that ended well. It was the conclusion of what B-V labeled as "the triumph of the largest moral interest the French genius ever had on a foreign land." (7) Of course, some minor obstacles remained, among which the ratification of the treaty by the countries themselves.

A day after the arrival of the Panamanian delegation in Washington, a stormy meeting took place between B-V, Amador and Boyd. They threatened to prevent the newly formed Panamanian Government from ratifying the Treaty, but B-V did not believe a word of it.

A day later, on November 20, he returned to New York, in his usual Waldorf Astoria Hotel, Suite # 1162. This suite does not exist today. The hotel was demolished in 1930, to make room for the construction of the Empire State Building, inaugurated in 1932. A new Waldorf Astoria Hotel was built on Park Avenue between 49th and 50th Streets. The famous Suite # 1162, "the cradle of the Panama Republic" (7) has thus disappeared.

On Monday November 23, the Panamanians returned to New York where they stayed at the *Fifth Avenue* Hotel, but, still angry at B-V, they did not see any reason to meet with him again.

In the meantime, B-V had urged the new Government of Panama to sign, explaining that all should be concluded before December 1st, the last day for all documents to be ready for Roosevelt's State of the Union, his annual speech to Congress.

In the evening, B-V received a negative answer from Panama, which did not surprise him at all. He then summoned the Panamanians to come to the Waldorf Astoria Hotel; he met with them on the next morning.

Time was of essence, as within a few hours Amador and Boyd would be on board a steamer, en route to Panama.

During this meeting, B-V convinced them of the urgency of the matter and gave them the Panama flag - sewn by B-V's wife Ida; the new Government would later select another one - and an original copy of the Treaty, contained in a small chest, sealed with Bigelow's arms. B-V wanted to associate his good friend Bigelow to the conclusion of his enterprise.

They Panamanian delegates left New York on the *City of Washington* at 1:30 p.m.

They would reach Colon on November 30, 1903, a day before the deadline set by B-V for Roosevelt's State of Union address. Such a tight schedule!

As the Panamanian Government did not answer B-V's request to agree on the Treaty, on November 26, he threatened to resign from his mission.

The Panamanians had accepted to appoint him Minister Plenipotentiary. What else could they do now, but accept the Treaty?

As for the Colombians, they continued their energetic protests, inundating Washington with complaints. On Saturday November 28, Generals Reyes and Nel Ospina arrived in Washington. They were now ready to let the Americans have the Panama Canal concession for free, if they were to reconquer Panama. They considered that a saving of $ 10 million - what Panama had obtained - would convince Uncle Sam. (15)

This change in the Colombians' attitude was surprising, a few months after the Senate's negative vote. They could not readily accept the independence of Panama and especially the fact that the United States had recognized her independence - followed by France, China, Austria-Hungary, etc.

The Colombians ignored that the *Hay/Bunau-Varilla* Treaty had already been signed by the Secretary of State and the Panamanian Minister Plenipotentiary, committing both countries to its application.

Finally, on December 2nd, the Panamanian Government ratified the Treaty, probably thanks to the influence of Amador and Boyd who had arrived in Panama a couple of days before.

All was well that ended well! Our story is near its end.

The only formality left to accomplish would be for the Senate to ratify the *Hay/Bunau-Varilla* Treaty.

On December 7, 1903, President Theodore Roosevelt related the entire story behind the signature of the Treaty, in his annual State of the Union address. He mentioned - one by one - the 53 "revolutions", which had taken place in Panama since 1846, and, so doing, justified the American official version of the last days events. The United States had to intervene 9 times in Panama since 1846, at Colombia's request (see Appendix 8).

That last intervention, in 1903, had totally overturned the political context in Central America.

Siegfried noted: "Without Bunau-Varilla, this revolution would never have happened. By insuring its success, with a marvelous fertility of resources, he had not been, as often said, the agent of the French New Company; on the other hand, the French Embassy in Washington has been careful not to intervene in the matter: all merit, and besides all responsibility, has to be attributed to him. The Canal of Panama has found in him a passionate, convinced and efficient champion." (13)

We will not add anything to this eulogistic discourse.

27

AMERICANS FINISHED WHAT THE FRENCH BEGAN
1904-1914

On January 8, **1904**, B-V, who had spent the holiday season with his family in Bigelow's New York home, was summoned by Root, the Secretary of War. He had been informed of an invasion of Panama by Colombian troops. Root believed that B-V could help him decipher Bogota's plan.

In fact, some 2,000 Colombian soldiers under the command of Generals Roa and Ortiz were getting ready to invade Panama by land, through the Darien Isthmus. B-V believed that it was a bluff: nobody could cross the Darien Isthmus by land! However, "Mr. Root was much preoccupied with the situation." (7) This matter was taken very seriously in Washington.

On January 12, Hay, the Secretary of State, called B-V and asked him whether a crisis could be avoided by paying an indemnity to Colombia. B-V assured him that an invasion by land was totally "impracticable, it will never take place.   . It can only frighten birds or men with birds' brains." (7) Colombia never really had the power to threaten the Americans.

When they had signed the *Mallarino-Bidlack* Pact in 1846, Colombia had put herself under the protection of the United States. With this security, they never had the opportunity to acquire a strong naval war fleet. It was that same Pact that caused the Colombians to lose Panama.

Since November 3, the day of Panama's independence, many American war ships had kept patrolling along her coasts and some landing exercises had even been reported. (6) Obviously, Roosevelt wanted to prevent Colombian troops to invade Panama, as Admiral Coghlan, the Commander of the U. S. fleet confirmed: "Our orders were to avoid any landing of hostile forces into Panama." (6)

B-V's confidence was not enough to allay the fears of Washington politicians. They were worried by warlike activities of Colombia, which gave new hopes to the adversaries of Panama.

On January 13, Senator Stone posted a motion, with the aim to "investigate and ascertain whether B-V . . . did aid or promote an insurrection in Panama." (7) B-V answered, in the newspaper *The Sun*, that Stone better investigate whether Palma Estrada had aided or promoted an insurrection in Cuba. It was an allusion to the way the United States had organized, from their territory, an insurrection against Spain. Annoyed by such recollection, Stone withdrew his motion. (7)

Suspicions against B-V did not stop. Was a persecution's delirium invading B-V's mind? B-V believed that "my person was to be the battle-field of the supreme efforts for killing the Treaty I had signed." (7)

On January 17, *The World* published an article "entitled in big letters: The Panama Revolution. A stock-gambler's plan to make millions."(7) It originated from a declaration of Jonas Whitley, a journalist manipulated by Cromwell, who later firmly denied that he had done such a thing. The rivalry between Cromwell and B-V was still active, despite the fact that Panama had won.

As the campaign for the ratification of the *Hay/Bunau-Varilla* Treaty by the Senate was underway, the climate became even more tense. Senator Morgan was still pulling the strings. Now 79, he was still working for the success of Nicaragua. The presence in Washington of the Colombian General Reyes and its delegation did not make things easy for the supporters of Panama.

As B-V had forecasted, the Colombians did not succeed in invading Panama: "the beaten enemy, mad with rage, is about to withdraw." (7)

"On January 28, the *New York Herald* announced that the Concentration Camp of Titumati, formed on the shores of the Atrato River, had been broken up. It was the point from which the Colombian troops were to march through about 200 miles of virgin forest and unexplored tropical territory to reach some point on the line from Colon to Panama City. . . Fever had decimated the troops to such an extent that they had to be recalled in haste." (7)

Their Generals had disagreed on the strategy. The surviving soldiers returned to their quarters in Bogota.

On February 15, Senator Hanna died of typhoid fever. B-V wrote to Hay: "Marcus A. Hanna's keen statesmanship and indomitable will (served) the cause of Panama, . . . of which he was the heroic and victorious defender." (7) He had defended Panama's cause until his last moments. We have to recall that his speech of June 1902 had been decisive - together with B-V's stamps.

On February 23, the Senate ratified the *Hay/Bunau-Varilla* Treaty by 66 votes for and 14 against.

Immediately after the vote, B-V informed the Government of Panama that his mission as Plenipotentiary Minister was over and that he requested this Government to "withhold the salary of my office, to form the nucleus of a fund for the erection of a monument to Ferdinand de Lesseps, the Great Frenchman," (7) the man B-V admired so much. This would be completed some twenty years later, in 1923. A group of statues would be inaugurated in the old part of Panama City (the *Casco Viejo*), in the French Square. Surprisingly, B-V's statue would not be in this group; we will soon learn why.

On that same day, February 23, recalled B-V: "as I was going through the hall of my hotel, somebody seized my hands to express his congratulations. It was the lawyer Cromwell. I had not seen him for three months. " (7)
Cromwell would soon after demand that his reward be paid by the New Company. After much disagreement, the parties resolved to submit their disagreement to arbitration. Almost three years later, on February 21, 1907, Cromwell produced a 200 pages-long letter to support his claim of $ 830,000. The arbitrators would only give him $ 230,000. This was evidently a sign that all his claims had not been fully justified. (6)
B-V concluded wisely that : "A plea for fees cannot be impartial for writing the story of any great event." (6)
Thereafter, Cromwell would carry such a great influence on the Panamanian Government that they named him "exclusive agent" of the country, a position he kept until 1937!

On February 26, at 11 a.m., Hay and B-V exchanged two copies of the treaty, as approved by the Governments of the United States and Panama. As B-V summed up the past ordeal: "Two strokes of a pen were sealing forever the Destiny of the Great Thought which had haunted Humanity during four centuries." (7)
This time, all was over and B-V returned to Paris, happy to have at last realized his childhood dream, to make the Panama Canal.

However, he had not done so as an engineer, as he had dreamed when he was a young graduate from Polytechnique, attending a conference by Ferdinand de Lesseps, but as a diplomat. History had repeated itself.

Lesseps himself was a diplomat and had not much regard for engineers.

The Colombian Government still did not believe that it had received an adequate compensation, and kept sending notes of protest to Washington.

"Reyes, having lost all hope, remained in Washington until the end of February." (15)

However, Luis Carlos Rico, the Colombian Minister of Foreign Affairs, sent on April 12, a 20 page-long letter to Hay, summarizing the November 1903 events; it accused the United States of violating the 1846 treaty, of which Rico detailed the history and how it had been implemented. As John Major pointed out: "The United States had no treaty right to prevent Colombia from putting down a rebellion." (20)

More than a year later, having not received any answer, Colombia asked for the difference of opinion to be submitted to arbitration. Elihu Root, Hay's successor, replied on February 10, 1906: "The ancient state of Panama, independent in its origin, and by nature and history a separate political community,   .   .   . never surrendered its sovereignty." (6) This was clearly an historical truth, as well as a flat refusal of having recourse to arbitration.

Colombia and the United States would debate for almost twenty years, before agreeing to a settlement of all claims for $ 25 million on December 22, 1921. It was a little less than what they asked for in 1903 ($ 32.5 million).

A month after the Senate ratification of the *Hay/Bunau-Varilla treaty,* on March 22, 1904, in Washington, took place the first meeting of the *Isthmian Canal Commission,* still chaired by Rear Admiral John G. Walker. Other members were: Major General George W. Davis - who would become later the first governor of the Panama Canal Zone -, William Barclay Parsons, Benjamin M. Harrod, Frank J. Hecker, Carl E. Grunsky and William H. Burr - the only member who participated in the former 1902 Commission.

They started working diligently and as soon as April 5, 1904, were holding a meeting in Colon, Panama. Later, they temporarily established their headquarters in Panama City, in the exact same building where the French had their offices.

To finalize the purchase of the assets of the French New Company, on April 22, 1904, in Paris, "two Assistant Attorneys General, W. A. Day and Charles W. Russell, came to sign the contract." (7)

On April 28, J.P. Morgan, the American Treasurer, on behalf of the United States, authorized the payment of $ 40 million. (7)

It is interesting to find out what the New Company did with this money.

261

Of course, its first priority was to pay back their share to the subscribers. They had bought shares at 100 francs in 1894 and these shares were worth on the market 130 francs (129.78 to be precise).

The subscribers were paid in three installments: June 1904, June 1906 and June 1908. They pocketed a profit of about 30 francs per share for a period of ten years, which amounted to less than 3% a year, a reasonable interest.

B-V had subscribed 5,000 shares. He received 650,000 francs, of which 150,000 francs was profit.

His brother Maurice had 15,000 shares, he received 1,950,000 francs and made a profit of 450,000 francs.

The total profit of the brothers (600,000 francs) was very small in comparison with ASC's profits (Artigue, Sonderegger & Co) where they earned about 8 million francs. Less than 10%!

As we have shown, B-V never had any intent to make a profit when he spent all these years negotiating the fate of Panama in Washington. His intentions were pure and disinterested. As another proof, if still necessary, let us examine his travel expenses for the period of 1890-1904. Their detail is shown in Appendix 3. B-V had spent almost a million francs or six times more than the profit he made by selling his shares of the New Company.

Quite magnanimous on his part!

His altruism is now fully demonstrated.

So far, only the New Company's shareholders had been compensated from the $ 40 million - 200 million francs, received from the United States. There were 650,000 shares, each paid by the New Company at market's value (129.78 franc each), for a total of 85 million francs. The remaining 115 million francs were used to indemnify the participants who had subscribed seven times between 1880 and 1888, as explicated in Appendix 2.

For all of them, it was a meager consolation, as they had paid 1035 million for bonds, more than twenty years ago and now received only: 115/1035 = 11% of what they had invested!

As for the 600,000 shareholders, who invested in the first subscription of December 1880, they lost their entire investment of 300 million francs.

After the completion of the sale of the New Company, all calculations made, we better understand the terrible reputation that the Panama affair carried for a long time in the French financial circles. It had effectively ruined almost a million small French investors. They had waited fourteen years - from 1889 to 1903 - to see their feeble hopes disappearing and their losses being confirmed.

B-V did not deemed his presence advisable at the signature ceremony, and he did not attend: "I refused because I did not want to allow people to confuse my work, which was to make the Panama's conception triumph, with this painful consequence, the sale of a thing the French people had created." (7) His nationalism would not accept the failure of the French in Panama.

However, he was proud of the honors bestowed on him: "The Government of the French Republic conferred upon me the Cross of Officer of Legion of Honor," he explained in his memoirs, adding that: "This promotion in the Legion of Honor from the rank of Knight to that of Officer possessed, in the circumstances, a significance particularly precious to me." (7)

He received all these tributes with an immense pleasure.

Hay wrote to him: "It is not often given to any man to render such a service to two countries and to the civilized world, as you have done." (7)

Later in 1909, B-V received a letter from Obaldia, then President of Panama. Amador had just died, on May 2nd, and B-V had written to show his admiration to the senior member of the *Junta Revolucionaria*, to which Obaldia responded: "Our people will keep eternally engraved in their memory your fruitful services and will put in a pre-eminent place the names of Amador and your own. The national gratitude gives them the title of Benefactors of Panama." (7)

B-V's interest in the Canal of Panama did not stop in 1903 with the Senate ratification of the Treaty. In the following years, he would continue to keep an eye on "his" Canal and to intervene whenever he deemed it necessary.

In July 1905, he received his friend Loomis and Senator Cabot Lodge in Paris. They dined at the restaurant of the Brighton Hotel.

On the following day, July 3, Loomis, Cabot Lodge* and B-V were hosted by Maurice Rouvier, the French Prime Minister. B-V was still considered a prestigious member of the Parisian society.

The beginning of the American work in Panama was quite slow, in order to adequately plan for the project. Until now, the American Government had discussed at length on the relative merits of Nicaragua or Panama, but the experts had not yet agreed whether to build a sea level or a locks canal. And neither had they decided which organization would build it: the U. S. Army Corps of Engineers or a private enterprise? That old debate still surged (see page 182).

John Findley Wallace, the first project director, was named by Roosevelt on May 4, 1904.

Wallace noticed wisely that : "a canal with locks is an absurdity . . . because of the constant increase in the dimensions of the ships, as well as the

---

* After the 1914-18 war, B-V will be invited by Cabot Lodge to join his group of militants for the defense of the World Peace.

enormous traffic which is bound to pass through the canal and the resultant scarcity of (fresh) water for lockages." (7) It was a very shrewd remark and a reader somewhat versed into the current project - to be effective in 2014/2015 - will understand that Wallace's remark was a clever vision of the future.

On February 14, **1905**, Wallace recommended to the *Panama Canal Commission* that the canal be built at sea level.

Aware of this absurd recommendation, B-V rushed to Washington, where he met with President Roosevelt on March 27. Roosevelt understood the problem, "with his characteristically quick intelligence." (7) Then on March 29, B-V met with the members of the *Commission* and easily persuaded them to study a canal with locks.

In September 1905, B-V returned again to America, where he spent, as he did every year, his summer vacation with his family on the Bigelow's estate.

During this summer of 1905, B-V and his wife Ida spent some time in Oyster Bay, on Long Island, New York State, where they were received by the family of President Roosevelt. "Teddy" had been re-elected in November 1904, thanks to his popularity and perhaps to some extent to his success in Panama.

He had not forgotten B-V and told him in confidence that:

"-   I have never been as astonished as I was when I read the article of *Le Matin,* of September 2 (1903), where you described exactly in Paris, what I was then preparing with Professor Bassett Moore at Oyster Bay.

-    But, Mr. President, it was purely a matter of logic.

-    Well, if that is so, you are the greatest logician I have ever known." (7)

B-V had to interrupt his vacation to go again to Washington, called by the *Panama Canal Commission,* its members had been personally appointed by Roosevelt himself - the President wished to follow closely its work - and composed of eight North-Americans and five Europeans. The *Commission* was hearing proposals from various experts to finalize the design of the project.

B-V was not a member.

On September 19, 1905, B-V made a presentation of his pre-canal project - the same as in 1898 -, which allowed for dredges to float on provisional lakes, with the objective of lowering the level of the lakes to the desired altitude. It was the famous method that he called "the transformation of rocks into dredgeable material." (7) Despite the help B-V received from a French expert, an eminent engineer of *Ponts & Chaussées*, Mr. Quellenec, his arguments were not heard.

Meanwhile, in Washington, the *Panama Canal Commission* was still debating the definition of the Canal: sea level or with locks?

In this Commission, Parsons, an ex-civil engineer, who directed the work of the New York subway, was convinced that the clay layers of the Culebra Hill were not as slippery as believed and that the underneath layers would be found much more stable. Parsons was a strong champion of a sea-level Canal.

Having followed the debate, B-V intervened to persuade Parsons that he was wrong: "the Culebra trench, once excavated, will be 125 meters deep. Do you know of any trench of that depth anywhere in the world? No. Please recall that in your New York underground work in 4th Avenue, the trench was 6 to 8 meters deep. . . and the hardness of the rock did not prevent some houses in the Fourth Avenue sliding towards the trench." (7)

After convincing Parsons, B-V also managed to persuade Roosevelt himself that the sea level canal was a bad choice.

B-V struggled to convince the members of the Commission to what he considered to be the only viable way of digging the Canal. He spent months in Washington, temporarily neglecting his engineering and investment businesses, specialized in railroads.

Wallace, the project Director, was still not convinced and continued to support a sea level canal. However, isolated in his opinion, he reckoned that he could not work with Washington's bureaucracy and resigned, after only a year in office.

President Roosevelt, who was following closely the project, named a new head of the *Panama Canal Commission*. But he did not meet any success. The chairman of the Commission, Theodore Shonts wanted the canal built by private contracts, while Roosevelt wanted the U. S. Army. Shonts resigned in 1906 and Roosevelt had it his way.

To explain Wallace's resignation, it should be said that in Panama reigned an indescribable disorder: there was nothing left than "the gloomy specter of the deluded hopes of the French people." (*The Panama Canal*, by Frederic Haskin, Doubleday, New York, 1914)

Haskin went on: "Here a long line of steam cranes, there a mass of purposeless machines, and there a dredge left after a flood on the banks of the *Rio Chagres*, every sight was full of the French defeat." However, Haskin specified that : "The equipment abandoned by the French was of a good quality and, despite the marks left by fifteen tropical summers, was having a real value."

Wallace's successor, named on July 25, 1905, was John F. Stevens, a U. S. Army engineer.

It is interesting to compare the American working methods - successful - and the French's - disastrous. To solve the great difficulties of such uncommon work, the Americans had special advantages:

1. The American organization was doomed to succeed. At its head was the President of the United States himself, supervising closely the *Commission*.

2. The supplier of funds was the American nation: Congress never hesitated to vote a budget for the canal.

3. As soon as the decision had been taken to have the canal built by the U. S. Army, it was obvious that the work would be done orderly and with discipline. It had been decided that the American workers, supervising the Jamaican workers, would be paid 50% more than they would in the continental United States. Their food was imported and sold to them at reduced prices - they were subsidized by the Government. As a result, many American workers came to work in Panama.

4. Soon after the yellow fever strike of 1904, Roosevelt decided that Gorgas should have *carte blanche* to eradicate this plague. The results would take time but Gorgas showed amazing results: in 1906, 82% of the workers had parasites in their blood; this percentage fell to 8% in 1913.

All conditions were set for success.

The *Panama Canal Commission* did not favor the scheme that B-V had recommended. On November 18, 1905, returning from a trip to Panama and contrary to all experts' opinion, the Commission recommended (again!) a sea-level Canal - without locks, by 8 votes against 5.

Moreover, on January 10, **1906**, this same Commission estimated the cost of this sea-level Canal at $ 247 million, 15% more than the Canal with locks, which had been estimated in 1902 at $214 million.

All this procrastination made no sense.

Would the Americans be as unlucky as the French? Would lack of preparation and indecision bring about the failure of the project?

In one respect, the Commission was pragmatic: they did not allow work to start before a healthy environment could be reached. In order to sanitize the Isthmus, the Commission brought Doctor Crawford Gorgas over from Cuba. He was the leading yellow fever specialist in the world. He was given *carte blanche* and used this opportunity to spend about $ 20 million - a huge sum, almost 10% of the total Canal estimate - to eradicate mosquitoes in a quasi-warlike campaign: he had the streets of Colon and Panama City paved; the inhabitants living along the Canal route were forbidden to have containers full of water, their houses were to be equipped with screening doors and windows; each house was fumigated carefully.

Gorgas used the Canal manpower to install safe water supplies and sewer systems; cisterns and cesspools were oiled; etc. These measures were successful.

In Washington, the Commission found Gorgas' expenses excessive and he was accused of squandering.* But, Gorgas had achieved his assigned goals. Yellow fever had been practically eliminated, dysentery had ceased and malaria had been abated.

The Americans had done exactly what the French had failed to do to maintain the morale and health of their workers. This time, the opening of the work could take place under much more propitious conditions.

Finally, in November 1906, Roosevelt approved B-V's recommendation after a trip to Panama and ordered that the canal be built with locks.

It was the first time that a President had gone abroad on an official visit. Such an honor for the new nation of Panama!

On February 5, **1907**, almost three years after the ratification of the *Hay/Bunau-Varilla* Treaty by the Senate, the Commission formally decided to adopt a canal with locks scheme.

These three years into the project had not been lost; they had been spent restoring sanitary conditions in the Isthmus, designing the works and recruiting manpower.

Although the Americans had learned much from the French mistakes, some mishaps would however be unavoidable.

In April 1907, Stevens, the American General Manager resigned for an unknown reason. According to McCullough: "What went sour for Stevens is a mystery, that Stevens chose never to explain." (16)

Stevens was replaced by Major G. W. Goethals, of the *U. S. Army Corps of Engineers;* he would stay at this position until the completion of the Canal in 1914. This was the last important setback in the great American effort that produced the Canal of Panama.

In April 1907, Goethals arrived in Panama. He acquired such a good reputation that he was called: the "Great Digger". However, he was to find an appalling situation: only 5 million cubic meters had been excavated since 1904; that was less than 3% of the total – estimated at 177 million cubic meters. He would give the project an enormous boost.

---

* It is said that Goethals, the U. S. Director of the Canal works in 1907, had complained to Gorgas about the high cost of killing a single mosquito (10 $!) and that Gorgas replied: "But if one of these mosquitoes bite you, what a loss it would be for the country." (28)

At the end of 1907, 32,000 workers were working on the Canal. Their number would reach up to 40,000 in the following years. (20) The French had never been able to gather such an enormous working force:
- 5,000 were Americans, paid 50% more than in their own country;
- A majority came from the British Antilles: 6,000 were from Jamaica; 20,000 from Barbados - the west Indies.
- On average, there were 3 to 4,000 Europeans.

The work continued without problems until November 20, **1908**, when a large part of the dam being built on the Gatun Lake collapsed. It was a minor incident, but B-V, who had remained attentive to the progress of the works, launched a controversy about the technical capabilities of Goethals.

Did B-V think that he could have done better than Goethals?

In order to defend Goethals, we must explain that this dam was a gigantic construction. The Rio Chagres was used to fill a large interior lake that the Canal would cross for a part of its way. On the Atlantic Ocean side, where the Chagres met with the Ocean, a dam was constructed. It was two kilometers long, 35 meters high, and had a base 600 meters wide. This huge dam, held by the weight of the earth accumulated, was at the time the largest in the world.

Such a gigantic dam perhaps could excuse Dingler for constantly postponing its design in 1885 and also explain why B-V never mentioned it in his memoirs.

On December 12, 1907, the *New York Herald* published an interview of B-V, where he announced that the project would cost $ 280 million. A few days later, the Canal Administration published the figure of $ 283 million. Almost exactly the same figure!

Both figures were noticeably higher than the $ 247 million initially calculated by the Commission. Here too, the engineers could not produce the right estimate. They rarely do.

Meanwhile, the matter of Panama's independence from Colombia - which had allowed the Americans to "grab" the Canal -, continued to trouble many minds.

On October 3, **1908**, - a month away from the presidential election - the *New York World* published a series of articles implying that a syndicate - it was the "black legend" - had been plotting to purchase the shares of the New Company and pocket part of the $ 40 million. The real scandal was that among the members of this syndicate were the names of Charles Taft, the brother of the future President and of Douglas Robinson, the brother-in-law of President Roosevelt.

Adding to these accusations, the *Indianapolis News* published on November 3, eve of the election, an article titled: "Who got the $ 40 million?" Despite its wide coverage, the article did not influence the election. Taft was elected, succeeding to Roosevelt, who had decided not to run for a third term.

Unfortunately, on December 1st, Roosevelt wanting to squelch the rumors, wrote to the *Indianapolis News* to confirm that: "the $ 40 million had been paid to the French Government." (6)

This blunder had serious consequences.

As a matter of fact, the newspaper remembered that Cromwell had testified in his February 1907 letter that the money had been transferred to the New Company, using the good offices of the J. P. Morgan bank. The liquidator, named by the French Government to represent the interests of the small shareholders, had been involved in that transfer.

Why did Roosevelt contest this version of the facts? Very much affected by the press attacks, Roosevelt lodged a complaint against both newspapers.

The matter had to be clarified. Reporters Earl Harding and Henry Hall were commissioned by Joseph Pulitzer, owner of the *World*, to gather all documents proving the merits of their case.(25)

The lawsuit was interrupted when most other newspapers took the President's side. They feared that that court action could create a precedent against them. The *World* had been forsaken by all other newspapers and had no choice but to yield to the President. Not surprisingly, the Federal Court Judges in a unanimous vote on January 3, 1911, declared the newspapers not guilty, because the motive: "Federal libel" was not recognized in American law.

Roosevelt lost his lawsuit.

The liberty of the press had been saved!

In Panama, the Americans were working on the completion of the Canal with no major setback. Now that the Isthmus had been cleaned by Gorgas, there were very few deaths from yellow fever. The laborers could work at full capacity. Almost two million cubic meters were extracted in January **1909**. During March 1909, 3 million cubic meters had been excavated - 3 times more than the French ever did in a month.

This intensive tempo will last until the end without any particular incident to mention.

The matter of the Panama revolution was still lurking in the press. When President Roosevelt's arrogance caused him to make another serious blunder on March 23, 1911, it arose again. "Teddy's" enormous power had probably gone to his head when he declared: "I took the Isthmus", (16) during a conference he gave at Berkeley University. Of course, he maintained that this sentence alone did not reflect the significance of his speech – which was true.

But, due to the press reports of the time, no one ever remembered the full contents of the speech - just this sentence. (6)

It was President Roosevelt himself who had encouraged the conspirators in Panama. Elihu Root used to pull the President's leg by saying: "You certainly have well defended yourself Mister President. You have shown that on being accused of seduction, you have conclusively proved that you were guilty of rape." (16)

This was a very serious matter. "I took the Isthmus" provoked political demonstrations throughout Latin America. It also revived the controversy initiated by the *World* in 1908. This time, Congress urged the Foreign Relations Committee to set up an inquiry. In January 1912, the *"House Committee on Foreign Affairs"*, chaired by Representative Henry Thomas Rainey, was ready to hear the witnesses.

Rainey invited all the personages he judged qualified to explain Roosevelt' attitude during the 1903 Panamanian Revolution. Rainey also wished to have the same inquiry investigate the validity of the proposals made by the Republic of Colombia, to resolve the dispute by naming arbitrators, proposals that the American Government had always eluded or refused.

Hearings were held from February 13 to 20, 1912. During the inquiry, the newspaperman Henry N. Hall presented the elements collected by Earl Harding at the time of the libel suit instigated by Roosevelt.

B-V could not attend the hearing chaired by Rainey and was excused by his friend Pavey. Thus the *Statement on behalf of Historical Truth*, which B-V wrote to express his disagreements with Cromwell's letter. (6)

Harding later gathered these arguments in a book: "The Untold Story of Panama" (Athene Press, New York, 1959).

However, the hearing eventually ran out of steam. Nobody was willing to directly attack President Roosevelt, who was still very popular. Under the influence of Henry Cabot Lodge, Congress abstained from passing a resolution and this marked the end of the witness' interviews. It was the last meeting of the *House Committee* on this case.

The Panamanian writer Juan David Morgan has written a novel covering most of this story. (23)

During the summer of **1910**, a series of large subsidences in the Culebra Hill caused the engineer in command of this sector, David Dubose Gaillard, to have a rage of madness. He was forced to resign. However, this time, the infamous Culebra Hill had nothing to do with it. Doctors would discover later that the poor engineer had a brain tumor. Gaillard lent his name to the trench dug in the Culebra Hill, known today as the *"Gaillard Cut"*.

Gaillard was quickly replaced and the American engineers masterfully completed the work.

On October 10, 1913, even though the Canal was not quite finished, President Wilson blew up a dike in Gamboa in a formal ceremony. The waters of the Gatun Lake flooded the Culebra Cut, causing the waters of both oceans to become mingled. B-V and Goethals were there, posing for a photographer on a hill overlooking the canal. This shows that B-V never lost interest in "his" canal.

The construction of the Interoceanic Canal was finally and successfully brought to an end.

It would soon allow steamers to pass from one ocean to the other.

Ten years had elapsed since the United States had purchased the French Company. Americans had extracted a total of 185 million cubic meters, which should be compared to the 55 million cubic meters extracted by the French - of which only 30 million were useful. (16)

In total, the Panama Canal construction had caused - in round figures – 12,500 casualties, 7,500 under the French supervision and 5,000 under the Americans.

These are not the figures one would find in History books: they generally quote a total of 25,000. As we have explained in chapter 9, page 100, our estimate is reasoned and not copied from other historians.

New research on this subject is consistent with our estimate.

Altogether, a little more than three billion francs had been spent.

We identify here the assertiveness of the first estimate uttered by Ferdinand de Lesseps (600 million francs) in 1879.

In reality, the Panama Canal had cost 600 million *dollars,* five times the Lesseps estimate!

On another subject, it is worth telling the ultimate fight that took place between the United States and Great Britain about the canal tolls. We have to remember that the *Hay-Pauncefote II* treaty, signed on February 21, 1902, called for equal treatment for the ships of all nations transiting through the Panama Canal.

On August 24, 1912, the Senate, following a demand from President Taft, voted the *Panama Canal Act,* exempting all American ships from toll when navigating in coastwise trade - from one U. S. port to another.

B-V joined the British to protest this exemption. The press campaign lasted for months, but President Taft was unmoved. It would be under Taft's successor, President Woodrow Wilson, that, after another campaign led by Elihu Root, Congress agreed to reconsider the exemption.

On June 15, 1914, a few days before the canal's inauguration, Wilson signed a revision to the amendment to the *Panama Canal Act,* cancelling the privilege granted to American ships, which the United States had abusively given to their own ships.

This showed to what extent the arrogance of this great country could reach.

B-V remained very active during that time. He was seen in Manchester, visiting the printing presses of the *Manchester Guardian,* which he recommended to his brother, Maurice, for *Le Matin*. B-V "was employing his scientific authority to the revision and improvement of *Le Matin*'s technical services. (30)

B-V was still the technical counselor for his brother's investments. In February 1913, he traveled to Mexico to visit oil fields;

However, B-V remained attached to his "dream".

On August 3, 1914, he narrated in his memoirs: "I went in the Isthmus, to cross the Panama Canal on the first steamer, the *Cristobal**, which floated on the Pacific Ocean a few hours after leaving the Caribbean seas. " (7)

This was a fortnight before the official inauguration, to which he had not been invited.

"On the same day, war was declared by Germany on France." (11)

Siegfried wrote: "This was a symbolic coincidence, as there will be from now on a new equilibrium of the continents." (13)

On August 6, B-V embarked again on the *Cristobal**, this time heading for New York.

On August 14, he caught the *City of Paris* from New York to Liverpool, from where he reached Paris on August 24.

On August 15, 1914, the Panama Canal was officially inaugurated.

Nicaragua was not totally out of the picture. Just a few days before this inauguration, on August 5, 1914, the United States and Nicaragua signed the *Chamorro-Bryan* Treaty, after the names of the Emiliano Chamarro, Minister of Foreign Affairs for Nicaragua - he will later become President from 1917 to 1921- and Secretary of State William Jennings Bryan.

---

* This ship is not to be mistaken with the war ship, which brought the Colombian troops in Colon on November 3, 1903.

This treaty was another abuse of power by the United States. For a meager fee of $ 3 million, it allowed the United States to lease for 99 years two islands off the coast of Nicaragua - the Corn Islands, where an American Navy base was never built - and to obtain a perpetual option to purchase the Nicaraguan Canal site. This was intended to exclude another country to build a canal in Central America.

The United States had really become a superpower, manipulating the "hemisphere" countries.

In 1909, the U. S. marines had intervened against the Government of President Zelaya, who had executed 500 prisoners; among them were two "gringos". The marines remained as an occupying force in Nicaragua until 1933.

The *Chamorro-Bryan* Treaty remained active until 1970, when the United States returned the Corn Islands to Nicaragua and abandoned their option to build a canal.

28

THE GREAT WAR
1914-1918

On August 24, 1914, B-V reached Paris and, on the same day, he wrote to the French Minister of War to obtain a mission in the French Army. At 54, he had been exempted from military duties, but he insisted to serve his country. The oldest men called to military service were born from 1866 to 1879 – 43 to 48 years old; they were called the "territoriale" - Maurice, born in 1856, was 58 years old.

His lifetime's achievement, the Panama Canal, had just been put in operation by the Americans. What else could he seek?

He could have quietly remained home, enjoying his fortune. However, he was a very courageous man and wanted to test his capabilities once again. He would play an important part in the allies' victory, a part which alone could see him in a good place in the French History books, independently of his achievements in the Panama Canal.

To defend the nation, the Minister of War needed every Frenchman he could draft. He granted B-V the right to keep his rank as Captain - since leaving his military school, he had remained in the reserve forces - and assigned him to be deputy of the Officer commanding the Paris Corps of Engineers. This was General Hirschauer, also an alumnus from Polytechnique – "two years older than B-V". (11) Thanks to his highly regarded experience in Civil Engineering, B-V was appointed to supervise the repair of the bridges prematurely destroyed by the French Army to stop the German invasion; "such a decision was equivalent to a refusal to fight", commented B-V. (11)

In April 1915, B-V was assigned as deputy to the Corps of Engineers supporting the 14th Armed Division in Caix on the Somme River.

He still worked on repairing bridges, but was now closer to the war front and more exposed.

On one occasion, he used part of his fortune to avoid administrative delays. He purchased some pumps and pipes necessary to supply water to a cavalry regiment, at a cost of 150,000 francs. It is not known whether he was later reimbursed by the French Government.

On February 21, 1916, after eighteen months in the war, B-V was assigned to the Corps of Engineers in charge of the Water Supply of Verdun, a city in the east of France, which would soon become a legendary battlefield between the German and French armies. Here, in Verdun, they fought a furious battle throughout 1916.

B-V was now in the heart of the combat zone.

One major problem he had to solve was to monitor the quality of available raw water and make it drinkable for the troops and horses. The current process used 2 to 4 milligrams of chlorine per liter of water. It was fine to kill all the colibacilli, but "it gave the water a repugnant smell and taste, which unfortunately recalled the smell of the disinfectants used in the camp toilets." (11)

After "ordering the laboratory of the army" to run tests, B-V discovered an original method to purify polluted water and make it potable. It was also a process using chlorine, but at a concentration twenty times lower. The colibacilli were still eliminated and the water had no after taste.

B-V's method was so successful that it was generalized to the entire French Army. B-V called this process: *Verdunization*, after the City of Verdun.

Without going as far as some authors, who sustained that, by this process, B-V had helped the French Army to win the battle of Verdun (18), we must recognize that this method played an important role in decreasing the soldiers' mortality due to typhoid fever.

After the war, the *Verdunization* process would be implemented in most of the French large cities.

After three years into the war, B-V was promoted to the rank of Lieutenant Colonel, but he remained assigned to the Verdun battlefield. As an engineer, he was not particularly exposed, but by a strike of bad luck, on September 3, 1917, he happened to be close to an impact of a German shrapnel. He was severely wounded, as he explained: "My friend, Major Devaux, was killed at my side. My right thigh and leg were shattered. My left foot was opened from side to side and its artery cut. A splinter from the bomb entered the flesh on my right side near the hip and opened an enormous wound which extended down to the base of the vertebral column where the coccyx was fractured." (7)

B-V's right leg had to be amputated. His left foot was salvaged. After 118 days in the hospital, he went back home to celebrate Christmas 1917 with his family.

Following this terrible accident, B-V would remain crippled for the rest of his life. He was nevertheless able to walk again with the help of a prosthesis that he designed - his creative genius never stopped.

Hero of the battle of Verdun, B-V received the War Cross medal.

He commented: "The war was finished for me but I could still serve France usefully"; (11) what he meant here was extending his *Verdunization* process to the major cities of France.

His Engineering Consulting firm had apparently ceased to exist because of the war. B-V filled his convalescence by writing a new book on the international politics around Panama and especially on the part that Panama played in the allies' victory. Here, he wrote that: "The history of Panama in the last thirty years . . . is also the history of the efforts developed to defeat the German machinations*." (9)

In this book, published in 1919, there was nothing new concerning the history of the Panama Canal, which he did not already mention in his 1913 book or in his *Statement on behalf of Historical Truth.*

After the war, B-V was a different man. Not only had he turned 60, but he now carried into his flesh the painful memories of the war. He was also affected by some new vicissitudes that appeared in his family. They are worth being mentioned briefly.

On July 19, 1913, Giselle - B-V and Ida's daughter -, married Viscount Charles Marie Devezeaux de Rancougne. It was a noteworthy Parisian wedding, celebrated by a bishop in Saint Pierre-de-Chaillot.

Only a year after the wedding, the Viscount was mobilized and captured by the Germans during the first months of the of war. He remained imprisoned for about three years in the fortress of Darmsdadt, in Germany.

During this time, his wife Giselle, with no child, kept herself busy by working as a volunteer in hospitals. Thanks to her father's friends, she was often seen in the American community of Paris, where she was known to have helped soldiers. As time passed, Giselle found it hard to be separated from her husband and her marriage suffered. In 1917, the divorce was effective.

---

* As an example, during WWI, the Panama Canal was used to bring nitrate ores from Chili to France; nitrates was a raw material for explosives. Germans did not need to import nitrates, as they manufactured them by chemical synthesis from air's nitrogen.

The Viscount remarried on July 26, 1919, with Ghislaine Elida Da Motta, of Belgian nobility. As for Giselle, she also remarried. Her daughter Mirella mentioned in a book that Giselle "after two failed marriages to fortune hunters, as she referred to them, took up the bohemian lifestyle of a single artist in Paris. . . She had tasted the nectar of freedom and moved into a studio at No.9, Rue Notre Dame des Champs," (24) a gift of her rich father. Giselle's hobby was sculpture and she was a student in Auguste Rodin's workshop, where she met Malvina Hoffman, an American artist, already known in New York, who agreed to sculpt a bust of B-V. A photo of this sculpture was reproduced on the first page of B-V's book, *"The Great Adventure of Panama"* published by Doubleday in 1920. It has also been used in the cover of the French version of the present book: "Philippe Bunau-Varilla. Panama Man" (Lulu Press Incorporated, 2012). See picture in page -1.

B-V was certainly happier with the achievements of Etienne, his son. Despite the fact that he did not follow his father's steps in his school studies, Etienne was a great fan of modern technology.

In July 1909, a Frenchman, Louis Blériot was the first aviator ever to cross the English Channel. It could well have been Etienne Bunau-Varilla!

In 1908, having successfully passed his school-leaving certificate, a requirement to enter University, B-V rewarded him with a biplane Voisin (worth 25,000 francs) on which he learned how to fly. He obtained one of the first French flying "brevet"(license): # 16. He made good progress and was able to participate in various meetings, one of which took place on August 22-29, 1909, in Reims. There he flew in company of the best aviators of the moment: Blériot, Latham, Farman and also Curtiss, an American who beat the world record at 77 kilometers per hour. More than half a million people were in Reims to witness the event. Aviation was the craze of the moment.

When war was declared, Etienne joined the French air force. His frail health - in 1903, he had traveled with his father to America to cure his asthma - was now forgotten.

On a bombing mission over the German territory, on May 27, 1915, his plane broke down and Etienne was forced to land. Captured by the Germans he was taken as prisoner of war in the Marienburg fortress, where he remained for two years.

For his bravery, the French promoted him to the rank of Lieutenant - officer -, but the Germans did not take this into account and treated him as the Sergeant Major he really was.

He remained in prison in Wurzburg, then later in Nuremberg and in Heidelberg, where his Lieutenant's rank was finally recognized by the Germans.

This was largely due to the intervention of his father, B-V, who pleaded his case with General Petain - the head of the 2nd French Army, where B-V served. Later, he was transferred with other prisoners of war to Mézières-les-Metz - in Lorraine, in the east of France, which had been occupied by the Germans since 1870. Prisoners were located there to deter French bombing in the area.

Finally, on June 19, 1917, after two years as a prisoner of war, Etienne was exchanged with some German soldiers and reached Switzerland where his uncle Maurice owned a sumptuous villa, next to the French border (see Appendix 5).

Etienne left the war with profuse amount of honors: Officer in the Legion of Honor, Military Medal, and War Cross. A hero!

The war period was not eventless for Maurice. Charles Humbert, one of his good friends, who had been editor in *Le Matin* from 1902 to 1906 and had started later a political career, bought in 1915 *Le Journal*, another major Parisian newspaper. For this purchase, Humbert had borrowed the money from a crook, called Paul Bolo, who had received funds from the German Embassy. Bolo, a spy, was discovered, judged and executed on February 14, 1918. Humbert had to resign from politics.

In 1918, *Le Matin* inopportunely criticized Georges Clemenceau*, who had become a very popular Prime Minister, an instigator in the victory against Germany and later nicknamed "Father Victory". *Le Matin* lost half a million readers, selling only 1 million copies at the end of the war.

The heydays were sadly over for Maurice, nicknamed the "Red House Emperor", because his Boulevard Poissonniere offices had been painted in red and gold,. He was 62 and would soon turn into a different person whom we shall describe later on.

Fortunately, the Bunau-Varilla family had survived to the Great War without any casualty.

The Second World War shall see the denouement of our story and the end of the Bunau-Varilla brothers' saga.

---

* B-V commented in his memoirs that "The relations between Clemenceau and my brother Maurice were extremely strained after having been, a few years before, very cordial."(11)

29

THE BROTHERS BETWEEN THE WORLD WARS

Just after the Great War, in September 1919, B-V published his third book of memoirs: *The Great Adventure of Panama, Its Essential Part in the Defeat of Germany.* (9) In it, B-V paid off old scores with his enemies, the Germans. He revealed, among other plots, that they intended to establish a naval base in Venezuela in 1900, from where they would have taken Panama, coveted because of its strategic location.

It was the book of a man who had been wounded in his flesh and had lost the use of a leg, which hindered his mobility. It was known that B-V's mobility had become his new obsession: he was measuring, on the maps of the cities he visited, the distance he had to walk every day - about one kilometer - to avoid phlebitis. Apart from his body pain, he was also wounded by the lack of gratitude from his compatriots, who had not yet recognized the merits of his *Verdunization*.

B-V was starting a new period of his life. He was getting old, - 60 - he was crippled with a wooden leg, he suffered from his peers' ungratefulness and he seemed to be at the verge of despair. His future seemed grim.

However, despite his physical impairment, he was often seen in the company of his American friends. They were actively working in the League of Nations with the objective of avoiding another bloody war. Despite his physical handicap, which he surmounted with his usual courage, B-V joined them and remained an active man.

Meanwhile in Central America, Colombians were still finding it difficult to accept the independence of Panama; Lemaitre commented that: "The shock inflicted had been so violent that it took four lustrums (Note: a lustrum is a period of five years) for the pain of the dismemberment to allow to tackle the problem with a cold head and to solve it with a certain friendliness, although with reluctance." (15) After having tried a couple of times - in 1909 and in 1914 -, to solve the dispute between Colombia and Panama, Americans sponsored an agreement in 1921. To make the loss of the Panama province easier to be accepted by the Colombians, "Uncle Sam" wrote a $ 25 million check to the order of Bogota.

This very "unfair" treatment provoked the rage of the Panamanians, as they had only received $ 10 million in 1904.

On August 20, 1924, Panama and Colombia signed the Treaty called *Velez-Victoria,* which restored diplomatic relations between the two countries; they had been interrupted after the 1903 coup. This new treaty also settled the problems remaining about the definition of those countries' common border.

In Panama, on December 4, 1923, the French Plaza was inaugurated. Set on a court surrounded by the old ramparts of Panama City, it boasted in its center a stone obelisk surmounted with a bronze rooster, symbol of France. In front of the obelisk, were aligned the busts of Ferdinand de Lesseps, Wyse, Sosa, Boyer and Reclus.

When he learned about this Plaza, B-V was bitterly offended not to find there his bust, as chiseled by Malvina Hoffmann, among the founding fathers of the Panama Canal. He was not alone to have been excluded: Godin de Lépinay, the French geographer who proposed the route for the Canal, was not in the Plaza either. For Godin, it was really an oversight, but for B-V, the explanation is simple.

In the 1920s, an anti-American movement had been gathering speed in Panama. It militated for the renegotiation of the 1903 Treaty, signed by Hay and B-V. This treaty was found "infamous" and even more so because it had been signed by B-V, who was not even a Panamanian.

The great difficulty that Panamanians expressed towards the 1903 Treaty found its outcome in a resolution voted by the Panamanian Chamber of Deputies, in January 1927, declaring B-V: "A foreigner prejudicial to our country . . . who is to be delivered to the mockery and hatred of the Panamanian people." To be honest, we have to mention that B-V had previously written in a letter published by *La Estrella* in Panama City, that: "The Isthmian Canal Convention was drafted and executed as a Protectorate Contract." (from Enrique Linares in the Political History of Panama) The word *Protectorate* had the faculty of infuriating the Panamanian political class and this really justified their resolution.

B-V found it very hard to accept this change of fortune. He was proud to have contributed to Panama's independence; he cherished - in his mansion of 53 Avenue d'Iéna -, the fountain pen which had been used to sign the 1903 Treaty, a gift from Hay. He had spent so many years of his life defending the cause of Panama, and, all of a sudden, there was no recognition of his work. All this added to his suffering.

However, he had reasons for rejoicing. The Panama Canal had become very successful:
- in 1920: just under 10 million tons of freight crossed the Canal,
- in 1924, on its tenth year of service: 22.9 million tons,
- in 1929, a record was reached with 30.6 million tons.

With a transit fee of $ 1.25 a ton, this represented around $ 30 to 40 million revenues a year. The Panama Canal had become a profitable enterprise and the Panamanians will not cease to request the end of the concession - granted for perpetuity to the United States in the *Hay/Bunau-Varilla Treaty*.

On his family's side, B-V was irritated by the escapades of his daughter Giselle. She could have been a good subject for today's "celebrity" magazines.

In 1926 Giselle, met a beautiful Italian, Mario Rocco, who was "wanted" by Interpol for having attempted to kidnap the daughter he had had in a former marriage. For Giselle, this third man seemed a satisfactory husband to be. Newly married, in 1929, Giselle and Mario decided to leave for a safari in Congo. After a few months, Giselle was pregnant and they moved to Nairobi - Kenya -to find a modern hospital. (24)

They settled in Kenya where their three children were born:

They lived on an allowance from B-V. Mario painted and Giselle carved.

They took residence in the outskirts of Nairobi, close to Lake Naivasha, where they built a sumptuous villa.*

B-V had kept contact with his American friends. Hay had died in 1905, John Bigelow in 1911, but Loomis, and others still lived.

In July 1920, Myron T. Herrick, the businessman who had introduced B-V to his Ohio friends, came to visit the site of the battle of Verdun – East of France. B-V served as his guide through the old battlefield.

They would meet again later, when Myron T. Herrick became the American Ambassador in Paris (1921 to 1929).

---

* During WWII, all transfer of money from France being almost impossible, and Mario being away from home as a prisoner of war, in order to survive, Giselle turned her villa into a farm.

B-V continued to be an enthusiastic supporter of the peace in the world. We may recall that at the end of the war, in 1919, the Treaty of Versailles was signed. The Senate, under a lobby led by the Secretary of State, Henry Cabot Lodge, refused to ratify this Treaty. Lodge was a friend of B-V and later they would work together for World Peace.

In May 1917, in the summer residence of his brother Maurice, in Brittany, B-V met Aristide Briand, who had been several times President of the French Council. Briand learned that Lodge was a friend of B-V and asked B-V to try to rally Lodge to the cause of peace.

When Myron T. Herrick became Ambassador in Paris, B-V asked for his support. However, his efforts were not successful.

In 1925, the Treaty of Locarno was signed between Germany on one side and France and Great Britain on the other side, to pledge for peace. But again, the United States refused to sign; this would last until 1928, after Lodge's death, and finally the United States would "mutually pledge to renounce to use war as a means of solving conflicts," as the treaty stipulated.

Americans were right in their hesitation to sign such treaty.

Ten years later, Hitler annexed Czechoslovakia!

B-V indeed had many disappointments during the period between the two world wars.

He however continued to successfully promote his special process for the treatment of water, that he had called *Verdunization,* the merits of which started to be recognized all over France - however very slowly. It took almost ten years for a public recognition of such process. It was, according to B-V's words, "the most extraordinary adventure of my life." (11)

In 1923, the City of Reims, which had been badly damaged during the war, was in full reconstruction and needed to find a water purifying process that did not leave a single trace of odor, because some of the water would be used to wash champagne bottles.

Having discarded the ozone process, - too expensive -, the City consulted with B-V: "They were embarrassed; they could not adopt the classic solution of *Javellisation,* because the smallest error in the dosage of dechlorurant left the water with the detestable taste of chlorine . . . it so happened that in the beginning of 1924, the new method, born on the battlefield of Verdun, was for the first time adopted by a large city." (7)

And following Reims' example, there would be many others.

The eleventh French Congress for Public Health held its meeting in Reims, on October 24, 1924. Doctor Techoueyres presented a paper to the French Medicine Academy, confirming the efficiency of B-V's *Verdunization.*

Later on, *Verdunization* was adopted by practically all large cities of France: Paris, Lyon, Marseille, Bordeaux, etc.

"Paris and Lisbon awarded B-V a gold medal, their highest decorations. The towns of Carcassonne, Reims, Lyon and Dieppe have had a medal coined for B-V. The towns of Auxerre, Bar-le-Duc, Calvi, Carcassonne and Dieppe granted B-V the title of Citizen of Honor. Two cities, Carcassonne and Calvi have each named one of their finest avenues after B-V." (11)

Medicine Nobel prize Alexis Carrel* wrote to B-V in September 1936: "You will thus – with *Verdunization* - have saved more human beings from disease and death than all the physicians of France together." (11)

As we have already mentioned, B-V loved to be honored.

Already rich, he did not need the money and generously abandoned the profits of the *Verdunization* to the company which marketed it. "My last word will be to congratulate the conscientious experts who have been responsible for the success of the *Verdunization*. In the last ten years, I recommend that the company S.A.V.I.S. be used for its implementation, as I did not want to take the patents to sell an invention I had made in France." (7)

The benefits of this process are recognized today as having contributed to the victory of the allies in Verdun by lowering considerably the fatalities from typhoid fever. The process also decreased child mortality from enteric fever.

B-V boasted that: "The gradual improvement in health at Paris is exclusively due to *Verdunization.* " (11) He meant the mortality rate due to typhoid fever.

However, you will remark logically, this has nothing to do with Panama. Well, it has, although in a remote way. B-V explained in his memoirs that "a curious phenomena is that yellow fever itself vanishes in front of the Verdunization. The reason is that the *Stegomya*, the mosquito carrying the yellow fever virus refuses to lay its eggs in a water without colibacilli, as it so happens with *Verdunized* water." (7)

Of course, Panama continued to obsess him . . . and, at the same time, would unfortunately destroy his fame.

In 1934, a pamphlet was published in Panama: "How Panamanians were betrayed, True History of the Treaty" by A. V. McGeachy. The traitor was obviously B-V. This sad image was now solidly anchored into Panamanian minds.

---

* B-V had a special recognition for Carrel who "invented the marvelous cure that saved me from death". (11) It was called the Carrel/Dakin liquor, a potent disinfectant, invented by Carrel and the British Chemist Henry Dakin.

Yet, we find another reason for Panama to be grateful to B-V. This same year 1934, the Pasteur Institute in Paris commercialized a vaccine against yellow fever, which it had invented. It had certainly been due to the philanthropy of the Bunau-Varilla brothers who had financially contributed to the fight of this terrible disease by subsidizing Gorgas and Finlay in Cuba.

Today, malaria continues to unfortunately affect people living in the tropical areas of our planet, as no vaccine has yet been developed.

It is estimated to kill one to two million people in Africa every year.

Just before the Second World War, after Americans had operated successfully for 20 years the Panama Canal, they examined how they could modernize it. President Franklin D. Roosevelt - a distant cousin of "Teddy" -, requested a study to widen the Canal. Construction of a second set of locks, to accept larger ships, in parallel with existing locks, started in 1939, but the project was suspended because of the war.

This project would not be brought out again after WWII, as Americans knew that Panamanians would repossess the Canal before long. Why invest when others would benefit from it? Particularly because several billion dollars were necessary.

After the war, in 1965, the arrival of atomic submarines decreased the strategic interest of the Canal, as their gauge did not allow them to transit through the locks. They could pass easily from one ocean to another via the North Pole. And the other units of the U. S. Navy - such as aircraft carriers, also atomic - had grown so much that they could not transit through the Panama Canal.

As for the commercial advantage, it had almost disappeared, because the United States had almost abandoned using the Canal: their own intermodal transport was more attractive; the transit of American goods through the Panama Canal represented only 10% of the coast-to-coast U. S. interstate traffic.

In 1937, B-V and his wife Ida were happy with the marriage of their son Etienne - he was 46 - with Nicole Merenda. They had two children: Prisca and Philippe II. Etienne was still flying or skiing as a hobby, but he had also tried a new sport, the VAM, a "Vehicle Activated by Man", for which he had taken a patent. It was an original invention, consisting of a streamlined bicycle. Races were organized, where cyclists reached 100 kilometers per hour. Unfortunately, there were several casualties and the International Cyclist Union banned it.

Etienne continued to fly his own airplanes and served again in the Air Force during the Second World War. (18)

On July 26, 1937, B-V published a book *"From Panama to Verdun"* (11), which obtained the *Marcelin-Guèrin* prize from the French Academy. He narrated once again his Panamanian adventure, without adding any new revelations with respect to his previous books. The last chapter of the book dealt with the *Verdunization* process, which B-V had developed during WW I.

The Second World War was near.

Although this did not appear clearly in B-V's memoirs, we can imagine that the relationship between the brothers Bunau-Varilla - Philippe and Maurice - had deteriorated.

This appears quite obviously. B-V was a true patriot and he lamented on the decadence of France: "If France had been really governed, it would have escaped easily from the spasms of the Dreyfus affair, which combined by a diabolic hand to the Panama scandal, would have led to its total destruction in 1905, if my efforts to defend my fatherland had not succeeded in preserving it from a fatal blow by inducing the powerful intervention of President Theodore Roosevelt, advised by my eminent friends Ambassador Francis B. Loomis and Senator Lodge." (9)

We notice here that his megalomania has grown up even more with age. He seemed to have appropriated for himself some actions, which were way above his ability.

His brother Maurice was a pacifist. He did not fight as a soldier in the First World War. He believed in a reconciliation between France and Germany. His newspaper *Le Matin* was strongly pro-German and also anti-Communist. Together with many Frenchmen, Maurice believed that the Germans were in a better position to fight the Russian Marxist ideology.

It was said of Maurice Bunau-Varilla that he had been a European before his time. But Maurice did not have the same virtuous reputation as his brother. Involved in many scandals due to the corrosive writings of *Le Matin,* Maurice was seen by his compatriots as the man who "between Panama and the Congo, . . . the future psychologists will ask if he was not a legend and if there really was a time where such a man could have governed the State, commanded to Ministers, telegraphed to the Tsar, rebuked Rockefeller and written painful insanities to the President of the Republic." (From Mouthon's book: "The Great Campaigns of *Le Matin*", 1910).

All of Maurice's personal attacks did not go without libel suits and condemnations that ensued; 50,000 francs for retributory damages in August 1907 and again the same condemnation in July 1908. (30)

Starting around 1930, the brothers were not as close as in the past. Their antagonistic political ideas stood between them.

Although Philippe (B-V) owned 30% of *Le Matin*, he had by choice never intruded in his brother's domain. The political line of the newspaper remained exclusively managed by Maurice, who owned 62% of *Le Matin*.

Maurice's newspaper turned resolutely against bolshevism by supporting the fascist regimes that appeared in Italy, Germany and Spain. *Le Matin* was one of the first newspapers to publish interviews of Hitler in November 1933 and of Mussolini in September 1935.

Le Matin's anti-Communist tendency was exacerbated. Maurice used to say: "Communists and terrorists are alike." (30)

The interviews of the fascist dictators and the unconditional support to Franco during the Spanish Civil War - 1936 to 1939 - marked a decisive turn in the newspaper's policy.

This move of *Le Matin* towards the extreme right isolated Maurice from his usual circle of friends. In 1931, Maurice broke his relationship with Aristide Briand, a friend of B-V - they had worked together on the *Locarno Pact* from 1920 to 1925, (see Appendix 5, page 327).

Le Matin had become a propaganda organ and would not be any more informative. It had really moved away from the original journal owned by Edwards in 1890, with the purpose of giving fresh news to privileged readers.

Its daily circulation dropped from one million after the war - 1919 - to 600,000 in 1934 and 300,000 in 1939.

As a consequence, its profits declined and it served no dividend to its stockholders after 1936. Maurice did not need the money, he had one of the largest fortunes in France, estimated to 100 million francs.

Despite these hard times, *Le Matin* continued its anti-communist, xenophobic and racist editorial course. It accused foreigners to be "international trash", "human rubbish", "garbage dumps", and they were associated to bolshevists, anarchists and terrorists.

In 1936, when a "Popular Front" came to power in France, *Le Matin* ceded to xenophobia and its motto became: "La France aux Français." (France to the French) It defended colonialist countries; Japan against China; Italy against Ethiopia. (30) Its positioning in the Parisian press was such in 1939 that, when Germans invaded France, it would be ready to accept its opinions and collaborate with the enemy.

Alike B-V, Maurice also believed in keeping people in good health, but for him, it was not philanthropic, but definitely profit oriented. He often pulled his brother's leg when he reminded him that *Verdunization* was more important to humanity than the Panama Canal.

Maurice's *Verdunization* was *Synthol*. This product, a mixture of alcohol, menthol and chloral, was invented in 1921 by Roger, a pharmacist; it was supposed to relieve all body pains. Maurice enthusiastically bought the rights from the inventor, founded the S.F.R.A.S. - *Société Française de Recherches et Applications Scientifiques* -; its laboratories were managed by Guy, Maurice's son.

In 1927, *Le Matin* launched a new weekly magazine *Le Siècle Médical* - The Medical Century - and started a huge marketing campaign to sell the *Synthol*. In France, the sales were all right and Guy appeared like a successful businessman. He also managed the new magazine.

However, in Germany - Maurice had sold the *Synthol* rights to one of his German friends - it was a complete failure. This disappointment did not affect Maurice's friendship with the Germans.

Maurice became a close friend of Joachim von Ribbentrop, the German Foreign Minister, who managed to include *Le Matin* among the foreign newspapers that the German Reich subsidized.

In 1939, Maurice was 82. His wife, Sophie Dorothée (Sonia) de Brunhoff had given him three sons:

- René, who died in 1907;

- Jean was 57. He had never taken any interest in *Le Matin*, apart from a subaltern position in 1910;

- Guy was 43; having studied engineering in the Alexander Hamilton Institute (New York), he had gradually taken over the management of *Le Matin*, and in 1939, he officially helped his aging father in running the newspaper.

Maurice had amassed a fortune estimated to 100 million francs, but had lost his compatriots' respect.

He was probably among the richest people in France. However, his heirs will not inherit much of it. It was a sad story.

30

THE STAIN

B-V felt the war coming. All his efforts for peace with his American friends had been in vain. It made him sick, in body and mind.

On May 10, 1940, the German Army entered Belgium, which had yet declared its neutrality. Hitler was not stopped by such a detail.

On May 16, Philippe Bunau-Varilla died, "having been through a new and dangerous surgical operation," (*Le Matin*, May 18, 1940). His funeral was attended by a few members of his family, in Passy's cemetery, in Paris. His daughter Giselle was in Kenya. His son Etienne was serving his country in the Air Force.

His wife Ida, his brother Maurice and his wife Sophie, and also his nephews Guy and Jean were the few to attend the ceremony.

Stephane Lauzanne, the chief editor of *Le Matin*, wrote an epitaph, on May 18, 1940, showing B-V's picture on the front page of the newspaper. It started with: "France has lost a great citizen, a man who from his first days to his last has always and everywhere magnificently served his country," and it was followed by three columns of an exhaustive panegyric, ending with: "What he did for the glory of France, here and in the New World, defies death and stands above all battles as the eternal testimony of what the will of a man can achieve." (2)

A few days later, happened an event that would cause Bunau-Varilla's name to be cursed forever.

B-V had been dead for nearly a month, when the German Army entered Paris on June 11, 1940. The occupation of France would last four years.

All French newspapers stopped being published until the new German order could be organized. However, some newspapers were more active than others were. On June 14, Marcel Knecht, a friend of Maurice, visited the German Headquarters in Paris - the *Kommandantur* - and obtained that *Le Matin* be published again. It had only ceased to be published for 4 days - June 13 to 16.

In a good understanding with the Germans, the friends he had cultivated for the last 30 years, Maurice continued to manage his newspaper *Le Matin*, with the help of his son Guy, who bore the title of "Assistant Political Counselor". Later, Guy would defend himself when accused of "collaboration", by stating that he "never involved himself in the editing or the political orientation of the newspaper".

All Parisian newspapers had been requisitioned by the Germans. Most of them refused to be submitted to the enemy's rule and retreated to the interior of the country, south of the demarcation line, where they enjoyed a relative freedom.

Maurice had always been anti-Communist and pro-German. He decided to collaborate with the enemy and his newspaper became the official voice of the occupying forces in Paris. At 83, the same age as the head of France, Marechal Petain, he could not see any harm in doing this. His pro-German and anticommunist ideas had blurred his patriotism.

Maurice went even further in his collaboration with the enemy. He decided to create a new weekly magazine, called *La Semaine*.

It was reported that Maurice maintained a red Nazi flag with the black swastika on the main wall of his newspaper's office, *Le Matin*, Boulevard Poissonnière.

During the war, *Le Matin* continued to be distributed at an average of 250,000 copies. Its profit, inexistent in 1939, skyrocketed to a record of 4 million francs a year. And this, after taking into account Maurice's and Guy's emoluments and representation expenses which amounted to 10 million francs yearly for each of them.

The war continued for four long years.

Etienne, B-V's son, came back unharmed and decorated with a medal of the Air Force, where he had acted as a hero. (18)

Giselle, his daughter, still in Kenya, saw his Italian husband come back from a prisoner camp in Tanzania. (24)

Their uncle Maurice died at 88 on August 1st 1944, a few days before the allied forces entered Paris as victors. The official medical statement mentioned a cardiac arrest. Some rumors mentioned suicide.

Maurice would not live to see the condemnation of his collaborating actions. His son Guy would pay dearly for his father.

On August 17, 1944, Paris felt that her freedom was near. The offices of *Le Matin* were occupied by the French *resistants*.

Paris was liberated on August 25.

A few days later, Guy was arrested, and later set free awaiting the investigation of his case.

In September, Guy was arrested a second time, but allowed to remain at home, for reasons of bad health. He was only 48 years old.

On November 3, 1944, his trial began. Mentally disturbed by the accusation of collaboration with the enemy, he managed to escape. On November 16, a warrant was set against him, on charges of collaborating with the enemy. On November 22, he was arrested when attempting to flee from France, with 20 kilograms of gold and 400,000 francs in cash.

As he returned to jail, his mother, Sophie (Sonia) , died on April 21, 1945.

All the chief editors of *Le Matin* were judged and condemned to 20 years of jail and the confiscation of their properties and belongings.

On January 3, 1946, after a year in jail, Guy's judgment was rendered. He was sentenced to life in jail. Like all the "collaborators", he was deprived of his civil rights and his fortune was confiscated. This brought an end to the enormous wealth accumulated by Maurice since his venture in Panama with *Artigue, Sonderegger & Co*, and later enlarged with his newspaper *Le Matin*.

The buildings, properties of the newspaper, were attributed to *L'Humanité*, a communist newspaper, which had interrupted publication when the war started and needed a new home.

Through Maurice's wrongdoings, Bunau-Varilla's name would be cursed forever.

What an unfortunate event for Philippe Bunau-Varilla - B-V - who had spent his whole life as a high-principled man.

This may explain why the name Bunau-Varilla has fallen into oblivion in France.

In 1953, after almost ten years in jail, Guy was paroled. According to some unconfirmed sources of information, he committed suicide some years later - 1984.

31
CAN PHILIPPE BUNAU-VARILLA
BE REINSTATED IN HIS OWN RIGHT?

On December 31st, 1999, according to their agreement with the United States (Treaty *Torrijos-Carter* of 1977), the Panamanians repossessed their Canal.

During the following years, the golden vs. black legend's controversy reappeared, mostly in 2003, during the celebration of Republic's Centennial. This was a political argument which questioned on one side the honesty of the *Proceres*, the Panamanian conspirators, Amador and his friends, and on the other side gave credit to the American power, represented by President Roosevelt and the investors of Wall Street.

Who were the men who really contributed to found the State of Panama in 1903? Our readers certainly by now have their own opinion.

This controversy has been covered in the theater play *El Veredicto* (The Verdict), which was performed from August 1st to 30, 2004, at the theater *La Cupula* in the capital City of Panama. Written by Juan David Morgan (author of *Con Ardientes Fulgores de Gloria*, (23) under the pseudonym of Jorge Thomas, it was a fictitious history of the 1903 independence of Panama). Co-authored by Ernesto Endara, this play presented both points of view:
- according to the black legend: Panama had been created by the financial power of Wall Street and by the capitalistic interests of the Americans. This thesis was the subject of Diaz Espino's book.(26)

according to the golden - sometimes-called white - legend: the independence of Panama was essentially due to the "conspirators" who had inspired the movement which led to the secession from Colombia.

J. D. Morgan declared of this play: "We had to convert each other, as accuser and defender of B-V." In *El Veredicto,* B-V was successively shown as the essential catalyst to the creation of the state of Panama and as the speculator who sold the Canal to the United States in order to increase his wealth. The theater owner, Eugenio Fernandez, commented about the play that: "Beyond entertainment, the aim is to put B-V in his proper dimension."

Of course, the authors of the play could only speculate on the real intents of B-V, as they were unaware of the origins of his wealth and did not know how much of this fortune he dedicated to Panama's independence.

But the simple fact of presenting both possibilities was a way to dismiss the image that B-V had acquired in Panama, that of a traitor.

In any case, in *The Verdict,* B-V was presented as fulfilling his childhood dream and helping Panama to be independent.

As the author put it: "This play intends to re-open the debate - which has been going on for a century - about the innocence or culpability of B-V, our first Panamanian Ambassador in America." Every evening, at the end of the play, the assistance in the theater was asked to vote to determine whether B-V was guilty or not. Most of the time, the spectators voted that B-V was not guilty.

More recently, in 2012, Rodolfo Leiton, a writer from Costa Rica, published: "Yo Tomé Panama " (I Took Panama), titled from the famous declaration of Teddy Roosevelt. Leiton showed that "B-V (who is shown on the book's cover) was a human being, with qualities and defaults; his only dream was to achieve the French Canal. . . Without B-V, the Canal and maybe the Republic of Panama would not be what they are today." *La Prensa,* a Panamanian newspaper, wrote that Leiton's book "resulted from a thoughtful literary work and a thorough documentation."(August 25, 2012)

Could these signs be precursory of a process to reinstate B-V in his own right in Panama and involve the re-writing of Panamanian history books, which still refer to Philippe Bunau-Varilla as the "infamous impostor who sold the Canal to the United States"?

We certainly hope that this book will contribute to this cause.

CONCLUSION

Today, the Republic of Panama is the exclusive owner of the Canal, after almost a century of North-American appropriation of the "Canal Zone".

The handing-over went smoothly. Some birds of ill omen had predicted catastrophes due to Panamanian *management's* inexperience.

They were proven wrong. Today, the Canal works even better than before and produces a substantial profit to Panama, contributing almost 10% of its Gross National Product. It is therefore essential to maintain its competitive nature in International Maritime Commerce.

Unexpectedly, at the turn of the 21st Century, Nicaragua prepared its last offensive to promote its Interoceanic Canal. With the advent of what is usually called "globalization", the world maritime flow of goods has increased to such an extent that a second Interoceanic Canal could be justified. Would this second canal be in Nicaragua? Its supporters claimed that this was where it should have been built in the first place.

A very serious proposal was prepared by the Government of Nicaragua. It resurrected the same scheme, which had been produced by Menocal in 1879, a Canal with locks, for a cost of $ 18 to 25 billion[*] and would take twelve years to build.

The *Panama Canal Authority*, aware of this competition, accelerated its modernization plans, much less onerous: only $ 5 billion, to be completed in 2014.

---

[*] The effect of inflation is clear: in a Century's time, the budget had grown from $250 million in 1906 to $18-25 billion in 2000.

This difference in cost is easily understandable, because the Panama Canal is already in operation and needs only to be enlarged to accommodate bigger ships, while in Nicaragua, everything has to be done.

Given the enormous sum required in Nicaragua for a new Canal, the investors were hesitant. The twelve years it would take to build seemed a very long time and the return on investment appeared remote. Still, the President of Nicaragua declared: "Our project is not a pure gamble, nor an adventure, but a very real project."

To which the *Panama Canal Authority*'s Director replied that: "We have fought during the whole 20th Century to get back the sovereignty of our Canal and it would be a big mistake today to let it become obsolete."

Pressed by the Nicaraguan project, the Panamanians hastened their studies to update Franklin Roosevelt's scheme: a second line of locks to be built in parallel with the existing one.

One may recall that the locks designed under Lesseps - those that Eiffel should have built - were 180 meters long and 18 meters wide. The locks of the existing American Canal are 300 by 33 meters. The future Panamanian project will have locks measuring 425 by 55 meters, with a draught increased from 12 to 18 meters. This shows the impact of the enormous increase in the size of commercial ships.

The future locks have been designed to handle the largest container ship that was being built at the time the project was launched (2006): a ship transporting 12,000 standard containers (TEU: twenty-foot equivalent units; 8*8*20 feet, about 39 cubic meters). Today, in 2013, ships are being built to transport up to 18,000 TEU. These gigantic ships would be too wide to cross the extended Panama Canal.

Where would this race end to build the largest possible ship?

On July 14, 2006, the Panamanian Parliament voted a law proposing the extension of the Canal. It had to be ratified by the people. On October 22, 2006, the Panamanian people voted by a large majority (78%) in favor of the project – however only 43% of all voters had cast a vote. The Panamanian Government was then authorized to proceed with the works.

This is a colossal project. To appreciate the enormity of it, one figure would permit to compare the progresses in earth excavation made since 1880. The Panama Canal's extension which will come into operation in 2015 will require moving 250 million cubic meters of earth, about 5 times more than the French had excavated with an average of 15,000 men; the current project will require only 5,000. The French had excavated 55 million cubic meters; the Americans completed the canal moving 185 million; for a grand total of 240.

The Panama canal extension is thus almost equivalent to digging a second canal.

Its total investment is estimated to $ 6 billion, of which 10% would be spent in basins to recycle the fresh water used by the locks.

Panama had won its last battle against Nicaragua and it is hoped that this final confrontation would indeed be the last. The fight had lasted for more than a Century and a half!

But history has its share of surprises.
Recently, in June 2012, Nicaragua's President, Daniel Ortega proposed a law to build "his" canal, based on a different route than recommended by Menocal - Rio Rama and Oyate, instead of Rio San Juan - and for a cost of $ 30 billion.
Newspapers commented: "Ortega revives Nicaragua canal fantasy."
And in September 2012, a Chinese company had declared to be interested to build such canal.

In 2015, just a Century after the inauguration of the Canal, the opening of a third line of locks will allow container-carrying vessels up to 150,000 tons, to cross the Panama Canal, instead of the usual 65,000 tons "Panamax".
The Panamaxes would continue to use the old line of locks, while the large container ships would transit through the giant locks today under construction.

Of course, we wish a successful life to the new enlarged Panama Canal.

But is it the end of the story? What could prevent such a marvel of human engineering to go wrong in the future?
Just a small detail.
As the earth's temperature is forecast to be slowly rising due to global warming - principally due to the effect of the increase in the concentration of carbon dioxide in our planet's atmosphere -, the polar cap of the North Pole would gradually melt within a few decades. Experts differ on a date, but agree that it would probably happen before 2030. Michel Rocard, ambassador of the poles, declared in May 2011: "Everybody has in mind that, in less than 20 years, half of the world trade could use the maritime routes of the North Pole." This would allow commercial shipping to take place across the Arctic Ocean, which could have a huge impact on the cost and route of all global shipping. Which means that a ship could go from Yokohama - Japan - to Hamburg - Germany – either in a westerly direction, along the north coast of Siberia; or in an easterly direction, along the passage north of Canada.
What effect would this have on Suez or on Panama ?

To be followed .   .   .

APPENDICES

APPENDIX 1.

CHARGES OF MR. LEMARQUIS AGAINST ASC

CHARGES OF Mr. LEMARQUIS, REPRESENTING THE SMALL SHAREHOLDERS OF THE INTEROCEANIC CANAL COMPANY AGAINST ARTIGUE, SONDEREGGER & Co.

(These documents are reproduced from the French National Archives, reference 7 AQ 22, 78 Avenue Leclerc, Roubaix, France.)
"Sums due by Artigue, Sonderegger & Co. (ASC) relative to the work they did in Panama."
(This document is dated December 18, 1893.)

1. CULEBRA (from kilometer 53.6 to kilometer 55.456)
A. Difference between the amounts called by ASC
   and the work effectively accomplished   536,512 francs
B. Unjustified work
       Advances transformed into fixed allocations   700,000 francs
       Unjustified move of the working equipment   200,000 francs
       Unjustified overheads   80,000 francs
       Withholding of 0.25 Francs/cubic meter
       on a previous contract   193,778 francs
       Payment of January 9, 1887; unjustified   387,204 francs
       Payment of March 5, 1888; unjustified   19,000 francs
C. "Lost" equipment   800,000 francs

2. PARAISO (from kilometer 55.456 to kilometer 57)
       Advance for 1.2 Million Francs transformed
       into a fixed allocation, which means that ASC
       has benefited of an unjustified rebate of   227,406 francs

3. MIRAFLORES (from kilometer 57 to kilometer 62.2)
       Unjustified move of the work's yard   1,105,000 francs
                                          _____

For a grand total of   5,548,270 francs

Accompanying this claim are several remarks from Mr. Lemarquis - the prosecutor - which are well indicative of the state of mind which was customary during this period:

"Mr. Philippe Bunau-Varilla, ex-Engineer Head of a Division and Director of the Works, had filled many positions in the High Management of the Company, which had allowed him to be fully aware of the work to be done by ASC. If anywhere the principle of responsibility should have been applied, it was in the Culebra Hill sector.

They (Note: it probably meant the parties involved: the Company and ASC) could have renounced to the damages, alleviated the burden of the contractor, by bringing the monthly targets of digging to more reasonable figures, instead of paying enormous indemnities, as if the Company had been the unique responsible for the non-execution of the contracts.

The prices paid to ASC were amply sufficient, exceeding those paid to the Anglo-Dutch Company, which did not receive such high allocations and advances.

ASC had received, by amending its contracts when the Canal with locks had been decided, some unjustified advantages, in the form of cancellation indemnities which should not have been payable.

Moreover, ASC never filled its commitments; the volumes extracted from the Culebra Hill being only at the end 1.9 million cubic meters instead of the 9 millions targeted for."

On its part, ASC claims that: "The work achieved was according to the contracts it signed with the Company and to the program defined in 1887, when it was decided to complete the Canal with provisional locks in four years. The work had been realized under the eyes of the Company's representatives, always permanently present on the work place."

In his charges against ASC, Mr. Lemarquis conceded however that: "the technical skill and qualities of the Directors of ASC existed without any doubt, and the same with their devotion to duty."

In the following lines of the same document, Mr. Lemarquis urged ASC to bring the financial help necessary to salvage the Company. In another document, ASC was proposed the following compromise: "ASC pledges to subscribe 22,000 shares of 100 Francs each in the capital of the New Company. These 2.2 million Francs will be divided into ASC's share holders in the form it will decide."

This compromise was not at all unreasonable, as the penalty only represented 5% of the revenues of ASC, which Vallé indicated to be 50.9 million francs (see page 125).

APPENDIX 2.

PUBLIC SUBSCRIPTIONS OF THE COMPANY

From Jean BOUVIER "The Second Scandal of Panama" (1964)

DATE	Number of shares	Interest	Nominal Value	Price Paid	Millions collected	% subscribed
Sep.7, 1882	250,000	5%	500 F	437.5F	109.375	100
Oct.3, 1883	600,000	3%	500 F	285 F	171.0	100
Sep.25, 1884	478,762	4%	500 F	333 F	145.19	91
Aug.3, 1886	458,802	3%	1000 F	450 F	206.46	100
July 26, 1887	258,887	3%	1000 F	440 F	113.91	50
Mar.14, 1888	350,000	3%	1000 F	460 F	35.031	22
Jun.26, 1888	2,000,000	prizes	400 F	360 F	254.588	35
TOTAL BONDS					1,035.554	

SHARES

Dec. 6. 1880	600.000		500 F		300.000	100

FUNDS COLLECTED FOR THE CONSTRUCTION OF
THE PANAMA CANAL **1,335 MILLION F**

Note:
The nominal value was the price at which each title would be refunded. (10)

It should be pointed out that the 1,335 million collected by the Company, corresponded, according to the calculations of Mr. Lemarquis to a nominal value of: **1,777 million francs.** This shows that the average discount per share was around 25%.

APPENDIX 3.

EXPENSES INCURRED BY B-V FROM 1890 TO 1914

A round-trip France (Le Havre) – USA (New York) in First Class of a Transatlantic Steamer was worth about $ 500.*

A "Suite" in the Waldorf Astoria Hotel was worth: $ 10/day.

B-V spent in meals, receptions, gifts, etc. : $ 10/day.

Every summer trip to the USA, for a three months period, B-V spent: 500 + 900 + 900 = $ 2,300

B-V came every summer to America from 1890 to 1904, in all:

15 trips * $ 2,300 =	$ 35,000
to which we should add the trip to Venezuela =	$ 5,000
And four trips from 1904 to 1914: 4* $2,500 =	$ 10,000
Cost of printing B-V's pamphlet:	
30,000 copies times at $ 0.20/ea. =	$ 6,000
Copies for the Senators:	
1,000 copies at $ 1/ea. =	$ 1,000
Notices published in a number of Parisian newspapers:	
140,000 Francs, or:	$ 28,000
Telegrams to Marroquin:	$ 5,000
Sum allocated to the conspirators of Panama:	$ 100,000
Cost of printing his 1892 book:	
1,000 copies at 10 francs/ea. (2 dollars)	$ 2,000
	————
For a grand total of:	$ 192,000
Or (at 5 French Francs per U. S. $):	**960,000 francs.**

---

* More precisely, a transatlantic round trip was worth from $ 200 to $ 500 in First Class (called Cabin Class), depending on the steamer and the shipping company. To this should be added $ 100 to $ 150 for the servant's trip, and also the Railway fares from Paris to Le Havre $ 10 (one-way) in 1st Class.
We have rounded up all these sums to $ 500.

APPENDIX 4.

BIBLIOGRAPHY

PRELIMINARY NOTE

We believe that, when an author covers a given historical subject, it necessarily implies that he/she has acquired full knowledge of the previous works on such subject and therefore his/her new book represents necessarily a step forward in the knowledge of such subject.

This is why we have classified our sources in chronological order and have selected a majority of historical works, rather than novels.

In the following list, the reader will appreciate how progress was made from one book to the next.

One note of caution: summarizing in a little less than 300 pages the 15,000 pages of this Bibliography, that is in a mere 2%, has been a very difficult exercise and the author implores all his readers to be particularly indulgent.

REFERENCES

1.   John BIGELOW Papers. MssCol 301.
       The New York Public Library. Manuscripts and Archives
       Division.
       1839-1912.

John Bigelow wrote an extensive diary, where he described in detail his trip to Panama - in February 1886 - and his relationship with B-V, which was related in a slightly different way than what B-V disclosed in his memoirs. Bigelow played an important part in the success of the Panama project. Convinced by B-V to act as "liaison" between France and America, Bigelow gathered a powerful lobby among his Republican friends to act in favor of the Panama Canal and against the Interoceanic Canal project of Nicaragua. Together with B-V, Bigelow had a pre-eminent role in the sale of the New Company to the American Government.

2.   French National Archives.

-    2.a Roubaix. Business Archives (*Archives du Travail*).
"Repertory of the Universal Company for the Interoceanic Canal of Panama," under the titles: 7 AQ 1 to 48, dated from 1878 to 1909, among which the most interesting are:
- 7 AQ 22: Trial of Artigue, Sonderegger & Co.
- 7 AQ 23 & 24: Lawsuits against the contractors; one of which was ASC.

Here in the French Archives we found the minutes of the trial of Maurice's company: Artigue, Sonderegger & Co., containing a list of violations committed by the contractors on the Panama Canal work place, the list of their unjustified profits and the cash advances they pocketed for no reason. The explanation of ASC's profit is clearly detailed.

Mr. Lemarquis' settlement - the prosecutor -, which required the banks, the contractors and all the parties involved in the bankruptcy of the Company to take part in its rescue and to contribute to the creation of the New Company.

The charges brought by Mr. Lemarquis against the various contractors were described *in extenso* in the Archives papers. There were documents showing the scurvy tricks of the Bunau-Varilla brothers and of other contractors, among which was Gustave Eiffel.

Several boxes full of documents brought the undeniable proof of the fraudulent actions of the contractors.

- 2.b Paris: 18AR/1 to 3.

Papers of Maurice Bunau-Varilla, where is found the letter of June 5, 1905, from B-V to Maurice, describing the agreement made by the brothers concerning the newspaper *Le Matin*, where they invested jointly.

- 2.c Paris. Numerical collection of the French Archives at the website : www:Gallica.bnf.fr, where have been digitized:

1. The report of General Vallé to the French Chamber of Deputies, dated July 4, 1893: Main text and 2 appendices for a total of almost 2,000 pages. This report covered the entire adventure of the Lesseps' Company in Panama. They were hearings of more than 100 witnesses, among them: Baïhaut, Clemenceau, Delahaye, Kohn, Oberndoerffer . . . and Philippe Bunau-Varilla (B-V).

Vallé's report has been one of our main sources for discovering the origin of the Bunau-Varilla brothers' wealth:
- the details of the trial of Artigue , Sonderegger & Cie,
- the scurvy tricks of the contractors working in Panama, their unjustified profits, their cash advances received unduly from the Company.
- the interview of B-V.

2. Daily copies of the newspaper *Le Matin,* from 1885 to 1944.

All these documents from the French Archives had been our major source of information, showing in detail the origin of the colossal fortune of the Bunau-Varilla brothers. The amount of their fortune coming from the profit made by ASC was detailed and calculated – down to one cent of a franc! - in Vallé's Report.

Vallé's Report gave the full account of Lesseps Company's misfortunes, with quotes from: Bulletins of the Company, Newspapers of the time, Reports of the Chamber's Commissions, etc.

Except for Jean Bouvier (10), we know - from their reference list - of no other author who had investigated the Archives of the Company in Roubaix.

3. Lucien Napoléon-Bonaparte WYSE. "The Panama Canal"
   Hachette, Paris. 1886

This book, written during the French Canal's construction, had two goals:
   1.   To summarize all the explorations made by Wyse in the Isthmus from
        November 1876 to February 1879.
   Of importance, in the appendices, are the full texts of :
        - the Bidlack-Mallarino treaty of 1846,
        - the Clayton-Bulwer treaty of 1850,
        - the Salgar-Wyse agreement of May 18, 1878,
        - the commitment letter of February 24, 1879, signed between Wyse
        and the Executive Committee of the Board of Directors of the Panama
        RailRoad Company: Trevor Park, G. Francklyn, and Jos. Ogden.
   2.   To report about the work of the French Company, as of October 1885.
Wyse's critics of the company's management were severe - he was not part of
it -; he had a dispute with Lesseps, who had promised him the General
Manager position in Panama and failed in keeping his word.

4.   Edouard DRUMONT. "La Dernière Bataille."
        ("The last Battle.")
        Dentu, Paris, 1890.

    It could be a surprise to the reader to find in the present book, which we
intended to remain decent and respectable, this reference to an infamous
volume - racist and anti-Semitic. We can only justify its presence here by its
great historical value. Drumont was an experienced journalist, curious to
explain all the intricacies of his time.
    In his book, he provided a lot of useful information about the work done
in Panama. In its third chapter, titled "A 19th Century Enterprise", we read
about Lesseps' lies: "this white elephant, a kind of majestic and greedy idol,
eating gold in a cloud of incense and returning golden excretions that newspapers were sharing among themselves." This extract also shows Drumont's
original style.
    This book contained many useful informations about the standard of
living of the period, the rumors which circulated in the Parisian society at the
time of the bankruptcy of the Lesseps Company, and many others.
    Of course, Drumont's book was a caricature of the situation in 1890.
Published just after the bankruptcy of the Company, with the aim to prepare
the public opinion to the trial of the culprits, this book more than reached its
objective. It raised a wave of hostility against the actors behind the Panama
affair.

B-V, fearing that it alluded to him, dedicated no less than three pages in his memoirs (134 to 137, Constable, London, 1913) to refute the famous word of Drumont: "It is a gigantic swindler's trick!" (7) He could not help rehashing the subject again in his book of 1937: "The campaign of calumny had begun on February 9, 1890, with a book by Mr. Drumont. His accusations seemed to be those of a hysterical man and were directed against the glorious and unfortunate Ferdinand de Lesseps . . . What he wrote is scarcely believable." (9) And, quite superfluously, B-V quoted half a page of Drumont's book.

Of course, Drumont's book has to be read with circumspection, but is this not the case with all our sources of information

5.   Philippe BUNAU-VARILLA
        Panama. Le Passé. Le Présent. L'Avenir.
        ("Past, Present and Future")
        Masson, Paris, 1892.

B-V's technical and historical book covered the activities of the Universal Company for the Interoceanic Canal of Panama. It had been written a few years after his adventure in Panama (1884-1889).

It was exceptionally large - 8 by 12 inches - and exhibited beautiful prints - with some foldouts in color - and enlightening photographs showing the French Company in action in Panama.

The first chapters dealt with the work achieved by the Company between 1881 and 1889. The rest of the book described in detail B-V's plan to complete the Canal with provisional locks; this plan would have allowed the Canal to be opened to ships within eight years and with 675 million francs of expenditures.

B-V exhorted: "all those who have risked their lives or their savings, have believed into the French talent and do not wish to abandon the fruit of so many sacrifices and so much work."

And he concluded: "if this wounded work was to be abandoned . . . how great would be the wrath of the nation against those who had contributed to its final session."

B-V distributed copies of his book to the French Parliamentaries. However, it did not meet any audience, as it was printed just when the Company's trial began; the Chamber of Deputies' members did not want to be involved again in the burning subject of the Panama Canal.

6.   " The Story of Panama. Hearings on the RAINEY's Resolution."
        Washington. Government Printing office. 1913.

        This huge volume - 736 pages - contains three important texts :

    1. "General Statement of Services Rendered by Sullivan & Cromwell, as
        General Counsel of the French Company, during the eight years -
        1896 to 1904 - in representation, defense, protection and advancement
        of the interests of said company."
        This document was addressed by William Nelson Cromwell, on Feb-
        ruary 21, 1907, to the arbitration judges, who had been named to de-
        cide whether the sums spent by Cromwell - $ 832,449 - were justified.
        The judgment validated only $ 228,282 (27% of what Cromwell re-
        quested).

    2. "Statement by Mr. Henry N. Hall, a staff correspondent of the New
        York World," before the Commission of Foreign Affairs of the House
        of Representatives, from February 9 to 20, 1912.
        Hall, a newsman of the *World*, was giving evidence in favor of Joseph
        Pulitzer the proprietor of the newspaper - with his sons -, whom The-
        odore Roosevelt had sued for libel.
        Hall had gathered an exceptional collection of documents and testi-
        monies, which he made public before the Committee on Foreign Af-
        fairs of the House of Representatives.
        Although Hall followed closely Cromwell's statement, he neverthe-
        less revealed interesting new facts.

    3. "Statement on behalf of Historical truth," a letter sent to the Commit-
        tee by B-V on March 29, 1912.
        "The origin of this statement was this: About the middle of last
        March, Mr. Bunau-Varilla received copies of these hearings. He at
        once saw the many fallacies that existed in the facts and conclusions."
        Probably written after (7) below had been published, this letter added
        a few useful details to help us understand better the part B-V had
        played in the 1903 Panamanian Revolution.

7.   Philippe BUNAU-VARILLA
        "Panama. La Création. La Destruction. La Resurrection."
        ("Panama. The Creation, Destruction and Resurrection.")
        Plon, Paris, 1913.

B-V's memoirs were a thick book, 600 pages long and with many photographs and graphics. It was the prime reference for the present book.

B-V seldom adulterated the facts, but often omitted what was detrimental to his interests. In addition, he never explained any of his motivations, which appeared obscure for an unfamiliar reader.

Just a quick example to illustrate this. It is hoped that after having read the present book, the reader easily understands why the period 1890-1895, during which ASC was judged and condemned has been almost totally left out from B-V's memoirs. Still, B-V appeared in front of the prosecuting Commission of the French Chamber of Deputies, but did not dwell on this in any of his books. This period was shameful for a man who amassed an enormous wealth in the Canal works from 1886 to 1889 and did not want anybody to criticize his accomplishments - or his brother's. This was another proof of his enormous vanity.

It took B-V almost ten years to write his book - 1904 to 1913. Knowing how meticulous he was, we can be sure that he weighed every single word of it. The book's highlight was the 1902- 1904 period, where B-V arrogated to himself the major part in the sale of the French Company's assets to the USA. As always, he showed a superior skill when he wrote about this episode. But, once again, he omitted important details such as to tell us who had called him in September 1903 to help the Panamanian conspirators.

Ambitious, arrogant, full of pride, in his books, B-V did not let anyone else have the first part. His attitude compelled us to take his declarations with extreme care. We had to check all the facts, crosscheck them, fill the blanks, and even compare the translations of both of B-V' his books with the French originals - one would be surprised how many times they differ!

However, B-V's books are *page-turners*, which we recommend vehemently.

Constable in London published a translation of this book in English in 1913 and Doubleday another translation in New York in 1920.

The quotes of this book have been extracted from the Constable edition.

8.   Theodore ROOSEVELT
        "An Autobiography"
        Charles Scribner New York 1912

This was one of the best books written by an American politician. Worth reading in its entirety, but we have taken our quotes from Chapter XIV "The Monroe doctrine and the Panama Canal", which described in Roosevelt words how he "took the canal": an amazing mixture of cleverness, pragmatism and cynicism.

9. Philippe BUNAU-VARILLA
"La Grande Aventure de Panama."
"The Great Adventure of Panama". Sub-titled: "The essential part
Panama played in the defeat of Germany.")
Plon, Paris, September 1919.

B-V fought in the Great War from August 1914 to the end of 1917, when
he was wounded, lost his right leg and was badly injured in his left foot. His
walk therefore became very painful and hazardous, despite a wooden leg of
his invention.

In his book, B-V expressed his bitterness towards the Germans (whom he calls
the "*boches*", according to the derogatory language of the time). He told us
about:
- "the insidious conspiration of the *boches*" (page ix)
- "the pervasive and treacherous hand of the *boche*" (page 47)
- "the criminal weapons of the *boches*". (Note: B-V alluded here to the combat
gases; page 90).

B-V also showed his contempt for the newspaperman Judet, who had the guts
to describe the bankruptcy of the French Company in Panama, as the "biggest
defeat of France since Fachoda." (page 65) This displeased B-V very much.
We found this book less interesting than the previous one. It had probably
been written when B-V was under the physical pain of his wounds and the
mental distress of the period. In 1919, his daughter Giselle divorced her first
husband, an exceptional and humiliating event in the high society of this
time. His brother, Maurice, had become anti-communistic and pro-German,
differing from B-V's strong nationalistic views. The brothers were not as close
as when they worked together in ASC.

This book did not bring any significant piece of information compared to the
previous book, published in 1913.

"The Great Adventure of Panama."
New York, Doubleday, 1920.
This was the English translation of the above-mentioned B-V's book of
memoirs. He probably translated it himself under the supervision of a Mr.
Richards. We did not find here any additional information, except for the
strange book's dedication, on the cover page: "To the great Ferdinand de
Lesseps, his eminent coadjutor Charles de Lesseps, the great Theodore
Roosevelt, and his eminent coadjutors John Hay and Francis B. Loomis, the
resurrectors of Panama," where B-V surprisingly gave a special place to his
friend Loomis, among men of great fame.

By surrounding Loomis with such prestigious personalities, B-V admitted in fact that he took a capital part in the success of the Panama Canal. Loomis was B-V's friend and acted as the intermediary with the American Government (Roosevelt and Hay).

10.   Miles DuVAL Jr. "Cadiz to Cathay"
           (Cadiz in Spain and Cathay, the ancient name for China)
           "The Story of the Long Struggle for a Waterway
           Across the American Isthmus"
           Stanford University Press. 1940.

In this most interesting book, written by a retired U. S. Marine Commander, we find:
-   A full list of the European and American explorers who visited the Central American Isthmus in the first years of the 19th century.
-   The description of the conflicts between the United States and Great Britain to gain control of Nicaragua. Great Britain had for centuries occupied the "Mosquito Coast" and Americans tried to negotiate her departure, putting forward the "Monroe Doctrine".

DuVal's book was prefaced by William Franklin Sands, the grand-son of Benjamin Franklin and a former American diplomat.

11.   Philippe BUNAU-VARILLA "De Panama à Verdun."
           ("From Panama to Verdun. Sub-titled: My fights for France.")
           Plon, Paris, 1937.

B-V told us again, in almost the same words as in his previous books, his contribution to the making of Panama and its Canal. However, we learned about his achievements during the 1914-18 War.

He pretended that without his water purification process, the *Verdunization,* the French Army would have lost the battle. It is not the purpose of our book to confirm the veracity of this statement. If it was true, B-V would have a statue in every city of France: he has just an Avenue in the city of Carcassonne, in the south of France.

This book did not bring any new fact to our story. B-V used quite the same words as in his 1913 book to narrate the Panama saga.

An English translation was issued exactly two years later, on July 26, 1939, and published in 1940 by Dorance and Co., Philadelphia.

12.   Dwight Carroll MINER
        "The Fight for the Panama Route"
        "The Story of the Spoooner Act and the Hay-Herran Treaty"
        New York. Columbia University Press. 1940

This is one of the best documented books on the Colombian negotiation. Based on:
- The "Libro Azul" (The Blue Book), written in 1904 and which related the story of that negotiation, as seen from Bogota's point of view,
- The "Story of Panama": an account of the Hearings before the Committee on Foreign Affairs of the House of Representatives. Washington. 1913 (see reference 6, above).

Of course, many more references are used by Miner, from the Library of Congress, the Bogota Archives, and about 200 books.

Miner spent almost 50 years teaching Contemporary Civilization at the New York Columbia University. He has produced here one of the most exhaustive study of the fight for the Interoceanic Route.

13.   André SIEGFRIED
        "Suez, Panama et les Routes Maritimes Mondiales"
        ("Suez, Panama and the World Maritime Routes.")
        Armand Colin, Paris, 1948.

It is not necessary to introduce André Siegfried, eminent historian, professor in the *College de France*, Member of the *French Académie*. His book had assembled the most important points concerning Suez and Panama.

Siegfried described B-V as a "persuasive and indefatigable man", who "took the matter in his hands with an incomparable brilliancy."

Siegfried summed up the 1903 treaty as follows: "By this treaty, the U. S. Government received a band of land 10 miles wide, with all the rights it would have had if it was its sovereign. In exchange, the United States guaranteed the independence of Panama, which received an indemnity of 10 million dollars, to which was added an annual rent of 250,000 dollars. Panamanians protested against this leonine Treaty, signed between an American and a Frenchman: one can ask whether Panamanians would have negotiated a better Treaty? What is probable is that without B-V, this revolution would never have occurred. The Panama Canal saw in B-V a passionate champion, convincing and efficient."

14. <u>Jean BOUVIER "Les Deux Scandales de Panama."</u>
("The Two Scandals of Panama.")
Julliard, Paris, 1964.

This most interesting book dealt mostly with the <u>financial scandal</u>, caused by the banks' commissions. The main French Banks - *Société Générale, Crédit Lyonnais, Crédit Industriel et Commercial* and many others - asked for exorbitant commissions, which contributed to the bankruptcy of the *Universal Company of the Interoceanic Canal of Panama,* and consequently annihilated the savings of hundreds of thousands of small investors.

This book, published in 1964, followed the opening of the French Archives - January 1st, 1950 - which had been restricted to the public since Lemarquis delivered the files in deposit in 1930. At that time, the archivist noted that many files were missing: all the Company's correspondence in and out, the list of the deceased, the bills and spending receipts and many others, which were destroyed in 1904 by an order of the Paris Court.

These 7 AQ files have nevertheless delivered some of the secrets we had been looking for.

This book narrated the scandals rather than telling the sad destiny of the Company. This book was absolutely indispensable to understand the trial of the instigators that were responsible for the bankruptcy. It was our inspiration, in particular in showing the way to the French National Archives in Roubaix, bundle 7 AQ, from which it took all of its information.

Our interest was in the sub-bundle 7 AQ 22, which related the trial of *Artigue, Sonderegger & Cie*, the company founded by the brothers Bunau-Varilla to work in Panama. Unfortunately, we do not know of any translation of this book in English.

15. <u>Eduardo LEMAITRE "Panama y su Separacion de Colombia".</u>
(in Spanish: Panama and its separation from Colombia)
Biblioteca Banco Popular, Bogota, 1971.

Written by an illustrious Colombian writer, this book - which to my knowledge has not been translated into English - analyzed the events of 1903 from the point of view of a Bogota citizen, who witnessed his/her country stupidly missing the *Deal of the Century.*

Lemaitre gave us many details about the Province of Panama before her 1903 independence. He covered in great depth the events that led to its secession and gave many interesting informations about the instigators of the independence.

Lemaitre also quoted many contemporary witnesses of the events of autumn 1903.

Lemaitre qualified B-V of "figura magnanima, generosa y omnipotente" (magnanimous, generous and omnipotent man).

He also recognized that the Panamanians "never admitted, justly, that he was the founder of their Republic."

Today, B-V's bust is not among the other personalities of the French Canal, which ornate the French Plaza, erected in 1923 in the old City of Panama.

We do not know of any translation of this book in English.

16.   David McCULLOUGH
         "The Path between Two Seas".
         Simon and Schuster, New York, 1977.

This was one of the most thorough and well-documented books about the making of the Panama Canal. However, in its avalanche of information, we noted that the period going from 1892 to 1898 was not covered; there was absolutely nothing about the trial of the contractors in 1894.

Unaware of the wealth accumulated by the Bunau-Varilla brothers, McCullough (like most authors) speculated on the motives of his intervention in the pro-Panama campaign in the United States. He indicated that B-V's expenses came "out of a private source that remains something of a mystery." Similarly, he wondered on page 290: "How could he afford the enormous house on Avenue d'Iéna? No one knew." And he added: "To his own descendants the origin of the family fortune would remain a mystery."

This book was nevertheless very much in favor of B-V. McCullough wrote on page 161: "It is fair to say that without B-V there would be no Canal at Panama." Practically, word for word, what Siegfried wrote.

A translation in Spanish was edited in Mexico (1979).

17.   A. BENARD de RUSSAILH.
         "Diary of a trip to California" (1850-1852).
         Published in its original French form in 1980,
         by Aubier Montaigne, Paris.

Russailh's French manuscript - written around 1860 - was discovered in 1931 and immediately translated and published in English by Westgate Press of San Francisco. The interest of this book lied in its detailed descriptions of the life aboard a sailing ship at the time of the great Californian mirage:

"The *Joseph* carried on board about 150 passengers, of which 40 in a single room (the First Class was 1,500 Francs, against only 500 in Third Class). The ship took about six months to cruise through the 6,000 leagues (about 15,000 miles) between Le Havre and San Francisco. There was only one stop to replenish in fresh food, in Brazil, Chile or Peru. The days on board were passed looking at the ocean, its fishes, sharks or birds, talking, sometimes in violent discussions, making fun of others as children do. . . . The passengers of the *Joseph,* landing in San Francisco were suddenly immerged in a climate of violence so characteristic of the first years of the Gold Rush, when revolvers or B*owie knifes* were an integral part of the men's costume."

This was how people traveled before the Panama Canal or even before the PRR.

Russailh's book immerged its readers into the atmosphere of the French pioneers emigrating to America, hoping for a better life.

18.   Gustave ANGUIZOLA
         "Philippe Bunau-Varilla. The Man behind the Panama Canal"
         Nelson Hall, Chicago, 1980.

Anguizola was a Panamanian historian who taught at the University of Texas. He wrote a book full of minute details. Its greatest interest and novelty came from the fact that Anguizola had interviewed various members of B-V's family: his daughter Giselle and his granddaughter Mirella Rocco Ricciardi, both providing some first-hand undisclosed information.

However, as always in the case of plethoric information, some minor errors were found in his book, which should for that reason be read with great care (Note of the author: this also applies to the present book: nobody is perfect.)

Anguizola did not question the origin of the Bunau-Varilla brothers' fortune, because he believed that they had inherited from a rich father: "Antoine (their father) died a few months after Philippe's sixth birthday, leaving his family well provided for, as he invested wisely in the Parisian real estate and in the mines of Asturias."

This was one of the only books to mention B-V's trip to Caracas in 1899, where he met with Loomis, who will later become Secretary of State, in 1903. B-V only mentioned briefly Loomis in his memoirs: "whom I had known while he was the American Minister Plenipotentiary in Lisbon." Here, Anguizola's source of information was an interview with B-V's granddaughter, Mirella Rocco Ricciardi. B-V has certainly omitted to mention this trip in his memoirs to avoid being accused of plotting with the revolutionaries in Panama.

315

As for B-V's family tree, described by Anguizola in pages 335-337, the reader will be the judge of its truthfulness. We believe that it is an amalgam of hypotheses, mostly unproven, but nevertheless very enlightening.

We have found the title of Anguizola's book to be absolutely relevant to the present book: "*Philippe Bunau-Varilla; The Man behind the Panama Canal*", but, to our judgment, Anguizola really went too far when he wrote page 332: "Philippe was one of the true geniuses of the late nineteen and early twentieth centuries. He ranks with such luminaries as Pasteur, Madame Curie, Marconi, Lindbergh, de Lesseps, ..."!

19.   Jean-Yves MOLLIER "Le Scandale de Panama."
        ("The Panama Scandal.") Fayard, Paris, 1991

Written by an illustrious professor of the Sorbonne University in Paris, a specialist of the Third Republic, this book quoted, among others, three important books: B-V's memoirs of 1913, Bouvier's and Siegfried's books.

It went in detail through the origins and consequences of the Panama scandal, which almost did away with the Third French Republic. The last and short chapter XIII (22 pages) dealt with the period 1894 -1903 and the sale of the French assets to the United States under the title "An American Canal," but did not reveal any new facts.

We read that B-V "was the only man who seemed decided to move heaven and earth to complete the Panama Canal", but found no explanation for B-V's motivations. We read also that B-V, "an engineer, has magnified his actions but omitted to explain the reasons behind them". And: "Without a doubt, the man had been the active, convinced and permanent champion of the enterprise from 1894 to 1906. It could however be incorrect to believe that B-V was acting by monomania or idealism, as he had acquired a considerable fortune thanks to Panama."

However, Mollier was not explicit about the origin of B-V's wealth.

He indicated that Maurice fled to England in 1897, to avoid the second inquiry Commission's investigation. He was accused of pocketing a commission of 2% on the contract the Company had signed with Eiffel for the manufacture of the locks - Reinach supposedly received another 3% and Hébrard 5%. Maurice was really a swindler!

Mollier saw B-V as the instrument of "a determined lobby, that of the bankers of the PRR, mainspring of the American part of the New Company." This theory was similar to the *leyenda negra* - in Spanish: the black legend - upheld by Diaz Espino. To substantiate his assumption, Mollier explained that Seligman, the New York banker, had purchased 3.6 million francs worth of shares of the New Company - on a total of 65 million francs.

Was this enough to prove that the PRR (Panama RailRoad Company) was the "bugle" which called B-V in September 1903?

We do not know of any English translation of this book.

20. John MAJOR.
"Prize Possession. The United States and the Panama Canal. 1903-1979." Cambridge University Press. 1993.

Although this highly documented book dealt essentially with the events posterior to 1903, its first chapter "Quest for a Canal. 1826-1903.", revealed a mass of useful information. John Major has read every possible piece of documentation from Panama City to Washington, D.C. His book is quite ignorant of B-V, the " Frenchman who had worked on the de Lesseps project in the 1880s and who was passionately committed to its completion."

Later in the book, B-V suddenly appears "on November 6, as envoy extraordinary and minister plenipotentiary" of Panama, without any other introduction. Of course, all along the book, B-V memoirs are quoted extensively.

21. Eduardo MANFUT. "Las Rutas del Canal. Historia de Nicaragua." (The Canal Routes. History of Nicaragua). 1997.

This long article, in Spanish, was illustrated by many photographs; it detailed the various phases of work, which took place in Nicaragua under the direction of the MCCN.

22. Ghislain de DIESBACH. "Ferdinand de Lesseps".
Perrin, Paris, 1998.

Written to celebrate the centennial of Ferdinand de Lesseps death (1894), this book was dedicated to the memory of the *Grand Français* (Great Frenchman) and disclaimed all his responsibility in the failure of the Company.
About B-V, de Diesbach wrote: "As he was born of an unknown father, some suspect that he is his - de Lesseps - son." Although there were some events from which one could deduce that B-V could have been Lesseps's son, we believe that there is not enough evidence to justify such parenthood.

This book often praised Lesseps, mentioning at length Suez rather than Panama, for obvious reasons.

However, we found there some material worthy of interest, among which the vivid description of the Panamanian weather, which we have quoted in the present book.

23.   Jorge THOMAS "Con Ardientes Fulgores De Gloria".
        (in Spanish: With Glittering Flashes of Glory)
        Grijalbo, Bogota, 1999.

A lawyer, historian, poet and novelist, Juan David Morgan - he wrote under a pseudonym -, has intensely re-created the atmosphere of the time. The plot, staged after 1903, presented us with the characters of the Panamani-an revolution. Among those are the *Proceres* - founding fathers of the nation - and B-V, who was the main character of the book.

This book advocated the "leyenda negra" (black legend), a Panamanian thesis according to which there had been a *hold up* on the 40 million dollars paid by the United States to the French *Compagnie Nouvelle du Canal de Panama*. According to Diaz Espino (26), an imaginary Syndicate of New York bankers had pocketed a major part of those millions, by buying shares of the French Company at a low price, just before it was sold to the U. S. Government.

Or was it a confusion with the Syndicate that Cromwell founded at the end of 1899?

24.   Mirella RICCIARDI "African Visions".
        Weidenfeld & Nicolson, London, 2000.

The author was Giselle's daughter, B-V's granddaughter. Born in Kenya, she published a book full of magnificent photographs, taken during her trips throughout Africa. We found in the text of this book some information about her grandfather, B-V, sometimes vague, but nevertheless interesting:
"The Panama project became Philippe's obsession and when de Lesseps French enterprise collapsed, Philippe managed to convince the President of the United States, Theodore Roosevelt, to continue with the work in Panama started by the French, rather than pursuing the original North American plan to build the canal in Nicaragua. He was thus able to save the French honor."

Here, the origin of the Bunau-Varilla fortune appeared clearly:
"Philippe's involvement in the Panama venture brought huge financial rewards to the family. . . Maurice, who with his brother had been born in abject poverty, (became) one of the stars of the Parisian political scene and the Bunau-Varilla name gained enormous status."

We have seen that "abject poverty" was highly exaggerated.

We found in this book how the brothers had used their wealth:
-       ". . . (my mother, Giselle) studied under Auguste Rodin and later prompted her uncle Maurice to launch an intensive campaign in *Le Matin* that led to the creation of the Rodin Museum in Paris",
-       Ms. Ricciardi mentioned "Uncle Maurice's yacht, the *Orion*",
-       "In 1933, the foundations of our home were laid, inspired by the design of the West African Pavilion at the 1932 Colonial Exhibition in Paris . . . A vast Mediterranean pink Italian-style palazzo rose against the barren African hills." This palace, built near Nairobi, Kenya, was converted into a lodge after the Second World War, when the Bunau-Varilla brothers' empire vanished.

25.   Edmund MORRIS. "Theodore Rex".
Random House, New York, 2001.

This was the second book of a trilogy covering in minute details the biography of our 26th President: Theodore Roosevelt. The third book has just been published (2010).

Of course, it also dedicated many pages to the Panama affair. Using a multitude of references, it revealed us a few facts not found in former books:
-       it told us about the interesting relationship between the President and his Secretary of State, John Hay, tempestuous at times,
-       it seemed to confirm Anguizola's theory about the friendship between B-V and Loomis: "As with the Venezuela episode, there seems to have been a concerted effort to create archival lacunae."
-       it suggested that Cromwell played an important part in the Panamanian Revolution, unfortunately to remain hidden forever, as: "Cromwell's papers have disappeared entirely."
-       it gave us a complete and entertaining record of Roosevelt's visit to Panama in November 1906. The story of Roosevelt inspecting the yams sold to the laborers in U. S. Army Commissaries was amusing.

26.   Ovidio DIAZ ESPINO   "How Wall Street Created A Nation".
       Subtitled: "J. P. Morgan, Teddy Roosevelt and the Panama Canal."
       Four Walls Eight Windows, New York, 2001.

This book told us all the details about the black legend - la "leyenda negra", in Spanish.

The author was a Panamanian lawyer, emigrated to the United States, who worked with the lawyers' firm of J. P. Morgan, New York. He took a sabbatical year to elucidate the real destination of the $ 40 million, paid by the United States to the French New Company in 1904.

According to his research, these millions have been pocketed - in part only, Diaz did not tell how much - by New York speculators who realized a tidy little profit: "it seems likely that American speculators had made a handsome profit", page 191.

Although this hypothesis of a speculation is credible, a simple look at the shareowners of the New Company (see chapter 15, above) suffice to prove that it must have been limited. It is hard to imagine that some of the largest shareowners - like Colombia or the large French banks - would have speculated or even less sold their stocks.

Of course, there were speculators among the small shareholders: Seligmann Frères, (a French bank affiliate of the New York Bank ran by the Seligman brothers Jesse and Joseph, later by Isaac) had invested 3.6 million Francs, which represented 3.6 / 65 = 5% of the capital of the New Company (*Compagnie Nouvelle du Canal de Panama*).

We should also consider that this so-called speculation had netted only an interest of 3% a year between 1894 and 1904 - Diaz confirmed this figure page 165 -, which did not unusually reward the speculators.

Our purpose here is not to dispute this hypothesis, but to show that this speculation was of such a magnitude that it could not have caused irreversibly the United States to select Panama instead of Nicaragua.

In fact, Diaz Espino was totally sincere when he wrote about the payment of the 40 million dollars:

-    page 171: "No record exists here of a single person who recovered the money." True, because most of the Archives of the French New Company have been destroyed. As Bouvier wrote: "It is the historian's work, with luck permitting, to reconstruct the puzzle with the available pieces that still exist." (**10**, page 13).

-    page 181: "The Hammond papers establish the existence of a conspiracy to buy the shares, but they do not prove that the speculators purchased any shares from the French shareholders."

Without the shadow of a doubt, it was a proven fact that Cromwell initiated a conspiracy (see Chapter 19, page 187). After he was discovered, we could not be aware of any sequel, as Cromwell would not have documented it.

This book was a source of useful information and showed the work of a clever man . . . the best evidence being the advertising masterpiece that was the title of the book.

A Spanish version was published in 2003 with "Editorial Planeta Colombiana" in Bogota, Colombia.

27.   Olmedo BELUCHE   "La Verdadera Historia
                    De La Separacion De 1903".
       (Spanish for: The true Story of the 1903 Separation;
       subtitled: Reflections at the turn of the Century)
       Imprenta Articsa, Panama, 2003.

This book explained the true nature of the two legends engendered by the politics in Panama:
-    the golden legend, which glorified the exemplary conduct of the secessionists, led by the *Proceres* (Amador and his friends),
-    the black legend, which assumed a plot by American capitalists.

Beluche, who flaunted his Marxist inclinations, regretted that November 3, 1903, the date selected by Panama as her National Holiday, was also the date of the invasion of the Canal Zone by the Americans.

This is purely an internal quarrel among Panamanians and it is not the purpose of this book to side with or against any of these so-called legends.

We have selected this book for its interest in describing the 1903 revolution, as seen by the Panamanians themselves and in particular its principal actors the *Proceres*.

Mr. Beluche hardly mentioned B-V. He indicated that B-V's account of the events of the autumn 1903 was hard to accept by the Panamanian oligarchy, because of the enormous ego exhibited by B-V, which reduced to nothing the part played by the "Proceres".

Obviously, B-V's part in Beluche's book was reduced to a minimum. But, his book was interesting in showing that a rehabilitation of B-V would not be an easy task.

28.   Fiammetta ROCCO
        "The Miraculous Fever-Tree. The cure that changed the world".
        Harper Collins, London, 2003.

Ms. Rocco is Mirella's niece and Giselle's granddaughter. A talented journalist, she published one of the most thorough histories of malaria and yellow fever.

This book was very helpful to understand the ravages of these diseases during the years of the French Canal. Ms. Rocco also provided us with precious information about the deaths of the workers in Panama. Quinine was expensive: "The officials of the Compagnie calculated that it was cheaper to let its workers die than to spend a lot of money trying to cure them," (pages 6 and 198). She explained among other things that 500 different species of mosquitoes were able to convey malaria, but that only 20 had been identified as able to transmit it to humans (page 23). She added that her great-grandfather (B-V) was protected against malaria thanks to the quinine doses that he regularly received from Paris (page 198); quinine protected him against malaria, but had no effect against yellow fever.
        According to Ms. Rocco, in 1929, B-V had moved: 1 Rue de la Grande Chaumière, (page 9) close to the crossings of Boulevards Raspail and Montparnasse. Maybe he desired to live closer to his daughter who had an apartment: 9 rue Notre-Dame des Champs?
        She also revealed the origin of the Bunau family: "B-V was an outsider, a protestant from the German borderlands . . . the son of a boarding house owner from Alsace" (pages 188 and 189). This is consistent with other reliable sources of information.

29.   Marc de BANVILLE. "Canal Français".
        (in French: The French Canal, 1880-1904.
        Subtitled: The Illustrated Adventure of the French in Panama.)
        Canal Valley, Panama, 2004.

This didactic book, illustrated with many photographs, maps and drawings, was the work of a French journalist, who had lived in Panama and who had access to the exceptional graphic documentation kept in this country. It told the sad story and the disappointed hopes of the French saga in Panama from 1880 to 1889. It displayed a multitude of documents, which re-created the small world of the 19th Century investors, making us fully realize the various unknowns they had faced.

It was nevertheless very kind with the French venture:
- Page 7. We read that: "The French were on the point of reaching their goals." At least, they believed it, because, at the end, they had really dug a mere 30% of the total!
- page 8: "The great majority of the funds had effectively been invested in the Isthmus." Actually, only 60% were used in the works.

A reader of Mr. de Banville's book would be fascinated with the graphic documents, which are absolutely exceptional. It is also the only book to show a picture of the Panamanian flag (page 138), as designed by B-V, sewed by Ida, B-V's wife, but rejected by the Provisional Government of Panama: two yellow suns against a blue sky are on the upper left corner, surrounded by red and yellow stripes, very much on the model of the American flag.

Moreover, Mr. de Banville was entirely in agreement with the present book when he wrote that B-V: "will take a stand against the general indifference in order to realize Lesseps' dream" (page 9) and that: "it is thanks to the determination of B-V, self-proclaimed champion of the Panama Canal, who started in 1901 a real crusade in the United States." (page 115)

Two other versions (Spanish and English) have been published with some minor changes with respect to the original French version.

30. Dominique PINSOLLE
"Le Matin 1884-1944. Une Presse d'Argent et de Chantage".
(in French)

An absolute "must read" to learn (almost) everything about *Le Matin,* the newspaper that Maurice ran from 1905 to 1944.
Although mainly oriented towards the analysis of the French press through the first half of the 19th Century, we have used many details concerning Maurice, worth being quoted in this book.

A NOTE FROM THE AUTHOR

Most of the quotations appearing in the present book have been extracted from books originally written in English.

Philippe Bunau-Varilla (B-V) published his memoirs and his subsequent books both in French and in English. We have chosen to reproduce all quotes from the English versions.

For books which had been written in French or Spanish, without any English translation (2, 3, 4, 13, 14, 15, 17, 19, 22, 23, 27 and 30), the author has done his best to translate accurately the meaning of the extracts quoted.

APPENDIX 5.

THE WEALTH OF THE BUNAU-VARILLA BROTHERS

We have to examine in the first place the profit made by the Bunau-Varilla brothers from the sale of the assets of the French New Company to the United States. This is to refute once for all the idea that B-V spent his time and his money to speculate and make a profit on his shares of the New Company.

It is true that the sale by the Bunau-Varilla brothers of their shares of the New Company netted them some profit. It is also true that this profit was quite negligible compared to the money they made with their company, ASC. Let us examine the figures.

In 1894, the brothers bought their shares at 100 francs each. In 1904, the New Company gave them 130 francs per share (129.78 exactly), which were paid in three installments: June 1904, June 1906 and June 1908. Their profit was thus 130 – 100 = 30 francs per share. For such period of ten years, it yielded slightly less than 3% per year, which was lower than for most investments of this time.

Thus, the investment required by Lemarquis in the New Company had been productive, but not spectacularly.

B-V had 5,000 shares; he made a profit of 150,000 francs.

Maurice had 15,000 shares; he made a profit of 450,000 francs.

Together their profit was: 150,000 + 450,000 = 600,000 francs, less than a half million francs, absolutely insignificant - less than 10% - compared to the 8 million francs they made with ASC - Artigue, Sonderegger & Co -, in only two years!

This clearly proves that the Bunau-Varilla brothers did not get involved in the sale of the New Company to the U. S. Government for pure reason of speculation.

Now, let us examine what the brothers bought with their money.

Eight million francs was a considerable fortune for the time. It was equivalent to 80 years of salaries of a Director of the Canal works or to 4,000 years of the salaries of a French worker.

The brothers did not keep this money idle in a bank.

They invested in the newspaper *Le Matin,* which produced profits totaling 70 million francs in 40 years.

Le Matin was a unique example of success in the Parisian press. Thanks to huge advertising campaigns - 500,000 francs in 1898 -, *Le Matin* increased its distribution from 285,000 copies in 1902 to 525,000 copies in 1910. Its cost was only 5 cents of a franc - 5 centimes.

Founded in 1883 by Edwards, the brother–in-law of Waldeck Rousseau, a politician, who would become President of the Council in 1899, *Le Matin* was sold in 1896 to Henri Poidatz and Maurice Bunau-Varilla. In 1905, Poidatz died and his share was acquired by Maurice and his brother B-V.

Many celebrities worked for *Le Matin*: Felix Fénéon, an art critique and anarchist; Jean Giraudoux, a writer; Gaston Leroux, a journalist and writer; Colette, a writer; Colette's husband, Henry de Jouvenel, a journalist and writer; Joseph Kessel, a writer; and many others.

Le Matin's success was due to a series of scandals, which made it very popular. In his book, titled *From Bluff to Blackmail; The great Campaigns of Le Matin*, published in 1910, F. I. Mouthon, a former journalist of the newspaper listed these scandals:

-   the campaign against Léopold II, King of Belgium, to speculate on the shares of the Belgian Congo Company, where B-V was the engineering advisor,
-   the campaign to defame Chaumié, a French Senator,
-   and many other campaigns against commercial products.

At that time, *Le Matin* was not the biggest newspaper in the French capital, it was surpassed by *Le Petit Parisien* (1.2 million copies), *Le Journal* (850,000) and *Le Petit Journal* (800,000). However, its distribution grew up to more than one million in 1913 and peaked at 1.6 million copies during the First World War.

The period between the two World Wars was not as favorable and, in 1939, its distribution had decreased to 300,000 copies. However, it climbed back to about 500,000 during WWII under Nazi's rule.

To conclude on this subject, in 1901, Maurice started an evening paper, *Le Français*, which never reached the same success as *Le Matin*. It stopped in 1903.

Other titles were property of *Le Matin*: *Pays de France* from 1914 to 1919; *Le Flambeau* in 1915 and 1916; *Medica*, a weekly magazine from August to December 1917; *The Morning*, an English edition specially edited for the Anglo-American troops from December 1917 to June 1918; *Le Ciné de France* in 1927 to 1929; *Le Siècle Médical*, from 1927 to 1944; *Minerva*, from 1935 to 1940;

La Semaine, a weekly magazine, copied on the American *Life,* with plenty of pictures.

Other than *Le Matin,* Maurice's investments are worth mentioning; they matched those of a multi-millionaire, totaling the enormous amount of 100 million francs ($ 200 million, equivalent to $ 600 million of today):
-        Shares in mining operations in Congo and in Spain (with B-V; Asturias Mining Company);
-        Shares in transportation companies; some with his Belgian friend Empain (Chemins de Fer du Congo);
-        Foreign financial trading companies: Lebanon, Laos, Soudan, China and Crimea.
-        Real Estate in Paris :
• 22 Avenue du Trocadero - today Avenue Georges Mandel (2) , which was Maurice's personal residence,
• 146 Rue du Faubourg Saint Honoré (2),
• 1 Rue de la Bourse (2),
• Avenue du Président Wilson (2),
• Avenue Henri IV (from: History of the Parisian Press),
and probably many other buildings in the newly developed 16th District of Paris with the *Real Estate Company of Trocadero and Passy.*
-        Château d'Orsay.
In 1906, Maurice bought 25 hectares - 60 acres - of land, near Orsay, at a place called *The Launay Mill,* with a large middle-class family house, built in 1840. Maurice reconditioned it and it became the Bunau-Varilla's family house. Giselle, B-V's daughter, explained that this mansion was used by his father to host his friends, among which we find the future President of France, Paul Doumer.
At the end of WW II, when Maurice's son, Guy was condemned for collaborating with the Germans, the Orsay land was seized and given to the French Atomic Energy Commission in 1951; a "cyclotron" had been built there.
-        Manor of Milliau.
In 1911, Maurice was in love with Lucie Jourdan and to hide their passion, he purchased the Island of Milliau (near the resort of Trégor, close to Lannion, in the Department of Morbihan, in the French Brittany), where he built a castle to host his mistress. One can learn more about this affair in the book: "Madame Jourdan and the Island of Milliau" - in French - by Yves Lales.
Their liaison lasted until 1920 and Miss Jourdan courted Aristide Briand, a political personality, who came to the Island of Milliau for his summer vacations, until his death in 1932.
This could explain how B-V became such a close friend of Briand.
-        Villa of Joux in Switzerland.
"In 1912, Maurice built another folly in Switzerland, near the village of Pont, in the Vaux canton, overlooking the Lake of Joux. Located on the railway line

Paris-Vallorbe, it was a villa with two wings on four levels, all made of concrete - a first in Switzerland, by the architect Hennebique, inventor of reinforced concrete. Its walls were cannon proof: one meter thick, made of a concrete frame containing stones. It was called the *Bunau-Varilla Villa* or the *Le Matin Villa* - after the newspaper. The villa saw for many years classy receptions with guests coming from Paris, but also from Nazi Germany.

The mystery about its guests, its impressive look and its isolated location in a forest clearing overlooking the lake, excited the imagination of the near-by Swiss villagers who pretended that in case of war, the manor will display a platform with guns pointed at the nearest French fort across the Swiss border."

(From Colette Raffaele, "The Manor of Haute-Roche au Pont." 2002.

A book related this story:

"The Guns of Bunau-Varilla" - in French - by the Swiss writer Claude Berney (1990).

It described the social life in the villa: "Every year, Maurice Bunau-Varilla came first with his mistress; never with his wife. Of course, with them came the servants. Later, but never together, came the legitimate spouse. And all the rest: Germain, the driver, Hortense, the catering manager, etc.   .   . Those people had millions and millions, gathered in Panama."

Maurice was pro-German, which would explain his choice of building a house in Switzerland.

-        A sumptuous villa in the village of Agay, near Cannes (France), on the Mediterranean Sea. And the obvious accessory to the villa, a private wharf where moored a yacht.

-        This yacht was *Meteor III.* In 1920, Maurice purchased it to a rich German. It had belonged to Edouard VII, King of England. It was a huge sailboat, 50 meters - 160 feet - long. Maurice re-christened it *Pays de France II.* He sold it in 1926 to buy another yacht: *Orion.* Later re-christened *Aldebaran, Orion* does not exist anymore. The *Meteor* still lives on.

-        Synthol.

Lastly, we have to mention that Maurice also owned a pharmaceutical production complex - now part of Glaxo-Smith-Kline - which produced Synthol, a well-known French "cure-all", invented in 1925 by a Mr. Roger, chemist in Orleans, south of Paris. Maurice saw in Synthol the panacea to cure all human illnesses and also a source of profit.

B-V's acquisitions were much less ostentatious.

In his memoirs, he mentioned that he lived since 1898 in a large mansion, near the Arch of Triumph, 53 avenue Iéna, in the heart of Paris. It was in the

16th ward, newly developed. His telephone was 527 88 and his cable address "BUNOVARILA", Paris.

However, he failed to mention that he bought an airplane to his son Etienne in 1908, to celebrate his school-leaving certificate. Etienne flew in an international meeting with Blériot in Reims in 1909, where all the famous aviators from all over the world were present.

This takes us far away from the lavish expenses of Maurice: Etienne's plane was only worth 25,000 francs.

B-V invested mostly in his steadfast idea: to make the Panama Canal. His many trips to the United States, Venezuela, and Cuba between 1890 and 1904, when he supported Panama against its rival Nicaragua, had cost him almost a million francs - see Appendix 3.

We shall not forget his investment in *Le Matin* or the other investments he shared with his brother Maurice: real estate, railways, mines, etc.

And last, Giselle's escapades made a hole in B-V's capital: an apartment in Montparnasse - Paris – a farm in Kenya, with a huge villa, etc.

The *Verdunization* process, he had invented to purify water, did not bring him a single franc (see page 282).

APPENDIX 6.

COMPARISON NICARAGUA – PANAMA

	NICARAGUA	PANAMA
VOLUME TO EXCAVATE Million cubic meters	174.1	72.5
STEEL QUANTITY Thousand of metric tons	36.7	29.6
DEPTH OF TRENCHES Meters	90.6 (Tamborcito)	31.4 (Culebra)
YEARLY MAINTENANCE COSTS Million Francs	17	10.3
NUMBER OF LOCKS	8	2 doubles 1 single
LENGTH OF THE CANAL Kilometers	228.3	67.7
Of which in a LAKE Kilometers	46.2	9.1
Of which in a CURB Kilometers	79.3	36.8
CURVATURE in degrees	2339	771
AVERAGE RADIUS meters	1950	2743
RADIUS OF STEEPEST CURVES Meters	1232	2500
CROSSING TIME hours	33	12
WIND ORIENTATION (the dominant winds are East/West)	E/W	N/S
RAIN meters per year	6.7	3.3

APPENDIX 7.

MAP OF THE CENTRAL AMERICAN ISTHMUS

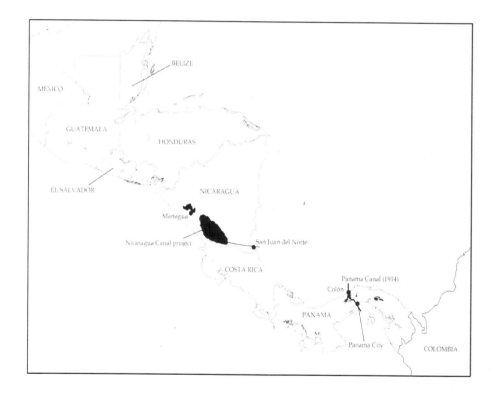

APPENDIX 8.

LIST OF DISTURBANCES ON THE ISTHMUS OF PANAMA
(FROM 1850 TO 1903)
Quoted from Theodore Roosevelt's "Autobiography" (8)
Charles Scribner & Sons, 1913. (pages 528 to 530)

"May 22, 1850. – Outbreak ; two Americans killed. War vessel demanded to quell the outbreak.

October 1850. – Revolutionary plot to bring about independence of the Isthmus.

July 22, 1851. – Revolution in four Southern provinces.

November 14, 1851. – Outbreak at Chagres. Man-of-war requested for Chagres.

June 27, 1853. – Insurrection at Bogota, and consequent disturbance on Isthmus. War vessel demanded.

May 23, 1854. – Political disturbances. War vessel requested.

June 28, 1854. – Attempted revolution.

October 24, 1854. – Independence of the Isthmus demanded by provincial legislature.

April 1856. – Riot and massacre of Americans.

May 4, 1856. – Riot.

May 18, 1856. – Riot.

June 3, 1856. – Riot.

October 2, 1856. – Conflict between two native parties. U. S. force landed.

December 18, 1858. – Attempted secession of Panama.

April 1859. – Riots.

September 1860. – Outbreak.

October 4, 1860. – Landing of U. S. force in consequence.

May 23, 1860. – Intervention of the U. S. force required by "intendente".

October 2, 1861. – Insurrection and civil war.

April 4, 1862. – Measures to prevent rebels crossing Isthmus.

June 13, 1862. – Mosquera's troops refused admittance to Panama.

March, 1865. – Revolution and United States troops landed.

August 1865. – Riots; unsuccessful attempt to invade Panama.

March 1866. – Unsuccessful revolution.

April 1867. – Attempt to overthrow Government.

August 1867. – Attempt at revolution.

July 5, 1868. – Revolution; provisional Government inaugurated.

August 29, 1868. – Revolution; provisional Government overthrown.

April 1871. – Revolution; followed apparently by counter-revolution.
April 1873. – Revolution and civil war, which lasted to October, 1875.
July 1878. – Rebellion.
December 1878. – Revolt.
April 1879. – Revolution.
June 1879. – Revolution.
March 1883. – Riot.
May 1883. – Riot.
June 1884. – Revolutionary attempt.
December 1884. – Revolutionary attempt.
January 1885. – Revolutionary disturbances.
March 1885. – Revolution.
April 1887. – Disturbance on Panama Railroad.
November 1887. – Disturbance on line of canal.
January 1889. – Riot.
January 1895. – Revolution, which lasted until April.
March 1895. – Incendiary attempt.
October 1899. – Revolution.
February 1900 to July 1900. – Revolution.
January 1901. – Revolutionary disturbances.
September 1901. – City of Colon taken by rebels.
March 1902. – Revolutionary disturbances.
July 1902. – Revolution.

The above is only a partial list of the revolutions, rebellions, insurrections, riots, and other outbreaks that occurred during the period in question; yet they number 53 for 53 years, and they showed a tendency to increase, rather than decrease, in number and intensity.

In short, the experience of over half a century had shown Colombia to be utterly incapable of keeping order on the Isthmus.

Had it not been for the exercise by the United states of the police power in her interest, her connection with the Isthmus would have been sundered long before it was."

LEVI Parsons Morton (1824-1920) American politician and banker.
Ambassador to France. Vice-President of Harrison (1889-1893).
Governor of New York State (1895-1897). **183,187**

LILLAZ   Contractor working in Panama. **84,99**
LINCOLN Abraham (1809-1865)   16th President.   **160,175**
LINDO Joshua   Panamanian banker living in New York.   **239,240,243,246**
LLOYD STEPHENS John (1805-1852)   U. S. explorer, writer and diplomat.   **10,14**
LOEB Solomon (1828-1903)   From a family of bankers. Partner with Kuhn.   **187**
LOOMIS Francis Butler (1861-1948) U. S. Minister. Acting Secretary of State (1905)
177-179,190,198,209,212,232,242-245,248,263,281,285

LOUBET Emile (1838-1929)
7th President of the IIIrd French Republic (1899-1906) **129,132**

LUDLOW William (1843-1901) U. S. Army Brigadier General,
Chairman of the Nicaragua Canal Commission (Apr.-Nov. 1895) **155,156**

LULL Edward Phelps (1836-?)
U. S. Navy Commander. Member of the Nicaragua Expedition (1872).
Commander of the Department of Alaska (1881). **21**

McCALL John A.
American Businessman, member of the Grace-Cragin-Eyre syndicate (1899). **183**
McGEACHY Alberto Victor (1890-1954) Panamanian editor of *Star & Herald*.
Author of "How Panamanians Were Betrayed" (1934) **284**

McKINLEY William (1843-1901) 25th President (1877-1901).
154,156,158,174-177,181,183,185,187,189-194,199,203-205

MALLARINO IBARGUEN Manuel Maria (1808-1872) Colombian politician.
President of Colombia (1855-1857). **12,17,45,75,227,237,258**

MARROQUIN RICAURTE Jose Manuel (1827-1908) Colombian politician.
President of Colombia (1902-1904). **30,202,210-212,227-236**

MARTIN Etienne   General Secretary of the Company. **91**
MARTIN Ferdinand   French Journalist.**130**
MARTINEZ SILVA Carlos (1847-1903).
Ambassador of Colombia in Washington (1901-1902). **202,209,210**

MENOCAL Aniceto Garcia (1836-1908) U. S. Navy Admiral, Cuban born engineer.
14,21,22,41-45,85,112,113,115,116,155,224,293,303

MICHELET Jules (1798-1874) French historian and writer.
MILLER Warner   (1838-1918)
U. S. Businessman, member of the Grace-Cragin-Eyre syndicate. **183**

MILLS Darius Ogden (1825-1910)   U. S. banker and investor. **183**
MITCHELL Edward Page (1852-1927)
Newspaper editor, successor of Dana at the head of the New York Sun (1926). **30,223**
MONCHICOURT Achille
Liquidator of the Company, successor of Brunet (March 1890). **128**

MONROE James (1758-1831)   5th President (1817-1825).   **11,20,45,48,181**
MORGAN John Tyler (1824-1907)   Democrat, Senator for Alabama (1877-1907).
114,115,150,152,154,156,174,176,182,187,198,199,211,213,224,232,246,253

MORGAN John Pierpont Sr., also called "J. P." (1837-1913)
American banker, instigator of the General Electric and U. S. Steel.
48,150,261,269,270

MORISON George Shattuck (1842-1903). Civil engineer.
Constructor of steel truss bridges. Member of 1st Walker Commission.
184-186,191,204,205

MOUTHON François Ignace (1869-1930) Journalist in *Le Matin*.
Author of "The Great Campaigns of *Le Matin*"(1910) **26-28,33,89,91,140,143,161,165,285**

PROCTER Harley Thomas (1846-1923)

Co-Founder of Procter &Gamble. **190,195,198**

POULTNEY Jane Tunis (1829-1889)   Spouse of John Bigelow. **98,160**

PULITZER Joseph (1847-1911)   U. S. publisher of the New York World. **269**

QUESNAY de BEAUREPAIRE (1834-1923).

President of the Paris Court of Cassation. **129,130**

RECLUS Armand (1843-1927)

1st General Manager of the Company (1881-1882). **37-39,43,59,64-66,280**

RECLUS Jacques Elisée (1830-1905). French geographer, brother of Armand.

REINACH Jacob Adolf called "Baron Jacques" de (1840-1892). German born banker.

33,39,40,42,45,81,106,109,128,130-134,141,167

REYES PRIETO Rafael (1849-1921)

Colombian politician.   President (1904-1909). **257,259,261**

ROA DIAZ Antonio   Colombian General. **258**

ROCCO Fiammetta (1955-) Great-grand-daughter of B-V.

Author of "The Miraculous Fever Tree". **56**

ROCCO Mario   Spouse of Giselle, B-V's daughter. **281**

RODRIGUEZ Manuel   Senator of Colombia (1902). **236**

ROOSEVELT Franklin Delano (1882-1945) 32nd President. **115**

ROOSEVELT James (1828-1900)

American businessman, father of Franklin D. Roosevelt. **115,152**

ROOSEVELT Theodore (1858-1919) 26th President.

5,75,178,181,197,203,204,207,208,211,215,
226,227,233,236,237,240,244-246,249,252,256,257,259,263-270,284,285,291,292,294

ROOT Elihu (1845-1937) U. S. Secretary of War (1899-1904).

Nobel peace prize (1912). **258,261,270,271**

ROTHSCHILD James de (1792-1868).

From a family of bankers, head of the Parisian branch. **36,163**

ROUSSEAU Armand (1835-1896)

Polytechnique (1854). French Senator (1895-1896). **60,80,81,83,85,86,97,127**

ROUVIER Maurice (1842-1911)

French politician. Prime Minister (1887 and 1905-1906). **105,135,263**

RUSSELL Charles W. (1856-1927) Deputy of W. A. Day, Attorney General. **227,261**

SADI CARNOT Marie François (1837-1894).

4th President of the French IIIrd Republic (1887-1894) . **170**

SALGAR MORENO Eustorgio (1831-1885)

President of Colombia (1870-1872). **41,45,209**

SOLOMON Augustin   French entrepreneur from the island of Guadalupe. **10,11**

SCHMIDLAPP Jacob Godfrey (1849-1919). Entrepreneur from Cincinnati (Ohio).

Friend of Herrick, Ohio Governor. **195,198**

SCHWAB Gustav H.   Agent of the German Lloyd Steamship Company. **196**

SELIGMAN Jesse (1827-1894). From a German family of Bankers.,

Head of the New York Branch, with his brother Joseph (1819-1880). **48,194**

SELIGMAN Isaac (1855-1912). Took over after Jesse's death.

The Seligman bank had affiliates in Paris, London and Frankfurt. **48,187,246**

SHERMAN John (1823-1900)   Senator (1861-1877 and 1881-1897). **152-154,176,190**

SIMMONS J. E. New York financier. Was Hanna's banker.

WESTINGHOUSE George Jr. (1846-1914).
American Businessman, pioneer in the electrical industry. **183**
WHITLEY Jonas   Press Agent of Nelson Cromwell.   **259**
WITTE Serge, de (1849-1915).   Finance Minister of Russia (1892-1903).   **170**
WOODWARD Benjamin Duryea (1868- ?)
Roman Languages Professor. Columbia University. **197**
WULSIN Lucien Bacas (1845-1912).
Partner and Head of the Baldwin Piano Co. (1873-1912). **190,192,195,198**
WYSE Lucien Napoleon-Bonaparte, (1844-1909). French engineer and explorer.
13,37,39-42,45,46,61,79,82,125,128,167,171,209

ZAVALA SOLIS Joaquin (1835-1906).   Minister of Nicaragua.   **112**
ZELAYA José Santos (1853-1919). President of Nicaragua (1893-1909). **21,155,224,273**

ACKNOWLEDGMENTS

This book is the result of a long process.

At first, this book had been written in French - and published in 2008 - then it was translated into English by the author, because it was thought that there might be a special interest for this book in Panama and the USA.

Very special thanks to Sara, who reviewed the English text, made it more legible and helped avoiding misinterpretations.

A notable mention to my friend Paul, who read meticulously the early French manuscript and suggested many wise changes. Many thanks to all my faithful friends who sent me a list of typos, errors, wrong dates, etc.

Last but not least, the author would like to thank all his family in France and in Panama for their constant support and patience. Their questioning of some of the author's findings has surely helped clarifying the story.